The Cruise
of the Alabama
and the Sumter

The Cruise of the Alabama and the Sumter
The Confederate Navy during the American Civil War

R. Semmes

*The Cruise
of the Alabama
and the Sumter*
The Confederate Navy
during the American Civil War
by R. Semmes

First published under the title
*The Cruise
of the Alabama
and the Sumterr*

Leonaur is an imprint
of Oakpast Ltd

Copyright in this form © 2009 Oakpast Ltd

ISBN: 978-1-84677-882-7 (hardcover)
ISBN: 978-1-84677-881-0 (softcover)

http://www.leonaur.com

Publisher's Notes

In the interests of authenticity, the spellings, grammar and place names used have been retained from the original editions.

The opinions of the authors represent a view of events in which he was a participant related from his own perspective, as such the text is relevant as an historical document.

The views expressed in this book are not necessarily those of the publisher.

Contents

Advertisement	7
Captain Semmes	9
Captain Semmes Joins and Assumes Command	13
Beginning the Cruise	20
A Hot Pursuit	33
A Visit to the President	39
In Hopes of a Fight	46
Sympathy for the South	52
Again at Sea	72
Up the Rock	79
A Daring Act	99
Appointment to the *Alabama*	105
Laws of Neutrality	111
Ready for the Cruise	115
A Fuitless Chase	121
Three Sacrifices in a Day	127
A Deserter Caught	131
Condemned!	138
Kindness Repaid	147
Temptation	151
Looking out for a Rich Prize	158

Prisoners of War	164
To Sea Again	170
Rescue of the Crew	179
Reinstating the Discipline	187
Patience Rewarded	193
Coaling at Sea Under Difficulties	200
Landing Prisoners	207
Homesick	214
Short of Provisions	219
The Capture off Cape Town	224
A Night Scene	230
Yankee Ships Scarce	242
Getting at the Truth	250
Off Again	259
At Cherbourg	264
The Informing Spirit	268
Appendix	277

Advertisement

The following account of the cruise of the two Confederate States steamers—*Sumter* and *Alabama*—is taken from the private journals and other papers of Captain Semmes. It has been found necessary occasionally to adopt a narrative form, but the endeavour has been throughout to adhere as closely as possible to that officer's own words.

Information has also been most kindly afforded by other officers of the two vessels, and especially Lieutenant R.F. Armstrong, and Master's Mate G. Townley Fullam, from whose private journals and other papers much valuable assistance has been obtained.

A good deal of controversy has arisen respecting the legality of the course pursued by the *Alabama*, in the case of certain vessels claiming to carry a neutral cargo. In all these cases, however, great care was taken by Captain Semmes to enter in his journal full particulars of the claims, and of the grounds on which it was refused admission. These cases will be found quoted in full in the following volumes.

CHAPTER 1

Captain Semmes

The President of the American States in Confederation was gathering an army for the defence of Southern liberty. Where valour is a national inheritance, and an enthusiastic unanimity prevails, this will not prove a difficult task. It is otherwise with the formation of a navy. Soldiers of Southern blood had thrown up their commissions in a body; but sailors love their ships as well as their country, and appear to owe some allegiance to them likewise. Nevertheless, if Mr. Davis had not a great choice of officers, he had eminent men to serve him, as the young history of the South has abundantly shown. To obtain experienced and trusty seamen was easier to him in such a crisis than to give them a command.

The Atlantic and the ports of America were ruled at that time absolutely by President Lincoln. The South had not a voice upon the sea. The merchants of New York and Boston looked upon the war as something which concerned them very little. Not a dream of any damage possibly to be inflicted on them, disturbed the serenity of their votes for the invasion of the South. Their fleets entered harbour proudly; their marine swam the ocean unmolested. Though there was war imminent, the insurance offices were content to maintain their terms upon a peace standard. What, indeed, was to be feared? The South had not a single vessel.

Here and there a packet-steamer might be caught up and armed, but what would they avail against such fleet and powerful ships as the *Brooklyn*, the *Powhattan*, and dozens of others? There was, then, a condition of perfect security, according to the ideas of all American commercial men. The arrangement, as they understood it, was that they were to strike the blow, and that no one was to give them the value in return.

It happened that Mr. Davis was of another mind. He perceived where a blow could be struck, on his part, with terrible emphasis, and how. The obstacles in his way were colossal; but we have learnt that obstacles do not appal his indomitable genius. On the 14th February, 1861, Captain Semmes, being then at his residence in the city of Washington, a Commander in the Federal navy, received the following telegram from Montgomery:—

Sir,—On behalf of the Committee on Naval Affairs, I beg leave to request that you will repair to this place at your earliest convenience.

Your obedient servant,
C.M. Conrad, Chairman.

The selection of Captain Semmes for the first hazardous service, whatsoever it might be, was due to his reputation and patriotism, as well as to the sagacity of the Confederate chief. He had already, in a letter to the Hon. Alexander H. Stephens, expressed his willingness to fight for the South: "his judgment, his inclinations, and his affections," all hurrying him, as he says, to link his fate with the first movement of the South. "My fate," he pursues, "is cast with the South; but I should be unwilling, unless invited, to appear to thrust myself upon the new Government *until my own State* has moved." This was at that time the feeling of many border statesmen. In another letter to Mr. Curry he had exposed sound practical views of the situation of the Confederates, as regards their marine, for defence and means of inflicting damage on their opponents.

Captain Semmes at once replied that he would attend upon the committee immediately. His next act was respectfully to resign his commission as Commander in the Navy of the United States; which resignation was accepted in the same terms. He ceased similarly to be a member of the Lighthouse Board. These matters concluded, he telegraphed to the Hon. J.L.M. Curry, in Montgomery, where the Confederate States' Congress was sitting, that he was now a free man to serve his struggling country. Forthwith he was deputed by President Davis to return to the Northern States, and make large purchases and contracts "for machinery and munitions, or for the manufacture of arms and munitions of war;" as also to obtain "cannon and musket-powder, the former of the coarsest grain," and to engage with a certain proprietor of powder-mills for the "establishment of a powder-mill at some point in the limits of our territory." This letter gives a good idea of the business-like qualities brought by Mr. Davis to his high office.

"At the arsenal at Washington," he writes, "you will find an artificer named Wright, who has brought the cap-making machine to its present state of efficiency, and who might furnish a cap-machine, and accompany it, to explain its operations." Throughout the letter, which is full of minute instructions and weighty commissions, Mr. Davis shows the fullest confidence in the loyalty and fitness of the man in whom he placed trust.

Captain Semmes was engaged in the performance of these immediate duties, when a confidential communication from Mr. S.R. Mallory, of the Navy department, gave him warning of two or more steamers, of a class desired for present service, which might be purchased at or near New York—"steamers of speed, light draught, and strength sufficient for at least one heavy gun."

> "The steamers are designed to navigate the waters and enter the bays and inlets of the coast from Charleston to the St. Mary's, and from Key West to the Rio Grande, for coast defences;" and Captain Semmes' judgment will need no further guide when he is told that "their speed should be sufficient to give them at all times the ability to engage or to evade an engagement, and that an 8 or 10-inch gun, with, perhaps, two 32, or, if not, two of smaller calibre, should constitute their battery."

The captain's appointment as Commander in the Navy of the Confederate States, and taking of the oaths, followed in April. On the 18th of that month, Mr. Mallory detached him from the post he held, by appointment from the President, of Chief of the Lighthouse Bureau, with orders that he should proceed to New Orleans and take command of the steamer *Sumter*. Captain Semmes saw clearly that war was coming. He perceived, at the same time, the means by which he could serve his country best. He set forth for New Orleans without delay.

Our readers will see, by-and-by, from the quotations we shall make from the Captain's Log, that he is as little the hungry fire-eater which many of his admirers suppose him to be, as he is the Black Pirate of the New York press. Captain Semmes is a native of Charles county, in Maryland, a State that has furnished numerous patriotic citizens to the South. Before accepting his new service he had taken honourable farewell of his old. The Federals had no charge to bring against him before the day when he stepped on the deck of the then unknown and insignificant *Sumter* steam-vessel. What they may have said later is of no particular consequence; nor can it be thought to be greatly to the discredit of Captain Semmes that they have cried out loudly, and as men in pain.

CHAPTER 2

Captain Semmes Joins and Assumes Command

The little vessel which now constituted the whole strength of the Confederate navy, was a merchant screw-steamer of 501 tons burthen. She had been hitherto known as the *Havannah*, and had plied as a packet-ship between the port of that name and New Orleans. She was now to be extemporized into a man-of-war, and in her new guise was to achieve a world-wide celebrity, and to play no unimportant part in the great struggle between North and South.

Arrived in New Orleans, Captain Semmes at once proceeded, in company with Lieutenant Chapman, to inspect his new command-of which he speaks with evident satisfaction as a "staunch and well-built" vessel. In her then condition, however, she was by no means fitted for her new duties; and he accordingly devoted all his energies towards effecting the alterations necessary for that purpose. The first step was to disencumber her decks of the long range of upper cabins, thus materially increasing her buoyancy as a sea-boat, and diminishing the area exposed to the enemy's shot and shell.

Then a berth-deck was laid for the accommodation of officers and crew, and the main deck renewed and strengthened to carry the heavy 8-inch shell-gun, mounted on a pivot between the fore and mainmasts, and the four 24 pounder howitzers of 13 cwt. each, to be mounted as a broadside battery. Additional coal-bunkers were also constructed, and a magazine and shell-room built in a suitable position, and these and a few other less important changes effected, the transformation was complete, and the little *Sumter* ready to proceed upon her work of devastation.

It must not, however, be imagined that all this was done without many and vexatious delays. The emergency had found the new Confederation altogether unprepared, and trouble and confusion were the inevitable result. Hitherto, everything had been done by the North. Up to the very last moment it had been believed that the separation of the two sections would be peaceably effected; and now the necessary works had to be hastily carried out by civilian workmen, under the direction of a department, itself as yet but provisionally and most imperfectly organized.

Sorely tried by the delays consequent upon this condition of affairs, Captain Semmes commences his *Diary* as follows:—

New Orleans, *May 24th*.—A month has elapsed since I began the preparation of the *Sumter* for sea, and yet we are not ready. Leeds and Co. have not given us our tanks, and we only received the carriage of the 8-inch gun today. The officers are all present, and the crew has been shipped, and all are impatient to be off. The river is not yet blockaded, but expected to be tomorrow. It must be a close blockade, and by heavy vessels, that will keep us in. Troops are being collected in large numbers in the enemy's States, marchings and counter-marchings are going on; and the fleet seems to be kept very busy, scouring hither and thither, but nothing accomplished. Whilst penning the last paragraph, news reaches us that the Lincoln Government has crossed the Potomac and invaded Virginia! Thus commences a bloody and a bitter war. So be it; we but accept the gauntlet which has been flung in our faces. The future will tell a tale worthy of the South and of her noble cause.

But the delays were not yet over. On the 27th May, the United States steamer *Brooklyn* made her appearance, and commenced the blockade of the river. The following day brought the powerful frigates Niagara and Minnesota to her assistance; and when on the 1st of June Captain Semmes began at length to look hopefully seawards, the *Powhattan* was discovered carefully watching the only remaining exit from the river.

One by one, however, the difficulties were fairly overcome, and the infant navy of the Confederate States was ready to take the sea. The *Sumter*'s crew consisted of Captain Semmes, commanding, four lieutenants, a paymaster, a surgeon, a lieutenant of marines, four midshipmen, four engineers, boatswain, gunner, sail-maker, carpenter, captain's and purser's clerks, twelve marines, and seventy-two seamen. Thus manned and equipped, she dropped down the river on the 18th

June, and anchored off the Barracks for the purpose of receiving on board her ammunition and other similar stores. From thence she again proceeded on the same evening still lower down the river to Forts Philip and Jackson, where she brought up on the following day, to await a favourable opportunity for running the blockade.

For three days she remained at her new anchorage, this period of enforced inactivity being diligently employed in drilling and exercising the crew, and bringing the vessel generally into somewhat better order than her hurried equipment had as yet permitted her to assume. On the 21st June, however, intelligence was received that the *Powhattan* had left her station in chase of two vessels, and that a boat from the *Brooklyn* had passed into the river, and was making for the telegraph station. Captain Semmes at once decided to avail himself of this opportunity to escape to sea, and getting up steam, proceeded to Pass à L'Outre, and despatched one of his boats to the lighthouse for a pilot.

Here, however, an unexpected difficulty occurred. The light-house-keeper replied that he knew nothing of the pilots, and the *Sumter* was accordingly compelled again to bring up, whilst the Confederate privateer *Ivy* ran down, at Captain Semmes' request, to the South-west Pass, to endeavour to procure a pilot for her there. This expedition, however, met with no better success, and the Ivy returned with the information that the pilots refused to take charge of the vessel. A further despatch was addressed to Captain Semmes, from the Captain of the House of Pilots, to the effect that "no pilots were now on duty."

It now became necessary to act with vigour, and the Ivy was accordingly again despatched to the South-west Pass. This time, however, she carried with her the first lieutenant of the *Sumter*, with the following peremptory message to the Master of the Pilot Association to repair immediately on board, and instructions, if any hesitation were evinced in complying with this command, to arrest the entire body and bring them off:—

C.S. steamer *Sumter*, Head of the Passes
June 22nd, 1861.

Sir,—This is to command you to repair on board this ship with three or four of the most experienced pilots of the Bar. I am surprised to learn that an unwillingness has been expressed by some of the pilots of your Association to come on board the *Sumter*, and my purpose is to test the fact of such disloyalty to the Confederate States. If any man disobey this summons, I will not only have his Branch taken away from him, but I will send an armed force and arrest and bring him on board. I have the honour to be,

>Very respectfully,
>>Your obedient Servant,
>>>(Signed)   R. Semmes.

This extreme measure, however, was not found necessary. The mere threat was sufficient, and on the following day the master, with several of his pilots, made their appearance on board the *Sumter*. After a brief consultation with Captain Semmes, they one and all, with the exception of the master, expressed their willingness to take the vessel to sea, and thereupon the captain, selecting one of the number for this service, permitted the remainder to depart.

Meanwhile, however, the golden opportunity had been lost; the *Powhattan* had returned to her station, and the harbour was again hermetically sealed. The *Sumter*, therefore, was again compelled to return to her anchors, and eight more days passed wearily away without affording another opportunity of evasion. The interval of expectation, however, was again occupied in drilling and exercising the crew, which was now beginning to get into good working order; measures being also taken for extinguishing and removing the lamps from the lighthouses at Pass à L'Outre and the South Pass, Captain Semmes addressing to the Navy Department at Richmond the following letter upon the subject:—

>C.S. steamer *Sumter*, Head of the Passes,
>Miss. River, June 30th, 1861.

Sir,—I have the honour to inform the department that I am still at my anchors at the "Head of the Passes," the enemy closely investing both of the practicable outlets. At Pass à L'Outre there are three ships—the *Brooklyn* and another propeller, and a large side-wheel steamer; and at the South-west Pass there is the *Powhattan*, lying within half-a-mile of the Bar, and not stirring an inch from her anchors night or day. I am only surprised that the *Brooklyn* does not come up to this anchorage, which she might easily do (as there is water enough, and no military precautions whatever have been taken to hold it), and thus effectually seal all the passes of the river by her presence alone, which would enable the enemy to withdraw the remainder of his blockading force for use elsewhere.

With the assistance of the Jackson and McRae (neither of which has yet dropped down), I could probably hold my position here until an opportunity offered of my getting to sea. I shall watch diligently for such an opportunity, and have no doubt that, sooner or later, it will present itself. I found, upon dropping down to this point, that the lights at Pass à L'Outre and South Pass had been strangely overlooked, and that they were still burning. I caused them both to be extinguished, so that if bad weather should set in, the blockading vessel will have nothing "to hold on to," and will be obliged to make an offing.

At present the worst feature of the blockade is that the *Brooklyn* has the speed of me, so that, even though I should run the bar, I could not hope to escape her unless I surprised her, which, with her close watch of the Bar, at anchor near to, both night and day, it will be exceedingly difficult to do. I should be quite willing to try speed with the *Powhattan* if I could hope to run the gauntlet of her guns without being crippled; but unfortunately, with all the buoys and other marks removed, there is a perfectly blind bar except by daylight. In the meantime I am drilling my gun-crew to a proper use of the great guns and small arms.

With the exception of diarrhoea which is prevailing to some extent, brought on by too free a use of the river water in the excessive heats which prevail, the crew continue healthy.

   I have the honour to be, &c., &c.,
    (Signed)   R. Semmes.
Hon. G.E. Mallory, Secretary of the Navy,
Richmond, Virginia.

The following orders were also issued:—

Orders to be Observed on Board the C.S. Steamer Sumter.

1. The deck will never be left without a lieutenant, except that in port a midshipman may be assigned to keep the first lieutenant's watch.

2. The quarter-deck will at all times be regarded as a place of parade, and no sitting or lounging will be permitted thereon. For the purposes of this order all the spar deck abaft the mainmast will be regarded as the quarter-deck.

3. Officers will wear their uniforms at all times when on board ship, and when on shore on duty.

4. No officer will remain out of the ship after ten p.m. without

the special permission of the commander.

5. Each division of guns will be exercised at least three times a week; and there will be an exercise at general quarters twice a week, *viz.*, on Tuesdays and Fridays.

6. The crew will be mustered at quarters for inspection every morning at nine o'clock (except Sundays), and every evening at sunset.

7. On Sundays there will be a general muster for inspection at eleven p.m., when the officers will appear in undress with epaulettes.

8. The chief engineer is to keep the commander informed at all times (through the first lieutenant) of the condition of his engines, boilers, &c.; and he is to see that his assistants, &c., are punctual and zealous in the performance of their duties, and report such as fail therein to the first lieutenant.

9. There will be an engineer at all times on watch in the engine-room when the ship is under steam, and the engineer on watch will report every two hours to the officer of the deck how the engines are working, &c.

10. The marine officer will drill his guard once every day when the weather is suitable, and the duty of the ship does not interfere therewith.

11. The firemen will be exercised once a week, when the pumps, hose, &c., are to be adjusted, and used as in case of actual fire.

On the morning of the 29th of June hopes were again excited by a report from the pilot that the *Brooklyn* had left her station; and steam being got up with all speed on board the *Sumter*, she again dropped down to Pass à l'Outre, but only to find that the report had been fallacious. The *Brooklyn* was still at anchor, though a slight change of berth had placed her behind the shelter of a mass of trees. Once more, therefore, the *Sumter* was brought to an anchor; but on the day following, her patient waiting was rewarded by the long-looked-for opportunity.

On the morning of the 30th of June the *Brooklyn* was again reported under way and in chase of a vessel to leeward; and no sooner was the fact of her departure fairly verified than steam was got up for the last time, and the little *Sumter* dashed boldly across the bar, and stood out to sea.

Almost at the last moment, however, it seemed as though the attempt to escape were again to be baffled by difficulties on the part of the pilot. The man on board of the *Sumter* lost courage as the moment of trial came, and professed his inability to take the vessel through the pass thus left free by the departure of the *Brooklyn*, alleging as his excuse that he had not passed through it for more than three months. Happily the man's cowardice or treachery produced no ill effects; for, as the *Sumter* dropped down the river on her way towards the open sea, another pilot came gallantly off to her in his little boat, and volunteered to carry her through the Pass.

The *Sumter* had not reached within six miles of the bar when her movements were perceived from the *Brooklyn*, which at once relinquished the far less valuable prize on which she had been hitherto intent; and, changing her course, headed at top speed towards the bar, in hopes of cutting the *Sumter* off before she could reach it. The narrow opening through the bar, distant about six miles from either of the opposing vessels, now became the goal of a sharp and exciting race.

The *Sumter* had the advantage of the stream: but the *Brooklyn* was her superior in speed, and moreover, carried guns of heavier calibre and longer range. At length the Pass is reached; and dashing gallantly across it, the little *Sumter* starboards her helm and rounds the mudbanks to the eastward! As she does so the *Brooklyn* rounds to for a moment and gives her a shot from her pivot gun. But the bolt falls short; and now the race begins in earnest! The chase had not continued long, when a heavy squall of wind and rain came up and hid the pursuing vessel from sight; but it soon passed away, and the *Brooklyn* was again descried astern, under all sail and steam, and evidently gaining upon her little quarry. On this the *Sumter* was hauled two points higher up, thus bringing the wind so far forward that the *Brooklyn* was no longer able to carry sail. And now the chase in her turn began to gain upon her huge pursuer. But she was now in salt water, and her boilers were beginning to "prime" furiously.

It was necessary to slacken speed for a time, and as she did so the *Brooklyn* again recovered her advantage. Then gradually the foaming in the *Sumter*'s boilers ceased, and she was again put to her speed. The utmost pressure was put on; the propeller began to move at the rate of sixty-five revolutions a minute, and the *Brooklyn* once more dropped slowly but steadily astern. At length she gave up the chase, and at four o'clock in the afternoon, just four hours after crossing the bar, the crew of the *Sumter* gave three hearty cheers as her baffled pursuer put up her helm, and, relinquishing the chase, turned sullenly back to her station at the mouth of the river.

CHAPTER 3

Beginning the Cruise

The *Sumter* had now fairly commenced her gallant career. The 1st July dawned bright and fair with, a light breeze from the south-west, and the little vessel sped through the water at an average speed of about eight knots an hour. All that day not a sail appeared in sight. Night settled down in all the calm splendour of the tropic seas, and nothing disturbed its serenity save the monotonous beating of the *Sumter*'s propeller as she steered a south-easterly course down the Gulf of Mexico. The following day brought her safely to Cape Antonio, which she rounded under sail and steam, and striking the trade-winds, hoisted up her propeller and stood away towards the west.

The afternoon of the 3rd July brought the *Sumter* her first prize. At about 3 p.m. a sail was descried in shore, beating to windward, and steering a course that would bring her almost into contact with the Confederate vessel. To avoid suspicion, no notice was taken of the stranger until the two vessels had approached within the distance of a little more than a mile from each other, when a display of English colours from the Confederate was answered by the stranger with the stars and stripes of the United States. Down came the St. George's ensign from the *Sumter*'s peak, to be replaced almost before it had touched the deck by the stars and bars, which at that time constituted the flag of the Confederate States. A shot was fired across the bows of the astonished Yankee, who at once hove-to, and a boat was sent on board to take possession of the *Sumter*'s first capture.

The prize proved to be the ship *Golden Rocket*, from the Yankee State of Maine—a fine ship of 690 tons burthen, only three years old, and worth from 30,000 to 40,000 dollars. She Was bound to Cienfuegos in Cuba, but had no cargo on board, and Captain Semmes, being unwilling at that early stage of his cruise to spare a prize crew, determined to destroy the vessel, and after taking the captain and crew on board the *Sumter* set the prize on fire and left her to her fate.¹

The following day saw two more prizes fall into the *Sumter*'s hands. These were the brigantines *Cuba* and *Machias*, both of Maine. The captures were taken in tow and carried off in the direction of Cienfuegos. The next day, however, the *Cuba* broke adrift from her hawser, and on being recovered, a prize crew was sent on board the vessel, with directions to carry her into Cienfuegos, for which port Captain Semmes was now shaping his course.

Arrived off that harbour on the evening of the same day, it was found too late to attempt to enter, and two more vessels being descried in the offing, the *Machias* was cast off, with orders to lay-to until the morning, and the *Sumter* started off in chase. On coming up with the two vessels, at about half-past nine o'clock, they proved to be the United States brigantines, *Ben Dunning* and *Albert Adams*. They were at once taken possession of, and ordered to make the best of their way in charge of a prize crew to Cienfuegos.

The night was passed in standing off and on outside the harbour, and with the earliest dawn preparations were made for running in. The weather was bright and clear, and the brief twilight of the tropics flushed rapidly into the full glare of day, and showed to the watchful eyes on board the *Sumter* the welcome spectacle of three more vessels being towed out to sea by a steamer, the stars and stripes floating gaily from their peaks. Warily and patiently the little *Sumter* lay in wait, under the shelter of the land, until the steamer had cast off her convoy, and the three unsuspecting vessels were fairly beyond the maritime

---

1. "It was about ten o'clock at night when the first glare of light burst from her cabin-hatch. Few, few on board can forget the spectacle. A ship set fire to at sea! It would seem that man was almost warring with his Maker. Her helpless condition, the red flames licking the rigging as they climbed aloft, the sparks and pieces of burning rope taken off by the wind and flying miles to leeward, the ghastly glare thrown upon the dark sea as far as the eye could reach, and then the death-like stillness of the scene—all these combined to place the Golden Rocket on the tablet of our memories for ever. But, notwithstanding the reluctance with which we did it, we would not have missed the opportunity for anything on earth. We wanted no war—we wanted peace; we had dear friends among those who were making war upon us, and for their sakes, if not for the sake of humanity, we hoped to be allowed to separate in peace; but it could not be; they forced the war upon us—they endeavoured to destroy us. For this, and for this alone, we burn their ships and destroy their commerce. We have no feeling of enmity against them, and all we ask is to be let alone—to be allowed to tread the path we have chosen for ourselves."—*Cruise of the Sumter*, from the *Index* May 1st, 1862.

league from the neutral shore, within which the law of nations forbids that captures should be made. Then suddenly her decks swarmed with men, the black smoke poured from her funnel, the sails filled, and out she came in pursuit. The chase was brief, and ere long the *barque West Wind,* the brigantine *Naiad,* and the *barque Louisa Kilham* were in charge of prize crews, and wending their way sadly back to the port they had so recently left in full expectation of a prosperous voyage.

So, with her little fleet of prizes, six in all, before her, the *Sumter* steered proudly into the harbour of Cienfuegos. As she passed the fort which guards the entrance, a hail was heard from the shore, accompanied by the almost simultaneous report of a couple of musket shots fired over the vessel, for the purpose, apparently, of enforcing the order to bring up and come to an anchor. The command having been obeyed, a boat was at once despatched in charge of Lieutenant Evans to call on the Commandant and ask an explanation of this inhospitable reception.

The message was brought back, that the flag of the new Confederacy had not been understood by him, and that the vessel had consequently been brought up in compliance with the standing order that no vessel, whether of war or otherwise, should be permitted to pass until her nationality had been ascertained. Explanations, of course, followed, and in the evening came the Commandant, with the Governor's permission either to land or go to sea, but accompanied by an intimation that the six prizes would be detained until instructions could be received from headquarters concerning them.

Lieutenant Chapman was now sent on shore with the following despatch for the Governor, and also to make arrangements for coaling and for the safety and ultimate disposition of the prizes:

C.S. Steamer *Sumter.* Cienfuegos,
Island of Cuba, July 6th, 1861.

Sir,—I have the honour to inform your Excellency of my arrival at the Port of Cienfuegos with seven prizes of war. These vessels are the brigantines *Cuba, Machias, Ben Dunning, Albert Adams* and *Naiad*; and *barques West Wind* and *Louisa Kilham,* property of citizens of the United States, which States, as your Excellency is aware, are waging an unjust and aggressive war upon the Confederate States, which I have the honour, with this ship under my command, to represent. I have sought a port of Cuba with these prizes, with the expectation that Spain will extend to cruisers of the Confederate States the same friendly reception that in similar circumstances she would extend to the cruisers of the enemy; in other words, that she will permit me to leave the captured vessels within her jurisdiction until they can be adjudicated by a Court of Admiralty of the Confederate States.

As a people maintaining a Government *de facto*, and not only holding the enemy in check, but gaining advantages over him, we are entitled to all the rights of belligerents, and I confidently rely upon the friendly disposition of Spain, who is our near neighbour in the most important of her colonial possessions, to receive us with equal and even-handed justice, if not with the sympathy which our unity of interest and policy, with regard to an important social and industrial institution, are so well calculated to inspire. A rule which would exclude our prizes from her ports during the war, although it should be applied in terms equally to the enemy, would not, I respectfully suggest, be an equitable or just rule.

The basis of such a rule, as, indeed, of all the conduct of a neutral during war, is equal and impartial justice to all the belligerents; and this should be a substantial and practical justice, and not exist in delusive or deceptive terms merely. Now, a little reflection will, I think, show your Excellency that the rule in question cannot be applied in the present war without operating with great injustice to the Confederate States.

It is well known to your Excellency that the United States being a manufacturing and commercial people, whilst the Confederate States have been thus far almost wholly an agricultural and planting people, the former had within their limits and control almost the whole naval force of the old Government, and that they have seized and appropriated this force to themselves, regardless of the just claims of the Confederates States to a portion, and a large portion of it, as tax-payers out of whose contributions it was created. The United States are thus enabled to blockade all the important ports of the Confederate States. In this condition of things, observe the practical working of the rule which I am discussing.

It must be admitted that we have equal belligerent rights with the enemy.

One of the most important of these rights in a war against a commercial people, is that which I have just exercised, of capturing his property upon the high seas. But how are the Confederate States to enjoy to its full extent the benefit of this right, if their cruisers are not permitted to enter neutral ports with their prizes, and retain them there in safe custody until they can he condemned and disposed of?

They cannot send them to their own ports for the reasons already stated. Except for the purpose of destruction, therefore, their right of capture would be entirely defeated by the adoption of the rule in question, whilst the enemy would suffer no inconvenience from it, as all his ports are open to him. I take it for granted that Spain will not think of acting upon so unjust and unequal a rule.

But another question arises, indeed has already arisen, in the cases of some of the very captures which I have brought into port. The cargoes of several of the vessels are claimed, as appears by certificates found among the papers, as Spanish property.

This fact cannot of course be verified, except by a judicial proceeding in the Prize Courts of the Confederate States.

But whilst this fact is being determined, what is to be done with the property? I have the right to destroy the vessels, but not the cargoes, in case the latter should prove to be, as claimed, Spanish property—but how am I to destroy the former, and not the latter? I cannot before sentence unlade the cargoes and deliver them to the claimants, for I do not know that the claims will be sustained; and I cannot destroy them, for I do not know that the claims will not be sustained.

Indeed, one of the motives which influenced me in seeking a Spanish port, was the fact that these cargoes were claimed by Spanish subjects, whom I was desirous of putting to as little inconvenience as possible in the unlading and reception of their property, after sentence, should it be restored to them.

It will be for your Excellency to consider and act upon these grave questions, touching alike the interests of both our Governments.

     I have the honour to be, &c., &c.,
      (Signed) R. Semmes.

His Excellency Don Jose de la Pozuela,
Governor of the City of Cienfuegos,
Island of Cuba.

At eight o'clock on the morning of the 7th July, Lieutenant Chapman returned, bringing with him Don Isnaga and Don Mariano Dias, two Cuban gentlemen, warm sympathizers with the Confederate cause. The latter of these gentlemen was at once appointed prize agent, and after partaking of the hospitality of the ship, they returned to shore, and the remainder of the day was spent on board the *Sumter* in replenishing the various stores that had begun to run low after her cruise. In the course of the day about 100 tons of coal and 5000 gallons of water were shipped, besides a quantity of fresh provisions for the crew; and at about 10 p.m. an answer arrived from the Governor to the despatch sent on shore the previous evening by Lieutenant Chapman.

It stated that the Captain-General of Cuba had given instructions as follows:—

1. No cruiser of either party can bring their prizes into Spanish ports.
2. If in any captures the territory of Cuba has been violated, the Spanish courts will themselves judge of the matter.
3. Any prizes will be detained until instructions can be had from the Queen.

These points being ascertained, the prizes already at anchor were left to the care of the prize agent, Don Dias, and at about midnight the *Sumter* hove up her anchor and again proceeded to sea. Nothing had as yet been seen of the prize brig *Cuba*, which had been left in charge of a prize crew a day or two before, nor, indeed, did she ever arrive at the rendezvous, being recaptured by the enemy, and carried off to the United States.

Shortly after leaving Cienfuegos, a sail was descried in the offing, which, however, on being overhauled, proved to be only a Spanish brig, and the *Sumter* accordingly kept on her course, between 9 and 10 p.m. passing the Cayman Islets, which, Captain Semmes remarks in his journal, are laid down some fifteen or sixteen miles to the westward of their real position. Daylight of the 9th July found the little *Sumter* struggling against a strong trade wind and heavy sea, off the western end of Jamaica, the blue mountains of which picturesque island remained in sight during the entire day.

At this period an accident occurred which for some time deprived the *Sumter* of the active supervision of her commander. Always of delicate constitution, and ill-fitted for the rough part he had now to play, he had lately been still further weakened by illness; and on mounting the companion-ladder, for the purpose of desiring that the vessel might not be driven at so high a speed against the heavy head-sea, a sudden giddiness came over him, and after leaning for a few moments with his head upon his arm, altogether lost consciousness, and fell heavily backwards down the companion to the cabin floor, where he lay for some time in a state of insensibility. The result of this fall was some very serious bruises, with a difficulty in breathing, which for some days kept him confined to his hammock. At this time, however, the *Sumter* was quite out of the ordinary track of commerce, and was labouring slowly through a heavy sea against the steady and tenacious trade-wind at the rate of little more than five knots an hour, making terrible inroads upon the small supply of coal which was so precious to her.

The 13th July found the trade-wind increased to a regular gale, the *Sumter* making literally no way at all against the heavy head-sea. In this state of affairs it was found necessary to abandon the previous intention of making for Barbados, as there was not sufficient coal on board to last the distance. This project, therefore, was given up, the vessel's head turned from the sea, the fires let down, the ship got under sail, and a new course shaped for Curaçao. Here it was hoped that a fresh supply of coal might be obtained, and the little *Sumter* staggered along under a press of canvas towards her new destination, the violent motion causing great distress to the captain, who was still confined to his cabin, and almost entirely to his hammock.

On the 15th July, the weather moderated for a time, and a warm sunny afternoon, with comparatively little sea, gave an interval of rest. The next morning saw the wind again blowing freshly, but at 9 p.m. land was seen on the starboard bow, and at four in the afternoon the *Sumter* passed the north end of the island of Curaçao, running down the coast to within about a mile of St. Anne's, where she arrived at a little after seven o'clock. A gun was fired as a signal for a pilot, and soon after one came off, promising to return again in the morning, and carry the vessel into harbour.

Morning came, and, true to his word, the pilot once more made his appearance upon deck. But the remainder of his promise he was unable to fulfil. "The Governor regrets," he said, in reply to Captain Semmes' inquiries, "that he cannot permit you to enter, he having received express orders to that effect." A little diplomacy, however, soon removed the difficulty, which had arisen from the urgent representations of the United States consul on the previous evening, aided, no doubt, by a defective description of the vessel from the pilot. Lieutenant Chapman was sent on shore with the following letter to the Governor:—

C.S. steamer *Sumter*, off St. Anne's,
Curaçao, July 17th, 1861.

His Excellency Governor Crol:

Sir,—I was surprised to receive by the pilot this morning a message from your Excellency to the effect, that this ship could not be permitted to enter the harbour unless she was in distress, as your Excellency had received orders from your Government not to admit vessels of war of the Confederate States of America to the hospitality of the ports under your Excellency's command. I must respectfully suggest that there must be some mistake here, and I have sent to you the bearer, Lieut. Chapman, C.S. Navy, for the purpose of an explanation.

Your Excellency must be under some misapprehension as to the character of this vessel. She is a ship of war, duly commissioned by the Government of the Confederate States, which States have been recognised as belligerents in the present war by all the leading Powers of Europe—*viz.*, Great Britain, France, Spain, &c., as your Excellency must be aware. It is true that these Powers have prohibited both belligerents from bringing prizes into their several jurisdictions, but no one of them has made a distinction either between the prizes or the cruisers themselves of the belligerents, the cruisers of both Governments being admitted to the hospitalities of the ports of all these great Powers on terms of perfect equality.

Am I to understand from your Excellency that Holland has adopted a different rule, and that she not only excludes the prizes, but the ships of war themselves of the Confederate States, and this at the same time that she admits the cruisers of the United States, thus departing from her neutrality in this war, ignoring the Confederate States as belligerents, and aiding and assisting their enemy? If this be the position which Holland has assumed in this contest, I pray your Excellency to be kind enough to say as much to me in writing.

I have the honour to be, &c., &c.

(Signed)   R. Semmes.

Governor Crol, St. Anne's, Curaçao.

This explanation removed all difficulties, and by 11 p.m. the requisite permission had been obtained, and the *Sumter* was safely at anchor in the lagoon.

Here she lay for some days, surrounded by bum-boats filled with picturesque natives of all colours, chattering like parrots, and almost as gaudy in their plumage. Meanwhile the crew were hard at work replenishing the coal-bunkers, filling up wood and water, taking in fresh provisions, and effecting the necessary repairs after the late cruise. While thus employed, a visit was received from a Venezuelan, who in very good English represented himself as a messenger or agent of President Castro, now in exile at Curaçao with four of his cabinet ministers. This emissary's object was to negotiate a passage in the *Sumter* for Don Castro and some twenty of his officers, with arms, ammunition, &c., to the mainland opposite. This proposition, however, Captain Semmes politely but very promptly declined, on the grounds, firstly, that he was not going in the direction indicated; and secondly, that if he were, it would be an undue interference on the part of a neutral with the revolutionary parties now contending for the control of Venezuela.

"It was remarked," he writes, "that Castro was the *de jure* President;" to which I replied, "that we did not look into these matters, the opposite party being in *de facto* possession of the government."

At Curaçao the *Sumter* remained until the 24th July, coaling, refitting, provisioning, and allowing each of her crew in turn a short run on shore, to recruit his spirits and get rid of his superfluous cash. At noon on the 24th she was once more under way, leaving behind her, however, one of her seamen, a worthless fellow of the name of John Orr, who, enticed away, as was suspected, by a Yankee captain and the Yankee keeper of a public-house, took the opportunity to make his escape from the ship. The loss, however, was not of importance; and after one or two slight attempts to trace him, the *Sumter* stood out of the harbour and shaped her course towards Venezuela.

Daybreak of the 25th July again presented to the eager eyes on board of the *Sumter* the welcome apparition of a sail. Chase was immediately given, and at half-past six the *Abby Bradford*, from New York to Puerto Caballo, was duly seized and taken in tow, her Captain proceeding with her upon her original course towards Puerto Caballo. It was late before that place was reached, and the night was spent standing off and on outside the harbour. With the return of day, however, the *Sumter* ran once more along the shore; and, without waiting for a pilot, steered boldly past the group of small, bold-looking islands, and dropped her anchor in the port. No sooner was the anchor down than the following letter was despatched to the Governor, asking permission to leave the prize until adjudication:—

C.S. steamer *Sumter*. Puerto Caballo,
July 26th, 1861.

Sir,—I have the honour to inform your Excellency of my arrival at this port in this ship, under my command, and with the prize schooner *Abby Bradford*, captured by me about seventy miles to the northward and eastward. The *Abby Bradford* is the property of citizens of the United States, with which States, as your Excellency is aware, the Confederate States, which I have the honour to represent, are at war; and the cargo would appear to belong also to citizens of the United States, who have shipped it on consignment to a house in Puerto Caballo. Should any claim be given, however, for the cargo, or any part of it, the question of ownership can only be decided by the Prize Courts of the Confederate States.

In the meantime, I have the honour to request that your Excellency will permit me to leave this prize vessel with her cargo in the port of Puerto Caballo, until the question of prize can be adjudicated by the proper tribunals of my country. This will be a convenience to all parties, as well to any citizen of Venezuela who may have an interest in the cargo, as to the captors, who have also valuable interests to protect. In making this request, I do not propose that the Venezuelan Government shall depart from a strict neutrality between the belligerents; as the same rule it applies to us, it can give the other party the benefit of, also. In other words, with the most scrupulous regard for the neutrality, she may admit both belligerents to bring their prizes into her waters; and of this neither belligerent can complain, since whatever favour is extended to its enemy is extended also to itself.

I have an additional and cogent reason for making this request, and that is, that the rule of exclusion, although it might be applied in terms to both belligerents, would not operate equally and justly upon them both. It is well known to your Excellency that the Northern United States (which are now making an aggressive and unjust war upon the Confederate States, denying to the latter the right of self-government, which is fundamental in all republics, and invading their territories for the purpose of subjugation) are manufacturing and commercial states, whilst the Confederate States have been thus far agricultural and planting states; and that, as a consequence of this difference of pursuits, the former States had in their possession at the commencement of this war almost all the naval force of the old Government, which they have not hesitated to seize and appropriate to their own use, although a large proportion of it belonged of right to the Confederate States, which had been taxed to create it.

By means of this naval force, dishonestly seized as aforesaid, the enemy has been enabled to blockade all the important ports of the Confederate States. This blockade necessarily shuts out the cruisers of the Confederate States from their own ports, and if foreign Powers shut them out also, they can make no other use of their prizes than to destroy them. Thus your Excellency sees that, under the rule of exclusion, the enemy could enjoy his right of capture to its full extent, his own ports being all open to him, whilst the cruisers of the Confederate States could enjoy it *sub modo* only, that is, for the purpose of destruction. A rule which would produce such effects as this is not an equal or a just rule (although it might in terms be extended to both parties); and as equality and justice are of the essence of neutrality, I take it for granted that Venezuela will not adopt it.

On the other hand, the rule admitting both parties alike, with their prizes, into your ports, until the Prize Courts of the respective countries can have time to adjudicate the cases as they arrive, would work equal and exact justice to both; and this is no more than the Confederate States demand. With reference to the present case, as the cargo consists chiefly of provisions which are perishable, I would ask leave to sell them at public auction for the benefit of "whom it may concern," depositing the proceeds with a suitable prize agent until the decision of the court can be known. With regard to the vessel, I request that she may remain in the custody of the same agent until condemned and sold.

    I have the honour to be, &c., &c.
    (Signed)   R. Semmes.
His Excellency the Governor and Military
   Commander of Puerto Caballo.

To this, however, that functionary could not be induced to assent, his reply being that such a proposition was altogether beyond his province to entertain, and that the *Sumter* must take her departure within four-and-twenty hours. At daylight, therefore, on the 27th, a prize crew was sent on board of the *Abby Bradford*, with orders to proceed to New Orleans, and at six o'clock the *Sumter* was again outside of the inhospitable port of Puerto Caballo.

The anchor was not fairly at the cathead when a sail was reported seaward, which on capture proved to be the *barque Joseph Maxwell*, of Philadelphia. The capture having taken place at about seven miles from the port to which she was bound, and half of the cargo being the property of a neutral owner, a boat was despatched with her master and the paymaster of the *Sumter* to endeavour to effect negotiation. The proposition was, that the owner of the neutral half of the cargo should purchase at a small price the remaining half and the vessel herself, which should then be delivered to him intact without delay. This little arrangement, however, was somewhat summarily arrested by the action of the Governor, who, much to Captain Semmes' astonishment, sent off orders that the prize should at once be brought into port, there to remain in his Excellency's custody, until a Venezuelan court should have decided whether the capture had or had not been effected within the marine league from the coast prescribed by international law!

This somewhat extraordinary demand did not receive the respect or obedience on which its promulgator had doubtless relied. Beating to quarters, and with his men standing to their guns in readiness for instant action, the *Sumter* stood out once more towards her prize; sent the master and his family ashore in one of his own boats, put a prize crew on board the *Maxwell*, and despatched her to a port at the south side of Cuba. It is believed that these unfriendly demonstrations on the part of the Governor of Puerto Caballo were owing to a fear that the *Sumter* was in truth employed upon some such enterprise as that on which the agent of Don Castro at Curaçao had vainly endeavoured to engage her, and was endeavouring to effect a landing for revolutionary troops.

The *Sumter* now again stood away upon her course towards the eastward, and at five in the evening came across an hermaphrodite brig, from whose peak floated the hated but welcome stars and stripes. This time, however, it was able to wave in safe defiance before the eyes of the dreaded foe, for the sagacious master had kept carefully "within jumping distance" of the shore, and the sacred "marine league of neutrality" protected the vessel from the fate that had befallen so many of her countrymen.

The afternoon of the 28th July found the *Sumter* off the island of Tortuga, and at eleven that evening the ship was hove to in thirty-two fathoms of water off the eastern end of Margaritta. Two more days' run along the Venezuelan coast, at times in so dense a fog that it was necessary to run within a mile of the shore in order to "hold on" to the land, and the Gulf of Bahia was reached. Following close on the track of a vessel just arrived from Madeira, and acquainted with the harbour, the *Sumter* held on her course through the Huero or Umbrella Passage, and shortly after noon anchored off the town of Port of Spain, receiving as she did so a salute from the ensign of an English brig passing out of the harbour.

Chapter 4

A Hot Pursuit

The arrival of the *Sumter* at Port of Spain appeared to create no small excitement among the inhabitants, official and non-official, of that little colony. The Governor at once proceeded to take legal opinion as to the propriety of permitting the suspicious stranger to coal, and a long leading article in the colonial paper gave expression to the editor's serious doubts whether the *Sumter* were really what she represented herself to be, a regularly commissioned vessel of war, and not, after all, a privateer. The legal advisers of the Governor seem to have reported favourably on Captain Semmes' request, for permission was given to take on board the requisite supplies, and the *Sumter*'s coaling proceeded, though not with much rapidity.

The morning of the 2nd August introduced on board a visitor of a new description. Through the heavy tropical rain which had been pouring almost incessantly since the arrival of the *Sumter*, covering the calm water of the harbour with little dancing jets, and drumming on the steamer's decks the most unmusical of tattoos, a little dingy was seen approaching, and in due time brought alongside of the Confederate man-of-war the master of a Baltimore brig, which, was lying at anchor some little distance off. The worthy skipper had heard of the terrible doings of his new neighbour, and in no little anxiety for his own fate had determined to take the bull by the horns, and inquire on board the *Sumter* herself whether he would be permitted to depart without molestation.

Great was the poor, man's delight when he was hailed as a native of a sister State, and informed that Maryland, though compelled by superior force to maintain an apparent allegiance to her enemy, was still considered a friend by her natural allies of the South, and that strict orders had therefore been given to let her commerce pass unharmed.

With a lightened heart he returned on board his vessel, and the Baltimore brig went on her way rejoicing.

The afternoon of the same day brought two more visitors in the persons of two English officers in mufti; but the international courtesy did not extend so far as returning the official visit made on Captain Semmes' behalf by Lieutenant Chapman, and Government-house remained unrepresented on board the *Sumter*. "His Excellency," it is to be feared, had taken offence at the slight passed upon his official position by Captain Semmes, in not having taken care to recover his health and strength sufficiently early to be able to make the official visit in person!

The morning of the 4th August would have seen the *Sumter* again under way but for some informality in the paymaster's vouchers, which had to be rectified; and during the delay thus occasioned, H.M. ship Cadmus entered the harbour, and the *Sumter's* departure was postponed with the object of communicating with her. Accordingly, a lieutenant was sent on board the new arrival, the visit being promptly returned by an officer of similar rank from the Cadmus, who, after exchanging the usual civilities, delivered himself of a polite message from Captain Hillyer, to the effect, that as the *Sumter* was the first vessel he had as yet fallen in with under the flag of the Confederate States, he would be obliged if Captain Semmes would favour him with a sight of his commission. To this, of course, the latter had no objection; and the demands of courtesy having been satisfied by the previous production of the English lieutenant's commission, that of Captain Semmes was duly exhibited, and the ceremonial visitor departed.

The next morning brought Captain Hillyer himself on board, and a long conversation ensued on the war and various kindred topics, the English captain leaving behind him a most agreeable impression. The visit over, steam was once more got up on board the *Sumter*, and at 1 p.m. she steamed out through the eastern or Mona Island passage, and running down the picturesque coast, with its mountain sides uncultivated but covered with numerous huts, passed at ten o'clock that evening between Trinidad and Tobago, and entered once more upon the broad North Atlantic.

For some days the time now hung somewhat heavily upon the hands of the little community. A solitary brigantine only was seen, and she so far to windward, that with the short supply of coal afforded by the not overscrupulous merchants of Port of Spain, it was not thought worthwhile to incur the expense and delay of a chase. The *Sumter* was now terribly in need of an excitement. Not a living thing was in sight, but the glittering schools of flying fish which ever and anon darted into view, and skimming rapidly over their surface sank again beneath the waves, only to be once more driven for a brief refuge to the upper air by their unseen but relentless enemies below. Drill and exercise were now the order of the day during the hours of light, and as the sun set and the tropic night came rushing swiftly up over the yet glowing sky, chessboards and backgammon-boards were brought out, and discussions, social, political, and literary, divided the long hours of inaction with the yarn and the song, and other mild but not ineffectual distractions of life at sea.

Still it was with feelings of no small satisfaction that "green water" was again reached, and the *Sumter* found herself within about ninety miles of the (Dutch) Guiana coast. Hopes were now entertained of soon reaching Maranham, but the next day showed them to be fallacious. A strong northerly current had set in, and, in addition to this drawback, it was discovered that the defalcations of the Port of Spain coal merchants were more serious than had been supposed, and there was not sufficient fuel left for the run. Next day matters were worse rather than better. The northerly current was running at the extraordinary rate of sixty miles in the twenty-four hours, a speed equal to that of the Gulf Stream in its narrowest part. Only three days' fuel remained, and making allowance for the northerly set, there were fully 550 miles to be accomplished before Maranham could be reached.

Still the *Sumter* held patiently on her course in hopes of a change; but no change came. Wind and current were as hostile as ever, and the observations of the 11th August giving lat. 2° 38' N., long. 47° 48' W., the question of the voyage to Maranham, or even to Para, appeared definitely settled, and letting his fires go down, Captain Semmes put up his helm, made all sail, and stood away on a N.W. course, hoping to find a fresh supply of coal at some of the ports of Guiana under his lee.

The afternoon of that day saw the sky clear, the sea almost calm, and the little *Sumter*, rolling along on the long, lazy swell, with all her starboard studding-sails set, at about three or four knots an hour, towards Cape Orange, from which point it was intended to make her way into Cayenne.

Here she arrived on the 15th August, but her hopes were again doomed to disappointment. On coming to anchor, officers were at once despatched with the usual complimentary messages to the Governor, and a request to be informed whether the vessel could be supplied with coal. These officers, however, were not permitted to land, the reason given being, that they were without a clean bill of health from their last port. It was in vain to represent the perfect state of health of the crew, and the length of time they had been at sea. The official mind was closed against any argument but that of the *consigne*. Five days' quarantine were ordered, and five days' quarantine must be undergone, before the salubrious shores of Cayenne could be exposed to the danger of infection from the new comers; and as the authorities accompanied this fiat with the statement, that there was no coal to be had in the place even for the supply of their own government vessels, our captain determined to make no further trial upon the discussion, but to seek his supplies elsewhere.

The afternoon of the next day brought the *Sumter* to the coast of (Dutch) Guiana; but there being no pilot to be found, she was compelled to come to an anchor in about four fathoms of water. Here, as the sun set, the dark smoke of a steamer was discovered against the glowing sky, and suspicion was at once aroused that the new comer must be a Yankee cruiser on the lookout for the Confederate "pirates." The drums beat to quarters on board of the little *Sumter*; decks were cleared for action; ports were triced up, guns run out, and every preparation made to give the supposed enemy a warm reception.

Darkness had closed in as the suspected vessel approached; the thump, thump, thump of her screw sounding plainly on the still night air. Silently she approached the watchful cruiser, steering completely round her anchorage, as though herself suspicious of the character of her new companion. No hostile demonstration, however, followed; the night was too dark to distinguish friend from foe; and the strange sail having come to anchor at some little distance from the *Sumter*, and evincing no disposition to assume the offensive, the guns were run in again, and the men were at length dismissed to the hammocks.

Early next morning steam was again got up on board the Confederate cruiser, which ran down under French colours for a closer examination of the stranger, who was lying quietly at anchor about two miles in-shore of her. As the *Sumter* approached she also mounted the tricolour, at the sight of which the pretended nationality of the cruiser was laid aside, and the stars and bars flew out gaily from her mizzen-peak. The Frenchman appeared much pleased at having thus fallen in with the celebrated *Sumter*; and being, like her, bound into Paramaribo, and of considerably lighter draught, invited her to follow him into the river, where a pilot might be obtained.

Arrived in Paramaribo the *Sumter* received tidings of the United States steamer Keystone State, which had been "in pursuit" of her for some time. This vessel was not very much larger than the *Sumter*, and their crews and armaments were very nearly equal, so there were great hopes on board the Confederate of a brush with the enemy on something like equal terms. These hopes, however, like so many others, were doomed to disappointment. By some fatality the Keystone State could never manage to come up with her quarry. While the latter had been coaling at Trinidad, she was performing a similar operation at Barbados, arriving thence at Trinidad after the *Sumter* had sailed. From this port she again started "in pursuit," but her chances of overtaking her enemy may perhaps have been somewhat affected by the fact, that on learning that the *Sumter* had started eastward, she at once followed upon a westerly track, which, doubtless to the great grief of her commander and crew, somehow failed to bring her alongside of the vessel of which she was in search.[1]

But if the United States war vessels were somewhat eccentric in their notion of a hot pursuit, it must be admitted that the United States consuls and other agents on shore were by no means equally scrupulous. Every possible expedient to prevent the *Sumter* from obtaining the necessary supplies of coal was tried by the consul at Paramaribo, but with less success than his strenuous exertions deserved. His first idea was to buy up all the coal in the port, and a handsome price was offered—in bonds on the United States government—for that purpose. But with singular blindness to their own interests the merchants of Paramaribo declined to put their trust in these bonds, and the ready money not being forthcoming the hopeful scheme was compelled to be abandoned. Undismayed by this first failure, the gallant Yankee next sought to charter all the lighters by which the coal could be conveyed on board, and here he was very nearly successful. One or two of the owners however declined to be bought up, and in the lighters supplied by them the process of coaling commenced. Still the persevering consul was not to be beaten. Failing the owners of

---

1. The writer of the Notes in the *Index* remarks on this curious proceeding:—"Rather a strange idea we thought. It put us in mind of a sportsman in California who was very anxious to kill a grizzly bear. At length he found the trail, and after following it for some hours gave it up and returned to camp. On being questioned why he did not follow in pursuit, he quietly replied that the trail was getting *too fresh*. It must have been so with the Keystone State—the trail was getting too fresh."

the contumacious barges, their crews were yet accessible to the gentle influences at his command, and some forty tons of coal found their way to the bottom of the harbour, instead of to the *Sumter*'s bunkers for which they had been destined.

At length, however, in spite of both active Yankee and dilatory Dutchmen, the operation was completed, and the little *Sumter* once more ready for sea. Even now, however, she was not to get away without a parting arrow from her indefatigable enemy. On the morning of her proposed departure the captain's negro servant went on shore as usual for the day's marketing, when he was waylaid by the worthy Yankee and persuaded indefinitely to postpone his return. Poor fellow! if his fate was anything like that of thousands of others "set free" by their so-called friends of the North, he must have long ere this most bitterly repented his desertion.

There was no time, however, to spare for searching after the runaway, so after a brief conference with the authorities, who were apparently not over anxious for his arrest, the *Sumter* got up steam and once more proceeded in the direction of Maranham.

CHAPTER 5

A Visit to the President

A whole month had thus been lost through the failure of the *Sumter*'s coal off the mouth of the Amazon. News, too, had been received at Paramaribo that six or seven large fast steamers were in hot pursuit; and as it was not likely that all of these—the larger, perhaps, more especially—would adopt the tactics of the Keystone State, it was an object with the solitary little object of their vengeance to make the best of her way to some safer cruising ground.

On the 31st August, then, she took her final leave of Paramaribo, and running some eight or nine miles off the coast in a northerly direction as a blind, altered her course to east half-south, with the intention of avoiding the current by which she had on the former occasion been so baffled, by keeping along the coast in soundings where its strength would be less felt.

The 4th September found her well past the mouth of the Amazon, bowling along under all fore-and-aft sails, with bright, clear weather, and a fresh trade-wind from about east by south. This was about her best point of sailing, and there being no longer any current against her, her log showed a run of 175 miles in the twenty-four hours. On the same day a strange sail was seen, but time and coal were now too valuable to be risked, and the temptation to chase was resisted. In the evening the equator was crossed, and the little *Sumter* bade farewell to the North Atlantic, and entered on a new sphere of operations.

The 5th September was a day of misfortunes. The weather was thick and lowering; the wind rapidly increasing; to half a gale, and the little vessel straining heavily at her anchor. In heaving up, a sudden jerk broke it short off at the shank, the metal about the broken part proving to have been very indifferent. She now ran very cautiously and anxiously towards the light, and into the bay, no pilot being in sight. For some time all went well, and the chief dangers appeared to be over, when suddenly the vessel ran with a heavy shock upon a sandbank, knocking off a large portion of her false keel, and for the moment occasioning intense anxiety to all on board.

Fortunately, however, the bank was but a narrow ridge, and the next sea carried the little vessel safely across it, and out of danger. Much speculation, however, was excited by this unlooked-for mishap, but a careful examination of the ship's position on the chart failed to elucidate the mystery: the part of the bay where the *Sumter* had struck being marked as clear ground. It was fortunate, at all events, that the vessel escaped clear, for within the next hour and a half the tide fell five feet, which with so heavy a load as that on board the *Sumter* could not but have occasioned a terrible strain had she been lying on the top of the bank.

Finding the soundings still so irregular as to threaten further danger, the *Sumter* now came to an anchor, and some fishing boats being perceived on the shore at a little distance, a boat was despatched which speedily returned with a fisherman, who piloted her safely to the town of Maranham. She was visited by a Brazilian naval officer, who congratulated her captain not a little on his fortunate escape, the Brazilian men-of war never thinking of attempting the passage without a coast pilot.

The day following that on which the *Sumter* arrived at Maranham was the Brazilian Independence Day. The town put on its gayest appearance; men-of-war and merchantmen tricked themselves out with flags from deck to truck, while the guns of the former thundered a salute across the ordinarily quiet bay. Amidst their universal demonstration the *Sumter* alone remained unmoved. The nation whose flag she bore had not yet been recognised by the Brazilian government, and it would therefore have been the height of incongruity to sport the slightest bunting on such an occasion. The more so as the good folks of Maranham, though to all appearance personally well disposed towards the Confederates, were in such dread of officially committing themselves, that they did not venture to invite the officers of the newly-arrived vessel to the grand ball given by the authorities in honour of the day.

On Monday, the 9th September, Captain Semmes took up his quarters on shore, and proceeded to make a formal call on the President of the Department. That functionary, however, pleaded indisposition, appointing the hour of noon on the following day for the desired interview. Meanwhile Captain Semmes had hardly returned to his comfortable quarters at the Hotel do Porto, ere he, in his turn, received a visit from Captain Pinto of the Brazilian navy, and the Chief of Police, a confidential friend of the President—the object of these gentlemen being to read to him a formal protest from the consul of the United States to the government, against the *Sumter*'s being permitted to receive coal or other supplies in the port. Amongst other equally bold statements this document asserted that the Confederate cruiser had not been permitted to enter the ports of any other European power. Assertions like these were of course easily disposed of, and it was agreed that the question should be discussed at the morrow's interview. The account of this discussion had, perhaps, better be given in Captain Semmes' own words:—

Tuesday, September 11th.—Called upon the President at twelve, and was admitted to an interview; the Chief of Police and Captain Pinto being present. I exhibited to the President my commission, and read to him a portion of my instructions, to show him that it was the desire of the Confederate States to cultivate friendly relations with other powers, and to pay particular respect to neutral property and rights; and the better to satisfy him that he might supply me with coal without a departure from neutrality, and to contradict the false sentiments of the United States Consul, I exhibited to him a newspaper from Trinidad, setting forth the fact that the question of the propriety of supplying me with coal in that island, had been formally submitted to the law officers of the Crown, and decided in my favour, &c.

The President then announced to me that I might purchase whatever supplies I wanted, coal included, munitions of war only excepted. I then stated to him that this war was in fact a war as much in behalf of Brazil as of ourselves, and that if we were beaten in the contest, Brazil would be the next one to be assailed by Yankee propagandists. These remarks were favourably received, the three gentlemen evidently sympathizing with us.

Captain Semmes continues his short diary as follows:—

Fresh wind and cloudy. Painting ship, and making preparations for the reception of coal. We are looking anxiously for the arrival of the Rio mail steamer, as we have a report brought by a Portuguese vessel from Pernambuco that a great battle has been fought; that we have beaten the enemy; and that we have marched upon Washington. God grant that our just cause may thus have triumphed! The whole town is agog discussing our affairs. Different parties take different views of them: the opposition party in the legislature, which is in session, being disposed to censure the government for its reception of us.

Thursday, September 12th.—Clear, with passing clouds; trade-wind fresh, as usual at this season of the year. Indeed, these winds will continue to increase in force until December, when they will gradually give place to the rains. It has been a favourite project of mine from the commencement of the cruise, to run off Cape St. Roque, and there waylay the commerce of the enemy in its transit both ways; but the strong gales and strong current which now prevail, will interfere for the present with my plan, and I must postpone it for awhile. If the war continues I shall hope to put it in execution at the proper time. It was at one time reported today that there were two United States vessels of war awaiting us outside, off Santa Anna; but the report proved to be the offspring of the excited imaginations of the townspeople. Had a conversation this evening with Senor Rodrigues, an intelligent lawyer and the Speaker of the Deputies, on the subject of the war. I found him pretty well informed, considering that he had received his information through the polluted channels of the Northern newspapers.

He seemed to think that we had been *precipitate* in breaking off our connexion with the North; but I told him we had been the most patient, long-suffering people in the world, and waited till the last moment possible, in hope that the fanaticism which swayed the North would have passed away; and that the responsibility of breaking up the once great government of the North rested entirely upon the propagandists of that section.

Friday, September 13th.—Cloudy, with the wind very fresh from the eastward. The town is still busy discussing our affairs. A deputy asked me seriously yesterday if the President had not ordered me to haul my flag down, as not being recognised. He said that the Assembly had called upon him for an explanation of the course he had adopted towards us, but that he had declined to respond.

It is reported, too, that there are two ships of war awaiting us outside near the Santa Anna light.

Saturday, September 14th.—Cloudy, with fresh trades. Having finished coaling and receiving our other supplies, we are engaged today in paying off our bills. I have been enabled to negotiate a draft for two thousand dollars upon the Secretary of the Navy; Mr. T. Wetson, one of our fellow-countrymen temporarily here, having been patriotic enough to advance me this sum on the faith of his government. He not only thus aided us, but was very anxious to come on board in person, if he could have wound up his business in time. In the evening at 7 p.m. I removed on board from the Hotel do Porto, preparatory to going to sea tomorrow.

On Sunday, the 15th September, the *Sumter* was again under way, and passed out of the harbour in charge of a pilot, Mr. Wetson accompanying her until she was fairly outside. No Yankee vessels were found, as had been reported, and the pilot being discharged, and a warm farewell exchanged with Mr. Wetson, the *Sumter* stood away upon a north-east course in the direction of her proposed cruising-ground in the calm belt between the trades, the Cape San Roque project being for the present abandoned. A dull time now commenced, great difficulty being experienced in forcing the vessel towards her cruising-ground against the current, which at times would carry her out of her course at the rate of more than fifty miles a day. Whilst thus beating wearily and patiently towards the station where it was hoped that more prizes might be obtained, a curious phenomenon was observed, of which the following account is given in the journal:—

Monday, September 23rd.—Clear, with passing clouds. Wind right from the south-east, veering and hauling two or three points. We have experienced in the last two or three days a remarkable succession of tide lips, coming on every twelve hours, and about an hour before the passage of the moon over the meridian. We have observed five of these lips, and with such regularity, that we attribute them to the lunar influence attracting the water in an opposite direction from the prevailing current, which is east, at the rate of some two miles per hour. We had a small gull fly on board of us today at the distance of five hundred miles from the nearest land. The tide lips came up from the south and travelled north, approaching first with a heavy swell, which caused us, being broadside on, to roll so violently that we kept the ship off her course from two to three points to bring the roller more on the quarter.

These rollers would be followed by a confused tumultuous sea, foaming and fretting in every direction, as if we were among breakers. We were in fact among breakers, though fortunately with no bottom near. No boat could have lived in such a cauldron as was produced by this meeting of the waters. They generally passed us in about three quarters of an hour, when everything became comparatively smooth again. No observation today for latitude, but by computation we are in latitude 5.25 N. and longitude (chronometer) 42.19 W. Current east by north 58 miles. So curious were the phenomena of the lips that the officers and men came on deck upon their approach to witness them.

It was many a long week now since the sight of an enemy had gladdened the eyes of the *Sumter*'s little crew, when, on the 25th of September, the welcome cry of "Sail, ho!" was once more heard from the masthead. Steam was at once got up, and the United States colours displayed from the Confederate cruiser. A short pause of expectation, an eager scrutiny of the stranger, as the blue and red bunting fluttered for a few moments upon his deck, while his men were busy with the signal halyards, and then a joyous cheer greeted the well-known stars and stripes, as they rose above her bulwarks, and mounted slowly to her mizzen peak.

She was not a very valuable prize, being merely a small brigantine, called the *Joseph Park,* of Boston, six days out from Pernambuco, in ballast. But she was the first fruits of a fresh cruise, and right joyously did the boat's crew pull on board her to haul down the enemy's flag, and replace it with the saucy stars and bars.[1]

This done, the crew were transferred to the captain's vessel, and a prize crew passed on board of the *Joseph Park,* with instructions to keep within sight of the *Sumter,* and signal her immediately on perceiving any suspicious sail. So the two cruised for some days in company, the *Joseph Park* keeping to windward during the day, and at night running down under cover of the *Sumter*'s guns. This capture was none the less welcome for the news she brought in a file of recent papers from Pernambuco, of the first victory of the South at Manassas, or Bull Run, as well as of the successes achieved in Missouri over the

---

1. The author of the "Notes" in the *Index* writes:—
"The officer who boarded the *Joseph Park* asked the captain if he had cargo. 'No.'—'Have you any specie?' 'Not a dollar.'—'Then, captain, you must get into the boat, and go with me on board the *Sumter.*' 'What are you going to do with me when I get on board?' The officer told him it would depend entirely upon circumstances; that if he behaved himself, and did not try to conceal anything, he would receive kind treatment; that it all depended upon himself 'Well,' said he, 'captain' (he called the officer who had boarded him captain) 'I *have* got a thousand dollars down below, and I guess I had better give it to you.' So he went below, and from out of some little hole took the bag containing the gold. The officer asked him why he had hidden the money, as we had the United States colours up. He said he thought it was the *Sumter,* and wanted to be on the safe side. The whole scene between the officer and the captain of the *Joseph Park* was ludicrous in the extreme. The answers to questions with that Yankee nasal twang and Yankee cunning, the officer seeing through it and enjoying it all the while, made many jokes in our mess afterwards."

troops of General Lyon. Poor *Joseph Park*! she had little anticipated her fate, and not a little amusement was created among her captors by an entry in her log of the day after leaving Pernambuco:—"We have a tight, fast vessel, and we don't care for Jeff. Davis!"

"My unfortunate prisoner," remarks Captain Semmes, "had holloa'd before he was out of the wood."

The journal continues:—

Friday, September 27th. "This is my fifty-second birthday, and so the years roll on, one by one, and I am getting to be an old man! Thank God, that I am still able to render service to my country in her glorious struggle for the right of self-government, and in defence of her institutions, her property, and everything a people hold sacred. We have thus far beaten the Vandal hordes that have invaded and desecrated our soil; and we shall continue to beat them to the end. The just God of Heaven, who looks down upon the quarrels of men, will avenge the right. May we prove ourselves in this struggle worthy of Him and of our great cause! My poor distressed family! How fondly my thoughts revert to them today! My dear wife and daughters, instead of preparing the accustomed "cake" to celebrate my birthday, are mourning my absence, and dreading to hear of disaster. May our Heavenly Father console, cherish, and protect them!

Chapter 6

In Hopes of a Fight

Another dull time now set in. On the 28th September the prize crew were recalled from the *Joseph Park*, which, after doing duty for some hours longer as a look-out ship, was finally at nightfall, set on fire, and burned to the water's edge. And now day after day passed by, unrelieved save by the little common incidents of a peaceful voyage.

One day it would be a flying-fish that had leaped on board, and paid the penalty of its indiscretion by doing duty next morning on the captain's breakfast-table; another day a small sword-fish performed a similar exploit; while on a third a heavy rain provided the great unwashed of the forecastle with the unaccustomed luxury of copious ablutions in fresh water. But not a sail was to be seen. Once only a simultaneous cry from half-a-dozen sailors of "Light on the starboard bow!" produced a temporary excitement, and caused the engineers to "fire up" at their utmost speed. But the alarm proved false.

The red light that had been so confidently reckoned on as the port lantern of some steamer moving across the *Sumter*'s bows, was at length set down as a mere meteor, or it might be some star setting crimson through the dim haze of the distant horizon. Luck seemed quite to have deserted the Confederate flag. They were lying in the very track of vessels between San Roque and New York. Allowing a space of seventy-five miles on either side of the *Sumter*'s station as the extent of this track, and calculating upon a radius of observation from her masthead of fifteen miles, one-fifth of the whole number passing should certainly have come within her ken. Yet in the course of seventeen weary days one vessel only had been seen, and the *Sumter*'s stock of patience was beginning to run very low.

At length, at ten o'clock on the morning of the 5th October, the welcome cry was again heard. "Sail, oh—h—h!" was shouted from the masthead with a lengthened emphasis, as though the look-out would mark the unusual fact with a special note of admiration. The stranger was dead to windward, and miles away, probably some seventeen or eighteen at the very least. But not a moment was lost in starting in pursuit. Steam was got up, sails furled, the vessel's head brought round in the direction of the chase, and in less than half an hour from the first announcement of her appearance, the *Sumter* was dashing through the water at top-speed in pursuit.

The chase was long and animated. At first starting the stranger had all the advantage of a stiff, steady breeze, whilst the *Sumter* was compelled to trust altogether to her powers of steaming; and the former, being a fine, fast vessel, appeared, if anything, rather to gain upon her pursuer. Gradually, however, as the two vessels changed their relative bearings, the *Sumter* also was enabled to avail herself of her fore and aft canvas, and now she began to gain rapidly upon the chase. Three hours and a quarter passed in this exciting contest; but at length the pursuer had come fairly within range, and the chase was over. Up went the Stars and Stripes to the *Sumter's* peak, and the usual pause of excited expectation ensued; when, after bungling awhile with his signal halyards, as though playing with his pursuer's hopes and fears, the red ensign of England rose defiantly from the deck, and there was to be no prize after all.

Very indignant was the captain of the *Spartan* at being hove-to by a Yankee, and great was the amusement of the boarding officer as he was welcomed with the observation that "the Northerners were catching h—"

"How so?" inquired he.

"Why by getting themselves so badly whipped by the Southerners."

It was observed that the worthy speaker appeared somewhat surprised at the perfect good-humour and satisfaction with which the intelligence was received.

The night now set in wet and wild. The wind increased to a moderate gale with a remarkably heavy sea, and violent rain-squalls passing at intervals over the vessel. The little *Sumter* rolled and pitched about as though she, too, were weary of the long period of inaction, and determined to effect some kind of diversion on her own account. Morning broke heavy and threatening, with the barometer at 29-87; and by noon it was blowing a whole gale, and the ship labouring so heavily that the ceremony of mustering the hands and reading the

Articles of War, customary on the first Sunday of every month, was perforce dispensed with, and "Jack"—as usual, when bad weather has fairly set in, and the ship has been made snug—got his holiday.

Towards night the gale, which had hauled gradually round from E.N.E. to S.E. and S.S.E. in the course of some eight or ten hours, began to moderate. By the next morning it had altogether broken, and though the clouds were still leaden, and the sea ran high after the blow of yesterday, the *Sumter* was once more able to make sail; and shaking the reefs out of her topsails, she stood away again towards the S.S.E.

The end of the week saw her well upon her way towards a new cruising ground, the Western side of the crossing having been fairly given up as a hopeless job, and Captain Semmes shaping his course for the Eastern crossing. At noon on Saturday, the 12th October, the new station was reached, the vessel's position on that day being in lat. 6.56 N., long. 44.41 W.; the weather calm, the sun shining dimly through a greyish veil of mist, and the little steamer rolling from side to side upon the long, heaving swells, her yards creaking and her sails flapping heavily against the masts with that dull, hopeless sound, more trying to the sailor than the fiercest gale.

Gales and calms—sunshine and rain-squalls—long rolling swell-heavy sea, and not a break in the monotonous round. Thirty-eight days out, and in all that time but two vessels spoken and one solitary prize!

Thursday, October 24th.—Cloudy, with the wind from the eastward. At half-past six in the morning descried a sail in the north east. Got up steam and gave chase. At nine came up with a brig, which proved to be a Frenchman, *La Mouche Noire*, from Nantes to Martinique. Sent a boat on board of him. He had no newspapers, and said he knew the United States were at war—we had the United States colours flying-but with whom he did not know. Enlightened Frenchman! Or this may teach us a lesson of humility, as showing us how little is thought in Europe of the American Revolution. The brig was a clumsy specimen of architecture, and was out forty-two days. We detained her less than half-an-hour, and permitted her to go on her course again. Our ill-luck seems to culminate; for two out of the only three sail we have seen in thirty-nine days have proved to be foreign.

Friday, October 25th.—Fresh breeze from the north, and trade-wind weather. Morning, a few rain-squalls, clearing, but with passing clouds, as the sun gained altitude. Afternoon heavy, overcast sky, with half a gale of wind. At 2.50 p.m. descried a sail on the starboard-quarter, bearing about S.E. Got up steam and gave chase, and at 5 p.m. came up with her. Fired a blank cartridge and spoke a Prussian ship, which I caused to heave-to for the purpose of sending a boat on board of him; but, as in the meantime the wind freshened, and considerable sea had arisen, and as I had no doubts of the character of the ship, I gave him leave to fill away and proceed on his course (to some one of the Windward Islands) without boarding him.

As I was rounding the ship to, near this vessel, we came so near a collision that my heart stood still for a moment as the bows of the huge, heavy-laden ship passed our quarter, almost near enough to graze it. If she had been thrown upon us by one of the heavy seas that were running, we should probably have been cut down to the water's edge and sunk in a few minutes. This will give me a lesson as to the space my long ship requires to turn in when she has a sea on the quarter or bow. We are forty days out today, have seen four sails, and three of the four have proved to be foreign. I am not discouraged, however, but I have had an excellent opportunity to practise the Christian virtue of patience, which virtue I think I am a little deficient in.

Sunday, October 27th.—A beautiful clear day, with a light breeze from the E.N.E., and a few summer-like passing trade-clouds. Mustered the crew. Two sail in one day! 8.30 p.m. A sail was descried in the S.E. We immediately gave chase with all sail, and added steam to sails in about an hour and a half. We came up with the chase about 3 p.m.; the vessel proving very fast. We showed, as usual, the United States colours, the chase showing the same. Fired a blank cartridge and ordered him to heave-to.

Sent a boat on board and captured him, hauling down the United States and hoisting our own flag as our officer got on board. She proved to be the schooner *Daniel Trowbridge*, of New Haven, Connecticut, from New York to Demerara, with a cargo of provisions; cargo belonging to same owner as vessel, *D. Trowbridge*, of Connecticut. Sent a prize crew on board, and left in pursuit of another sail that had been descried in the meantime, with which we came up at dark. She proved to be a brigantine from Nova Scotia to Demerara (English). Permitted her to proceed on her course. Banked fires, and put the ship under sail, with a light at the peak, and the prize in company.

Monday, October 28th.—Fine clear weather, with a moderate sea and a light breeze. Called the prize within hail; hoisted out the longboat and sent her alongside and commenced receiving provisions. I felt truly thankful to a kind Providence for this windfall, for we were running short of provisions—beef bad, and weevily bread. And here were more than we needed, and of the best. Pork, beef, hams, flour, bread, crackers (biscuits), &c.; this was truly a Yankee cargo, there being a large number of pigs, sheep, and geese on board. A busy, bustling day, with boats passing to and fro, and men busy on both ships with boxes, barrels, &c. To get at the cargo we threw overboard the superincumbent articles, and strewed the sea with Connecticut wooden ware and brooms.

Tuesday, October 29th.—Another favourable day for unloading the prize. Wind light from the East, and not too much sea on. We are filling up with five months' provisions. In the meantime we are enjoying the luxury, far away out at sea and forty-three days from port, of fresh meat; the sheep on board the prize being in excellent condition, and I have them slaughtered in sufficient numbers for the crew. At noon the sky becoming overcast; lat. 16.54 N., long. 57.33 W.

Wednesday, October 30th.—A beautiful serene day, with a light breeze from the S.E. and a smooth sea. At 7 p.m., "Sail, ho!" from aloft. Despatched a couple of boats to the prize schooner to bring away some of the live stock, and sent orders to the prize master to set fire to the prize and return on board. These orders being all executed and the boats run up, at 8.30, steamed in pursuit of the strange sail. At eleven came up with, and sent a boat on board of the Danish brig *Una*, from Copenhagen to Santa Cruz, sixty-nine days out. Permitted her to proceed on her course after a detention of about half-an-hour. We showed her the United States colours.

This evening, having directed the junior lieutenant to send to the master of the prize schooner *Daniel Trowbridge*, for the log slates of the schooner which he, the master, had put among his private baggage, it was reported to me that the master in delivering these articles to the messenger, the sergeant of marines, used this insolent language-"D—— them. I hope they will do them no good, and if they want a shirt I can lend them that too." I had the man seized and put in double irons. Lat. 16.40 N., long. 58.16 W.

Thursday, October 31st.—Beautiful clear weather, with a light breeze from the North and East. Got up and sunned the ball cartridges, some of which had been damaged by the damp, and overhauled the pumps which had gotten out of order. At 2 p.m. a light having been reported to me, I ordered steam gotten up and made pursuit. As we came up with it, we found it to be a burning fragment of the schooner which we had fired eighteen hours before. Banked fires. We have been greatly interested since our last capture in examining a lot of newspapers found on board. They are as late as the 8th October, and give us most cheering accounts of the war.

We have gloriously whipped the enemy at all points, and have brought Missouri and Kentucky out of the Union. The tone of the European press is highly favourable to our cause, and indicates a prompt recognition of our independence. And all this cheering information we get from the enemy himself! Lat. 16.54 N., long. 57.59 W. The master of the prize schooner *Trowbridge*, having made a very humble apology for his conduct of yesterday, and asked to be released from confinement, I directed him to be discharged from close custody and to have his irons taken off.

The *Daniel Trowbridge*, however, was the last prize that fell to the *Sumter*'s lot on this cruise. She was now in the full track of vessels crossing the Line, and scarcely a day passed without one or more being overhauled; but the Stars and Stripes appeared to have vanished from the seas. Vessel after vessel was brought-to, now English, now French, now belonging to someone or other of the innumerable neutral nations, but not a Yankee was to be seen, and the ship's company began almost to weary of their profitless task.

One brief morning's excitement there was, as a large steamer was descried in the offing, evidently a man-of-war. All was at once alive and eager on board the little *Sumter*. The drums beat to quarters, decks were cleared for action, and every preparation made for combat, as the Confederate cruiser stood boldly out to meet her expected foe. But again the eager crew were doomed to disappointment. They were no more to fight than to capture prizes. As the stranger drew near, the white ensign of St. George fluttered gracefully to her peak, and after the customary interchange of civilities, the two vessels went on their respective courses, and the little *Sumter* was once more alone on the wide ocean.

A change of cruising ground was now again resolved on, and a course shaped for the West Indies. Still, however, without success, and at length the supply of water beginning to fail, the cruise was abandoned, and on the 9th November the *Sumter* steamed into Fort de France in Martinique, having been fifty-seven days at sea.

CHAPTER 7

Sympathy for the South

Saturday, Nov. 9th.—Weather fine during the morning. At daylight, got up steam and stood in for the land northward of Fort St. Louis' Bay, running down the coast as we approached. The coast, all the way into the anchorage, is bold and clear. Ran within three hundred yards of Point Negro, passing a passenger steamer bound to St. Pierre, and anchored in six fathoms water, with the south end of the fort bearing E. 1/4 S., and the wharf about N. by E. A pilot soon after came on board, and we got up anchor and went in to the anchorage E. of the fort, the health officer visiting us in the meantime, and giving us *pratique.*

Sent a lieutenant to call on the Governor, and afterwards visited him myself. I stated in this interview that I had come into Martinique to refresh my crew, and obtain such supplies as I needed, coal included. The Governor replied that he could not supply me with coal from the Government stock, but I was free to go into the market and purchase what I wanted, he, the Governor, *not knowing anything about it*; and that as to my prisoners, if the United States consul at St. Pierre would become responsible for their maintenance, I might land them. With his consent, I sent the two masters up to St. Pierre in the packet to see this consul, and arrange the matter.

I despatched also the paymaster to look after coal and clothing for the crew, giving leave to Lieutenant Chapman to accompany him. The Governor at one time ordered me to shift my berth, by returning to my first anchorage; but countermanded the order upon my demanding an explanation of it. He seemed disposed, too, to restrict my procuring supplies *at this place*, on the ground that it was merely the seat of government and a military and naval station; but upon my insisting upon my right, under the Imperial proclamation, to be treated in all respects as a lawful belligerent, be abandoned his point. The French colonies are governed by the minister of Marine, naval officers being the governors and chief officials. The Governor of Martinique is a rear-admiral.

Sunday, Nov. 10th.—Rain in the early morning, clearing towards eight o'clock. Went on shore and accompanied M. Guerin to the Governor's mass, at 8 p.m. The interior of the church is very pleasing, with rare valuable paintings. The congregation was small. A detachment (one company from each regiment), entered the main aisle, and formed in double lines, a few minutes before the commencement of the service. The Governor and his staff entered punctually, and the service lasted about three-quarters of an hour. Fine music from a band in the orchestra. The blacks and whites occupy pews indiscriminately, though there is no social mixture of the races.

All colours have the same political rights, notwithstanding which the jealousy and hatred of the whites by the blacks is said to be very great. Was visited by M. Guerin. and a number of gentlemen—members of the Colonial Legislature and others—to whom I explained the true issue of the war—to wit, an abolition crusade against our slave-property; our population, resources, victories, &c.—to all of which they listened with much appearance of gratification, and which they also expressed from time to time, lamenting the blind policy of their Home Government. Mustered the crew, and read Articles of War. Three of the prisoners have shipped.

Let another batch of liberty-men go on shore. Two of yesterday's batch did not come off in time this morning. Since came on board. Visited the Savannah to hear the music, which is given every Sunday evening. It was a gay and beautiful scene: the moon, the shade, the trees, the statue of Josephine, the throng of well-dressed men and women, the large band and the fine music, the ripple of the sea; and last, though not least, the Katy-dids, so fraught with memories of home, dear home! Visited M. Guerin after the music, and made the acquaintance of his charming family, consisting of wife, daughter-in-law, and niece, who gave some music on the piano and a song. M. Guerin's mother died a nun in the city of Baltimore, where M. Guerin was himself educated. He retains his early impressions of Baltimore very vividly.

Monday, November 11th.—Weather clear and pleasant, with refreshing trade-winds; watering ship. Visited the town, and went a-shopping in company with M. Guerin. Found French manufactured clothing, &c., reasonably cheap. In the afternoon strolled on the heights in rear of the town, and was charmed with the picturesque scenery on every hand. The little valleys and nooks in which nestle the country houses are perfect pictures, and the abrupt and broken country presents delightful changes at every turn. I saw but few signs of diligent cultivation.

The negro race is here, as everywhere else, an idle and thriftless one; and the purlieus of the town where they are congregated are dilapidated and squalid. The statue of Josephine in the Savannah is a very fine specimen of sculpture. It represents her in her customary dress, and she appears, indeed, a charming woman. This is her native island. The United States consul came down today from St. Pierre, and I landed the remainder of the prisoners, twelve in number, putting them on parole. I had them all assembled in the gangway, and questioned them as to their treatment on board. They all expressed themselves satisfied with it. The officers returned from St. Pierre, and reported that coal was to be had, but that the Collector of Customs had prohibited the merchants from sending it to us. Wrote to the Governor on the Subject:—

Confederate States' steamer Sumter,
Port Royal, Nov. 12th, 1861.

Sir,—In the interview which I had the honour to hold with your Excellency on Saturday last, the 9th inst. I understood your Excellency to assent to the proposition that I might go into the market at St. Pierre, and purchase such supplies as I might stand in need of, coal included. The precise position assumed by your Excellency was, that you would neither assent nor prohibit. On the faith of this understanding, I despatched one of my lieutenants and my paymaster to St. Pierre, to make the necessary purchases, and they have returned and reported to me that they found an abundance of coal in the market, and at reasonable rates, and that the owners of it are anxious to supply me with it, but that your Collector of the Customs had *interposed*, and prohibited the merchants from selling or delivering it to me.

For the information of your Excellency, I will here state that I have been permitted to coal in all the ports I have heretofore visited, except only at the French port of Cayenne, where I was informed that there was no coal in the market, and where it was insisted that I should undergo a quarantine of five days before communicating with the town. As it was not convenient for me to undergo this quarantine, I sailed immediately. I have coaled at Cienfuegos in the island of Cuba, at Curaçao, at Trinidad, at Paramaribo, and at Maranham. It appears that Spain, Holland, England and Brazil have each deemed it consistent with their neutrality in the present war to permit me freely to supply myself with coal.

Am I to understand from the action of your officers at St. Pierre that you have withdrawn the implied assent given me on Saturday last, and that France, through your agency, adopts a different and less friendly, rule? Will France drive a vessel of war of the Confederate States from one of her islands to a British island to procure coal? And if she does this, on what principle will she do it? It is a well-settled rule of international law, that belligerent cruisers have the right to enter freely into neutral ports for the purpose of replenishing their stores of provisions, or replacing a lost mast or spar; and why should not they be equally permitted to receive on board coal?

Coal is no more necessary to the locomotion of a steamer than is a mast or spar to a sail-ship; it is no more necessary to a cruiser than provisions. Without a mast or without provisions a sail-ship could not continue her cruise against the enemy; and yet the neutral permitted her to supply herself with these articles. Nor can such supplies as these be placed on the ground of humanity. It would be inhuman, it is true, to permit the crew of a belligerent cruiser to perish in your ports by debarring from access to your markets, from day to day; but it does not follow that it would be inhuman to prevent her from laying in a stock of provisions to enable her to proceed to sea, and continue her cruise against the enemy. It is not humanity to supply a vessel with a lost mast or a spar, and yet no one doubts that this may be done. Humanity, then, being out of the question, what possible distinction can your Excellency draw between supplying a vessel with the articles above mentioned, and supplying her with coal?

Without any one of them she would be unable to prosecute her cruise against the enemy—why, then, will you supply her with a part, and not with the whole?

Without troubling your Excellency further, however, with an

argument of the question, I will content myself with stating what I believe to be the true rule of law, and it is this:—A belligerent ship of war *cannot increase her armament or her crew in a neutral port, nor supply herself with ammunition; but with these exceptions she may procure whatever supply she needs.*

Although it would be an easy matter for me to run to one of the British, or Danish, or Dutch Islands, I should regret to be obliged to do so, and to have to inform my Government of the reason. I would not willingly have France adopt a rule which would effectually shut us out of her ports, whilst Holland, Great Britain, Spain, and Brazil admit us freely into theirs. The rule, prohibiting us from bringing our prizes into neutral ports, operates very harshly upon us, as the weaker naval power of the belligerents, without adding to it one still more harsh, and which has the sanction of neither law nor precedent. If, however, it be the determination of your Excellency to insist upon my departure without coal, I beg that you will have the goodness to say as much to me in writing. Your Excellency is the best judge of your instructions, and of what they require of you.

  I have the honour to be,
    With much consideration,
      Your obedient Servant,
       (Signed)   R. Semmes.
To his Excellency M. Maussion de Condé,
 l'Amiral et Gouverneur de la Martinique.

We have the gratifying intelligence that Captain Hollins, with some armed steamers, had driven the enemy from the mouth of the Mississippi, sinking the *Preble*, and driving the other vessels on the bar of the S.W. Pass. Mr. Seward has issued a proclamation, desiring the Governors of the Northern States to put their forts, &c., in condition, "as well on the seaboard as on the lakes!" This, with Fremont's abolition proclamation, will be of great service to us. *Quem Deus*, &c. The Governor consents to my coaling at St. Pierre.

Friday, November 12th.—Fine, pleasant weather. Watering ship. I did not visit the shore today; some of the officers are on shore dining, &c., with the French naval officers. There is evidently great sympathy for us in the island. We have got on board all our "liberty-men," no one of them having shown a disposition to desert. At 9 p.m., a drunken fireman jumped overboard and swam ashore, in spite of the efforts of a boat to catch him. He thus braved the discipline of the ship solely for a glass of grog!—so strong upon him was the desire for drink. We sent an officer for him and caught him in a grog-shop. It is reported to us, as coming from the Captain of the Port, that there is a frigate cruising off the Diamond Rock. The ship *Siam* arrived today, with 444 *coolies*!

Translation of Reply received from the Governor, in Answer to the preceding.

Fort de France, 12th November, 1861.

To the Captain—

I have the honour to send you the enclosed letter, which I ask you to hand to the Collector of Customs at St. Pierre, in which I request him to permit you to embark freely, as much coal as you wish to purchase in the market.

I do not change at all from the position which I took with you on Saturday last. I do not consider that I am empowered any more to give you coal from the Government supply of this division, than I am to interfere with the market to prevent its being sold to you there.

With the expression of my highest regard for the Captain,

    (Signed)   Maussion de Condé.

Wednesday, November 13th.—Got up steam, and unmoored ship at daylight; and at half-past six passed out of the harbour of Fort Royal, or rather now Fort de France. The pilot repeated the intelligence that there was a frigate off the Diamond Rock. As we passed the picturesque country-seat of the Governor, perched upon a height overlooking the sea, we hoisted the French flag at the fore. Passed the St. Pierre steamer on her way down. At eight, came to, in the harbour of St. Pierre, at the man-of-war anchorage south of the town. Several of the custom-house officers visited us, saying that they had not come on board officially, but merely out of civility, and from curiosity to see the ship. Sent a lieutenant on shore to call on the commandant, and make arrangements for the-purchase and reception of coal, despatching to the collector the Government order to permit us to embark it.

At 1 p.m., shifted our berth nearer to the shore, for the convenience of coaling, mooring head and stern with a hawser to the shore. Received on board thirty tons by 9 p.m.; sent down the foreyard for repairs. Quarantined the paymaster and surgeon for being out of the ship after hours, but upon the explanations of the former, released them both. The market-square near the water is thronged with a dense crowd, eagerly gazing upon the ship; and the newspaper of today gives a marvellous account of us, a column in length. Among other amusing stories, they claim me to be a French officer, formerly serving on board the *Mereuse*!

Thursday, November 14th.—Rain in the forenoon. Busy coaling, and getting on board a few necessary stores. It is reported that the *Iroquois* sailed from Trinidad on the 2nd November, and that there are three ships of war of the enemy at St. Thomas', one sail vessel, and two steamers; and that one of these was expected here last night. She has not yet made her appearance. It will be difficult for her to prevent our sailing. At 2.30 p.m. the steam-sloop *Iroquois* of the enemy made her appearance, coming round the north end of the island. She had at first Danish colours flying, but soon changed them for her own. She steamed ahead of us very slowly, and, taking up a position some half to three-quarters of a mile from us, stood off and on during the afternoon and night.

Finished receiving our coal and provisions (sugar and rum) at about 9 p.m., when I permitted the crew to have their hammocks as usual. Directed everything to be kept ready for action. Visited in the afternoon by the mayor of the city and some gentlemen, who assured me of the sympathy of the citizens, and of the colony generally. At 1.30 p.m. I was called by the officer of the deck, and informed that the *Iroquois* was standing in for us, and approaching us very close. Called all hands to quarters, and made all preparations to receive the enemy in case he should attempt to run us on board. He sheered off, however, when he came within three or four hundred yards. He repeated this operation several times during the mid-watch, imposing upon us as often the necessity of calling the men to quarters; indeed, from about half-past two they slept at their guns. Great excitement pervades the entire city. The market-square, the quays, and the windows of the houses, are thronged by an eager and curious multitude, expecting every moment to see a combat. The enemy approached us at one time within a ship's length.

Friday, November 15th.—Fine, bright morning. At 7.30 a French steamer of war, *L'Acheron,* Captain Duchaxel, came in from Fort de France, and made fast to one of the buoys. The *Iroquois* about a mile from us. At 8.30 sent a boat on board the Frenchman to pay the usual ceremonial visit. The throng in the town unabated, multitudes being gathered near the water, looking out at the two ships. At 10 the French captain paid me a visit. He came up, he said, with orders from the Governor, to preserve the neutrality of the port between the two belligerents, and in case the *Iroquois* came to an anchor, to demand of the captain a promise that he would not proceed to sea for twenty-four hours after our own departure. I wrote to the Governor, informing him of the violation of the neutrality of the port by the *Iroquois*, and desiring him to apply the proper remedy:—

C.S. steamer *Sumter*, St. Pierre,
Island of Martinique,
November 15th, 1861.

Sir,—I have the honour to inform your Excellency that I am closely blockaded in this port by the enemy's steam sloop-of-war *Iroquois*, of twice my force. This vessel, in defiance of the law of nations, and in contempt of the neutrality of this island, has boldly entered the harbour, and without coming to anchor is cruising backwards and forwards in a menacing attitude, not only within the marine league of the shore, but within less than a ship's length of this vessel, which is moored not more than one hundred yards from the beach. During the past night she several times approached me within fifty or a hundred yards.

I deem it my duty to acquaint your Excellency with these facts, and to invoke your authority for the preservation of my just rights within your waters. I take the following principles, applicable to the present case, to be well settled by the law of nations:—Firstly, that no act of hostility, proximate or remote, can be committed by any belligerent in neutral waters; secondly, that when a cruiser of one belligerent takes refuge within the waters of a neutral power, a cruiser of the opposite belligerent cannot follow her into those waters for purposes of hostility, proximate or remote. It is not only unlawful for her to approach within the marine league, for the purpose of watch and menace, but it is equally unlawful for her to hover about the coast of the neutral, at any distance within plain view, for the same purposes.

All these are remote or prospective acts of war, and as such, offensive to the neutral power. Thirdly, that when opposite belligerents meet by accident in a neutral port, if one of them departs therefrom, the other is bound to wait twenty-four hours before departing. For the opposite belligerent to depart immediately in pursuit, is to avail herself of the neutral territory for the purpose of war. She commits, by the very fact of sailing, a remote act of hostility which is offensive to the neutral state.

In view of the foregoing facts and principles, I respectfully request that your Excellency will cause the *Iroquois* to cease hovering about the coast of the island for the purpose of watching my movements; in other words, to withdraw herself out of plain sight. Or if she prefers to come in, to anchor, to direct either that she shall depart twenty-four hours before me, or wait twenty-four hours after my departure, whichever she may prefer. I shall be ready for sea in four or five days, as soon as my engineers make some necessary repairs to my machinery.

In conclusion, it is quite possible that the captain of the *Iroquois* may arrange some signals for giving him intelligence of my movements, with the United States consul at this port, and I have therefore to request that some officer may be charged with the prevention of any such act of hostility.

I have the honour to be, &c.,
(Signed) R. Semmes.
To His Excellency
M. Maussion de Condé,
Admiral and Governor of Martinique,

During this night the *Iroquois* did not approach us so near as on the past night. Closed in the gun-deck ports, got the swinging booms alongside, and directed the crew, in case of being called to quarters during the night, to repair to the spar-deck as boarders, boarding being the mode in which the enemy would attack us, if at all.(See note following.)

Note: On the 14th, at 4 p.m. when we had nearly finished coaling and other arrangements for sea, a steamer was seen rounding the north point of the island. She was under Danish colours, and had made, it was evident, some ludicrous attempts at disguising herself—such, for instance, as a studied disarrangement of her yards, and some alteration of her head-booms. I was under the impression at the time that we were very old birds to be caught with such chaff. She came up slowly at first, evidently not seeing us as we lay concealed in the shadow of the hills; but when within about two miles, we could see, with the aid of our glasses, the water curling from her bows, and we knew that the Yankee had scented his prey; or, to employ the expressive phrase of our rough old signal quartermaster, "she had got a bone in her mouth." All the good citizens of St. Pierre came down to the beach to witness the scene, and a great many indulged their aquatic instincts by swimming out to us to await the *dénouement*. The *Iroquois* was now close on to us, and when about a hundred yards distant, hauled down the Danish colours, and set the stars and stripes in their place. Thus we were once more in the presence of our hated foe.

The *Iroquois* is one of the new class of gunboats, powerfully armed with nine and eleven-inch guns, and is about 1000 tons burden. Her crew consists of about 200 men; and we knew it was useless for the *Sumter* to think of fighting her, our only hope of escape being by strategy. The enemy stood in close to the land, and sent a boat on shore to communicate with the U.S. Consul and the French authorities, being, however, very careful not to drop anchor. Captain Palmer informed his Excellency the Governor that there was a pirate at anchor in the port of St. Pierre, and requested permission to destroy her; but this was refused emphatically, and the irate commander furnished with the proclamation of his Imperial Majesty Napoleon III., according belligerent rights to the Confederate States, and decreeing strict neutrality on the part of France.

He was informed that it was necessary for the *Iroquois* either to cast anchor, or leave the waters of the isle, and if accepting the former alternative, that an interval of twenty-four hours must elapse between the departure of either belligerent; also that, in case of any breach of neutrality occurring, the forts would open on the offending party. After remaining stationary for some two hours, her boat returned. The *Iroquois* stood out of the harbour, taking a position a short distance ahead of us, and commenced backing and filling across our bows. Meanwhile the crew of "the pirate" were not idle; every preparation was made to repel boarders, and to defend our ship to the last extremity. The crew were inspected, and every man seen to be properly armed and equipped for action.

We fully expected an attack that night, and remembered the threats and loud pretensions of not respecting any neutrality which prevented them from destroying the *Sumter*, as made by the commander of the *Niagara*, and the redoubtable Porter of the *Powhattan*,—this latter gentleman having actually followed us as far as Maranham, only to find the people *Sumter*-mad on his arrival. Very few on board the *Sumter* that night felt any inclination for slumber; the men were sitting about in groups, commenting in low tones on the contest which now seemed to be imminent; while those officers who were at leisure were gathered on the quarter-deck, engaged in the same interesting discussion.

At 2 p.m. the word was passed by the lookouts forward that the Yankee was bearing down close upon us; and the order passed, almost in a whisper, "to go to quarters." I never saw men obey an order with more alacrity. In a few minutes the boarders, pikemen, and small-arm men were ranged in three lines close to our low rail, to await his attack, all preserving a perfect silence that seemed death-like. When about twenty feet distant from us, we heard the deep tones of her bell in the engine-room, as it rang the order to back; but not before we had discovered her men at quarters, and, in fact, presenting every appearance of a ship intending to board an enemy.

A single stray pistol-shot would have brought on the engagement, and to judge from the lights and signals glancing along the fortifications, the Frenchmen would have taken a hand, too. The appearance of our decks next morning was amusing. The men were strewn about promiscuously fully armed and accoutred for battle, endeavouring to obtain some rest; a stranger might easily have imagined us to be a buccaneer. Captain Palmer stated next day that he was afraid we would board him in boats, when asked the meaning of his threatening manoeuvres; but it was difficult to believe that the commander of a ship of war would make such a flimsy excuse; and let us hope for his own credit that he did not really believe his own statement.

The demeanour of the crew was most satisfactory. No noise or bustle could be noticed; but a quiet, firm determination was expressed in the countenance of each man to defend our noble little ship to the bitter end, and never strike our flag to the foe. These flagrant violations of neutrality greatly irritated the inhabitants, and the better portion of them threw off their thin mask of indifference, and openly expressed sympathy for us. Some were so excited as to volunteer to go with us; but their kind offers were not accepted. The negroes, however, did not seem to recognise us for what we really are, their best friends, but were somewhat opposed to the *Sumter*, and their allegiance to our enemy was made the subject of one of Captain Palmer's voluminous despatches to Mr. Gideon Welles.—*Index*.

Saturday, November 10th.—The *Iroquois* ahead of us, about a mile distant. At 10 p.m., I returned the visit of the French commander. I pointed out to him the insolent manner in which the *Iroquois* was violating the neutrality of the port. No additional order had been received from the Governor. Scraping and painting ship, and repairing the engine to put it in thorough condition for service. At meridian the *Iroquois* came to anchor about half a mile from us, at the man-of-war anchorage. The captain of the *Acheron* visited me, to say the Governor had directed him to inform me that if I preferred it, he would be glad to have me visit Fort de France with my ship, where he could afford me more ample protection, and whither, he presumed, the *Iroquois* would not follow me; and if she did, that he would compel her to depart from French waters.

I replied that before deciding upon this invitation, I would wait and see whether the *Iroquois* accepted the condition of remaining twenty-four hours after my departure, or departing twenty-four hours before me. The *Iroquois* got under way again immediately after anchoring, and in the evening the captain of the *Acheron* sent a lieutenant on board of me, to say that the commander of the *Iroquois* refused to accept the condition, and that he had been directed to withdraw himself beyond the marine league in consequence. She remained a few hours to supply herself with refreshments, and as night fell took her station; but not at the distance of a marine league *during the night.*

We have thus taught this ignoramus Yankee captain some knowledge of, and some respect for, the laws of neutrality. In the afternoon I took a delightful stroll along the beach northward.

Sunday, November 17th.—Morning fine. Visited the church opposite the ship, and heard mass. The congregation was very large, composed chiefly of blacks—women. We were politely shown into the trustees' pew. A short sermon, chiefly addressed to some young persons who had just made their first communion, was delivered by a good-looking young priest, who had fair command of language, and was easy and graceful in his manner.

A sort of police officer or fugleman officiated here, as at Fort Royal—a feature which I did not like. The *Iroquois* preserves her distance by daylight.

Monday, November 18th.—The enemy cruising off the harbour as usual. During the morning a French man-of-war schooner arrived from Fort de France, with the Governor on board (who visits St. Pierre to distribute premiums to the schools), and about one hundred troops to reinforce the fort. Repairing our machinery and painting ship. Some boatmen have been imprisoned by the authorities for going out to the enemy. At nightfall the Director of the Customs came off to see me, and said that the Governor had told him he expected to see the captain of the *Sumter* at his (the Director's) house; adding, that he said this of his own accord—the Governor not having authorized him to say as much to me. I took the hint, and went on shore at 8 p.m., accompanied by my clerk, to call on his Excellency.

He did not seem to have anything in particular to say, except to renew his invitation for me to go to Fort de France in my ship, which I declined, on the ground that this would be a more convenient port from which to escape, and one affording more facilities for the repairs of my engine. He told me that the captain of the *Iroquois* pleaded ignorance as to his violation of the neutrality of the port; but added, he knew better. An American (enemy) schooner got under way at dusk, and stood out to the *Iroquois*, where she remained about an hour before proceeding on her cruise to the northward and westward.

Tuesday, November 19th.—Some surf observable this morning, increasing until about 4 p.m.; the wind variable, settling for a short time in the south-east. I became anxious on account of my berth, which was represented to me as insecure, in case of a blow from seaward. I sent and got a pilot on board, but when he came he said he thought we should not have bad weather; and as by this time the sea had gone down, I was of his opinion, and concluded to remain at my anchors for the present, especially as the repairs to our machinery would be finished by tomorrow evening.

Heavy rain in the evening. The *Iroquois* within the marine league. Visited by the commander of the French schooner of war, whom we called on yesterday. About 10 p.m. the British mail steamer arrived from St. Thomas. Sent a boat on board of her, and got English papers to the 1st November. She brings intelligence of the enemy's steamer *St. Jacinto*, having boarded an English steam-packet, and taken out of her Messrs. Slidell and Mason, who had been carried to the *Havannah* by the *Nashville*. The English people will regard this as an insult to their flag, and in this way it may do us good. Night clear; moon rising a little before eight. Not quite darkness enough for our purpose yet.

Wednesday, November 20th.—Morning clear; wind variable. The *Iroquois* never loses sight of us, violating the neutrality of the port by night by coming within the marine league to observe us. Sent the engineer on shore to hurry the repair of his pumps. Loosed sails. Furled at meridian, and ordered the fires to be lighted at 1 p.m.; the weather looking unsettled, heeled the ship and scraped the grass off her port side near the water-line. The *Iroquois* crawled in again last night within about a mile and a half. As it was cloudy we lost sight of her in the early part of the night for the first time.

Thursday, November 21st.—Cloudy, with slight showers of rain. Drew the charges from the battery and reloaded it; and examined and put in order for action the small arms. Got up some barrels of salt provisions and arranged them on each side of the quarter-deck to trim ship. She lay an inch or two too much by the head. A boat employed filling up our water. Changed our fasts to the shores in readiness for a move. Hurrying the engineer with his work. I fear every moment to see another enemy's ship arrive. During the morning the Governor returned in the *Acheron* to Fort de France. In the afternoon the *Acheron* came back. Wrote a note to the latter complaining of the continued violation of the neutrality of the port by the enemy's ship. Engineer not ready, so we are obliged to lie over another day.

C.S. Steamer *Sumter*, St Pierre,
Nov. 21st, 1861.

Sir,—It becomes my duty to complain of the continued violation of the neutrality of this port, and of my right of asylum, by the enemy's steam sloop of war the *Iroquois*.

This vessel, in shameful disregard of the warnings she has received from his Excellency the Governor, comes every night, under cover of the darkness, within a mile and a half, or less, of the anchorage. Last night, at nine o'clock, she was seen from my deck with the naked eye, assisted by an occasional flash of lightning; and as the night was comparatively obscure, no vessel, not being under sail, could have been seen at a greater distance than from a mile to a mile and a quarter.

I have besides to inform you, that two small boats communicated with the enemy in broad daylight yesterday, one of them pulling, upon leaving her, to the north point, and the other to the south point, of the harbour.

I have, &c., &c.,
(Signed)   R. Semmes.

To M. Duchaxel,
Commander of His French Majesty's
Steamer, L'*Acheron*.

Friday, November 22nd.—The enemy about two and a half miles distant. The engineer will be ready today, and, God willing, we will get out tonight. Wrote to the captain of the *Acheron*, in reply to the position assumed by the governor:—

C.S. Steamer *Sumter*, St. Pierre,
Nov. 22nd, 1861.

Sir,—I have had the honour to receive your letter of yesterday, in which you communicate to me the views of the Governor of Martinique relative to the protection of my right of asylum in the waters of this island; and I regret to say that those views do not appear to me to come up to the requirements of the international code. The Governor says, "that it does not enter into his intentions to exercise towards the *Iroquois*, either by night or by day, so active a surveillance as you desire." And you tell me that "we ought to have confidence in the strict execution of a promise made by a commander in the military marine of the American Union, so long as he has not shown to us evidence that this engagement has not been scrupulously fulfilled."

It would appear from these expressions that the only protection I am to receive against the blockade of the enemy is a simple promise exacted from that enemy, that he will keep himself without the marine league of the land; the Governor in the meantime exercising no watch by night or by day to see whether this promise is complied with. In addition to the facts related by me yesterday, I have this morning to report that one of my officers, being on shore in the northern environs of the town last night, between eight and nine o'clock, saw two boats, each pulling eight oars, the men dressed in dark clothing, with the caps usually worn by seamen of the Northern States, pulling quietly in towards the beach.

He distinctly heard a conversation between them in English, one of them saying—"Harry, there she is; I see her"—in allusion, doubtless, to the presence of my vessel. These boats, no doubt, have orders to make signal to the *Iroquois* the moment they discover me under way. Now, with all due deference to his Excellency the Governor, I cannot see the difference between the violation of the neutrality of these waters by the enemy's boats, and by his ship. And if no strict surveillance is to be "exercised either by night or by day," I am receiving very much such protection as the wolf would accord to the lamb. Is it an act of love for the enemy to approach me with his boats for the purpose of reconnaissance, and especially during the night? and I have the same right to demand that he keep his boats beyond the marine league as that he keep his ship at that distance.

Nor am I willing to rely upon his promise, that he will not infringe my rights in this particular. It appears to me further, especially after the knowledge of the facts which I have brought to your notice, that it is the duty of France to exercise surveillance over her own water, "both by night and by day," when an enemy's cruiser is blockading a friendly belligerent, who has sought the asylum in those waters accorded to him by the law of nations. I have, therefore, respectfully to request that you will keep a-watch by means of guard boats, at both points of this harbour, to prevent the repetition of the hostile act which was committed against me last night; or, if you will not do this yourself, that you will permit me to arm boats and capture the enemy when so approaching me.

It would seem quite plain, either that I should be protected, or be permitted to protect myself. Further, it is in plain violation of neutrality for the enemy to be in daily communication with the shore, whether by means of his own boats, or boats from the shore. If he needs supplies, it is his duty to come in for them; and if he comes in, he must anchor; and if he anchor, he must accept the condition of remaining twenty-four hours after my departure. It is a mere subterfuge for him to remain in the offing, and supply himself with all he needs, besides reconnoitring me closely by means of boats.

I protest against this act also. I trust you will excuse me for having occupied so much of your time by so lengthy a communication, but I deem it my duty to place myself right upon the record in this matter. I shall seize an early opportunity to sail from these waters; and if I should be brought to a bloody conflict with an enemy, of twice my force, by means of signals given him in the waters of France, either by his own boats or others', I wish my government to know that I protested against the unfriendly ground assumed by the Governor, that "it does not enter into his intentions to exercise towards the *Iroquois* either by night or by day, so active a surveillance as you [I] require."

I have the honour to be, &c., &c.,
   (Signed)   R. Semmes.
M. Duchaxel, Commander of H.I.M. Steamer, L'*Acheron*.

C.S. Steamer *Sumter*, St. Pierre,
Nov. 23, 1861.

Sir,—I have the honour to inform you that the pilot of the enemy's steamer *Iroquois* habitually spends his time on shore in this port; and that last night he slept on board the enemy's topsail schooner moored near the beach, in the vicinity of the English *barque Barracouta*. I have ample evidence outside of my ship to establish these facts. Now, it must be obvious to you that the enemy has sent this man into French waters to act as a spy upon my movements; and he has, no doubt, in his possession rockets or other signals, with which to communicate my departure to his ship. This man, though only a pilot, and temporarily employed on board the *Iroquois*, is in law as much an officer of that ship, for the time being, as any one of her lieutenants.

The case, then, may be stated thus:—A lieutenant of the *Iroquois* not only spends his time *habitually* on shore, but sleeps at night on board another vessel of the enemy, instead of sleeping at a hotel, the better to enable him to observe my movements, and communicate them to his ship. And yet all this is permitted by the authorities!

I most respectfully but earnestly protest against this violation of my rights. As I stated in my letter of yesterday, an act of reconnaissance (and still more an act of reconnaissance for the purpose of giving information by signal) is an act of war; and will France permit an act of war to be committed against me in her own waters, and under the eye of her authorities, civil and military?

In conclusion, I request that you will issue an order, requiring this spy to depart to his ship, and that you will also take the proper steps to prevent the schooner in which he stays from making any signals to the enemy.

    I have the honour to be, &c., &c.,
    (Signed)   R. Semmes.

M. Duchaxel,
Commander of H.I.M. Steamer, *L'Acheron*.

Note.—The *Sumter* went to sea from the port of St. Pierre on the evening (8 o'clock) of the date of the preceding letter, and, as was predicted, the light was burned on board the American schooner to signal her departure to the *Iroquois*.   R.S.

Muffled the windlass. Getting on board some water. Last night, between eight and nine o'clock, the engineer being on shore, near the north end of the town, saw two of the *Iroquois'* touts, and heard one of them say to the other, "Harry, that's she—I see her:" in allusion, doubtless, to the presence of this vessel. We were all very anxious as the night approached as to the state of the weather; and lo! for the first time in five or six days, we had a beautiful star-light night, without a speck of cloud anywhere to be seen. The enemy continued plain in sight, and our black smoke, as it issued from the stack, would have betrayed us at a distance of five miles. We were therefore reluctantly compelled to give up the attempt.

Saturday, November 23rd.—Beautiful clear morning, with every appearance of settled weather. Fine starlit nights and clear settled days, though very pleasant to the lover of nature, are not quite such weather as we require for running a blockade by a ship which keeps herself in plain sight of us, and which has the heels of us. But we must have patience, and bide our time. Several sail have come in and departed during the last twenty-four hours. The enemy in the offing as usual. Towards noon it began to cloud up, and we had some rain, and I had strong hopes that we should have a cloudy, dark night.

The moon would not rise until seven minutes past eleven, and if we could be aided by a few clouds we should have sufficient darkness; for be it known that in these tropical climates, where almost every star is a moon, there is no such thing as darkness when the firmament is clear. But my hopes began to fade, with the day, for one cloud disappeared after another, as the sun went down, until the night promised to be as serene and bright as the last.

Venus, too, looked double her usual size, and being three hours bright at sunset, poured forth a flood of light, little less than that of the moon in a northern latitude. Notwithstanding all these discouragements, however, I resolved to attempt the run, and having made all the necessary preparations silently, so as not to awaken the suspicions of the townspeople, who were always on the alert, at about five minutes before eight o'clock gun-fire, I directed the chain to be slipped, and the fasts to the shore cut, and put her under steam.

The enemy being on my starboard bow, and apparently standing towards the north point of the roadstead, I headed her for the south point, giving her full steam. So much on the *qui vive* were the townspeople, that we had scarcely moved twenty yards when a shout rent the air, and there was a confused murmur of voices, as if Babel had been let loose.

As we neared the French steamer of war, *Acheron*, signals were made to the enemy by means of blue lights from one of the Yankee schooners in port: perceiving which, and knowing that the signals were so arranged as to designate our direction, after moving a few hundred yards further, I doubled, and came back under cover of the land, while I stopped once or twice to assure myself that the enemy was continuing his course in the opposite direction, in obedience to his signals; when, as soon as the engineer could do so (for he had to cool his bearings, and this was truly an anxious moment for me), I gave her all steam, and stood for the north end of the island.

As we approached it, the Fates, which had before seemed unpropitious to us, began to smile, and the rain-squall, which had come up quite unexpectedly, began to envelope us in its friendly folds, shutting in our dense clouds of black smoke, which were really the worst telltales we had to dread. The first half-hour's run was a very anxious one for us; but as we began to lose sight of the lights of the town and to draw away from the land, we knew that the enemy had been caught in his own trap, and that we had successfully eluded him. I had warned the French authorities that their neutrality would be disregarded, and that these signals would be made.

The commander of the *Iroquois* had been guilty of a shameful violation of good faith towards the French naval officer, to whom he made a promise that he would respect the neutrality of the port, by sending his pilot on shore, and arranging these signals with the Yankee skippers. Yankee faith and Punic faith seem to be on a par. Our ship made good speed, though she was very deep, and by half-past eleven we made up with the south end of Dominica. Here the wind fell, and we ran along the coast of the island in a smooth sea, not more than four or five miles from the land. The moon by this time being up, the bold and picturesque outlines of this island, softened by the rains and wreathed in fleecy clouds, presented a beautiful night-scene.

The sleeping town of Rousseau barely showed us the glimmer of a light, and we passed but one coasting schooner. At 2 p.m., we were off the north end of the island, but now heavy rain-squalls came up, and rendered it so thick, that we were obliged to slow down, and even stop the engine, it being too thick to run. The squall lighting up a little, we endeavoured to feel our way in the dark; mistook the south for the north end of Prince Rupert's Bay, and only discovered our mistake when we had gotten fearfully near the shore, and had whitened our water!

Hauled her broad out, and again put her under very slow steam. The weather now lighting up more, we put her under headway again, doubled the island, and shaped our course E. by N. It was now 4:30 p.m., and I went below and turned in. *Deo gratias.* Poor D., the quartermaster, I had to depose him from his high office of night look-out this night. He had been remarked for his keen vision by night; but on this occasion he was so perturbed, that he saw a steamer bearing down upon him from every direction—even magnifying small sloops into frigates.

The evening of this day was lovely, and I think I have never seen a more beautiful, sedative, poetic, love-in-a-cottage landscape, than the valleys and hills presented in which lies the town of St. Pierre. All these charms were heightened by the presence of grim-visaged war. Our run took everyone by surprise—several of the officers had breakfast and dinner, appointments for several days ahead. My crew seem to be highly delighted at our success in "doing the Yankee;" but I am not sure that an old boatswain's-mate, and a hard, weather-beaten quartermaster, who had shaved their heads for a close fight, were not disappointed that it did not come off.

CHAPTER 8

Again at Sea

Once more afloat on the open sea; and at 4 p.m. of Monday November 25th, a promising commencement was made in the capture of the fine ship *Montmorency*, of 1183 tons, laden with Welsh coal for the English Mail Packet service. And, fortunately so for her, or she would have shared the fate of the *Golden Balance*, the *Daniel Trowbridge*, and other "burnt offerings" of the little *Sumter*. As it was, she paid a light toll in the shape of small supplies of paint, cordage, &c., and entering into a ransom bond for 20,000 dollars, to be paid to the Confederate States Government at the end of the war, her captain and crew were paroled, and she herself permitted to proceed on her voyage.

At 1.30 p.m., on the 26th November—writes Captain Semmes—showed first the United States and then our own colours to an English schooner, probably from the Bahamas to the Windward Islands, and at three captured the United States schooner *Arcade* from Portland, Maine, to Port au Prince, Guadaloupe, loaded with stores. The master and half-owner of the schooner was Master of the *barque* Saxony at the time of the loss of the Central America, and was instrumental in saving lives on that occasion, for which a handsome telescope had been presented to him. I had the pleasure of returning the glass to him, captured among the other effects of his vessel.

Took the master and crew on board (a rough sea running), and set fire to her. At 4.40 stood on our course. The blaze of the burning vessel still in sight at 8 p.m. During the night the wind lulled and became variable. Hauled down the fore and aft sails, and steered N.E. The prize had no newspapers on board, but we learned from the master that the great naval expedition which the enemy had been some time preparing had struck at Beaufort, South Carolina, on Fort Royal Sound. No result known.

After five days of hard fighting with the strong N.E. trade, blowing for the most part half a gale of wind, and with thick and dirty weather, the enemy is at length overcome, the sky clears, and the *Sumter's* head is turned towards Europe. And now for a time Yankee commerce was to have a respite, its relentless little enemy directing its attention exclusively towards maturing her voyage across the Atlantic. She had at this time but sixty days' water for her own crew, in addition to whom there were now the six prisoners taken from the schooner.

The passage, too, would have to be made for the most part under canvas, and would probably not occupy less than fifty days. Of course, she had now but six or seven days' supply of coal—a small reserve in case of emergency, and hardly sufficient to enable her to cruise a few days on the other side, and, if possible, not go quite "empty-handed" into port.

Still the days were not altogether uneventful, and before the week was out, a fine prize ran, as it were, into her very arms. Of this capture the journal gives the following account:—

Tuesday, December 3rd.—At 6.30 p.m. Sail, ho! a point on the starboard bow. At 7.30 the sail, which was standing in nearly the opposite direction from ourselves, approached us within a couple of miles. We hoisted French colours, when she showed United States'. Took in all the studding sails, hauled by the wind, tacked, and fired a shotted gun. The stranger immediately hove to. Lowered a boat, and sent a lieutenant on board of him.

Stood on and tacked, and having brought the stranger under my guns, I began to feel sure of him (our smoke stack was down, and we could not have raised steam in less than two hours and a half). He proved to be the ship *Vigilant*, of Bath, Maine, bound from New York to the guano island of Sombrero, in ballast. Captured him. Took from on board chronometer, charts, &c., and a nine pounder rifled gun, with ammunition, &c. Set him on fire, and at 3 p.m. made sail. This was a fine new ship, being only two years old, and worth about 40,000 dollars.

Lat. 29.10 N., Long. 57.2-2 W. Steering E. by N. We received a large supply of New York papers to the 21st November. We learned from these papers that the *San Jacinto* was in search of us when she took Messrs. Mason and Slidell from on board the *Trent*. The enemy has thus done us the honour to send in pursuit of us the *Powhattan*, the *Niagara*, the *Iroquois*, the *Keystone State*, and the *San Jacinto*.

Dirty weather now for several days, the little vessel rolling and straining, and withal beginning to leak to an extent which caused no small anxiety to those in command. Still, however, she was quite up to mischief, and on the 8th December, the *Ebenezer Dodge*, twelve days from New Bedford, bound to the Pacific on a whaling voyage, was added to the fatal list. Forty-three prisoners were now on board, cooped up with the crew in the narrow berth deck, when the weather forbade their appearance on deck, and the little *Sumter* was beginning to feel herself overcrowded.

It became necessary to adopt precautions, and one-half the prisoners were now kept constantly in single irons, taking it turn and turn about to submit to the necessary but disagreeable infliction. The wind, too, hung perseveringly in the east, and things were getting uncomfortable. They were destined, as the following extracts will show, to be yet more so.

Wednesday, December 11th.—As ugly-looking a morning as one could well conceive. Thick, dark, gloomy weather, with the wind blowing fresh from the east, and threatening a gale (bar. 29.70 and falling) and a steady but moderate rain falling. Put the ship under short sail. Our large number of prisoners renders the crew very uncomfortable during this bad weather. At meridian, gale blowing, with thick, driving rain. Lat. 32° 48' N., Long. 49° 32' W.D.R. At 2 p.m., dense clouds hanging very low all around the horizon in every direction. Wind about E.S.E., inclined to haul to the southward. Bar. 29.59. The pall of clouds is not so dense as at noon, and the rain comes only occasionally in squalls. The clouds are rifted, and appear to be on the point of rapid motion.

Wore ship to the northward and eastward. The wind soon after backed to the northward and eastward, and we had to run the ship off N.W. for a while. Towards night, however, the wind went back to E., and blew very fiercely, raising very heavy and irregular sea-squalls of rain. The lightning was very vivid. It blew very heavily until about 1 p.m., when it abated for more than two hours, blowing only in puffs, and then not very hard. Near the centre of the cyclone, lowest barometer. A little past midnight a quartermaster entered with the report that the starboard-bow port had been stove in! It was then blowing furiously. I immediately despatched the first lieutenant to barricade the port and stop out the water as effectually as possible, in which he succeeded pretty well.

This report gave me considerable anxiety, as the ports in the gun-deck and the uppermost works of the ship are her weak points at which the gale would assault her with most effect. In the meantime the barometer has been gradually settling, settling, settling—sometimes remaining stationary for several hours and then going down as before. At 8 p.m. it was 29.53. We had an awful night—no one able to sleep.

Thursday, December 12th.—Thick, gloomy weather, with the gale raging as fiercely as ever. It blew very heavily all the morning. The barometer continued to sink until it reached 29.32—at 6 p.m. its lowest point. The wind has hauled to the south. We are evidently in a cyclone, having taken it in its northern quarter, the gale travelling north. On the starboard tack, its centre has passed to the west of us. Ordered the donkey engine to be got ready for use last night, in case the ship should make more water than the small bilge pumps could throw out. Carried away the flying jib-boom at 7.30 p.m.—saved the sail. As the gale progressed the wind hauled to the south and west; and at 4 p.m., judging that the strength of the gale had passed us, I kept the ship on her course, E. by S., which gave a quartering wind and sea; and although the sea was heavy, and the wind yet blowing a gale, she made beautiful weather of it, scudding as well as she had lain to. The wind blew fresh all night, with a slowly rising barometer.

Escaped the "cyclone," a fresh danger threatened, and from the element more feared by the sailor than either wind or water in their wildest moods. It was about midnight of December the 14th that the watch on deck were startled by the smell of fire, soon followed by the appearance of smoke pouring out of the ventilator leading up from the berth deck. The alarm was immediately given; hands turned up and sent to quarters, and a strict investigation made. Fortunately no damage was done except to a mattress and pea-jacket which were partly consumed; but the escape was a narrow one, and the sentries on duty below no doubt considered themselves well off, to escape with no other punishment for their carelessness than a week's stoppage of their grog.

On went the *Sumter* with varying fortune, now running pleasant races with some huge whale, that left a track upon the water almost as broad as her own; now rolling and tumbling in a gale, with ports barricaded to keep the water out, and donkey engine ringed to keep it under. And at last the continued bad weather and consequent confinement to the crowded lower deck, began to tell upon the health of the crew, and no less than twelve were at one time upon the sick list. The little vessel herself, too, was getting rapidly invalided. The leak increased terribly, and fully half the day was taken up at the pumps. The Christmas-tide entries in the *Journal* are as follows:—

Tuesday, December 24th.—An unpropitious Christmas-eve; the gale of last night continuing, with rain and a densely overcast sky. The barometer is rising, however, which is a portent that the gale will not last long. I have abandoned the idea of attempting to run into Fayal. These Azores seem to be so guarded by the Furies of the storm, that it would appear to be a matter of great difficulty to reach them in the winter season. We have thirty-eight days of water on board, allowing a gallon to a man; but still I have put the officers and crew on the allowance of three quarts per day. I will run for the Straits of Gibraltar, which will carry me in the vicinity of Madeira, should I have occasion to make a port sooner.

Weather breaking somewhat at noon, but still thickly overcast. No observation. Lat. 37° 31' N., Long. 31° 71'W. by computation. It freshened up from the N. at 2 p.m., and blew a gale of wind all night from N.N.E. to N.N.W. Running off with the wind a little abaft the beam very comfortably; but the two small pumps were kept going *nearly all night*. They do little more than keep her free.

Wednesday, December 25th.—Christmas-day! Bringing with it, away here in mid-ocean, all the kindly recollections of the season and home, and church and friends. Alas! how great the contrast between these things and our present condition. A leaky ship filled with prisoners of war, striving to make a port through the almost constantly recurring gales of the North Atlantic in mid-winter! Sick list—ten of the crew, and four prisoners. Wind fresh from the N.W. We are making a good run these twenty-four hours. Lat. 36'08 N., Long. 28-42 W.

Weather cloudy, and looking squally and ugly, with a falling barometer, it being at noon 29.70; 29.80 is the highest it has been since the last gale. A series of gales commenced on the 19th inst. Altered our course from S.E. by E. to S.E. to avoid the St. Mary's bank; a Captain Livingstone having reported, about forty years ago, that he saw white waters hereabouts, and no nation having thought it worthwhile to verify the report. Thermometer 63°. Heavy rain-squalls. The weather during the night was dirty and squally, with lightning all around the horizon by turns, and heavy rain.. Spliced the main-brace.

The 26th December brought the *Sumter* off Cape Flyaway, and once more she was rapidly approaching the ordinary track of commerce.

Monday, December 30th.—Sail, ho! at daylight, and Sail, ho! in succession during the whole day, until as many as thirty-five were reported. There were as many as nine or ten in sight at one time, all standing on the same course for the tide and wind. Got up steam and began chasing at 8 p.m., and chased until 4 p.m. The first vessel we overhauled was a Dutch *barque*, clipper-looking, on board which we sent a boat; and we afterwards overhauled, and caused to show their papers, fifteen others of the fleet, every one of which was European!—*Viz.* Dutch (ships), 4; English (2 *barques* and 5 brigs), 7; French (1 ship and 1 brig), 2; Swedish (brig), 1; Prussian (*barque*), 1; Hamburg (brig), 1. One of the results of the war is, that in this whole fleet, as far as we could ascertain, there was not a single Yankee! So many ships at the same time so far out at sea, is a sight not often seen. The weather was very thick and rainy, and from the S. to E., a real dirty day; and in such a state of weather, with so many ships running down our track, we had serious apprehensions of collisions as the night set in. To guard against which we set out masthead as well as side lights. At 4.30 p.m., let the steam go down and made sail. No observations. Lat. 35° 39'; Long. 17° 33' D.R.

We first showed the United States colours to all these vessels, and the only one which saluted it was the Prussian. We afterwards showed our own flag to a number of them, and they all, with one or two exceptions, saluted it. The stream of vessels still continued after nightfall—two having passed us showing lights, one ahead and the other astern. At 6.15 p.m., or about one hour after dark, the wind was blowing fresh from the E., and they came down upon us with fearful rapidity.

Friday, January 3rd, 1862.—Ugly looking morning, with a falling barometer. Several sail were reported from the masthead during the morning watch. We shortened sail to permit one of them, which was steering the same course with ourselves, to come up with us. She proved to be a Spaniard. We then gave chase to another ahead of us, running before the wind for the Strait of Gibraltar. We chased her some two hours, when it began to blow a fierce gale from the west, which obliged us to give over the chase and to haul up to prevent running to leeward of our port, and to put the ship under short sail and steam. It blew very fiercely until near sunset, and raised a heavy, short, abrupt sea, in which the ship rolled more heavily than I had ever seen her before.

This shook our propeller so as to cause the ship to increase her quantity of water considerably—so much so that the engineer reported that under short steam he was just keeping her free with his bilge-pumps, and that if anything happened to these, he feared the other pumps would not be sufficient. Under these circumstances, I ran in for the land, cutting short my cruise by a day or two, as I had still two or three days' coal on board. We made the Cadiz Light in the mid-watch—(my fine chronometers!)—a beautiful red flash, and soon after got soundings.

Ran in for the light under low steam, and at 7 p.m. we were within four or five miles of it. The morning was wet and gloomy. Fired a gun, and hoisted the jack for a pilot; and soon after, having received one on board, we ran into the harbour and anchored. As we approached, the scene was most beautiful, in spite of the day. The city of Cadiz is a perfect picture as you approach it, with domes, and towers, and minarets, and Moorish-looking houses, of a beautiful white stone.

The harbour was crowded with shipping—*very thinly* sprinkled with Yankees, who could get no freights—and a number of villages lay around the margin of the bay, and were picturesquely half hidden in the slopes of the surrounding mountains, all speaking of regenerate old Spain, and of the populousness and thrift of her most famous province of Andalusia. Visited by the health-officer, who informed us that unless we were specially exempted, we should be quarantined for three days, for not having a certificate of health from the Spanish Consul at Martinique. A number of merchant ships hoisted their flags in honour of our arrival, and one Yankee showed his in defiance.

Chapter 9

Up the Rock

During the stay of the *Sumter* at Cadiz, and her subsequent arrival at Gibraltar, Captain Semmes made the entries in his *Journal* which will be found in this chapter.

Saturday, January 4th.—Harbour of Cadiz—ancient Gades—with its Moorish houses and *feluccas*, or latteen vessels. Some fine oranges alongside—the product of this latitude, 36° 32' N., about the same parallel with Norfolk, Virginia. It is one hundred and eighty-eight days today since we ran the blockade at New Orleans, and of this time we have been one hundred and thirty-six days at sea. We are informed this evening that the question of our being admitted to *pratique* (and I presume also the landing of our prisoners) has been referred to Madrid by telegram.

Sunday, January 5th.—Sky partially overcast, with a cool north wind. Thermometer 56°. Early this morning the health officer came alongside, and brought me the order from the Government to depart within twenty-four hours, and a tender of such supplies as I might need in the meantime. I replied as under:—

C.S. Steamer *Sumter*, Cadiz,
January 5, 1862.

Sir,—I have had the honour to receive, through the health officer of the port, an order from the Government of Spain, directing me to proceed to sea within twenty-four hours. I am greatly surprised at this unfriendly order. Although my Government has not yet been favourably recognised by Spain, it has been declared to be possessed of the rights of belligerents in the war in which it is engaged; and it is the practice of all civilized nations to extend the hospitality of their ports to the belligerents of both parties alike—whether the belligerents be *de facto* or *de jure*. I am aware of the rules adopted by Spain, in common with the other great powers, prohibiting belligerent cruisers from bringing their prizes into her ports; but this rule I have not violated. I have entered the harbour of Cadiz with my single ship, and I demand only the hospitality to which I am entitled by the law of nations—the Confederate States being one of the *de facto* nations of the earth, by Spain's own acknowledgment, as before stated.

I am sorry to be obliged to add, too, that my ship is in a crippled condition. She is damaged in her hull, is leaking badly, is unseaworthy, and will require to be docked and repaired before it will be possible for her to proceed to sea. I am therefore constrained, by the force of circumstances, most respectfully to decline obedience to the order which I have received, until the necessary repairs can be made. Further, I have on board forty-three prisoners, confined within a small space, greatly to their discomfort, and simple humanity would seem to dictate, that I should be permitted to hand them over to the care of their consul on shore without unnecessary delay.

I have, &c.
(Signed)   R. Semmes.

To his Excellency
The Military Governor of the Port
of Cadiz, Spain.

At 11.30, a boat with the Spanish flag anchored a short distance from me, evidently a guard upon my movements. The Yankees have been at work, no doubt, to bring all this about. The military governor is telegraphing my reply back, and we shall see what the answer will be.

I was mistaken in the above. The order to proceed to sea was begotten in the wise brains of the local authorities. My reply to it having been telegraphed to Madrid, the authorities were overruled; and the Queen despatched an order to permit me to land my prisoners, and to make such repairs as I needed. So this business, which has troubled us a couple of days, is at an end. This evening, just before dark, a Spanish steam-frigate came down from the Navy Yard, and anchored near us.

Monday, January 6th—Last night I was aroused at 2.30 p.m., by a boat from the shore, with a note from the military governor, requesting me to delay proceeding to sea, that the *benevolent* intentions of her Majesty's Government in regard to me might be carried out. The "muddy heads" on shore had received a despatch from Madrid, in reply to my letter to them. Weather clear and bracing. Wind from the North. Thermometer at noon 59.° The steam-frigate disappeared somehow during the night. Protested, as under, against the presence of a health guard-boat:—

C.S. Steamer "*Sumter*," Cadiz,
January 6th, 1862.

Sir,—I have had the honour to receive your Excellency's note of today, in which you inform me that the proceedings of the local authorities of Cadiz, commanding me to proceed to sea within twenty-four hours, have been overruled by the Government at Madrid, and that the Queen had graciously permitted me to land my prisoners, and to remain to put the necessary repairs upon my ship. Do me the favour to communicate to her Majesty my thanks for her prompt and friendly action in the premises.

In the meantime, allow me most respectfully to protest against the presence of the guard-boat which has been placed in surveillance upon my movements, as though I were an ordinary ship of commerce.

Compliance with the laws of quarantine should be left with me as a matter of honour, and the presence of this boat implies the suspicion that a ship of war of a friendly Power could so far forget herself as to infringe the regulations of the port—a suspicion as unworthy the health authorities of the port of Cadiz as it is offensive to me.

I have the honour to be, &c. &c.
(Signed)   R. Semmes.

Señor Ignacio Mendez de Vigo,
Military Governor of the Port of Cadiz.

Tuesday, January 7th.—Today I received a note from Senor de Vigo, the military Governor, informing me that the Queen's Government had consented to permit me to land my prisoners, and to remain for repairs. He puts my remaining, however, on the ground of necessity arising out of my crippled condition.

Received also a reply from the Yankee Consul to my note about the prisoners: declined to receive it on account of its being improperly addressed.[1] Landed all the prisoners. Received another note from the Governor, requesting me to hurry my repairs, &c. Sent to the Captain of the port on the subject. Referred by him to Captain-General.

Wednesday, January 8th.—Complained to the Civil Governor of the paymaster and surgeon having been called alongside the guard-boat (whilst coming on board in a shore boat). Despatched a lieutenant to San Fernando to see The Captain-General about docking the ship. He returned at nightfall, with word that The Captain-General would reply in the morning.

Thursday, January 9th.—Visited by Engineer of docks at San Fernando, to learn the extent of the repairs which we shall require, and to take the dimensions of the ship, to ascertain whether she can enter the only dock that is empty. A fine, clear day, with a pleasant wind from the N. Bar. 30'34., the highest that I have ever seen. No answer from the Captain-General yet (noon), as to our being docked. Besides the six ships which Mr. Welles says have been in pursuit of me—*viz.*, the *Powhattan*, the *Niagara*, the *San Jacinto*, the *Iroquois*, the *Keystone State*, and the *Richmond*—the *Ino* and the *Dacotah* are also employed in this fruitless business.

We are fairly in the hands of the circumlocution office. I suppose they are telegraphing Madrid. The greatest excitement prevails all over Europe to learn the result of the English demand for the Commissioners. The general impression is, that the Yankees will give them up, and that there will be no war. The packet from New York is expected in England today. In the meantime, Great Britain is calling home her ships of war; the Mediterranean fleet arrived at Gibraltar on January 2nd, and threw the commercial community into the greatest consternation. Received final permission this evening from the Captain-General to enter dock.

Saturday, January 11th.—Visited the shore. Cadiz full of life and bustle. Met Mr. Oliver; he is from the East. He says Russia is laying deep schemes for uniting the whole Sclavonic race under her rule;

---

1. Captain Semmes, C.S.N., to U.S. Consul, Cadiz,
C.S. Steamer *Sumter*, Cadiz, January 7, 1862.

Sir,—Your note of this morning having been sent off to me by a common boatman, I could not learn the name of the writer without breaking the envelope. Having done so, and ascertained it to be from yourself, I decline to receive it, as being improperly addressed. My address is as follows:—
Commander H. Semmes, Confederate States Navy, Commanding C.S. Steamer *Sumter*. E.S. Eggleston, U.S. Consul.

and that the *cotton* pressure is felt at Constantinople, up the Danube, and, in short, all over Eastern Europe. Received permission from the Governor to land the marine who was sentenced by court-martial to be discharged. News of the great fire in Charleston. Rumour that the Yankees have given up the Commissioners. Can scarcely credit it as yet. Yankee-dom can hardly have fallen so low.

Sunday, January 12th.—Landed the discharged marine. The news that Messrs. Mason and Slidell have been given up appears to be confirmed. The subtle diplomacy, notifying the Yankee Government *unofficially*, that the ultimatum would be withheld a short time, to allow them time to give up the prisoners *voluntarily*, was resorted to! The Yankee Consul here gave a dinner on the occasion! The Cadiz papers comment very unfavourably upon this back-down, and insist that notwithstanding, it is the duty of the great Powers to interpose and put an end to the war. In the afternoon we got under way, and passing through the fleet of shipping, went up to the dock at Caracca, some eight miles east of the city. The harbour is perfect, the water deep, and the buildings extensive. The pilot who took me up, says he is the man to run me out by the enemy, when I am ready—that he was in New Orleans sixty years ago, and remained a year in Louisiana, where he learned to speak the language, which he has not yet entirely forgotten.

Monday, January 13th.—At about 10 o'clock the dockyard people came on board of us, and at 10.30 we were safely docked, and at noon the dock pumped dry. We suffered very little damage from running ashore at Maranham. We indented a small place under the forefoot, and knocked off only a small portion of our false keel instead of the whole of it, as we supposed. We are now knocking away bulk-heads, and removing magazine and shell room to get at the shaft. At 1 p.m. called officially upon the Naval-Commandant, and returned him my thanks for the handsome manner in which he had docked my ship. I spoke of the back-down of the Yankees, which he asserted would make them lose caste in Europe.

The great fire at Charleston was alluded to by him, whereupon I remarked that Europe could see from this incident—(the work of incendiarism prompted and paid for, no doubt, by the enemy)—the barbarous nature of the war waged upon us, and told him we were in fact fighting the battles of Spain as well as our own; for if the barbarians of the North succeeded in overcoming the South (which, however,

I pronounced an impossibility), and destroying our slave property, in their wild fanaticism and increasing madness, they would next make war on Cuba and Porto Rico. He replied that this war could not continue much longer; there were people and territory enough in North America to make two great governments, and Europe would, no doubt united, soon interpose. I was treated with great civility and kindness.

Tuesday, January 14th—Had an interview today with the Naval-Commandant, who explained to me the orders he had received from the Government in relation to my ship, which were to put upon her only the *indispensable* repairs, without essential alterations. I expressed myself satisfied with this; told him I knew the solicitude of his Government to avoid complication; and, that so far as depended upon me, he might rely upon it that I would permit nothing to be done which might involve it in any way. Proceeding with the necessary repairs. Some thousand workmen, many of them convicts, are employed in this yard. They have in dock, receiving her copper, a heavy steam frigate constructed here, and another still larger on the stocks. Immense quantities of timber are in the docks, and though the water is salt it is not attacked by the worm, the ebb and flow of the tide preventing it. Timber which has been forty years in these docks is perfectly sound. Five of my seamen deserted yesterday—all foreigners, I am glad to say. The Commandant has promised to put the police on the scent, but I have no expectation I shall get them.

Wednesday, January 15th.—Having had the plank replaced in the bilge, and re-coppered and overhauled the propeller, we were let out of dock at 1 p.m. These repairs were done with a very bad grace by the Spanish officials, who seemed in a great hurry to get rid of us, lest the affair of our being docked should compromise them! This I suppose was due to official timidity, not to any want of good feeling, as the Commandant of the yard expressed to me his regret at not being able to put me in complete repair; personally offering to render me any service in his power. Our engine not being ready for use, the Captain-General sent a small steamer to tow me to Cadiz, where we anchored at about 4 p.m.

Whilst lying in the dock, a stampede took place amongst my crew, nine of them having deserted. Two were brought back; the rest escaped. Some of these men had behaved themselves very well, but none of them, of course, had any attachment to the flag, not being natives, or, indeed, citizens at all, and, sailor-like, they had got tired, and wanted a change. Some, no doubt, shrank from the arduous and perilous duties of the service in which they had engaged. They took refuge with the Yankee Consul, and it was useless to ask to have them given up. The enemy is certainly good at burning cities by means of negro incendiaries, and at enticing away our seamen. Another lad ran away from a boat this evening. Have directed no boat should leave the ship without an officer, and that the officer be armed, and ordered to shoot any men who attempt to desert.

Thursday, January 16th.—Called my crew aft and had a talk with them about the bad conduct of their shipmates who had deserted. Told them I did not believe I had another man on board capable of so base an act; that men who could run under such circumstances would run from their guns; and that I did not want such, &c., &c.; and ended by telling them that when funds arrived they should be permitted to go on liberty.

At 9 p.m., the *aide-de-camp* of the Military Governor came on board, bringing a pilot with him, with a peremptory order for me to go to sea. I replied as under:—

C.S. Steamer *Sumter*, Cadiz,
Jan. 16, 1862.

Sir,—I have the honour to inform you that whilst my ship was in the dock at Caracca eight of my seamen deserted, and I am informed that they are sheltered and protected by the United States Consul. I respectfully request that you will cause these men to be delivered to me, and to disembarrass this demand of any difficulty that may seem to attend it, permit me to make the following observations:—[2]

3. It has been, and is, the uniform custom of all nations to arrest and hand over to their proper officers, deserters from ships of war; and this without stopping to inquire as to the nationality of the deserter.

4. If this is the practice in peace, how much more necessary does such a practice become in war; since, otherwise, the operations of war—remote, it is true—but still the operations of war, would be tolerated in a neutral territory.

5. Without a violation of neutrality, an enemy's consul in a neu-

---

2. The paragraphs omitted, contain merely a recapitulation of the claim of the Confederate States to full belligerent rights.

tral territory, cannot be permitted to entice any seamen from a ship of the opposite belligerents, or to shelter or protect the same; for, if he is permitted to do this, then his domicile becomes an enemy's camp in a neutral territory.

6. With reference to the question in hand, I respectfully submit that the only facts which your Excellency can take cognizance of, are, that these deserters entered the waters of Spain under my flag, and that they formed a part of my crew. The inquiry cannot pass a step beyond, and Spain cannot undertake to inquire, as between the United States Consul and myself, to which of us the deserters in question more properly belong. Such a course would be tantamount to an interposition between two belligerents, and it would be destructive of the essential rights of ships of war in foreign ports, as well in peace as in war.

7. I am inclined to admit that if a Spanish subject serving under my flag should escape to the shore, and should satisfy the authorities that he was held by me by force, and either without contract, or in violation of contract, that he might be set at liberty, but such is not the present case. The nationality of the deserters not being Spanish, Spain cannot, as I said before, inquire into it. To conclude, the case which I present is simply this:- Several of my crew, serving on board my ship under voluntary contracts, have deserted, and taken refuge in the consulate of the United States. To deprive me of the power, with the assistance of the police, to recapture these men, would convert the consulate into a camp, and the consul would be permitted to exercise the right of a belligerent on neutral territories.

I have the honour to be, &c., &c.

(Signed) R. Semmes.

Exmo. Sr. Don J. Mendez de Vigo,
Military Governor, Cadiz.

Friday, January 17th.—Before I had turned out this morning the Governor's aid again came on board, stating the order was made peremptory, that I should go to sea in six hours, or I should be forced. I called in person on the Governor, a not over bright official, and endeavoured to make him understand how I was situated, but it seemed impossible. He promised, however, to send a despatch to Madrid, to the effect that I had no coals, and was awaiting funds to procure the same; but, he added, if he received no despatch in the six hours he should require me to depart. I returned on board, and gave the necessary orders to get ready for sea. At 4 p.m., whilst I was weighing my anchor, the General's aide came alongside, and said to me that the Madrid Government had consented to let me remain twenty-four hours, that a despatch was being written to me on the subject, to which the Governor desired that I would reply in writing.

I told the officer that, if his Government had politely acceded to my request, permitting me to remain until my funds arrived, I could have appreciated it; but that being restricted to forty-eight hours, I declined to avail myself of the privilege, and should go to sea; and that the general need not trouble himself to read me the written despatch, as I had no other reply to make. I got under way in a few minutes afterwards, and as I was passing out a boat was seen pulling in great haste towards me, one of the crew holding up a letter in his hand. I did not stop to receive it; I felt too indignant at the manner in which I had been treated to be very civil. We passed outside of the harbour a little before sunset, and held on to the light until midnight, when we steamed for the Strait of Gibraltar.

Saturday, January 18th.—We entered the Strait of Gibraltar at about 5 p.m., passing the Tarifa Light, and with the bold shores of both Africa and Europe in plain sight, in the bright moonlight—bright, notwithstanding the passing clouds. We made the Gibraltar light about daybreak, and saw at the same time a number of sail. We gave chase to two that *looked* American, which they proved to be, and which we captured. The first was the *barque Neapolitan*, of Kingston, Massachusetts, from Messina to Boston, laden with fruit and fifty tons of *sulphur*. The whole cargo was stated by the master, in his depositions, to belong to the Baring Bros., consigned to their agents in Boston—a falsehood, no doubt.

Without stopping to look into the *bona fides* of this claim of neutral ownership, it was enough that the sulphur was contraband, and that the fruit belonged to the same owner; I destroyed both ship and cargo. No papers as to the latter were produced. The second vessel was also a *barque*, the *Investigator*, of Searsport, Maine. She being laden with iron ore, the property of neutrals (Englishmen), I released her on a ransom bond; she was bound to Newport, Wales. One fourth of the vessel was owned in South Carolina, and the share of the South Carolina owner was omitted from the ransom bond—amount of bond being less one-fourth fifteen thousand dollars. Having burned the *Neapolitan*, I steamed in for Gibraltar at 2.30 p.m. Passed under Europa point at about dusk, and stood in, and anchored in the bay at about 7.30 p.m.

Boarded in a few minutes by a boat from an English frigate, with an offer of service. Sent a boat alongside the health ship.

Sunday, January 19th.—We found early this morning we had *pratique*. A number of English officers and citizens came on board. At 10 I called on board the frigate that had sent the boat on board of us last night, but was informed that the captain (who was absent) was not the commanding officer present, and that the latter lived on shore. At 2 p.m. I landed at the arsenal and called upon the commanding naval officer, who received me very politely. I asked the loan of an anchor, having but one, and the captain promised to supply me with one if there should be no objection on the part of the law officers of the Crown! Walked from the captain's little oasis—scooped out as it were from the surface of the Rock, with a nice garden-plot and trees, shrubbery, &c.—down into the town, and called on Lieutenant-General Sir W.J. Codrington, K.C.B., the Governor, an agreeable type of an English gentleman of about fifty to fifty-five years of age.

The Governor tendered me the facilities of the market, &c., and in the course of conversation said he should object to my making Gibraltar a *station*, at which to be at anchor for the purpose of sallying out into the Strait and seizing my prey. I told him that this had been settled as contrary to law by his own distinguished judge, Sir William Scott, sixty years ago, and that he might rely upon my taking no step whatever violative of the neutrality of England, so long as I remained in her ports, &c. The garrison is about seven thousand strong, and it being Sunday, the parade-ground and streets were thronged with gay uniforms. Spain, with her hereditary jealousy and imperiousness of character, is very formal and strict about intercourse with the Rock. The Duke of Beaufort visited us today.

Monday, January 20th.—Very fresh, threatening a gale. Ship reported as having dragged her anchor. Ordered steam to be got up and the berth shifted. Ran in nearer to the eastern shore into four fathom water and where it was smoother.

Tuesday, January 21st.—The westerly wind is bringing a fleet of ships into the bay. Today Colonel Freemantle came on board to return my visit on the part of the Governor, and to read to me, by the latter's direction, a memorandum of the conversation which had passed between us on Sunday. The points noted were—first, that we had agreed that I should receive all necessary facilities for the repair (from private sources) and supply of my ship, contraband of war excepted; and, secondly, that I would not make Gibraltar a station at which to lie at anchor, and sally out upon my enemy. I assented to the correctness of the Governor's memorandum.

The first lieutenant and paymaster ashore making arrangements for the purchase of an anchor and chain. The house of Peacock and Co. refused to supply us, because it would offend their Yankee customers. They made arrangements with another party. The town of Gibraltar, from the fact that the houses are built on the side of the Rock, and stand one above the other, presents the beautiful spectacle every night of a city illuminated. Colonel Freemantle politely requested me to visit the various batteries, &c.

Wednesday, January 22nd,—Wind still from westward. Received on board an anchor and chain. Received a letter from Captain Warden, on a point of international law, to which I assented—to wit, that vessels should have twenty-four hours' start.

Thursday, January 23rd.—Visited by Captain Warden, the Senior Naval Officer. Received a letter from Hon. Mr. Yancey, who does not believe that the blockade will be raised for three months. Ordered a survey upon the ship.

Friday, January 24th.—Invited to dine with the 100th, a Canadian regiment. Some of the officers went. Captain Palmer has been relieved by De Camp.

Saturday, January 25th.—We hear a rumour that the *Nashville* has been sold. Ships constantly arriving and departing.

Sunday, January 26th.—A charming, balmy day, resembling April in *Alabama*. At 10, went on shore to the Catholic church; arrived as the military Mass ended: many Catholics in the army. Small church, with groined arches—remnant of Spanish times. After church took a delightful stroll into the country, just above the Alameda. It is a labyrinth of agave and flowers and shrubbery, among which the path zigzags up the mountain-side; geraniums, and jonquils, and mignonette, and lilies are wild. One is only surprised, after looking at the apparently barren face of the rock, to find so much sweetness of Mother Earth.

I clambered up a couple of hundred feet, and from that height the bay, the coasts of Spain, and sleeping Africa, robed in the azure hue of distance, and the numerous sail, some under way, and others lying like so many cock-boats, as seen from the height, at their anchors— the latteen craft speaking of the far East, &c. Statue of General Elliot. A number of fine-looking Moors in the streets, picturesque in their loose dresses and snowy turbans. Gibraltar is, indeed, a city of the world, where one sees every variety of costume, and hears all tongues. Spanish is the predominant language among the commercial classes. Major-General Sir John Inglis (the hero of Lucknow), of the English army, Governor of Corfu, having arrived on his way to the Ionian Islands, visited us today to see our ship, which he was kind enough to say had become "quite distinguished."

Monday, January 27th.—A general exodus of the shipping this morning out of the Straits, within which they had been detained some ten days by a head wind. The English mail steamer from Southampton arrived. Received from her a *Times* of the 20th, from which we learn that England had protested against the barbarity of blocking up the harbour of Charleston, by sinking a stone fleet. We feel some anxiety for the safety of Messrs. Mason and Slidell, they having embarked on board the English gunboat *Rinaldo*, at Princetown, on the 2nd instant, and not having been heard of on the 10th, although bound to Halifax. A heavy gale blew on the eve of their embarkation.

Tuesday, January 28th.—Preparing the ship for sea, surveying machinery, and impatiently awaiting news from London.

Wednesday, January 29th.—Visited the shore, and went to the Military Library and Reading Room, where I found the principal London journals. Reported that the English Government will consult Parliament about recognising us. Took a long stroll to the east end of the Rock—exceedingly broken and picturesque. Came upon a Moorish burying-ground, looking out upon Africa. Some of the marble slabs had become almost disintegrated by the weather, so old were they. What a history of human affections, hopes, aspirations, tribulations, and disappointments lay buried here! New works, adding additional strength to this renowned fortress, are still going on.

Thursday, January 30th.—Visited, in company with Colonel Freemantle, the famous fortifications, passing through the galleries—three tiers, one above the other—in the north end of the Rock. These are huge tunnels, extending from a third to half a mile, with embrasures from space to space for cannon—the solid Rock forming the casemates. From these galleries we emerged out on a narrow footway cut in the rock, and stood perpendicularly over the sea breaking at our feet, and had a fine view of the N.E. face of the Rock rising in a magnificent mass some 1500 feet. From this point a tower, called the Queen of Spain's Chair, was pointed out to me—on the height opposite, to the northward.

The legend connected with which is, that during one of the sieges of 1752, the Queen of Spain came to this eminence to witness the assault and capture of the place, and vowed she would not descend therefrom until the flag of Spain should wave from the Rock. The assault failed, and the Queen in performance of her vow refused to descend, until the Governor of Gibraltar, hearing of the determination of her Majesty, sent her word that he would at a given hour hoist the Spanish ensign that she might descend. This was done, and the Queen was rescued from her predicament without breaking her word.

Having finished our inspection of the Rock, we went through the town, and passed out on to the neutral ground, from which I returned after a four hours' ride completely broken down. On the south end, under a perpendicular wall of rock, that in summer breaks the sun from an early hour in the afternoon, is the Governor's summer residence, to which he resorts for protection against the heat. We met his Excellency and lady, who had come out to look at their summer home, &c. Colonel Freemantle told me that the Spanish Consul, whom he pointed out as we passed the Alameda, had stated that I was a Spaniard, or at least that my father was—a native of Catalonia—that I spoke Catalan as well as English, and that my name was a common one in that province.

Saturday, February 1st.—Witnessed a review of about five thousand troops in the Alameda. Drums draped with black, and the ornaments of the officers covered with black crape in respect to the memory of the Prince Consort.

Sunday, February 2nd.—Received letters from N——, informing me, that as my ship was unseaworthy, Mr. Yancey had determined to send me the new one built at Liverpool, if I desired it.

Wednesday, February 5th.—A United States merchant ship came in and anchored. Ready for sea. Mr. Joyce came on board, and went afterwards with the Engineer on shore to look at some coal. Mr. Joyce sent word that he could not purchase any, there being a combination against us. Sent the first lieutenant to the Governor to represent the facts to him, and to ask for a supply from the public stores. He replied he had no coal under his control, that it belonged to the naval officer, but that he did not think it could be supplied. Expressed his astonishment at the combination of the merchants. Sent a number of men on shore on liberty.

Friday, February 7th.—Liberty-men staying over their time. Two of them have deserted and gone over to the U.S. Consul. One of them has been badly beaten by the rest of the men. Eleven of them came on board later. Visited by a Spanish Lieutenant, who had been directed by the Spanish Naval Commander at Algeciras to see me and state that the U.S. Consul had complained to the Spanish government that I had violated the neutrality of Spain by capturing the *barque Neapolitan* within a mile and a half of Ceutra, on the Morocco coast, and that the Government had given the Admiral orders to see that both belligerents in the war should respect Spanish neutrality.

I stated to him in reply that any question which the capture might present was a matter between our two Governments, and that I did not recognise the right of the Spanish Admiral to inquire into the matter. To this the lieutenant assented. I then said that I would take the pleasure of showing him, however, for the information of the Admiral, that the truth had not been represented to his Government by the United States Consul. I then called my clerk, and showed him the deposition of the Master of the captured vessel, in which it was stated that the capture was made within five miles of Gibraltar! The officer seemed equally astonished and pleased, and expressed his satisfaction.

Saturday, February 8th.—Early this morning the British frigate *Warrior* came in, and anchored near us. Sent a lieutenant on board to make the usual complimentary call. Awaiting the arrival of a vessel with coal, consigned to Mr. Joyce, who promises to supply us. My coxswain ran off today, and I was pulled off by a drunken crew.

Sunday, February 9th.—Did not go to church, but remained on board to be present at muster. Eleven of my vagabonds still on shore. Some of these, we learn, have gone to the United States Consul, and claimed his protection. This official has been seducing them off by an emissary. Wrote to the Governor charging this on the Consul, and wrote also to Captain Warden, asking to be supplied with coal from the Government dockyard.

C.S. Steamer *Sumter*, Bay of Gibraltar,
Feb. 10, 1862.

Sir,—I have the honour to state for the information of his Excellency the Governor of Gibraltar, that I am informed and believe that the United States Consul, at this place, has, by means of his emissaries, tampered with, and seduced from their allegiance, several of the crew of my ship who have visited the shore on liberty. The impropriety and illegality of such conduct is so manifest that I take it for granted his Excellency will interpose his authority for my protection. Great Britain, having proclaimed a strict neutrality in the war now pending between the United States and Confederate States, is under the obligation, I respectfully suggest, not only to abstain herself, from any un-neutral conduct, but to see that all persons whatsoever within her dominions so abstain.

No act of war, proximate or remote, should be tolerated in her waters by the one belligerent against the other, or by any citizen or resident against either belligerent. His Excellency will doubtless concur with me in the justice and propriety of the rule thus stated. To apply this rule to the present case. Being prompted by motives of humanity to send my crew on shore, in small detachments, for exercise and recreation, after a long confinement on shipboard, my enemy, the United States Consul, sends his agents among them, and by specious pretences persuades them to desert their ship, and take refuge under his Consular flag.

This has been done in the case of the following seamen:—Everett Salmon, John G. Jenkins, Thomas F. Kenny, and perhaps others. Here is an act of war perpetrated against me in neutral territory, and the consular residence, or office, has become *quoad hoc* a hostile camp. And this conduct is the more objectionable in that the nationality of most of these men is not American. His Excellency, as a soldier, knows that no crime is regarded with greater detestation in the present civilized age of the world, than the one here described. As between contending armies in the field, an offender caught in the perpetration of such an act, would be subjected to instant death; and this, not only because the act is an act of war, but because it is a dishonourable act of war.

And can an enemy make use of neutral territory to do that, which would subject him to an ignominious death, if he were without such territory, and within reach of the opposite belligerent? When my men come within his Excellency's jurisdiction I lose all control over them, and must rely upon his comity to regain possession of them. If they leave me of their own free-will, in the absence of the recognition of my Government, and of treaty stipulation, perhaps I have no remedy. But when I permit them to go on shore, and enter the jurisdiction of a neutral and friendly power, I do so with the just expectation that they will receive the shelter and protection of the neutral flag; and that they will not be permitted to be run off by my enemy; and to wheedle and entice a sailor from his ship, and that too when, perhaps, he is half drunk, is little better than kidnapping him.

In the present case, the violation of the neutral jurisdiction is as complete as if the Consul had seized my men by force; for he has accomplished the same object; to wit, weakening his enemy by stratagem—a stratagem practised by one belligerent against another. If this act had been committed by a military or naval officer of the enemy, transiently within the limits of Gibraltar, everyone would have been surprised at it, and would have exclaimed against it as a flagrant violation of the law of nations. And is the offence of less magnitude when committed by a Consul, who is peculiarly favoured by the law of nations, as an officer of peace, and one whose pursuits lie wholly in the walks of commerce?

Mr. Sprague, the United States consul, is a gentleman whom I have heard favourably spoken of, and it is barely possible I may do him injustice in imputing to him the conduct described, but the evidence came to me in a very satisfactory shape, and I shall be ready to produce it if the allegation be denied. Should the proof be made out to his Excellency's satisfaction, I shall deem it my duty to request that the Consul be suspended from his functions, and that the question of withdrawing his Exequatur be referred to the British Government.

   I have, &c., &c.,
     (Signed) R. Semmes.
To Capt. J. Freeling, Col. Sec.

      C.S. Steamer *Sumter*, Bay of Gibraltar.
           Feb. 10th.

Sir,—I have the honour to inform you that I have made every effort to procure a supply of coal, without success. The British and other merchants of Gibraltar, instigated I learn by the United States Consul, have entered into the un-neutral combination of declining to furnish the *Sumter* with coal on any terms. Under these circumstances, I trust the Government of her Majesty will find no difficulty in supplying me. By the recent letter of Earl Russell (31st January, 1862), it is not inconsistent with neutrality for a belligerent to supply himself with coal in a British port. In other words, this article has been pronounced, like provisions, innoxious; and this being the case, it can make no difference whether it be supplied by the Government or an individual (the Government being reimbursed the expense), and this even though the market were open to me.

Much more, then, may the Government supply me with an innocent article, the market not being open to me. Suppose I had come into port destitute of provisions, and the same illegal combination had shut me out from the market, would the British Government permit my crew to starve? Or, suppose I had been a sail ship, and had come in dismasted, and the dockyard was the only place where I could be refitted, would you have denied me a mast? and if you would not deny me a mast, on what principle will you deny me coal, both articles being declared by your Government innoxious? The true criterion is, not whether the Government, or an individual may supply the article, but whether the article itself be noxious or innoxious.

The Government may not supply me with powder—why? Not because I may have recourse to the market, but because the article is noxious. A case in point occurred when I was in Cadiz recently. My ship was admitted into a Government dock, and there repaired; firstly, because the repairs were innocent, and, secondly, because there were no private docks in Cadiz. So here, the article is innocent, and there is none in the market (accessible to me); why then may not the Government supply me?

In conclusion, I respectfully request that you will supply me with 150 tons of coal, for which I will pay the cash; or if you prefer it, I will deposit the money with an agent, who can have no difficulty, I suppose, in purchasing the same amount of the material from some one of the hulks, and returning it to her Majesty's dockyard.

     I have, &c.,
     (Signed)   R. Semmes.

Captain E. Warden,
Senior Naval Officer, Gibraltar.

Monday, February 10th.—Received a visit from Captain Cochrane, of the *Warrior*, son of the late Earl of Dundonald, notorious in the war of 1812, and distinguished in the South

American service. Wrote the following letter:—

C.S. Steamer *Sumter*, Bay of Gibraltar,
Feb. 10, 1862.

Sir,—I have the honour to inform you that I have this day caused to be paid to the Spanish Consul at this port the amount of the bill contracted by this ship under my command while in the dock at Caracca.

   I have, &c.,
     (Signed)   R. Semmes.
To the Captain of the Port, Cadiz.

Tuesday, February 11th.—Five men in confinement! The d—— seems to have got into my crew. I shall have to tighten the reins a little.

Wednesday, February 12th.—Called on the Governor to have a talk with him on the subject of my deserters. He took the ground that in the absence of treaty stipulations he could not deliver a fugitive unwilling to be returned. Whilst I was with him the *Tuscarora* was announced by the telegraph. This ship came in and anchored near us about 12 noon, disguised with her mainyards down, so as to resemble a merchant steamer. I saw Captain Warden on shore also. He informed me that the question of my being coaled by the dockyards had been referred by telegraph to London.

Thursday, February 13th.—Blowing a levanter. In the morning a *barque* dragged foul of the *Tuscarora*, and carried away her (the *barque's*) foreyards. Later in the day the *Tuscarora* shifted her berth over to the Spanish shore, near San Roque. Several vessels took shelter in the harbour from the gale. Among them a French line-of-battle ship, and a Spanish side-wheel man-of-war. Shut up in my little cabin by the wet weather, I have time to brood gloomily over home and the war, and the prospects of our dear South.

Friday, February 14th.—At noon the *Tuscarora* got under way, and stood over to Algeciras.

Saturday, February 15th.—Anniversary of the day of my resignation from the navy of the United States; and what an eventful year it has been! The Northern States have been making a frantic and barbarous war upon thirteen states and nine millions of people; in face, too, of Madison's words:

If there be a principle that ought not to be questioned in the

United States, it is that every nation has the right to abolish an old Government and establish a new one. This principle is not only recorded in every public archive, written in every American heart, and sealed with the blood of a host of American martyrs, but it is *the only lawful tenure* by which the United States hold their existence as a nation.

And then what flood-gates of private misery have been raised by this war—overwhelming families without number in utter ruin and desolation.

Reduced my worthless sergeant to the ranks, and promoted a corporal in his stead. The British Parliament met on the 6th, and we have in the papers today the address to the Queen, and the speeches of the Earl of Derby and Lord Palmerston. From the general tone of all these papers we shall not be acknowledged at present. They say the quarrel is no business of theirs, and we must fight it out. Astute Great Britain! she sees that we are able to fight it out, and thus her darling object will be accomplished without the expenditure of blood or money.

Sunday, February 16th.—Visited by the Captain of the *Scylla* frigate.

Monday, February 17th.—Visited the *Warrior*. The Governor and suite and a number of naval and other officers, civilians, and ladies visited her by appointment at the same time. The *Warrior* is a marvel of modern naval architecture, and for a first experiment may be pronounced a success. She is a monstrous, impregnable floating fortress, and will work a revolution in shipbuilding. Wooden ships, as battleships, must go out of use. With this single ship I could destroy the entire Yankee fleet blockading our coast, and this is the best illustration I can give for the necessity of this revolution in shipbuilding. The British Government has declined to supply me with coal from the dockyard, and I must make arrangements to get it from Cadiz. The London, ship-of-the-line steamer, arrived.

Tuesday, February 18th.—The Southampton mail steamer arrived, bringing news from London to the 12th. The news of the defeat and death of General Zollicoffer is confirmed.

Wednesday, February 19th.—Called on Captain Warden, and had a conversation with him on the subject of our blockade by the *Tuscarora*. Called his attention to the prevention of signals, the *Tuscarora* communicating with Gibraltar by boats. Gave notice if the *Tuscarora* came in I should claim precedence of departure, &c. The *Warrior* went to sea.

Judging from the tone of the English journals there is no prospect of our immediate recognition. Sent to Cadiz-for coal.

Thursday, February 21st.—The newspapers state that there are seven Yankee ships in pursuit of us—four steamers and three sail-ships. Three of the steamers were at Teneriffe on the 11th of January. A report has reached us that our Paymaster and ex-Consul Tunstall are prisoners in Tangier! Received a letter from Captain Warden, informing me that the Governor had prohibited all vessels in the harbour from making signals, and had prohibited the *Tuscarora* from communicating with the harbour by boats so long as she remained in Spanish waters, &c.

Saturday, February 22nd.—The report is confirmed of the illegal imprisonment in Tangier of Paymaster Myers and Mr. Tunstall.

CHAPTER 10

A Daring Act

The imprisonment of the two gentlemen alluded to at the conclusion of the last chapter, is an episode in the history of the *Sumter* which demands something more than mere passing notice. When the news of the occurrence reached England it excited a considerable amount of attention, as not only did the case exhibit some curious phases of the working of the law of "strict neutrality," but it also afforded a very excellent idea of the marvellous loyalty of one of the United States Consuls. Reference has been previously made to the zealous conduct of the consular officials of the North.

It has been shown that at Maranham, Cayenne, Paramaribo, Cadiz, and Gibraltar, the respective Yankee Consuls acted upon the broad principle that every Confederate was the natural enemy of the United States, and a rebel to boot. Not content with simply holding this opinion, the task these gentlemen set themselves was, to indoctrinate the Governments of the several countries in which they were located with the same views of the case. In some cases they succeeded so far as to cause considerable vexation to Captain Semmes; and if they failed to convince the authorities, that the *Sumter* was a piratical craft, they at least succeeded in occasionally entailing needless delays in obtaining those necessary supplies, which as an officer in the service of a country recognised as a belligerent, the commander of the *Sumter* had a right to demand.

The Tangier Consul, however, went far beyond his brethren, for he not only demanded, but succeeded in effecting the arrest and imprisonment of an officer and a citizen of the Confederate States. These gentlemen, Mr. Myers, the paymaster of the *Sumter*, and Mr. Tunstall, a private Southern gentleman, had been despatched by Captain Semmes from Gibraltar to Cadiz, in search of coal. The vessel in which they embarked touched at Tangier, and the two Americans landed for the purpose of inspecting the curious old Moorish city.

No sooner were they on shore than the United States Consul hastened to the authorities, denounced his enemies, and demanded their arrest, alleging that it was authorized by treaty stipulation with the United States. After vainly imploring advice from the representatives of the Christian Powers, the sorely perplexed authorities complied with this demand, and the two Confederates were seized, heavily ironed, and kept prisoners in the Consul's house. At the very first opportunity they communicated with Captain Semmes, and he with his usual promptitude at once despatched the following letter to the Governor of Gibraltar:—

C.S. Steamer *Sumter*, Bay of Gibraltar,
February 22nd, 1862.

Sir,—I have the honour to ask the good offices of His Excellency the Governor of Gibraltar in a matter purely my own. On Wednesday last, I despatched from this port, in a French passage-steamer for Cadiz, on business connected with this ship, my paymaster, Mr. Henry Myers, and Mr. T.T. Tunstall, a citizen of the Confederate States, and ex-United States Consul at Cadiz. The steamer having stopped on her way at Tangier, and these gentlemen having gone on shore for a walk during her temporary delay there, they were seized by the authorities, at the instigation of the United States Consul, and imprisoned. A note from Paymaster Myers informs me they are both heavily ironed, and otherwise treated in a barbarous manner.

I learn further that the pretence upon which the unlawful proceeding was had, is, that it is authorized by treaty stipulation with the United States. Unfortunately I have not a copy of this treaty in my possession; but I presume it provides in the usual form, for the extradition of criminals, and nothing more. I need not say to his Excellency that treaties of this description are never applied to political offenders—which I presume is the only category in which the United States Consul pretends to place these two gentlemen. An occurrence of this kind could not have happened, of course, in a civilized community.

The political ignorance of the Moorish Government has been shamefully practised upon by the unscrupulous Consul. I understand that the British Government has a diplomatic agent resident at Tangier, and a word from that gentleman would no doubt set the matter right, and insure the release of the unfortunate prisoners. And it is to interest this gentleman in this humane task that I address myself to his Excellency. May I not ask the favour of his Excellency, under the peculiar circumstances of the case, to address Mr. Hay a note on the subject, explaining to him the facts, and requesting his interposition?

If any official scruples present themselves, the thing might be done in his character as a private gentleman. The Moorish Government would not hesitate a moment, if it understood correctly the facts and principles of the case; to wit, that the principal powers of Europe have recognised the Confederate States as belligerents, in their war against the United States, and that, consequently, the act of making war against these States by the citizens of the Confederate States, is not an offence, political or otherwise, of which a neutral can take cognizance; and even if it were the former, no extradition treaty is ever meant to apply to such a case.

I have the honour, &c. &c.
(Signed)   R. Semmes.
Capt. S. Freeling, Col. Sec.

This letter was unattended with success, the maintenance of strict neutrality being a barrier in the way of any interference on the part of the British authorities at Gibraltar. Accordingly, Captain Semmes penned the subjoined formal protest, and despatched it to the Governor of Tangier.

C.S. Steamer of war *Sumter*, Bay of Gibraltar,
February 23rd, 1862.

His Excellency the Governor of Tangier, Morocco:

I have the honour to inform your Excellency that intelligence has reached me of the imprisonment by the Moorish Government at Tangier, of Mr. Henry Myers, the Paymaster of this ship, and Mr. T.T. Tunstall, a citizen of the Confederate States, and late United States Consul at Cadiz. I learn further, that these gentlemen are heavily ironed, and otherwise treated with inhumanity. I am utterly at a loss to conceive on what ground this illegal imprisonment can have taken place; though I learn that the United States Consul demanded it, under some claim of extradition treaty stipulation.

A word or two will suffice to set this matter right. It must, of course, be known to your Excellency, that the Confederate States have been acknowledged by the principal powers of Europe, as belligerents in the war in which they are engaged with the United States; and that, consequently, the Paymaster of this ship, in any act of war in which he may have participated, can have been guilty of no offence, political or otherwise, of which any neutral power can take cognizance. Indeed, as before stated, the neutral powers of Europe have expressly recognised the right of the Confederate States to make war against the United States.

No extradition treaty therefore can apply to Paymaster Myers. Mr. Tunstall not being in the military or naval service of the Confederate States, can no more be brought within the terms of any such treaty than Paymaster Myers. I have, therefore, respectfully to demand, in the name of my Government, and in accordance with the laws and practice of nations, that these two citizens of the Confederate States be set at liberty.

I have the honour, &c., &c.

(Signed) R. Semmes.

Determined to leave no stone unturned, the Commander of the *Sumter* sought to interest the British Charge d'Affaires in the fate of the two prisoners, as will be seen by the annexed letter:—

C.S. Steamer *Sumter*, Bay of Gibraltar,
February 23rd, 1864.

Sir,—May I ask of you the favour to act unofficially for me in a matter of humanity, by handing to the proper officer the enclosed communication, demanding the release from imprisonment in Tangier of the Paymaster of this ship, and of Mr. T.T. Tunstall, a citizen of the Confederate States. The Moorish authorities have evidently been imposed upon by false representations as to the character and status of these gentlemen. I hear that the United States Consul demanded their imprisonment under some extradition treaty. The absurdity of such a claim will of course be apparent to you.

We are recognised belligerents; our acts of war are legal therefore, so far as all neutrals are concerned, and it cannot be pretended that any officer of this ship can have committed any offence in any act of war in which he may have participated against the United States, which Morocco can take cognizance of, or bring under the terms of any extradition treaty.

I have the honour to be, &c., &c.

   (Signed)   R. Semmes.

John Hay Drummond Hay, C.B.,
H.M. Charge d'Affaires, Tangier, Marocco.

On the 24th Mr. Hay replied, and the following extract from his communication will best explain the grounds he assumed:—

"You," he writes, "must be aware that Her Britannic Majesty's Government have decided on observing a strict neutrality in the present conflict between the Northern and Southern States; it is therefore incumbent on Her Majesty's officers to avoid anything like undue interference in any questions affecting the interests of either party which do not concern the British government; and though I do not refuse to accede to your request to deliver the letter to the Moorish authorities, I think it my duty to signify distinctly to the latter my intention to abstain from expressing an opinion regarding the course to be pursued by Morocco on the subject matter of your letter."

To this despatch Captain Semmes forthwith replied, and his letter is remarkable for the able manner in which the question of neutrality is dealt with. After thoroughly reviewing the transaction, he sums up as follows:—

"Upon further inquiry I learn that my first supposition that the two gentlemen in question had been arrested under some claim of extradition (unfortunately I have not a copy of the treaty between Morocco and the United States) was not exactly correct. It seems that they were arrested by Moorish soldiers upon the requisition of the United States Consul, who claimed to exercise jurisdiction over them as citizens of the United States, under a provision of a treaty common between what are called the non-civilized and the civilized nations. This state of facts does not alter in any degree the reasoning applicable to the case. If Morocco adopts the *status* given the Confederate States by Europe, she must remain neutral between the two belligerents, not undertaking to judge of the nationality of the citizens of either of the belligerents, or to decide any other question growing out of the war which does not concern her own interests. She has no right, therefore, to adjudge a citizen of the Confederate States to be a citizen of the United States, and not having this right herself she cannot transfer it by treaty to the United States Consul."

The communication, however, produced no effect; and, meanwhile, another step was taken at Tangier. The United States frigate *Ino* no sooner learnt the news of the capture made by the Consul than it ran over to Tangier, sent a boat on shore with armed men, and carried off the prisoners. This proceeding was not, however, allowed to be performed quite so quietly as the Yankees could have wished. The Christian population, exasperated at the arrest, turned out in force, and fears were entertained that even the forty men from the *Ino* would not be able to secure the safety of their prize. But here the neutral powers were of assistance: their representatives, with Mr. Drummond Hay at their head, came to the aid of the captors, calmed the mob, and thus averting the threatened rescue, enabled the United States to carry off the two Confederates on board the *Ino*.

Captain Semmes, finding he could do nothing with the authorities at Tangier, communicated with Mr. Mason, the Confederate commissioner in London, and that gentleman made strong representations at the Foreign Office, with what results the following statements of facts will show.

It was on the 28th of February that the captives were finally carried off from neutral territory, by an armed force from an enemy's ship. On the 8th of March, Mr. Mason was informed by the Under-Secretary, that the British Government was under the impression that they had been released from confinement. On the 6th of March, just two days before Mr. Mason received this intelligence, the *Ino*, which had run back to Cadiz, transferred the two unfortunate prisoners to the Yankee merchant ship, *Harvest Home*, which carried them away to a prison in the United States.

Such was the history of the Tangier difficulty—a question which, at the time, created considerable stir in Europe, and which is likely to leave a lasting impression upon the Southern mind.

CHAPTER 11

Appointment to the *Alabama*

Meanwhile the search for coal had been continued by the *Sumter* and at length a promise of a supply had been obtained. It so happened, however, that this supply, so long sought and so hardly won, would after all never be required.

The little *Sumter*'s days as a cruiser were numbered. By no means a new boat when first converted by Captain Semmes into a vessel of war, the hard work and rough usage she had experienced in her seven months at sea, had been too much for her already enfeebled constitution, and she was now little better than a wreck. At last she fairly broke down altogether, was surveyed by a board of her officers, pronounced unseaworthy, and on the 24th of February Captain Semmes makes the following entry in his journal:—

"And so the poor old *Sumter* is to be laid up. Well! we have done the country some service, having cost the United States at least a million of dollars, one way or another!"

And so she unquestionably had. Eighteen vessels captured; seven burned, with all their cargo on board; and two released on heavy ransom bonds, represent in themselves no inconsiderable amount of damage. Add to this the amount really expended in pursuit of her; the enormously increased rates of insurance; the heavy losses from reluctance to entrust goods in United States bottoms, or to send ships themselves to sea under the United States colours, and we have an aggregate of loss that a million of dollars can hardly cover.

Her career was now over; but she was ere long to find a successor under the same command, beside whose exploits her own were to sink almost into insignificance. The events of the few months that elapsed between the final abandonment of the *Sumter* and the *Ala-*

bama's start on her adventurous career, may best be gathered from Captain Semmes' own official report to the Secretary of the Navy at Richmond.

> Nassau, New Providence,
> June 15 to 20, 1862.

Sir,—I have the honour to inform you of my arrival at this place, on the 8th instant, in twenty days, from London. I found here Lieutenants Maffit and Sinclair, and received from the former your letter of May 29th, enclosing a copy of your despatch to me of May 2nd. As you might conclude from the fact of my being here, the original of the latter communication had not reached me; nor, indeed, had any communication whatever from the department. As you anticipated, it became necessary for me to abandon the *Sumter*, in consequence of my being hemmed in by the enemy in a place where it was impossible to put the necessary repairs upon her-to make her fit to take the sea.

For some days after my arrival at Gibraltar, I had hopes of being able to reach another English or a French port, where I might find the requisite facilities for repair, and I patched my boilers, and otherwise prepared my ship for departure. In consequence of a combination of the coal merchants against me, however, I was prevented from coaling; and, in the meantime, the enemy's steamers, *Tuscarora* and *Kearsarge*, and the sailing sloop *Ino*, too, arrived and blockaded me. Notwithstanding the arrival of these vessels, I should have made an effort to go to sea, but for the timely discovery of further defects in my boilers, which took place under the following circumstances:—An English steamer, having arrived from Liverpool with an extra quantity of coal on board, offered to supply me. I got steam up to go alongside of her for the purpose, when, with a very low pressure, my boilers gave way in so serious a manner as to extinguish the fires in one of the furnaces.

I was obliged, of course, to "blow off;" and upon a re-examination of the boilers, by a board of survey, it was ascertained that they had been destroyed to such an extent as to render them entirely untrustworthy. It was found, indeed, to be necessary either to supply the ship with new boilers or to lift the old ones out of her, and renew entirely the arches and other important parts of them, which could only be done in a machinist's shop, and with facilities not to be found at Gibraltar. In this state of things, it became necessary, in my judgment, either to lay the ship up, or to sell her.

Of course, the remaining by her of myself, my officers and crew, in her disabled and useless condition, was not to be thought of. Still, I felt that the responsibility was a grave one; and deeming it more respectful to the department that it should be assumed by someone higher in authority than myself, I reported the facts to the Hon. James M. Mason, our commissioner in London, and requested him to assume the power. (The following is the letter here referred to:—

C.S. Steamer *Sumter*, Bay of Gibraltar,
March 3rd, 1862.

Sir,—I had the honour to address you a note a day or two ago, requesting you to assume the responsibility of giving me an order to lay the *Sumter* up, that my officers and myself may return to the Confederate States, to take a more active part in the war. I now enclose you a copy of a letter addressed to me by the wardroom officers of this ship on the same subject, by which you will perceive that there is no difference of opinion between us as to the policy and propriety of the step indicated. Each succeeding mail is bringing us intelligence that the enemy is pressing us on all sides, and it would seem that we shall have occasion for every arm and all our energies and resources to defend ourselves.

The most that we could hope to accomplish by remaining where we are would be, perhaps, to occupy the attention of an additional steamer of the enemy. One steamer will always remain to watch the ship, in whatever condition she may be; and probably no more than two would continue the blockade if the officers remained by her. The enemy, having some 300 armed ships afloat, one ship would seem to make no appreciable difference in his offensive force. I would not press this matter upon you so earnestly if there was any certainty of my hearing from the Secretary of the Navy in any reasonable time; but my despatches are liable to capture, as are his despatches to me, and many months may therefore elapse before I can receive his orders.

I can readily understand how, under ordinary circumstances, you might hesitate about giving me this order, but there are frequent occasions in which responsibility must be assumed, and I respectfully suggest that this is one of them. To lay the *Sumter* up without an order from the naval department involves responsibility either in you or in me; and, as I stated to you in my last note, it appears to me that the responsibility may be assumed by you with more propriety than by myself, as you are a high functionary of the Government, while I am a mere subordinate of a department.

The question of expense, too, is to be considered—the expenses of the ship, with the utmost economy, being, in round numbers, 1000 dollars per month. Should you decide upon giving me the order, do me the favour to telegraph me as follows, *viz.*:— "Your request is granted—act accordingly." Address me also by mail, as it will take some days to wind up affairs, and I shall have ample time to receive your letter before leaving for London.

    Respectfully, &c. &c.
      (Signed)   R. Semmes

Hon. Jas. Mason, Com., &c., London.

This he did very promptly, and in a few days afterwards I discharged and paid off in full all the crew, except ten men, and detached all the officers, except Midshipman Armstrong and a Master's Mate. I placed Mr. Armstrong in charge of the ship, supplied him with money and provisions sufficient for himself and his diminished crew for ten months, and departed myself for London, whither most of the officers also repaired on their way to the Confederate States. Upon my arrival in London, I found that the *Oreto* (*Florida*) had been despatched some weeks before to this place; and Commander Bullock having informed me that he had your orders to command the second ship he was building, himself, I had no alternative but to return to the Confederate States for orders.

It is due to Commander Bullock to say, that he offered to place himself entirely under my orders, and even to relinquish to me the command of the ship he was building; but I did not feel at liberty to interfere with your orders. Whilst in London, I ascertained that a number of steamers were being prepared to run the blockade with arms, &c., and instead of despatching my officers at once for the Confederate States, I left men to take charge of these ships, as they should be gotten ready, and run them in, deeming this the best service they could render the Government under the circumstances. I came hither myself (accompanied by my First-Lieutenant and Surgeon), a passenger in the British steamer *Melita*, laden with arms, &c., with the same intention.

It is fortunate that I made this arrangement, as many of my officers still remain in London, and I shall be able to detain them there, to take them with me in the execution of your order of the 2nd of May, assigning me to the command of the *Alabama*. In obedience to this order I shall return by the first conveyance to England, when the joint energies of Commander Bullock and myself will be dedicated to the preparation of this ship for sea. I will take with me Lieut. Kell, Surgeon Galt, and Lieutenant of Marines, Howell—Mr. Howell and Lieut. Stribling having reached this port a few days before me, in the British steamer *Bahama*, from Hamburgh, laden with arms, &c., for the Confederacy. At the earnest entreaty of Lieut. Commanding Maffit, I have consented to permit Lieut. Stribling to remain with him as his First Lieut., on board the *Florida*; and the *Florida's* officers not yet having arrived, Mr. Stribling's place on board the *Alabama* will be filled by Midshipman Armstrong, promoted.

It will, doubtless, be a matter of some delicacy and management to get the *Alabama* safely out of British waters without suspicion, as Mr. Adams, the Northern envoy, and his numerous satellites are exceedingly vigilant in their espionage. We cannot, of course, think of arming her in a British port. This must be done at some concerted rendezvous, to which her battery (and the most of her crew) must be sent in a merchant vessel.

The *Alabama* will be a fine ship, quite equal to encounter any of the enemy's sloops of the class of the *Dacotah, Iroquois, Tuscarora*, &c.; and I shall feel much more independent in her upon the high seas than I did in the little *Sumter*. I think well of your suggestion of the East Indies as a cruising-ground, and hope to be in the track of the enemy's commerce in those seas as early as October or November next, when I shall doubtless be able to make other rich "burnt-offerings" upon the altar of our country's liberties.

Lieutenant Sinclair having informed me that you said, in a conversation with him, that I might dispose of the *Sumter* either by laying her up or selling her, as my judgment might approve, I will, unless I receive contrary orders from you, dispose of her by sale upon my arrival in Europe. As the war is likely to continue for two or three years yet, it would be an useless expense to keep a vessel so comparatively worthless so long at her anchors. I will cause to be sent to the *Alabama* her chronometers, charts, &c., and I will transfer to the vessel her remaining officers and crew.

In conclusion, permit me to thank you very sincerely for this new proof of your confidence, and for your kind intention to nominate me as one of the "Captains" under the new Navy Bill.

I trust I shall prove myself worthy of these marks of your approbation.

        (Signed)   R. Semmes.

Hon. S. Mallory, Sec. of the Navy.

CHAPTER 12

Laws of Neutrality

The vessel to which Captain Semmes was now appointed had been built expressly for the Confederate navy, by Messrs. Laird and Sons, of Birkenhead. She was a small fast screw steam-sloop, of 1040 tons register, not iron-clad, as was at one time erroneously supposed, but built entirely of wood, and of a scantling and general construction, in which strength had been less consulted than speed. Her length over all was about 220 feet, length of keel, 210 feet; breadth of beam, 32 feet, and 18 feet from deck to keel. She carried two magnificent engines, on the horizontal principle, constructed by the same firm, and each of the power of 300 horses; while her coal-bunkers were calculated to accommodate about 350 tons of coal.

The *Alabama*, or as she should as yet be called, *No. 290*, was barque-rigged, her standing gear being formed throughout of wire rope; thus combining strength with lightness to the utmost possible extent. Her ordinary suit of sails consisted of the usual square sails in the foremast, fore topmast staysail and jib, large fore and main topsails, maintop sail, topgallant sail and royal, and on the mizzen-mast spanker and gaff topsail. Occasionally, this rig would be varied, as was the case in entering Cherbourg, just before the close of her eventful career, when a crossjack yard was got up across the mizzen-mast, with mizzen topsail and topgallant yards to match; and the *Alabama* assumed for a time the appearance of a full-rigged ship. This, however, was only a temporary *ruse*, and her ordinary cruising sails were similar to those commonly in use with vessels of her class.

A little forward of the mizzen-mast was placed the steering apparatus, a large double wheel, inscribed with the significant words: *Aide toi et Dieu t'aidera*; a motto which, in the case of the *Alabama*, has been better acted up to than such legends usually are. Just before the funnel, and near the centre of the vessel, was the bridge, at either side of which hung the two principal boats, cutter and launch; a gig, and whale-boat, being suspended from the davits on either side of the quarter-deck, and a small dingy over the stern.

On the main deck she was pierced for twelve guns, with two heavy pivot guns amidships. Her lines were beautifully fine, with sharp flaring bows, billet head, and elliptic stern. The cabin accommodation was perhaps somewhat scanty, but this, in so small a vessel, built altogether for speed, not comfort, was scarcely to be avoided. The semicircular stern-cabin was, of course, appropriated to the captain, with a small state-room opening out from it in the starboard side. Forward of this came the companion ladder, and forward of this again the wardroom, or senior officers' mess, with small cabins on either side for the lieutenants, surgeon, and other officers.

Passing through the wardroom, the visitor entered the gunroom, or "steerage," allotted on the starboard side to the midshipmen, and on the port to the engineers. Next came the engine-room, occupying an unusual space for a vessel of the *Alabama*'s size; the coal bunkers, &c.; and finally, the berth-deck, or forecastle, with accommodation for 120 men. The lower portion of the vessel was divided into three compartments, of about equal dimensions. In the aftermost were store-rooms, shell-rooms, &c.; the midship section contained the furnaces and fire-rooms; whilst the forward compartment was occupied by the hold, the magazines, and the boatswain's and carpenter's stores.

Such was the *Alabama*, or, as she was long called, *No. 290*; and considering the peculiar circumstances under which she was built, the numerous requirements to be satisfied, and the perfection of the workmanship throughout the vessel, the cost of her construction and armament cannot but be considered marvellously small. The builder's charge for hull, spars, sails, boats, cable, and all equipment, except armament, was £47,500. To this must be added the cost of her batteries, £2500; magazine tanks, £616; ordnance stores, £500; and small arms, £600, making a total cost of £51,716, or in American money, of 250,305.44 dollars.

It must not be supposed, however, that in leaving the building-yard of Messrs. Laird, the *Alabama*'s equipment was by any means complete. The strictest injunctions had been given both to Captain Bullock and Captain Semmes, to avoid doing anything that would by any possibility be construed into an infringement of either the municipal law, or the anxiously-guarded neutrality of England; and as the Foreign

Enlistment Act clearly forbade the *equipment* of ships of war for belligerent uses, it was necessary that the new cruiser should leave England unarmed, and take her chance of capture, until some safe place could be found for taking her armament on board.

This was, of course, a delicate operation, and one requiring the preservation of strict secrecy, that the cruisers of the United States might at least not be enabled to pounce upon their new enemy, until she had been placed to some extent in a condition for self-defence. Nor was this the only ground on which caution had to be observed. The career of the *Sumter* had given Captain Semmes a clearer idea than he had probably before possessed of the precise meaning of the word neutrality, as applied to the present war, and there was too much at stake to run the risk of detention from any such views of its obligations as had been put forward in the case of his captive officer at Tangier. The law of the case might be—he certainly thought it was—clear enough; but there was no use in throwing temptation in the way of those by whom it was to be interpreted. The recent cases of the *Alexandria*, the *El Tousson*, and the *El Monassir*, have shown with sufficient clearness that this calculation was tolerably correct.

Accordingly, the reticence which has so distinctively marked the men of the South throughout the struggle, was most religiously observed in the case of the *Alabama*. It was impossible, of course, altogether to conceal from the diligent researches of Mr. Adams' spies the fact of her destination. But beyond having a strong suspicion that the vessel so rapidly approaching completion in Messrs. Laird's yard was intended for the Confederate States, these astute gentlemen were altogether at fault. This, however, was enough, and on the application of Mr. Adams an order was despatched to the Customs' authorities at Liverpool to seize the ship, and prevent her from going to sea.

Fortunately for the Confederate vessel her friends were equally on the watch, and tidings of the projected seizure were promptly conveyed to Birkenhead. It was necessary now to act with promptitude, and the final preparations were pushed on with the utmost speed. At length, at a quarter past nine on the morning of the 29th July, 1862, the anchor was got up for the first time since she had been afloat, and the *No. 290* dropped slowly down the Mersey, anchoring that afternoon in Moelfra Bay.

Even this, however, could not be carried out without considerable precaution, and it was necessary, as a blind to the suspicious eyes so constantly employed in watching every movement of the sorely suspected vessel, to announce that she was merely proceeding for a short trial trip. To give colour to this pretence, to which her even then unfinished condition lent a *prima facie* sanction, a gay party was assembled on board. A number of ladies, friends and acquaintances of the builders, enlivened the narrow, and as yet rough and unfinished deck with their bright costumes, and seemed to afford a sufficient guarantee for the return of the vessel to port. Luncheon was spread in the cabin, flags decorated the seats hastily improvised on the sacred quarter-deck, and all seemed bent upon making holiday.

Suddenly, however, the scene changed. At a signal from the *Alabama* a small steam tug came puffing alongside, and to the visitors' great astonishment they were politely requested to step on board. Relieved of her gay cargo, the transformation of the *Alabama* proceeded with rapidity. The luncheon had been already cleared away, and now seats and flags, and all the rest of the holiday paraphernalia began speedily to disappear. Late that evening and all the next day the bustle of preparation continued, and at two o'clock in the morning of the 31st July the anchor was once more weighed, and with a strong breeze from the S.W. the *No. 290* started off, ostensibly on a voyage to Nassau in the Bahamas.

Just in time. That morning the seizure was to have been made. At the very moment that *No. 290* was heaving up her anchor, a huge despatch "On Her Majesty's Service" was travelling down to Liverpool, at the top speed of the north-western mail, commanding the Customs' authorities to lay an embargo on the ship. The morning was still but very slightly advanced when through the driving south-westerly squalls came the gold-laced officials in search of their prize, only to return in outward appearance considerably crestfallen, inwardly perhaps not altogether so deeply grieved as a good neutral should have been at the ill success of their uncomfortable trip.

Two days more and another actor appeared upon the scene. Like her colleague at Tangier, the United States frigate *Tuscarora* had got scent of a valuable prey, and hurried round to the Mersey at full speed of sail and steam to secure it. But by the time she arrived at Moelfra Bay, the *No. 290* was already a couple of days upon her outward voyage. The game was up, and the only resource of the baffled Yankee now lay in scolding poor Earl Russell, who certainly had been no willing agent in the escape of the daring little Confederate cruiser.

CHAPTER 13

Ready for the Cruise

No. 290 ran rapidly before the S.W. gale up the Irish Channel, and past the Isle of Man and Ailsa Crag, till as the columns of the Giant's Causeway began to loom dimly through the driving rain she rounded to, laid her main-topsail to the mast, and sent a boat on shore with the pilot and Captain Bullock, who up to this time had been in command of the vessel. She was now transferred to the charge of Captain J. Butcher, late of the Cunard service, her other temporary officers being—Chief Lieutenant, J. Law, of Savannah, Georgia; second, Mr. G. Townley Fullam, of Hull, England; Surgeon, D.H. Llewellyn, of Easton, Wilts; Paymaster, C.R. Yonge, of Savannah, Georgia; and Chief Engineer, J. McNair, an Englishman. The crew, the greater number of whom had been taken on board in Moelfra Bay, numbered about seventy men and boys, and were shipped for a feigned voyage, the Confederate captain trusting to the English love of adventure, to induce them to re-ship when the true destination of the vessel came to be declared.

Bidding *adieu* to the Irish coast she now shaped her course for Terceira, one of the Western Islands, where she was to meet her consort, and receive on board the guns and other warlike stores, she had been restrained by respect for English law, from shipping in Liverpool. Throughout this run, which occupied nine days, the wind still continued blowing a strong gale from the southward and westward, with a heavy sea running, through which *No. 290* dashed along sometimes at a speed of upwards of thirteen knots an hour. It was not, however, without a certain amount of risk that this pace was maintained.

Amongst other less serious damages the bow port was stove in by a heavy sea, and altogether the vessel showed manifest symptoms of the speed at which she had been driven. But accidents of this kind were of minor importance compared with the supreme value of time. Once fairly off, and the news of the escape must spread rapidly through the kingdom. The first whisper of it would bring the enemy's ships in pursuit, and a single hour's delay in reaching her destination and placing herself in a condition for self-defence, might bring one of them alongside, and the career of the new cruiser be cut short before it had fairly begun. So *No. 290* "crashed on" at top speed, and on the 10th of August "Land, ho!" was called from the foremast-head, and she brought up at Porto Praya in Terceira.

During this trying voyage the new vessel had given full promise of those splendid qualities as a sea-boat, on which depended so much of the extraordinary success of her after career. She was, of course, by no means in the best trim for sailing, whilst everything about her being bran new was in the worst possible condition, short of being quite worn out, in which to enter on so severe a trial. She came through it however most triumphantly, exhibiting a speed and ease of motion rarely to be found in combination. All hands arrived at Terceira in the best spirits, and highly delighted with their new ship.

The bay of Porto Praya, in which *No. 290* was anchored is of no very great extent, but presents excellent holding ground for vessels, and is sheltered from all but easterly winds. Three or four small forts occupy positions on the shore, but appear never to have been armed, and are at present falling rapidly into decay. The bay itself is secluded, and not particularly well supplied with the means of sustenance, fruit and vegetables being tolerably plentiful, but water very scarce, and beef a luxury only to be obtained by importing it from Angra, on the other side of the island. The officers however were kindly and hospitably received by the inhabitants, and the best the place afforded placed at their disposal.

As yet the expected consort of the Confederate vessel had not arrived, and some anxiety was felt by Captain Butcher and his brother officers, as day after day passed by, and no signs of her appeared. On the 13th August, expectations were aroused by the cry of "Sail, ho!" but the new comer proved to be only a Yankee whaling schooner, from Provincetown; and additional anxiety was occasioned on her arrival by the indiscretion of one of the ship's company, by whom the real character and design of *No. 290* was betrayed to the United States schooner, the speedy departure of which, after learning the news, seemed ominous of trouble.

At last, on the 18th, a large *barque* was observed steering for the brig, and on a nearer approach proved to be the long-looked-for ship. She was the *Agrippina*, of London, Captain McQueen, with a cargo of ammunition, coal, stores of various descriptions, and six thirty-two pounders. Once lashed alongside the sloop, and all haste was made to transfer her cargo, and the crews of the two vessels were busily engaged in this operation when, on the 20th of August, the smoke of another steamer was seen on the horizon, and after a brief interval of suspense, lest the new comer should prove to be a United States vessel of war, in search of the escaped Confederate, the *Bahama*, Captain Tessier, made her number, and three hearty cheers from the crew of *No. 290* gave welcome to Captain Semmes, and the other officers late of the *Sumter*.

Captain Semmes embarked on board the *Bahama* at Liverpool, on the morning of Wednesday, 13th August, joining the ship in a steam-tug, the *Bahama* having dropped down towards the mouth of the Mersey a few hours previously. Captain Bullock, who, as it has been said, had seen the new ship safely off upon her voyage before leaving her at the Giant's Causeway, and had reported the happy commencement of the adventure, accompanied him on board the *Bahama*, in which were also a number of seamen, shipped, like those on board *No. 290*, for a feigned voyage, in the hope of inducing them to join when the ship was fairly in commission.

As the tug left us to return to the city—writes Captain Semmes-the crew gave us three hearty cheers, to which we responded. After a passage of seven days, we made the island of Terceira, and soon afterwards the port of Praya, at the eastern end of the island, our appointed rendezvous. As we approached the port we looked with eager eyes for *No. 290*, and her consort, the *Agrippina*, which had been despatched to her from London with the armament. Greatly to our satisfaction we soon discovered the spars, and then the hulls of both vessels lying snugly in the bay, and apparently in contact, and indicating the transhipment of the battery, &c.

At about 11.30 p.m. we steamed into the harbour, and were immediately boarded by Captain Butcher, who reported that he had already gotten on board all the heavy guns, and many of the paymaster's stores, &c. As the harbour is open to the east, and as the wind was blowing from the N.E., driving a considerable swell in, which caused the two vessels to lie very uneasily alongside of each other, I gave orders that they should both follow me to the bay of Angra, where we all anchored about 4 p.m. Hauled the two steamers alongside, and commenced discharging the two additional guns.

After having shown the new vessel to the seamen I had on board the *Bahama* (numbering thirty-seven), I addressed them, telling them that they were released from the contract they had entered into at Liverpool, and were now perfectly free to dispose of themselves, and that I invited them to enter with me on board my ship. I spoke of the war, explained to them the object of my contemplated cruise, and the inducements held out to them of prize-money, &c. This afternoon about one-half the number shipped; the others hung back, perhaps, for better terms. There are, perhaps, some sea-lawyers among them influencing their determination. I moved my baggage on board, and slept my first night on board my new ship. Warned by the authorities that West Angra was not a port of entry, and that we must move to East Angra.

Thursday, August 21st.—Clear fine weather. I am charmed with the appearance of Terceira. Every square foot of the island seems to be under the most elaborate cultivation; the little fields divided by hedgerows of what appeared to be sugar-cane. The white one-storied houses are dotted thickly among all this cultivation, giving evidence of great populousness in this primitive paradise—so far removed away from the world, and so little resorted to by commerce. Wind inclined to haul to the S.E., which will open us to the sea again, and I am, of course, quite anxious.

Received a letter (or rather Captain Butcher, who is still the nominal commander of the ship, did) from the English Consul, informing us that the authorities still insisted upon our going round to East Angra. Replied that we had come in to receive coal from the *barque* in our company, &c., and that as the day seemed fine, and we should probably have a good lee for the purpose, I would go to sea without the marine league for the purpose. I knew they suspected me of arming as well as coaling, and hence I resorted to this step to quiet their apprehensions of my infringing their neutrality.

Stood along the island—the *Bahama* in company and the *barque* alongside—and hoisted out the gun-carriages, and mounted as many of the guns as we could. Returned during the afternoon, and after nightfall anchored in East Angra, with the *barque* still alongside. We were hailed very vociferously as we passed in very bad English or Portuguese, we could not make out which, and a shot was fired at us.

The *Bahama*, which was following, hauled off and stood off and on during the night; we continued our course, and anchored about

8.30 p.m. Near midnight I was aroused from a deep sleep into which I had fallen after the fatigue and exertions of the day, and informed by the officer of the deck very coolly that the man-of-war schooner was firing into us. As I knew they did not dare to fire *into* me but were only firing at me, perhaps to alarm me into going out of the harbour, I directed the officer to take no notice of the proceeding. In the morning we learned that this had been a false alarm, and that the firing had been from the mail steamer to bring on board her passengers.

Had a talk with the old boatswain's-mate, who consented to go with me, and to use his best exertion to bring over to me all the good men over whom he could exercise influence.

Friday, August 22nd.—Wind from the S.W., promising us a smooth day for our work. Called all hands at 6 p.m., and commenced coaling. At 7 p.m. a number of Custom House officers and the English Consul came on board. Our coaling was suspended until the two ships could be entered at the Custom House. We lost a couple of hours by this visit, but I was gratified to learn as the result of it that we might remain quietly and continue our coaling, &c.

We got the remaining guns into position; got up and loaded some of the rifles; opened a barrel of cartridges, and made sundry other hasty preparations for defence, in case any attempt should be made to seize the ship. At 11.30 p.m. signalled the *Bahama*, and brought her in to her anchors. Towards night the weather became rainy, and considerable sea setting in to the harbour, we shoved the *barque* off to an anchor. During the night she dragged her anchor, and we were obliged to send a party on board her to let go another, to prevent her from dragging on shore. There was quite a row this evening on board the *barque*, ending in a general fight, the sailors by some means or other having managed to get drunk.

Saturday, August 23rd.—Morning cloudy and rainy. We were unable to get the *barque* alongside, so as to continue coaling before 9 p.m. Still we are hurrying the operation, and hope to be able to get through by night. We have all sorts of characters on board, but the crew is working quite willingly; now and then a drunken or lazy vagabond turning up. The sharp fellows thinking I am dependent upon them for a crew are holding back and trying to drive a hard bargain with me.

Getting the battery to rights, and caulking the screw-well, which leaks badly when she is under way. Made some acting appointments to fill up my officers. Received on board a fine supply of fresh provisions and vegetables for the crew. In this beautiful island all the fruits of the temperate and many of the torrid zone are produced. Pine-apples, pears, plums, and melons were brought off to us.

We finished coaling, except seven or eight tons, by working until 9 p.m., when the men were fairly fagged out. Hauled the *barque* off, and resolved to go out with what coal I had on board, as to finish entirely would involve a delay of Sunday.

CHAPTER 14

A Fruitless Chase

Sunday seemed destined from the very first to be a notable day in the annals of the new Confederate cruiser.

The morning of Sunday, the 24th August, found her afloat ready for sea; the delicate operation of transhipping stores in an open roadstead safely accomplished, a supply of coal on board sufficient for some weeks of average steaming, and six of her guns mounted and ready to cast loose for action at a moment's notice. The early hours of the morning were occupied in washing down the decks which were covered thickly with coal, and making matters above board as shipshape as under the circumstances could be managed. By noon this was finished, and all was ready for sea. A brief space was then devoted to the no less necessary operation of dining, and at noon steam was got up, the anchor weighed, and *No. 290* stood out to sea, the *Bahama* still keeping her company.

For about four or five miles the two vessels kept silently upon their course, until well beyond all possibility of dispute as to the too well-remembered maritime league of neutrality. Then as four bells sounded from the forecastle the crew were summoned aft, all heads were bared, and stepping in full uniform on to the quarter-deck, Captain Semmes proceeded in a voice clear and firm, but not altogether free from emotion, to read aloud to the assembled ships his commission from the President as Commander of the Confederate States Steam Sloop, *Alabama*.

As he proceeded, the English flag which had been carried by the vessel during her days of *incognito*, was slowly lowered to the deck, and three little black balls might be seen wriggling their way swiftly but cautiously to the mastheads and mizzen peak of the *Alabama*. Boom! goes the starboard forecastle gun as the reading is ended. The three black balls are "broken out," the long pendant uncurls itself at the main, the red cross of St. George flutters at the fore, and the pure white ensign of the Confederacy, with its starry blue cross upon the red ground of the corner, floats gracefully from the peak, as the little band breaks into the dashing strains of "Dixie," and three ringing cheers peal out over the sparkling sea.

So far all had gone well and hopefully, and the enthusiasm of the moment had brought a flush to the cheek and a dimness to the eye of many a weather-beaten tar among the little crew. But enthusiasm is fleeting in these practical days, and the sound of the last cheer had scarcely died away upon the summer breeze ere the scene changed, and the true nineteenth century spirit resumed its sway. The ceremony of hoisting the flag and taking command completed, Captain Semmes called all hands aft upon the quarter-deck, and addressed them as he had previously addressed the crew of the *Bahama*, inviting them to ship with him in the *Alabama* for the cruise.

The address is described by those who listened to it as most spirited and effective. It frankly avowed that the principal object of the *Alabama* was to cripple the commerce of the enemy. But this would not be her only aim. Prudence was essential, and he was not to fight a fifty-gun ship, but when the opportunity offered of engaging on anything like equal terms, the *Alabama* would be prompt enough to accept the combat. "Let me once see you," he said, in conclusion, "proficient in the use of your weapons, and trust me for very soon giving you an opportunity to show the world of what metal you are made."

The address was greeted with an unanimous burst of cheers, and then came the anxious moment. "It may be supposed," writes Captain Semmes, in recording the events of that memorable day, "that I was very nervous about the success of this operation, as the management of the ship at sea absolutely depended upon it." And of this fact the men were at least as fully aware as himself. Nor had they any scruples as to availing themselves most fully of the advantages of their situation. "The modern sailor," continues Captain Semmes, "has greatly changed in character. He now stickles for pay like a sharper, and seems to have lost his recklessness and love of adventure."

However this latter proposition may be, the truth of the former was most amply proved on the day in question. Jack niggled and haggled, and insisted pertinaciously on the terms he felt his would-be Captain's necessity enabled him to command; and in the end Captain Semmes was fain to consent to the exorbitant rates of £4 10s. a month for seamen, £5 and £6 for petty officers, and £7 for firemen! "I was glad," he writes, "to get them even upon these terms, as I was afraid a large bounty in addition would be demanded of me."

Very curious was the contrast afforded by this scene with the enthusiasm that had preceded, and the gallant, dashing, reckless career that followed it. These men who thus stood out for the last sixpence they could hope to wring from their employer's necessity, were the same who subsequently dashed blindfold into the action with the *Hatteras*, and later yet, steamed quietly out of a safe harbour with a disabled ship, to meet an enemy in perfect trim and of superior force, and as their shattered vessel sank beneath their feet, crowded round the very captain with whom the hard bargain had been driven, imploring him not to yield.

Finally, the bargaining resulted in the shipping of a crew, all told, of eighty men; a larger number, perhaps, than Captain Semmes had himself anticipated, but still not so many by at least twenty-five as were required for properly manning and fighting the vessel. With these, however, the Captain was fain to be content, trusting to volunteers from future prizes to complete his complement. A hard evening's work followed in preparing allotments of pay to be sent home to the sailors' wives, and also in paying their advance wages, and sending small drafts for them to agents in Liverpool. It was not till 11 p.m. that this task was completed, and then Captains Bullock and Butcher took a final farewell of the ship, and returned on board the *Bahama*, which with the remainder of the two crews steamed away for Liverpool, and the Confederate cruiser was left alone upon the wide ocean, and had fairly started on her adventurous career.

No sooner had the two steamers parted company than sail was made on board the *Alabama*. The fires were let down, fore and main topsails were set, the ship's head turned to the N.E., and by midnight Captain Semmes was able to leave the deck, and thoroughly worn out with the day's excitement and exertions, turn in to an uneasy berth in search of a few hours' repose.

Of this, however, there was not much to be obtained. The *Alabama* was no sooner under way than the wind began to freshen, and soon increased to a moderate gale. This was accompanied by one of those ugly seaways so common in the North Atlantic, and the vessel rolled and tumbled in a manner sufficiently trying, without the addition of the manifold discomforts inseparably attendant on a first start. These, too, were, as may well be supposed, not a little aggravated by the hurried manner in which the transhipment of stores from the *Agrippina* and *Bahama* had perforce been conducted. Everything, in fact, was in the wildest confusion. The ship herself was dirty and unsettled, and her decks below lumbered in all directions with all manner of incongruous articles.

No one was berthed or messed, nothing arranged or secured. Spare shot-boxes, sea-chests, and heavy articles of baggage or cabin furniture were fetching away to the destruction of crockery and other brittle ware, and the no small danger of limbs. While to crown all, the upper works of the vessel which had been caulked in the damp atmosphere of an English winter, had opened out under the hot sun of the Azores through every seam, and the eternal clank, clank of the pumps, which it was fondly hoped had been heard for the last time when the poor, worn-out little *Sumter* had been laid up, played throughout the long night a dismal accompaniment to the creaking of the labouring vessel, and the wild howling of an Atlantic gale.

So passed the *Alabama*'s first night at sea. The next day the gale still continued, and hindered not a little the energetic exertions of the First Lieutenant, who, whilst Captain Semmes endeavoured, by snatching a few hours' sleep, to quiet his worn-out nerves, took his turn in the endeavour to bring something of order out of the apparently hopeless chaos, and gradually reduce the vessel to the trim and orderly condition proper to a well-commanded man-of-war. On the Tuesday the gale abated, though there were still the remains of a heavy sea. Topsails and gallant-sails were set, and the propeller, which had hitherto been merely disconnected, and left to revolve, was hoisted up out of the water.

Several days now passed in setting matters to rights, passing spare shot below, laying the racers for the pivot guns; overhauling and stowing the magazines; securing furniture, baggage, and other loose articles that had hitherto pretty well "taken charge" of the deck below; and otherwise making things somewhat snug and shipshape, and preparing the vessel for self-defence in case of need.

By Friday, August 29th, these preparations were nearly completed, and in the early morning of that day the cry of "Sail, ho!" was heard for the first time from the look-out at the fore-topgallant crosstrees of the *Alabama*. The ship was at once kept away towards her, and after a long chase, approached at near nightfall to within five or six miles of the strange sail. The vessel proved to be a brig, and on nearing her

Spanish colours were shown by the *Alabama*.

The brig made no response, and the cruiser proceeded to fire a blank cartridge, as an intimation of her character. Still the stranger kept doggedly upon her way, without response, and it became a question whether ulterior measures should be taken. After careful examination, however, of all those various indications by which a sailor can judge of the nationality of a vessel, almost as effectively as from a sight of her colours, it was decided that she was, at all events, not an American; and Captain Semmes, being anxious to haul by the wind, and make his way with all speed to the westward, the chase was abandoned, and the *Alabama* proceeded again upon her course.

The next day, Saturday, August 30th, saw the preparations for the battery complete, and the pivot guns finally mounted, and ready for action. The men were now allotted to the various stations, and mustered at quarters, when it was found, that by telling off half a dozen of the junior officers to complete the crew of the rifled gun, there were just hands enough to fight the ship. This was satisfactory; and altogether the five hard days' work since quitting Terceira had resulted in something more like success in the way of order, comfort, and efficiency, than it had at first sight appeared possible to anticipate.

Sunday, August 31st, was a welcome day of rest to all on board; the only break being a brief run off after a brig to leeward, which on being challenged with French colours, proved to be a Portuguese. During the day the *Alabama* made good running to the westward, under topsails, with a fresh breeze well on her starboard quarter; and at midnight made all snug, and brought by the wind on the port tack. The next day was passed for the most part in quietly lying to under topsails, with her head to the southward and eastward, whilst the crew were employed in finishing the fittings of the battery, and scraping the deck and bulwarks clear of some of the accumulated dirt, till 3 p.m., when she filled away again, and started upon a N.W. course.

By Tuesday, Sept. 5th, the *Alabama* had run into the thirty-eighth parallel, and the temperature was sensibly altering. Up to this period no prize had been captured, the few vessels overhauled having all been under a neutral flag. On this day, however, whilst in chase of a brig, whose extraordinary swiftness enabled her fairly to show the *Alabama* a clean pair of heels, a vessel was descried in the offing, and the Confederate bore up and made towards her. On approaching she was found to be lying-to, with her foretopsail laid to the mast, and on a somewhat nearer inspection, proved evidently to be a whaler.

English colours were hoisted on board the *Alabama*, and a cheer was with difficulty suppressed as the Stars and Stripes rose in answer to the stranger's deck. Arrived within boarding distance, a boat was at once sent on board the prize, the *Alabama*'s red ensign giving place to the Confederate flag as the boarding officer gained her deck. She proved to be the *Ocmulgee*, of Edgartown, her captain, by name Abraham Osborn, being a thorough specimen of the genuine Yankee. She was, of course, taken possession of, her crew brought on board the *Alabama* and placed in irons, and a quantity of rigging, of which the latter was much in need, together with some beef, pork, and other small stores, transferred to the captor. A light was then hoisted at her peak; her helm lashed hard a-lee; the prize crew re-transferred to their own ship, and the *Ocmulgee* left to her own devices, the *Alabama* lying by her during the night.

The next morning another sail hove in sight, so the prize was fired, and the *Alabama* again started off in chase, having taken from the prize thirty-six prisoners besides the stores, rigging, &c., before alluded to. The new chase proved to be a Frenchman, bound to Marseilles; and this fact having been ascertained, the *Alabama* was kept away N. 1/2 W., and in two hours afterwards was in sight of the island of Flores.

CHAPTER 15

Three Sacrifices in a Day

From the 7th to the 18th of September was a busy time on board the *Alabama*. Prize after prize was taken, and Captain Semmes' *journal*, as will be seen, is chiefly taken up with records of successful chases.

Sunday, September 7th.—Running in for the island of Flores. At 11 p.m. mustered the crew for the first time, and caused to be read the Articles of War, to which they listened with great attention. At 3.30 p.m., having approached sufficiently near the town of Lagens, on the south side of the island, we sent all the prisoners on shore, having first paroled them in the three whale-boats belonging to the prize, *Ocmulgee*. At 4 p.m. filled away upon the starboard tack to head off a schooner that appeared to be running in for the island.

Having approached her within a mile, we hoisted the English colours. The chase not showing her colours in return, fired the lee bow gun. Still paying no attention to us, but endeavouring to pass us, fired a shot athwart her bows. Not yet heaving-to, or showing colours, fired a second shot between her fore and mainmast; she then hoisted the United States colours and rounded-to. Sent a boat on board and took possession. The captain coming on board with his papers, she proved to be the *Starlight*, of Boston, from Fayal to Boston *viá* Flores. She had a number of passengers; among others, some ladies. Put a prize crew on board of her. Brought on board all the United States seamen, seven in number, including the captain, and confined them in irons, and ordered the prize to remain close to us during the night. Some dark clouds hanging over the island, but the wind light and the sea smooth.

Among the papers captured were a couple of despatches to the Sewards, father and son, informing them of our operations at Terceira.

This small craft left Boston only six days before we left Liverpool in the *Bahama*. How strangely parties meet upon the high seas! The master was the cleverest specimen of a Yankee skipper I have met, about twenty-seven or twenty-eight. He avowed his intention of trying to run the gauntlet of my shot, deprecated the war, &c., &c.

Monday, September 8th.—Again stood in to the town of Santa Cruz, in company with the prize; lowered the cutter, and sent the prisoners on shore, with a note addressed to the Governor. In the meantime the Governor himself with several citizens came on board us. The Governor offered us the hospitalities of the island, and in return I expressed to him the hope that his fellow-citizens who were passengers, had suffered no inconvenience from her capture.

In the afternoon, gave chase and showed English colours to a Portuguese brigantine. We then wore ship, and chased a *barque* in the north-west, with which we came up about sunset. She proved to be the whaling *barque Ocean Rover*, from Massachusetts, forty months out, with a cargo of 1100 barrels of oil. Laid her to for the night, and permitted the captain and his crew to pull in to the shore (Flores) in his six whale boats. The sea being smooth, the wind light off shore, and the moon near her full, this was a novel night procession!

Tuesday, September 7th.—I was aroused in the mid-watch, having had about only three hours' sleep, after a day of fatigue and excitement, by the announcement that a large *barque* was close aboard of us. We were lying to at the time in company with our two prizes. Wore ship very quietly, and gave chase. The chase rather got the wind of us, though we head-reached upon her, and at daylight we hoisted the English flag. The *barque* not responding, fired a blank cartridge. She still not responding, fired a shot astern of her, she being about two miles distant. This brought her to with the United States colours at her peak; put a boat on board, and took possession of her. She proved to be the *Alert*, from New London, sixteen days from port; bound, *via* the Azores, Cape de Verde, &c., to the Indian Ocean. Supplied ourselves from her with some underclothing for the men, of which we stood in need.

About 9 p.m. fired the *Starlight*; at 11 fired the *Ocean Rover*; and at 4 p.m. fired the *Alert*. Boarded a Portuguese whaling-brig, the master of which I brought on board with his papers. These proving to be regular, I dismissed him within a few minutes. Sent the captain and crew of the Alert on shore, to the village on the north end of Flores, in their own boats, four in number.

Sail, ho! at 5 p.m. Filled away, and gave chase to a schooner in the N.E. She was standing for us at first, but tacked on our approach, and endeavoured to run. We had shown her the United States colours, and she also had hoisted them, but she distrusted us. A blank cartridge brought her round again, and hove her to. Sent a boat on board, and took possession of the schooner *Weather Gauge*, of Provincetown, six weeks out. The last two captures supplied us with large numbers of Northern newspapers as late as August 18th.

Saturday, September 13th.—Gave chase to a sail reported on the weather bow, and upon coming up with her, and heaving her to with a blank cartridge, she proved to be the hermaphrodite whaling brig *Altamaha*, from New Bedford, five months out. Little or no success. Captured her, put a prize crew on board, and made sail in chase of a *barque* to windward.

Sunday, September 14th.—Last night at a quarter past eleven I was aroused by the report that a large ship was close on board of us. Hurried on deck, wore ship, and gave-chase; the strange sail being about two to two and a half miles from us, partially to windward. Made all sail, held our wind, and gradually eat him out of the wind, as well as head-reached on him. Fired a blank cartridge, which he disregarded. Continued to overhaul him, and when we had gotten on his weather-beam, distant about half a mile from him, fired a second gun, which speedily brought him to the wind with his main-topsail to the mast.

Sent a boat on board, with an order to the officer to show me a light if she should prove to be an American; and in a few minutes after the officer got on board a light was shown at the peak. Lay by him until daylight, when the captain was brought on board. The ship proved to be the United States whaler *Benjamin Tucker*, from New Bedford, eight months out, with about 340 barrels of oil. Crew thirty. Brought everybody on board, received some soap and tobacco, and fired the ship. Made sail to the S.E.

Monday, September 15th.—Caulking the decks, which are already quite open. Made the island of Flores from the masthead late in the afternoon. Exercised the crew at quarters. Shipped one of the prisoners from last prize—a Hollander.

Tuesday, September 16th.—At daylight made a schooner on the starboard bow. Gave chase, and at 7.30 hove her to with a blank cartridge, and sent a boat on board, she showing United States colours. She proved to be the whaling schooner *Courser*, of Provincetown, Massachusetts. Took possession of her as a prize. Stood in towards Flores, within four or five miles, and sent all the prisoners from the last three prizes on shore in their own whale boats, eight in number. Number of prisoners sixty-eight. About 5 p.m., having taken the prize some eight or ten miles distant from the land, hove her to, called all hands to quarters, and made a target of her, firing three rounds from each gun. The practice was pretty fair for green hands for the first time. We hulled the target once, and made a number of good line shots. At dark fired the prize, and made sail to the westward.

Wednesday, September 17th.—At 7.30 p.m. gave chase to a sail on the starboard bow, and at meridian came up with and took possession of, the United States whaling *barque Virginia*, twenty-one days from New Bedford. Received papers as late as the 28th August. Got on board from the prize a large supply of soap, candles, &c.; and after bringing the prisoners on board, fired her; filled away, and made sail to the N.W.

Thursday, September 18th.—Gave chase to a *barque*, which, discovering our purpose, made all sail and tried to escape. Came up with her at 2 p.m., after a chase of about three hours. Hoisted the English ensign, to which she refused to respond. Fired the starboard bow gun, and ran up our own flag, when she shortened sail and hove-to. Sent a prize crew on board, she showing the United States ensign. Brought the master on board. She proved to be the whaling *barque Elisha Dunbar*, of New Bedford, twenty-four days out. As it was blowing fresh and threatening a gale of wind, we got all the prisoners on board in the course of about a couple of hours, and set fire to the *barque*. Reefed topsails, set the fore trysail with the bonnet off, and stood on a wind on the starboard tack to the S. and E.

CHAPTER 16

A Deserter Caught

After this burst of good fortune in the way of prizes, during which the *Alabama* had destroyed upwards of 230,000 dollars' worth of United States property—or an amount very nearly equal to her own entire cost—in eleven days, a lull was experienced. A succession of gales from various points of the compass now prevailed with more or less violence for seven or eight days, during a great portion of which the *Alabama* was lying to, in a heavy sea under close-reefed main-topsail and reefed trysails.

These were hard times for the prisoners; huddled together on deck, with no shelter but an extemporized tarpaulin tent between them and the pelting of the pitiless storm, which drenched the decks alternately with salt water and fresh, as the heavy rain-squalls came down, or the sea, glittering with phosphoric light, came dashing over the weather bulwarks. There was, however, no alternative. The berth-deck was already fully occupied by the *Alabama*'s own crew, and the unlucky prisoners were compelled to make the best of their uncomfortable position, and console themselves with the hope that some vessel with a neutral cargo might fall on the same ill-fortune with themselves, and afford them a chance of being paroled and sent ashore.

As the sun crossed the line the weather moderated, and by the 25th of September all was again calm and fair, and the crew busy caulking the decks, which had leaked terribly during the gales. They were followed by a succession of calms and light baffling winds, the delay occasioned by which was turned to advantage in practising the crew at the battery, and with small arms.

With the commencement of another month the rough weather returned. The 2nd October was a real ugly-looking day, with dense black clouds and a Newfoundland north-easter blowing freshly. No observation was to be had, the thick clouds altogether shutting out the sun, and the ship being in the current of the Gulf Stream, the most she could do was to guess at her position within some thirty or forty miles.

On the 3rd the weather moderated, and fortune again smiled upon the *Alabama*. The morning watch was not yet over when two sails were descried, the one ahead, the other on the lee bow, each of which in its turn was overhauled and captured; the one proving to be the *Emily Farnum*, from New York for Liverpool; the other, the *Brilliant*, from the same port for London, with a valuable cargo of grain and flour.

The cargo of the *Emily Farnum* being neutral property, the vessel was released as a cartel, the prisoners from the *Brilliant* being transferred to her, as also those already on board from the other prizes, a change, as may well be imagined, sufficiently acceptable to those unfortunate beings who had now been exposed for nearly three weeks to all the vicissitudes of an autumn in the North Atlantic. This done, the *Emily Farnum* was permitted to proceed upon her way. The *Brilliant* was then stripped of everything that could be of use to her captors, set on fire, and left to her fate.[1] From the papers taken on board of this vessel the crew of the *Alabama* learned the good news of the Confederate victories in Virginia, and also of the successful run of the screw-steamer Florida into a Confederate port. The two vessels also brought to the *Alabama* a prize, in the persons of four new recruits, which, in the short-handed condition of the ship, was of more real value to her than the vessels themselves.

The *barque Wave Crest*, of and from New York, for Cardiff, with a cargo of grain, was the *Alabama*'s next victim. She was chased and captured on the 7th of October, and having no evidence of the neutral ownership of her cargo, was condemned and set on fire, after serving for some time as a target, at which her captors might practise their firing. She was still blazing merrily, when another vessel was descried from the masthead, and at 9.30 p.m. of a beautiful moonlight night, a blank shot from the *Alabama* brought up the smart little brigantine *Dunkirk*, from New York, for Lisbon, also loaded with grain. A boat

---

1. One of the *Alabama*'s officers writes in his private journal:— "It seemed a fearful thing to burn such a cargo as the *Brilliant* had, when I thought how the Lancashire operatives would have danced for joy had they it shared amongst them. I never saw a vessel burn with such brilliancy, the flames completely enveloping the masts, hull, and rigging in a few minutes, making a sight as grand as it was appalling."

was sent on board of her, and her papers handed over to one of the *Alabama*'s officers. No evidence of neutrality, however, was to be found, and before midnight she too was a blazing wreck, and her captain and crew prisoners on board the Confederate steamer.

The *Dunkirk* proved noteworthy in two ways. On searching through her papers, it appeared that besides her ostensible cargo she was also employed in what may be termed a kind of religious smuggling. Some Portuguese copies of the *New Testament* were discovered, together with a number of tracts in the same language, tied up in large bundles, on the back of one of which was the endorsement:- "Portuguese Tracts; from the 'American Tract Society,' for distribution among Portuguese passengers, and to give upon the coast to visitors from the shore, &c. When in port, please keep conspicuously on the cabin table for all comers to read; but be very careful not to take any ashore, as the laws do not allow it."

It appeared, however, that the conscience of the society had pricked them for this concession to the majesty of the law, and a pen had been carefully run through the last sentence. A little lower down, upon the same packet, was written, "As may be convenient, please report (by letter, if necessary) anything of interest which may occur in connexion with the distribution; also take any orders for Bibles, and forward them to John S. Peerin, Marine Agent, New York Bible Society, No. 7 Beekman Street."

The other noteworthy fact in connexion with the Dunkirk was the capture on board of her of one of the seven sailors who had deserted from the *Sumter* whilst lying at Cadiz ten months before. This man, whose name was George Forrest, was at once recognised, and on the day but one after his capture on board the enemy's vessel, a court-martial, consisting of the first lieutenant (president); senior second lieutenant; master, chief engineer, and lieutenant of marines, with the captain's clerk as judge-advocate, was assembled in the wardroom to try the prisoner for the crime of desertion. The evidence was, of course, simple enough, and the man was found guilty, and sentenced to lose all pay, prize money, etc., already due to him, and to fulfil his original term of service, forfeiting all pay and allowances, except such as should be sufficient to provide necessary clothing and liberty money.

That same afternoon another sail was descried and chased, and just before sunset the *Alabama* came up with and brought to, the fine packet ship *Tonawanda*, of Philadelphia, belonging to Cope's Liverpool line, and bound from Philadelphia to Liverpool with a full cargo of grain, and some seventy-five passengers. Here was a serious matter of embarrassment; of the seventy-five passengers, some thirty or more were women, and what to do with such a prize it was hard to know.

It was, of course, impossible to take the prisoners on board; yet Captain Semmes was, not unnaturally, reluctant to release so fine a vessel if he could by any possibility so arrange matters as to be able to destroy her. It was therefore determined to place a prize crew on board, and keep the ship in company for a time, in hopes that ere long some other vessel of less value to the enemy, or guarded from destruction by a neutral cargo might, by good luck, be captured, and thus afford an opportunity of sending the prisoners away upon cartel.

Accordingly, a bond was taken of the captain for eighty thousand dollars, as a measure of precaution, in case it should be found necessary to let the ship go without further parley, and a prize master having been put on board the *Tonawanda*, was ordered to keep company, and her captor started off on a chase after a brig, which on being overhauled proved to be English. One transfer, however, was made from the prize, being nothing less than a well-grown and intelligent negro lad, named David White, the slave of one of the passengers, who was transferred to the *Alabama* as waiter to the wardroom mess, where he remained until the closing scene off Cherbourg, by no means disposed, so far as his own word may be taken for it, to regret the change of masters.

The following day, as an additional security, the master of the *Tonawanda* was brought as a hostage on board the Confederate steamer, the prisoners from the last two ships burned being at the same time transferred to the prize. In this manner the two vessels cruised in company for two or three days—an anxious time enough for the crew and passengers of the unlucky *Tonawanda*, who spent most of their time in eagerly scanning the horizon, in the hope that some armed vessel of their own nation might appear in sight, and rescue them from their unpleasant predicament. No such luck, however, was to be theirs; but on the 11th October, a fresh addition was made to their numbers in the crew of the Manchester, a fine United States ship from New York to Liverpool, the glare of which as she, like so many others, was committed to the flames, by no means alleviated their anxiety, as they thought how soon a similar fate might befall their own vessel, should fortune not interpose to arrest the disaster.

At length, on the 13th October, excitement prevailed on board of both vessels, and the hopes of the anxious passengers on board the *Tonawanda* rose to fever pitch, as a large vessel was seen bearing down under topsails only, her easy-going style of sailing seeming to prove conclusively to a sailor's eye, that she must be either a whaler or a man-of-war. On board the *Alabama* the former was the favourite supposition, and hopes ran high of another glorious bonfire fed by tons of brightly burning sperm oil. The aspirations of the *Tonawanda* were naturally in favour of the man-of-war, and it was with difficulty that considerations of prudence restrained the open exhibition of their delight as the stranger drew near, and the long pendant floating proudly from her masthead seemed to assure them that their hopes were to be fulfilled.

But disappointment was equally in store for all. The big easy-going ship proved to be nothing more or less than an ordinary Spanish merchantman, who, with more regard for personal appearance than maritime etiquette, had quietly appropriated to herself the distinguishing ornament of a man-of-war. So the guns of the *Alabama*, which had been cast loose and loaded, were again secured, and the crew dismissed from quarters; while the disconsolate *Tonawanda*s, balked of their fondly anticipated rescue, shook their fists at the deceptive Spaniard, and went below to digest as best they might their grievous disappointment.

At last, however, this time of suspense was over, and kind fortune came to their assistance in the shape of a threatening gale of so ugly an appearance that the captain determined not to run the risk of parting company, and thus altogether losing his awkward, but not the less valuable prize. Accordingly, having accepted from the master a ransom bond for eighty thousand dollars, he dismissed him to his ship, and amid the wildest demonstrations of delight from the closely-packed prisoners on board, the *Tonawanda* filled away, and was seen no more.

The wind now freshened to a tolerably fresh gale. Not sufficient, however, for the next two days to prevent the *Alabama* from chasing and capturing, on the 15th October, the United States *barque Lamplighter*, of Boston, from New York to Gibraltar, with a cargo of tobacco, which, however, as it proved, was never destined to soothe the *ennui* of the British soldier at that not very lively station. The sea was running high, and the boats had a rough time of it in boarding the *barque*, and returning with prisoners, &c. However, it was managed at last; the unlucky vessel was fired, and after burning fiercely for some time, went headforemost to the bottom, leaving behind her a savoury cloud that almost tempted her destroyers to regret their work.

And now it proved indeed fortunate for the prisoners who had so lately been discharged, that they were not doomed to weather out on the *Alabama*'s deck the gale that came upon her. The 17th of October saw the culminating of the bad weather that had prevailed during the last four or five days, and for some hours the *Alabama* was exposed to a perfect hurricane. The storm did not last long, but for about four hours it blew furiously. It was not yet at its height, and the ship was still carrying her close reefed main-topsail with reefed main trysail and fore topmast staysail, when a sharper lurch than usual threw a sudden strain upon the bumpkin to which the weather main brace was led, and in a moment it had snapped in two. The main-yard no longer supported by the brace, and pressed by the whole power of the straining topsail, flew forward and upward till it was bent nearly double, when with a loud crash it parted in the slings, splintering the topsail into ribands with a noise like thunder.

The ship was now in the greatest peril, for there was no longer sufficient after canvas to keep her head to the wind against the powerful pressure of the foretopmast staysail, and in another moment she must have fallen into the trough of the sea, and probably been at the least dismasted, if not altogether swamped. But the quick eye of the captain of the foretop saw the danger, and springing to the staysail halyards he cut the sail away, and the ship relieved of pressure forward, again came up to the wind.

The main trysail was now lowered, though not without splitting the sail, and a small three-cornered storm trysail hoisted in its place. Even under this minimum of canvas the tremendous pressure of the gale upon her spars forced her down in the water several streaks, and the idlers and boys were lashed for safety under the weather bulwarks, life-lines being stretched before them to prevent them from falling to leeward.

So far as it was possible under the circumstances to estimate the probable extent of this cyclone, its greatest diameter would appear to have been from about one hundred and sixty to two hundred miles, whilst the diameter of the vortex, through a considerable portion of which, if not actually through the centre, the *Alabama* appears to have passed, would probably be from about thirty to five-and-thirty or perhaps forty miles.

The *Alabama* took the gale at S.W., the wind hauling afterwards to S., and the vessel passing completely through the vortex. During that time it lulled for about half or three-quarters of an hour, then hauled in a few minutes to about N.N.W., which was the severest portion of the gale, commencing with the squall by which the main-yard was carried away. The barometer sank as low as 28.64. At 2 p.m. it had risen to 29.70, but fell again a little, and then rose gradually. The rise and fall of the barometer were both very rapid.

During the violence of the gale, the birds flew very low, and with great rapidity, and some rain fell, though not a great deal. The surface of the sea was one sheet of foam and spray, the latter completely blinding all on deck. A curious result of the gale was a huge knot into which a strip of the main-topsail, the clew line, and chain sheet had twisted themselves in a hundred involutions, defying any attempt at extrication except by aid of the knife.

During this tremendous storm the *Alabama* behaved splendidly, proving herself as fine a sea-boat as ever swam.

By the evening the storm had lulled, but the sea was still running fearfully high, and it was not until the next day that it was possible to set about repairing the damage suffered in this by far the severest trial through which the *Alabama* had as yet passed.

CHAPTER 17

Condemned!

The *Alabama* was again out of luck. For the second time since her departure from Terceira, nearly a fortnight passed without bringing a single prize. It was, indeed, hardly to be expected that the splendid success which had attended the first three weeks of her cruise could be maintained. From the 1st to the 18th of September, she had captured and destroyed no less than ten vessels, of an aggregate value of nearly two hundred and fifty thousand dollars. Then had followed an interval of a fortnight, during which one vessel only was overhauled, and proving to be French, permitted to proceed.

This dull period over, the 3rd October had seen the commencement of another run of good fortune, extending over nearly a fortnight, during which she succeeded in capturing five more vessels, all of considerable size, and for the most part with valuable cargoes. In this fortnight alone damage was inflicted upon United States property to the amount of more than half-a-million of dollars; and it was but natural that, after so splendid a gift, fortune should for a time hold her hand.

Accordingly, for the next ten or twelve days the *Alabama* lay helplessly on the ocean, tossed and beaten about by a succession of gales from every point of the compass, culminating, as we have seen, in the hurricane of the 16th October. The season was, indeed, most unusually severe, this month of October being commonly one of calm and fine weather. A gale at this time is a most unusual occurrence; but for more than a week a succession of storms was experienced of the most violent description, while for fully three weeks the weather continued dark, rough, and gloomy, with strong shifting winds and heavy rain, the thick clouds rarely separating sufficiently to afford the chance of an observation.

Occasionally a break in the murky canopy would give promise of a change for the better; but a very few hours served to dissipate the rising hope. The sky would be again overcast, the wind breeze up from a fresh quarter, and another night of discomfort set in. In addition to this adverse weather, a still further difficulty was experienced in the strong current that appeared to set continuously from the westward, drifting the vessel bodily out of her course at the rate of sixty or seventy miles a day. During this period, the barometer ranged from 28.64 to 29.70. It was remarkable that the winds appeared to succeed each other with perfect regularity, rotating, as nearly as possible, once in every two days, or at the utmost, in two days and a half. The course taken by these rotatory storms was always the same, and it was a rare occurrence for the wind to remain stationary in one quarter during eight or ten successive hours.

On the 23rd October the gale at last finally broke, and with the return of better weather the *Alabama*'s luck seemed also about to revive. At noon a brief break in the clouds just gave time for an observation for latitude, and this was barely worked out, when "Sail, ho!" was heard from the masthead; and a fine brig was discovered hull down on the lee bow. Running down to her under close-reefed topsails, she proved to be English; but though not destined herself to become a prize, the deviation in the *Alabama*'s course, occasioned by the chase, proved most fortunate for her. She had scarcely luffed up again, after ascertaining the brig's nationality, when again the welcome cry was heard, and the helm shifted in pursuit. Soon the new chase became clearly discernible from the quarter-deck, when she proved to be a large ship running to the northward and eastward under a press of canvas. So determinedly was she "cracking on" as to have everything set, even to her main-royal, notwithstanding that the wind was still blowing very nearly half a gale.

The course of the stranger being diagonal to that of the *Alabama*, the speed at which she was travelling soon brought her within speaking distance, and, as usual, a feint was made for the purpose of extorting a confession of her nationality. The flag chosen this time was the English blue ensign, and it was speedily answered by the Stars and Stripes, which fluttered gaily from the merchantman's peak as she dashed along under her towering mass of canvas before the breeze, right across the *Alabama*'s path.

Another moment and the scene was changed. The Yankee ensign had hardly reached her peak, when down came the beguiling signal from the *Alabama*'s flagstaff, and the white folds of the Confederate ensign unfurled themselves in its stead. A flash, a spurt of white smoke, curling for a moment from the cruiser's lee-bow, and vanishing in snowy wreaths upon the wind, and the loud report of a gun from the *Alabama*, summoned the luckless Yankee to heave to.

In a moment all was in confusion on board the merchantman. Sheets and halyards were let go by the run, and the huge cloud of canvas seemed to shrink and shrivel up as the vessel was rounded to with folded wings like a crippled bird, and with her foretopsail to the mast, lay submissively awaiting the commands of her captors.

She proved to be the ship *Lafayette*, of Boston, bound to Belfast, with a full cargo of grain, &c. Of her own nationality there was, of course, no doubt; but a question now arose about the ownership of the cargo, and some hours of patient investigation were necessary before Captain Semmes could determine upon the course to pursue. Finally it was determined that the claim of neutral ownership was a mere blind to insure against capture; and at 10 p.m., the ship having been formally condemned, the crew were transferred to the *Alabama*, and the prize fired and left to her fate.

The following is Captain Semmes' memorandum of the:

CASE OF THE *LAFAYETTE*

Ship and cargo condemned. The cargo of this ship was condemned by me as enemy's property, notwithstanding there were depositions of the shippers that it had been purchased by them on neutral account. These *ex-parte* statements are precisely such as every unscrupulous merchant would prepare, to deceive his enemy and save his property from capture. There are two shipping houses in this case; that of Craig and Nicoll, and that of Montgomery Bros.: Messrs. Craig and Nicoll say that the grain supplied by them belongs to Messrs. Shaw and Finlay, and to Messrs. Hamilton, Megault, and Thompson, all of Belfast, to which port the ship is bound, but the grain is not consigned to them, and they could not demand possession of it under the bill of lading, it being consigned to *order*, thus leaving the control in the hands of the shippers.

The shippers, farther, instead of sending their grain as freight in a general ship, consigned to the owners, they paying the freight, charter the whole ship, and stipulate themselves for the payment of the freight. If this property had been *bonâ fide* the property of the parties in Belfast named in the depositions, it would undoubtedly have been consigned to them, under a bill of lading authorizing them to demand possession of it, &c., &c.; the agreement with the ship would have been that the consignees and owners should pay the freight upon delivery. Even if this property were purchased, as pretended, by Messrs. Craig and Nicoll, for the parties named, still their not consigning it to them and delivering to them the proper bill of lading passing the possession, left the property under the dominion of Craig and Nicoll, and as such, liable to capture.

The property attempted to be covered by the Messrs. Montgomery, is shipped by Montgomery Bros. of New York, and consigned to Montgomery Bros., in Belfast; and the title to the property, so far as appears in the bill of lading, is in the latter house, or in the branch house in New York. Further, the mere formal papers of a ship and cargo prove nothing, unless properly verified, and in this case the master of the ship, although a part owner of the ship, whose duty it was upon taking in a cargo in time of war, to be informed of all the circumstances attending it, and connected with the ownership, knew nothing, except what he learned from the face of the papers.

These certificates, therefore, were pronounced a fraud, and the cargo as well as the ship, condemned. 3rd *Phillimore* 610-12 to the effect, that if the goods are going for account of the shipper, *or subject to his order or control* (as in this case), the property is not divested *in transitu*. The goods shipped by Craig and Nicoll, were consigned to their *order*, as has been seen.

As to the Montgomery's, see 3rd *Phillimore* 605, to the effect that if a person be a partner in a house of trade in an enemy's country, he is, as to the concerns and trade of that house, deemed an enemy, and his share is liable to confiscation as such, notwithstanding his own residence is in a neutral country. Further, the property consigned to Montgomery Bros., even admitting the Belfast house not to be a partner in the New York house, is liable to the same objection, as in the case of Craig and Nicoll; since, although the property is described as belonging to a party in Sligo, there is no bill of lading among the papers authorizing that party to demand the possession. The property is not divested, therefore, *in transitu*.

3rd *Phillimore*, 599, to the effect, that "further proof" is always necessary when the master cannot swear to the ownership of the property (as in this case). And as I cannot send my prizes in for adjudication, I must of necessity condemn in all cases where "further proof" is necessary, since the granting of "further proof" proceeds on the presumption that the neutrality of the cargo is not sufficiently established; and where the neutrality of the property does not fully appear from the ship's papers and the master's deposition, I had the right to act upon the presumption of enemy's property.

By midnight the *Lafayette* showed only a dim glare on the distant horizon, but the event formed a topic of discussion for the next two days, more especially as from the newspapers found on board it was ascertained that news of the captures on the banks of Newfoundland had already made its way to the United States, and that the Yankee cruisers were, therefore, probably by that time in full pursuit.

The 26th October, however, provided the crew of the *Alabama* with a fresh excitement. The weather had cleared beautifully, the wind was light from the eastward, and the vessel was gliding smoothly and swiftly, with studding-sails set alow and aloft, over the long, easy swell, which alone remained to tell of the heavy gales of the past fortnight. Everyone was enjoying the change, and even the strict discipline of the man-of-war was, for the moment, in some measure relaxed, as officers and men gave themselves up to the full pleasure of a period of sunshine and tranquillity, after the long spell of gloom and storm. The lookout-man alone, high up on the fore topgallant crosstrees, still swept the horizon as eagerly as ever in search of a prize.

At about noon his vigilance was rewarded by the sight of a sail on the port-quarter, and in a moment all was again bustle and excitement on board. Quick as the word could be given, the "flying kites" were furled, yards braced in, and the ship hauled up on a taut bowline in chase.

But the stranger was now well to windward, and fully four or five miles distant. The *Alabama* flew through the water with the freshening breeze, flinging the spray over her sharp bows, and stretching to her task as though she herself were conscious of the work before her, and eager in chase. But the strange sail was almost, if not quite, as fast as herself, and her position so far to windward gave her an immense advantage. The day, too, was wearing on, and the sky beginning to cloud over, giving every token of a dark if not a stormy night. If the chase could only hold on her course till dusk she was safe, and already the hopes of another prize were beginning to fade, and the anxious speculators on the forecastle were expecting the order to up helm and relinquish the chase.

On the quarter-deck, too, the idea was gaining ground that the affair was hopeless, and that it was not worthwhile to keep the ship longer from her course. But the *Alabama* was not given to letting a chance slip, and before finally abandoning the pursuit it was determined to try the effect of a shot or two upon the nerves of the stranger. A slight cheer, quickly checked by the voice of authority, rose from the eager crowd on the forecastle, as the weather bow gun was cast loose and loaded, and in another minute the bright flash, with its accompanying jet of white smoke, leaped from the cruiser's bow, as the loud report of a 32 pounder rang out the command to heave to.

A moment of breathless suspense, and another cheer rose from the delighted throng of sailors, as the stranger's sails were seen for a moment to shiver in the wind, and the frightened chase luffed to the wind, and then lay motionless with the Stars and Stripes at her mizzen-peak. Another sharp hour's beating and the *Alabama* was alongside, and had taken possession of the United States schooner *Crenshaw*, from New York to Glasgow, three days out.

And now began another investigation into the character of the cargo, and notes were once more carefully compared, lest any *bonâ fide* neutral property should become involved in the fate that would otherwise befall the captured enemy. Finally, however, the case was decided against ship and cargo, and both were accordingly committed to the flames, the following entry being made by Captain Semmes of the grounds of his decision:—

Case of the Schooner *Crenshaw*

This vessel was captured under the North American flag, and had on board a North American register—there is, therefore, no question as to the ship. There has been an attempt to cover the cargo, but without success. The shippers are Francis Macdonald and Co., of the city of New York; and Mr. James Hutchison, also of New York, deposed before the British consul, that "the goods specified in the annexed bills of lading were shipped on board the schooner *Crenshaw*, for, and on account of, subjects of Her Britannic Majesty, and that the said goods are wholly and *bonâ fide* the property of British subjects." No British subject is named in the deposition, and no person is therefore entitled to claim under it.

Further: even admitting the goods to have been purchased on British account, the shipper has not divested himself of the possession by a proper consignment, under a proper bill of lading. The property is consigned to the *order of the shipper*, which leaves it entirely under his control; and it having left the port of New York as his property, the title cannot be changed while the property is *in transitu.*

As to the first point—to wit, the failure to point out some particular British owner of the property—see 3rd *Phillimore* 596, to the following effect:—"If in the ship's papers, property, in a voyage from an enemy's port, be described 'for neutral account,' this is such a general mode as points to no designation whatever; and under such a description no person can say that the cargo belongs to him, or can entitle himself to the possession of it as his property," &c.

And as to the second point—to wit, the failure on the part of the shipper to divest himself of the title and control of the property by a proper bill of lading—see 3rd *Phillimore* 610-12, as follows, *viz.*: "In ordinary shipments of goods, unaffected by the foregoing principles, the question of proprietary interest often turns on minute circumstances and distinctions, the general principle being, that if they are going for account of the shipper, or subject to his order or control, the property is not divested *in transitu*" &c.

Monday, October 27th.—Another gale of wind! In the mid-watch last night the barometer commenced falling, and by 3 this afternoon it had gone down to 29.33, where it remained stationary for a time, and then began to rise slowly, being at 29.45 at 8 p.m. The wind began to blow freshly from the south, and hauled gradually to the westward, the barometer commencing to rise when the wind was about W.S.W. In the early part of the gale we had the weather very thick, with heavy squalls of rain, clearing about nightfall, with the wind from the W.S.W.

In the midst of a heavy squall of wind and rain, and with a heavy sea on, we discovered a brig close aboard of us, on our weather quarter; but as we were on opposite tacks we soon increased our distance from each other. Wore ship, and hove to, under close-reefed topsails on the starboard tack. Being about a degree to the southward of St. George's Bank, got a cast of the lead at 7 p.m., with no bottom at eighty-five fathoms. Lat. 39.47 N., Long. 68.06 W., a little over two hundred miles from New York.

Tuesday, October 28th.—Weather cloudy; wind light from the north, hauling to the eastward. The heavy sea, from the effects of the gale yesterday, continued all day rolling and tumbling us about, and keeping the deck flooded with water. In the morning watch descried a brig running off to the southward. She being some distance off, and running in the wrong direction, we did not chase. Soon afterwards another sail was reported to the westward, standing in our direction; shaped a course to head her off, and at 11 p.m., having approached her within half a mile, hoisted the English blue. The stranger showing United States colours, we hoisted our own, and hove him to with a gun. Brought the master on board with his papers, and finding the cargo condemnable, got the crew on board, fired the ship, and filled away.

The prize proved to be the *barque Lauretta*, of Boston, from New York, for Madeira and the Mediterranean. Received papers as late as the 24th. The intelligence of our captures (as late as the *Brilliant*) seems to have created great alarm for the safety of commerce in New York.

CASE OF THE *LAURETTA*

This ship being under American colours, with an American (U.S.) register, no question arises as to the ship. There are two shippers of the cargo, Messrs. Chamberlain, Phelps, and Co., and Mr. H.J. Burden, both houses of New York city. Chamberlain, Phelps, and Co. ship 1424 barrels of flour, and a lot of pipe staves, to be delivered at Gibraltar or Messina, to their own order; and 225 kegs of nails to be delivered at Messina, to Mariano Castarelli. The bill of lading for the flour and staves has the following indorsement, sworn to before a notary: "State, city and county of New York: Louis Contenein being duly sworn, says, that he is a clerk with Chamberlain, Phelps, and Co., and that part of the maize in the within bill of lading, is the property of subjects of the King of Italy."

This certificate is of no force or effect for its generality; it points to no one as the owner of the merchandise, and no person could claim it under the certificate. See 3rd *Phillimore*, 596. Farther: the property is consigned to the *order* of the shipper. The title, therefore, remains in him, and cannot be divested *in transitu*. See 3rd *Phillimore*, 610-12. The contingent destination of this property, too, shows that it was property for a market. It was to be delivered either at Gibraltar or Messina, as the shipper might determine—probably on advices by steamer, before the ship should reach her destination. She was to stop, as we have seen, at Madeira, which would give ample time for the decision.

The bill of lading for the 225 kegs of nails has a similar indorsement, except that it is asserted that the whole of the property belongs to subjects of the King of Italy. It is not sworn that the property belongs to Castarelli, the *consignee*, and for aught that appears, Castarelli is the agent of the shipper to receive this consignment on his, the shipper's account. The presumption being, that notwithstanding a consignment in due form by an enemy shipper to a neutral, the property is enemy's property, until the contrary be shown. The consignment alone does not show the property to be vested in Castarelli, and the certificate does not indicate him as the owner.

Although Castarelli could demand possession of the goods, under this consignment, he could not claim to hold them as his property under the certificate. There is, therefore, no evidence to show that he is not the mere agent of the shipper. What renders this consideration still more clear is, that if the goods had really belonged to Castarelli, it would have been so stated in the certificate. Why say that the goods belonged to "subjects of the King of Italy," when the *consignee* was the real owner?

The property shipped by H. Jas. Burden consists of 998 barrels of flour and 290 boxes of herrings, and is consigned to Charles B. Blandly, Esq., at Funchal, Madeira. The shipper, H.J. Burden, makes the following affidavit before the British consul in New York, to wit: "That all and singular the goods specified in the annexed bill of lading, were shipped by H.J. Burden, in the *barque Lauretta*, for and on account of H.J. Burden, subject of Her Britannic Majesty." Now, Burden may be a very good subject of Her Britannic Majesty, but he describes himself as of 42 Beaver Street, New York, and seems to lose sight of the fact, that his domicile, for the purposes of trade, in the enemy's country, makes him an enemy, *quoad* all his transactions in that country.

Further: if the H.J. Burden, the shipper, is not one and the same person with the H.J. Burden for whom the property is claimed, then there is nothing in the papers to show that property is vested in the latter, since it is not consigned to him, nor is it shown that the consignee, Charles B. Blandly, Esq., is his agent. The presumption, in the absence of proof, is, that the consignee is the agent of the shipper.

Wednesday, October 29th.—At 10 p.m. hove to; let down the propeller, and put the ship under steam. Chased and overhauled a Dutch *barque*, and towards nightfall came up with the United States brigantine, *Baron de Custine*, from Bangor, with lumber for Cardenas. The vessel being old, and of little value, I released her on ransom bond, and converted her into a cartel, sending some forty-five prisoners on board of her, the crews of the last three ships burned.

CHAPTER 18

Kindness Repaid

The month of October went out as it came in with severe and blustering weather. The *Alabama* was still upwards of two hundred miles from New York, and it seemed as though a change would become necessary in her plans. Ever since starting upon his adventurous cruise, it had been a favourite scheme with Captain Semmes to make his appearance off this the very chief of the enemy's ports, and, if not strong enough actually to threaten the place itself, at all events to make a few captures within sight of the capital city of the North. It had been, therefore, a special disappointment to find himself baffled by a continued succession of hostile winds and contrary currents; and even the brilliant success that had thus far attended him in the capture of twenty-one vessels and the destruction of property to very nearly a million of dollars, seemed hardly to compensate for the failure of his pet project.

It was fast becoming evident, however, that the scheme for putting in an appearance off New York must be abandoned, at all events for the present; and on the 30th October the chief engineer was consulted as to the amount of coal remaining in the bunkers. The report was unfavourable. Four days' fuel only was left; and it was clear that even had the vessel been nearer than she was to her intended cruising ground, this would have been rather a short supply with which to venture on so dangerous an experiment. Reluctantly, therefore, the scheme was relinquished, the fires let down, propeller hoisted up again, and sail made to the southward and eastward *en route* for the coal *depôt*.

The ship was now out of the track of commerce, and for some time scarcely a vessel was seen. The 2nd November, however, brought a prize in the shape of the ship *Levi Starbuck*, five days out from New Bedford, on a whaling voyage of thirty months to the Pacific Ocean.

Like all whalers, she carried a stronger crew than is common with other vessels of similar tonnage, and twenty-nine prisoners were transferred from her to the *Alabama*. Being bound, too, on so long a cruise, she was well furnished with all necessaries, and the captor was enabled to supply himself from her with various articles of which, by this time, and after the rough weather he had experienced, he had begun to stand somewhat sorely in need.

Not the least highly-prized among the spoils of the *Levi Starbuck* was a noble collection of cabbages and turnips, fresh from their native soil! These were, indeed, invaluable. The *Alabama* had now been upwards of seventy days at sea, and during nearly the whole of that period her crew had subsisted entirely on salted provisions. Happily, as yet, no ill effects had appeared; but the fresh vegetables came most opportunely to ward off any danger of that scourge of the sailor's existence, scurvy, to which a longer confinement to salt diet must inevitably have exposed them.

Indeed, but for the consciousness of how vitally necessary a change of diet is to the health of a ship's crew, there would have been something almost ludicrous in the delight with which the men, who for the last six months had been almost daily destroying thousands of pounds' worth of the most valuable property of every description, now hailed the acquisition of a sack or two of turnips and a few strings of humble cabbages. But abstinence is a wonderful quickener of apprehension; and for teaching the true value of the good things of this life, there are few recipes more effectual than a voyage in the forecastle of a cruising man-of-war.

Besides the cabbages and turnips, which were so welcome forward, the Levi Starbuck contributed not a little to the comfort of the after-part of the vessel by her contribution of newspapers, which passed eagerly from hand to hand, through wardroom and steerage, affording a pleasant change from the worn-out topics of discussion that had now grown threadbare through the wear-and-tear of many a dull day and stormy night. The *Starbuck's* papers brought news from Yankeeland as late as the 28th of October, and not the least important item was that which told of the excitement occasioned among the enemy by the little craft whose officers were now jesting merrily over the consternation she had raised, and the measures that were being taken for her destruction.

It was certainly not a little amusing to read in the angry columns of Yankee newspapers, the magnificently-exaggerated accounts of the depredations of the dreaded Confederate "pirate." It was difficult sometimes to recognise the events referred to under the gorgeous embellishments with which they were invested. Occasionally, too, an exclamation of disgust would be heard from some officer, more excited or less philosophic than his comrades, as with his head half-buried in some broad, ill-printed, vilely-smelling sheet, he would declaim from its columns, for the edification of the mess, paragraph after paragraph of abuse of the vessel and her officers, and withering denunciations of the barbarity with which their unfortunate prisoners were treated while on board.

Among those who thus revealed their true nature by abusing and vilifying the men, who, though enemies, had endeavoured while they had them in their power to alleviate in every possible way the inevitable hardships of captivity, the master of the ship *Brilliant* obtained for himself an unenviable pre-eminence, by the grossness of the falsehoods with which he retaliated upon his captors for their mistaken kindness; and many a vow was registered in the wardroom and gunroom of the *Alabama*, that should this gentleman ever again fall into their hands, they would be wiser than to waste courtesy on one who could so little appreciate it.

The *Levi Starbuck* having been disposed of in the usual manner, sail was again made upon the *Alabama*, and on the 5th November, Bermuda, "the still vexed," was passed, though at too great a distance to sight the land.

Saturday, November 8th.—In the mid-watch a sail was reported—a schooner, standing south. Wore ship (1.30 p.m.) and gave chase. Soon after daylight, the chase being some five miles dead to windward of us, a ship was discerned standing to the northward and westward. Discontinued the chase of the schooner, and gave chase to the ship. At 10 p.m., the latter having approached to within a mile of us (we having United States colours flying), hove her to with a gun, and a change of flags. Sent a boat, and brought the master on board. She, proved to be the ship *T.B. Wales*, of Boston, from Calcutta for Boston.

There being no claim of neutral property among the papers, and the master having no knowledge on the subject, except that the linseed belonged to the owner of the ship, condemned both ship and cargo. A large portion of this cargo was consigned to Baring Brothers, Boston, including 1704 bags of saltpetre—contraband of war—which would have condemned all the property of the Barings, even if proof of ownership had been found on board, which was not the case.

We are to be embarrassed with two females and some children, the master having his wife with him, and there being also a passenger and his wife. I shall bestow them upon the wardroom, having a couple of state rooms vacated for them. Poor women! They are suffering for the sins of their wicked countrymen who are waging this murderous war upon us.

About nightfall another sail was descried from aloft, and a light was seen after dark; but we did not get hold of the sail. Just at dark, having taken all the prisoners on board from the prize, and got her main-yard on board to replace ours, carried away in, the storm of the 16th ultimo, we set fire to her, and filled away on our course. Nine of the crew of this ship volunteered, and were shipped as part of our own crew—an acquisition more valuable than the prize herself.

Sunday, November 9th.—My *ménage* has become quite home-like with the presence of women and the merry voices of children. We have had a quiet Sabbath-day, there being nothing in sight.

For some time from this date quiet days preponderated. The *Alabama* was now in the region of the trade winds, but it was some time before they were fairly taken. From the 9th November, in Lat. 27.52 N., Long. 58.24 W., to the 15th November, in Lat. 21 N., Long. 57.49 W., the wind continued light and variable, sometimes even for a few hours blowing directly from the southward. On the 15th November the N.E. trade appeared to have fairly set in, and from this time fine weather and favouring breezes became the order of the day.

Sunday, November 16th.—Beautiful clear weather, with a moderate trade from about east by south. Woollen clothes becoming uncomfortable. At 11 p.m. mustered the crew, and inspected the ship. A quiet Sabbath-day, with nothing in sight. Our ship begins to look quite like a ship of war—with her battery in fine order, her decks clean, freshly-painted outside, masts scraped, &c., &c., and the crew well disciplined. Thus far I have never seen a better disposed or more orderly crew. They have come very kindly into the traces.

Monday, November 17th.—Running before the wind, with studding-sails set on both sides. At 2 p.m. made the island of Dominica, half a point on the starboard bow.

CHAPTER 19

Temptation

The 18th November saw Captain Semmes again off Martinique, which he had visited in the *Sumter* just twelve months before. Making the north end of the island at about 4 p.m., the propeller was lowered and steam got up, the day breaking just as the *Alabama*'s screw began to revolve. At 10 p.m., having run past St. Pierre, she anchored in the harbour of Fort de France.

Here she found her faithful consort, the *Agrippina*, from whom she had parted at Terceira on the 24th of August. On her departure from that port, she had returned with all speed to Cardiff, from which she had again sailed for the rendezvous at Martinique, and was now ready with a fresh supply of coal for the *Alabama*, and had been waiting her arrival just eight days. In addition to the much needed supply of coal, the *Agrippina* brought a small mail for the *Alabama*'s officers, who thus received news from friends at home for the first time for more than three months.

No sooner was the anchor down than a lieutenant was sent ashore to pay the usual visit of ceremony to the Governor, carrying with him a note, informing his Excellency of the arrival of the Confederate steamer *Alabama* in French waters. A few hours brought a courteous reply, extending to the *Alabama* the hospitality of the port; and the health officers having visited the ship, arrangements were made for laying in a stock of provisions, and such other articles as were required after the cruise. Nor were the amenities of the *Alabama*'s reception confined to the authorities alone. An enthusiastic greeting awaited her from almost every one; the clubs were placed at their disposal, and invitations *à discretion* poured in from every side.

It would, perhaps, have been better for the discipline of the *Alabama* had the welcome extended to her crew been somewhat less cordial. Weary of their long confinement, and bent, as the sailor always seems to be on first putting into port, on a "good spree," a considerable number of her men fairly succumbed to the hospitality of the worthy islanders, a result that was not a little aggravated by the exertions of the deserter, Forrest.

This man appears to have entertained a deliberate purpose of exciting a mutiny on board of the vessel, and with this object in view, managed to slip overboard unobserved, swam to a boat, and returned on board with a quantity of spirits, which he distributed through the forecastle. The result was a disturbance, which at one time wore a serious aspect, and which, but for the energy and promptitude of the means taken to subdue it, might have had very awkward results.

The captain of the *Alabama*, however, was not a man to be intimidated or taken off his guard. No sooner was the disturbance reported than the drums beat to quarters, and the sober portion of the crew were at once directed to seize the rioters. Placed in double irons, and effectually drenched with buckets of cold water by their laughing comrades, the unlucky mutineers soon came to their senses, and order was restored. The ringleader, Forrest, was then triced up in the mizzen-rigging, "two hours on and two off," to await the punishment of his crimes.

The next day brought a fresh vision of the Stars and Stripes, but this time from the mizzen-peak of a heavily-armed steamer, which appeared early in the morning, standing in towards the harbour. The *Alabama* was at once cleared for action, and, as a precautionary measure, her funds were despatched on shore for deposit in the event of the engagement which appeared likely to ensue. This, however, was not to be. The merchants, thinking evidently that Captain Semmes was in their power, and must pay their price for taking charge of his treasure, refused to have anything to do with it at a lower rate than five *per cent*.

To this the officer in charge would not agree, and the money was again carried on board. Fortunately, as it turned out, for when the true character of the stranger came to be ascertained, he proved to be the United States steamer *San Jacinto*, of fourteen guns—*viz.*, twelve 68 pounders, and two eleven-inch shell-guns, and therefore much too heavy for the *Alabama* to venture on an attack. This point was but just settled when the merchants appeared alongside with an abatement in their charges for taking care of the Confederate treasure; but the chance was gone, and they were compelled to return as empty-handed as they had come.

Meanwhile, the authorities ashore had been bestirring themselves to prevent any violation of the neutrality of their port. A boat was despatched to the *San Jacinto* with orders either to come to an anchor, in which case she must remain in the harbour full twenty-four hours after the departure of the *Alabama*, or else to proceed again to sea, and cruise beyond the limits of the maritime league from the harbour. The latter alternative being preferred by the United States Captain, the *San Jacinto* put her helm aport, and came slowly round, returning to the prescribed distance from the shore, where she proceeded to steam slowly backwards and forwards, in the hope of intercepting her little enemy, should the latter venture to leave her anchorage.

Pending this submission on the part of the United States cruiser to the orders of the Governor, the French gunboat *Fata* received instructions to get up steam, and shifting her berth, took up her position close alongside of the *Alabama*, fully prepared to offer her own contribution to any controversy that might arise between the two rival vessels. Her captain and officers were very friendly, offering every assistance, and pointing out on the chart the best means of eluding the enemy, the superiority of whose size and weight put an end to all idea of a deliberate attack, though there were still some among the crew of the *Alabama* who could not relinquish the hope that in making their way out of the harbour an engagement might be forced upon them.

All the vigilance of the authorities, however, though extending to the prohibition of any intercourse whatever between the *San Jacinto* and the shore, was unable to prevent the Yankee from establishing a code of signals by which he might at once be put in possession of any movement on the part of the Confederate steamer, which he now, no doubt, fully looked on as his prize. Two of his boats were, as was afterwards discovered, on the look-out during the night, and an understanding had been come to with the master of the Yankee vessel lying in the harbour to signal the *Alabama*'s departure.

By dusk, Captain Semmes' preparations were completed; the funds, which the Martinique merchants had allowed to slip through their too-widely-opened fingers, were safely despatched on their way to Liverpool; the necessary supplies were on board; and, with decks cleared for action, all lights carefully extinguished, and all hands at quarters, the *Alabama* stole quietly from her anchorage, and steamed cautiously across the harbour on her way to the open sea.

It was a period of intense anxiety as the *Alabama* slipped silently through the tranquil water of the harbour, each moment bringing her nearer to the powerful enemy, who, when dusk had shut him from their view, had been planted in the very centre of the entrance, eagerly looking out for the expected prize. Presently it was found that her movements were, at all events, known to the spies of the enemy, and a succession of signals from the Yankee vessel they had left at anchor were evidently intended to warn the *San Jacinto* of the attempted escape.

Momentarily now was expected the flash of the enemy's gun, and the hoarse roar of his shot, and each crew stood by its loaded gun ready with a prompt reply. Not a word was uttered on the crowded deck, and so deep was the silence, that the low throbbing of the *Alabama's* propeller, as it revolved slowly in the water, seemed to strike on the ear with a noise like thunder. But the minutes passed by and the expected broadside never came. The straining eyes of the look-outs could see no sign of the *San Jacinto*. Either she had misunderstood the signals of her accomplice on shore, or by some strange fatality they had altogether escaped her; and the *Alabama* held on her course unmolested, until, at twenty minutes past eight, less than an hour after the start, she was considered fairly out of danger of interception.

The guns were now run in and secured, the word passed to the engineers to fire up and give her a full head of steam; the men were piped below, and the *Alabama*, throwing off the silence in which for the last hour she had been wrapped fore and aft, darted off merrily over the rippling waves, in the direction of the island of Blanquilla, at the rate of fourteen knots an hour. It subsequently transpired that, notwithstanding all her vigilance and all her pre-arranged signals, the *San Jacinto* had been totally unaware of the escape of her agile foe, and actually remained for four days and four nights carefully keeping guard over the stable from which the steed had cleverly stolen away.

The morning of the 21st of November found the *Alabama* off the Hermanas, and by 1.30 p.m. she was in sight of the island of Blanquilla, the appointed rendezvous of the *Agrippina*, who had already, about nine o'clock that morning, been descried on the port bow making all speed towards her destined anchorage. Here both vessels arrived in the course of the afternoon; the *Alabama*, which was a far swifter sailer than her merchant tender, being the first to drop anchor, and the *Agrippina* following her in.

As the two vessels neared the shore, a schooner was discovered at anchor in the little bay, and on the approach of the strangers she hoisted the Stars and Stripes. On being overhauled by a boat, despatched for that purpose from the *Alabama*, she proved to be the United States whaling schooner, *Clara L. Sparks*, of Provincetown; and great was the grief and astonishment of the unlucky master when the white flag of the Confederacy was discovered floating at the new comer's peak.

The temptation was great to seize her, and devote her to the flames, but Captain Semmes was anxious for nothing so much as to avoid all possible ground of complaint with regard to any infringement of neutrality. It happened, fortunately for the *Clara Sparks*, that a few herdsmen from Venezuela were supporting a miserable existence in the barren island off which she was anchored, and to make prize of the vessel under these circumstances, might possibly be construed into a breach of neutral privilege.

In the end, therefore, it was determined not to molest the whaler; and her master was informed, much to his relief and delight, that so soon as the *Alabama*'s arrangements were completed, he would be free to continue his course. Meanwhile, however, it was peremptorily necessary that he should not be permitted to escape, and reward the forbearance of his captors by giving her enemy information as to her whereabout. Orders were therefore given that the master and mate of the schooner should repair every evening on board the cruiser, remaining with her till the morning, when they were permitted to return on board, and resume their avocations.

At 8 p.m. of Saturday, the 27th November, the operation of coaling commenced, the men working in groups, which were relieved every two hours, and by nightfall about seventy tons had been got on board. The wind was fresh enough to raise a slight sea, causing the two vessels to chafe considerably as they lay closely locked together for the purpose of transhipping the coal. But notwithstanding the breeze, the day was so hot as to deter Captain Semmes from visiting the shore, despite the inevitable longing, after a confinement on board of more than three months, to find the foot once more planted on solid ground. Some of the other officers, however, explored the island, which they found a barren place enough; the three herdsmen, who constitute the entire population of the country, maintaining themselves after a fashion, by rearing a few goats. They must, indeed, lead a life of privation, the island producing scarcely anything; and even the water supply being extremely scanty, and so brackish as to be hardly fit for human use.

Although today is the Sabbath—writes Captain Semmes, in his

journal of the following day—I did not consider it any violation of Christian duty to continue coaling, as we are liable to be surprised at any moment, and to have our purpose defeated.

So, too, thought the *Alabama*'s crew, who worked cheerfully on throughout the day, completing their task by half-past eleven on the Monday morning. The *Alabama* had now on board about 285 tons, nearly 200 tons having been received from the *Agrippina*. Estimating her consumption at sixteen tons a day, which would give a moderate rate of steaming, she had, therefore, in her bunkers fuel for about eighteen days.

This important matter arranged, the next thing to be done was to send down the main-yard, which had been carried away in the cyclone, and roughly fished together, and to supply its place with the second new spar taken from the ship *T.B. Wales*. This occupied the greater portion of the 25th, and Captain Semmes then proceeded to "break out" the hold, for the purpose of taking stock of his provisions, no opportunity having yet offered, since the hurried shipment of stores off Terceira, to ascertain the precise amount in hand of salted provisions, and other necessaries. Batches of liberty-men were also sent on shore to recruit themselves with a run upon *terra firma*—an amusement in which such of the officers as could be spared were but too glad to join.

Wednesday, the 26th November, saw all these arrangements completed, and the last batch of liberty-men safely on board again after their run. The *Alabama* was now ready for a fresh cruise, but before taking leave of Blanquilla, there was an act of justice to be done. Accordingly, that afternoon a court-martial was summoned for the trial of George Forrest, the seaman who had originally deserted from the *Sumter*, and who, on his recapture, had been sentenced to serve out his time, forfeiting all pay, prize-money, &c. His present offence was that of endeavouring to incite the crew to mutiny, and of procuring with that object the liquor with which the rioters of the 18th November had been made intoxicated.

The case was clearly proved, and after some consultation judgment was passed, sentencing him to lose all prize-money, and to be dismissed the ship in disgrace. At a quarter past seven in the evening, all hands were mustered aft to hear the sentence read; and after a short but effective address from Captain Semmes, the prisoner was informed that he was now dismissed the Confederate service with the stain of infamy upon him, and bundled over the side into the boat that was to convey him to the shore.

This ceremony over, and the ship rid of the incorrigible scoundrel who had so long disgraced her, the men were dismissed, and preparations made for the *Alabama*'s departure. She had been already preceded by the *Agrippina*, three of whose hands had volunteered in exchange for three from the steamer, and on the return of the boat no time was lost in getting her under way. The captain and mate of the Yankee schooner were released, and the *Alabama* stood out to sea under easy sail.

Chapter 20

Looking out for a Rich Prize

The *Alabama* was now on the look-out for a Californian steamer, and it was quite possible that in so doing she might run into a fight. However, should that be the case, there would be no disposition to shirk it. The vessel was already three months in commission; and though some of her crew had no doubt been originally a rough lot—the boys especially picked up in the streets of Liverpool, being designated by Captain Semmes as most incorrigible young rascals-three months of steady, strong-handed discipline had done wonders in reducing these rough elements to order, and making out of a set of merchant sailors, gathered here and there at random by the prospect of high pay and stirring adventure, as orderly and well-trained a crew as could be found on board many a man-of-war of twice her length of service.

All hands, then, were ready and eager for a brush with the enemy. It was necessary, of course, that the relative strength of the two ships should not be too disproportionate; but the approach of an United States ship of anything like their own force would have been hailed with delight by all on board.

Considerable excitement was occasioned when, on the second day after leaving Blanquilla, a prospect of an encounter seemed to present itself. It was still early morning when a sail was reported on the lee bow, and soon the stranger was made out to be a large side-wheel steamer, *barque*-rigged, and standing towards the *Alabama*. She was of considerably superior size, but it was determined at least to see what she was made of; and the *Alabama* was luffed to the wind, while preparations were made for lowering her propeller and getting her under steam. It was soon perceived, however, that the stranger was keeping quietly on her course, without paying the slightest attention to these manoeuvres; and as it was pretty certain that no enemy's ship, so greatly superior in size, would lose so tempting an opportunity, it was at once clear that she must needs be a neutral, probably some French war-steamer bound for Martinique. So the propeller was left where it was, and the *Alabama* slipt away again upon her course.

At nine o'clock the same morning, the coast of Porto Rico was in sight, and a few hours afterwards the *Alabama* entered the Mona Passage, shortening sail as she did so to permit a *barque* to run up with her for the purpose of ascertaining her nationality. The *barque*, which proved to be English, dipped her ensign as she passed to the Stars and Stripes which were flying from the peak of the *Alabama*; but the compliment not being really intended for the Confederate vessel, but for her enemies, was, of course, not returned.

The Mona Passage being the regular track of United States commerce, it was looked upon as almost a certainty that at least one cruiser would be stationed for its protection. A bright look-out, therefore, was kept, and hopes again ran high of a speedy brush with the Yankees. Nothing, however, appeared; and the attention of the *Alabama* was for the most part devoted throughout the day to strictly domestic affairs.

Today—says Captain Semmes, in his *journal*—has been a great "house-cleaning" day with the first lieutenant, who, regardless of Mona Passages, strange sails, &c., is busy with his holy-stones and sand.

Gave an order to the paymaster today, authorising him to pay the increased rates agreed upon with the crew off Terceira, *viz*.

		£	s.	Dollars.
Master-at-arms	per month	6	0 —	29.04
Yeoman	"	6	0 —	29.04
Ship's steward	"	6	0 —	29.04
Ship's corporal	"	6	0 —	26.62
Armorer	"	6	0 —	29.04
Ship's cook	"	5	10 —	26.62
Chief boatswain's mate	"	6	0 —	29.04
Second ditto	"	5	10 —	26.62
Gunner's mate	"	6	0 —	29.04
Carpenter's mate	"	6	0 —	29.04
Sailmaker's mate	"	5	10 —	26.62
Quartermaster	"	5	10 —	26.62
Quarter gunners	"	5	10 —	26.62
Cockswains	"	5	10 —	26.62
Capt. of forecastle	"	5	10 —	26.62

Capt. of top	"	5	0 — 24.20
Capt. of aftguard	"	5	0 — 24.20
Capt. of hold	"	5	0 — 24.20
Cabin steward	"	5	0 — 24.20
Ward-room steward	"	5	0 — 24.20
Seamen	"	4	10 — 21.78
O. Seamen	"	4	0 — 19.36
Landsmen	"	3	10 — 14.94
Boys	"	2	0 — 9.68
Firemen	"	7	0 — 33.38
Trimmers	"	5	0 — 24.20

Sunday, November 30th.—Mustered and inspected the crew. At 9 p.m., sent a boat on board of a Spanish schooner twenty days from Boston, bound to the port of San Domingo. Received some newspapers by her as late as to the 13th inst. Soon afterwards another sail was discovered to leeward, beating up the coast. Ran down for her, and when within proper distance hoisted United States colours. The stranger responded with the same; whereupon, in accordance with our usual practice, we hoisted our own colours and fired a blank cartridge. This hove her to, when we sent a boat on board of her. She proved to be the *barque Parker Cook*, of and from Boston, bound to Cayes. This was a very timely capture, as we were running very short of provisions, and the prize was provision-laden. Got on board from her a quantity of pork, cheese, crackers, &c.; and at 10 p.m. illuminated the shores of San Domingo with a *flambeau* furnished by wicked men who would gladly see another San Domingo revolution in our unhappy country.

In the afternoon the weather became angry, and the wind blew fresh, raising a considerable sea. As we were in the bight of Samana, I felt a little uneasy about drifting too near the shore. These are some of the anxieties of a commander that his officers scarcely ever know anything about. Our prize was burned off Cape Raphael. I did not turn in until near midnight; was called two hours afterwards, upon having run a prescribed distance; turned in again, and had just fallen comfortably asleep, when the officer of the deck came down in great haste to inform me that a large ship was standing down directly for us. We were hove to, and as the moon had gone down, and the night was dark, I knew she must be close aboard of us. I immediately ordered the main-topsail to be filled, and hurrying on a few clothes, sprang on deck. At a glance I saw that the danger was passed, as the intruder was abaft the beam, running to leeward. Wore round and followed him.

Monday, December 1st.—A stiff trade, with squall clouds. A whirlwind passed near us. We had just time to take in the port studding sails, which had been set in chase of the unwelcome disturber of my rest last night. The chase proved to be a Spanish hermaphrodite brig. Land in sight on the port beam, and at noon the cape just ahead.

Tuesday, December 2nd.—Running down the land. Off the Grange at noon. Last night, at ten o'clock, a sail was reported on the port quarter, nearly astern, running down before the wind like ourselves. Having lights up, and looming up large, I called all hands to quarters and cleared the ship for action, pivoting on the port side, and loading the guns. As the stranger ranged up nearly abeam of us, distant about eight hundred yards, we discovered him to be a heavy steamer, under steam, and with all studding sails set on both sides. Here was a fix! We had no steam ourselves, and our propeller was triced up!

A few minutes, however, decided our suspense. From the quiet movement of the steamer on her course, without shortening sail, or otherwise, so far as we could see, making preparation for battle, it was quite evident that he was not an enemy. He was a ship of war—probably a Spaniard, bound from San Domingo to Cuba. My first intention was to range up alongside and speak him, and for this purpose I set the foresail and topgallant sails. But we were soon left far astern, and the stranger was out of sight long before we could have got up steam and lowered the propeller in chase.

About 3 p.m. made the island of Tortuga. A sail reported on the starboard bow, standing across our bows on the *port* tack. Through the stupidity of the lookouts the next thing we knew was that she was off on the starboard quarter, and to windward of us, she having been on the *starboard* tack all the while! I turned in tonight, hoping to get some rest, as I had been up the greater part of last night. But after undressing, and before getting into my cot (10 p.m.), the officer of the deck came below in a great hurry to say there was a large vessel running down on us—we were hove to—which appeared to be a steamer. Immediately ordered the officer to fill away; went on deck, and at a glance perceived that the sail was a brig running clear of us, and some distance astern.

Went below again, and this time succeeded in actually getting into bed, when I was again aroused by the announcement that a vessel, with very white canvas, was running down upon us, a little forward of our weather beam. Went on deck, filled away again, and ran on under easy sail to assist the stranger's approach. The night squally, with showers of rain, and the wind fresh. At 1.30 p.m. the stranger approached, and we spoke him. He was a small schooner—white, as almost all the West Indian schooners are—Spanish, &c. Turned in at two o'clock, and at daybreak down came intelligence again that there were two sail in sight, and at 7 p.m., one of them being within signal distance, I had again to turn out. This night will serve as a specimen of a great many spent by me in my cruises.

Wednesday, December 3rd.—We are cruising today, with the weather very fine and clear, in the passage between San Domingo and Cuba. Caused two neutral vessels to show their colours, and at noon squared away for the east end of Cuba. Where can all the enemy's cruisers be, that the important passages we have lately passed through are all left unguarded? They are off, I suppose, in chase of the *Alabama!*

At 10 p.m. a *barque*, having come quite near us in the bright moonlight, we fired a blank cartridge to heave him to, and wore ship. As he disregarded our signal, I directed a round shot to be fired at him above his hull. This had the desired effect, our shot passing—as we learned from him afterwards—between his fore-stay and foremast. He proved to be the French *barque, Feu Sacré*, from Port au Prince to Falmouth.[1] When asked why he did not heave to at the first shot, he replied that he was a Frenchman, and was not at war with anybody! At midnight made the light on Cape Maise.

Thursday, December 4th.—Standing off and on Cape Maise, waiting for our Californian friend, who should have left Aspinwall on the 1st, and should pass this point today or tonight. Fires banked, so as to give us steam at a short notice. Several sail passing during the day. Exercised the crew at the battery at sunset. A beautiful bright night, with the wind somewhat too fresh from the N.E. Lying to off Cape Maise. Everybody on the tiptoe of excitement, and a good many volunteer look-outs. As for myself, having put the ship in the right position, I turned in at 10 p.m., giving orders not to call me for a sail-ship, and got a good night's rest, of which I stood very much in need.

Friday, December 5th.—A very fine morning, with highly-transparent atmosphere. The west side of Haiti visible, though distant ninety miles. On this fine balmy morning I enjoyed exceedingly the cheerful notes of our canary. This is a little prisoner made on board one of the

---

1. From the boarding officer's memoranda it appears that the master of this vessel protested vehemently against being annoyed by United States vessels—the *Alabama* passing in this case as the U.S. ship *Wyoming.*

whalers; and sometimes at early morning I fancy myself amid "jessamine bowers," inhaling the fragrance of flowers and listening to the notes of the wild songsters so common in our dear Southern land. May God speedily clear it of the wicked, fanatical hordes that are now desolating it under pretence of liberty and free government!

If the Californian steamers still take this route, the steamer of the 1st must have been delayed, otherwise she should have passed us last night. Several sail in sight, but I cannot yet leave my station to overhaul them, lest my principal object should be defeated. At noon, a schooner would insist on stumbling right into my path, without the necessity of a chase. I brought her to, and she proved to be United States property. She was the *Mina*, of and from Baltimore, for Port Maria, on the north side of Jamaica. Her cargo being English, I released her on a ransom bond for 15,000 dollars. She was of ninety tons, and thirteen years old. Kept her by me until sunset, and then permitted her to depart, having sent on board her the prisoners from the *barque Parker Cook*.

Our hopes of capturing a Californian steamer were considerably damped by the intelligence given us by the mate of this schooner, that these steamers no longer ran this route, but that the outward bound took the Mona Passage (?), and the homeward bound the Florida gulf passage. Still, I will wait a day or two longer to make sure that I have not been deceived.

Saturday, December 6th.—At 9 p.m. hoisted the propeller, and made sail to the northward and eastward. The outward-bound Californian steamer is due off the Cape today, if she takes this route at all; I will therefore keep the Cape in sight all day. I glean the following paragraph from a New York letter, published in a file of the *Baltimore Sun*, received from the schooner *Mina*:—

> The shipments of grain from this port during the past week have been almost entirely in foreign bottoms, the American flag being for the moment in disfavour in consequence of the raid of the rebel steamer *Alabama*!

CHAPTER 21

Prisoners of War

Sunday again! The *Alabama*'s lucky day; and this time, at least, destined to be especially marked with white chalk in the annals of the ship. The morning passed calmly enough; the ship in her quiet Sabbath trim; and nothing giving token of what was about to follow, save here and there a group anxiously scanning the horizon, or eagerly discussing the chances of a rich capture before nightfall.

The forenoon wore slowly away, and five bells had just sounded, when the cry of "Sail, ho!" from the masthead put everyone on the *qui vive*, the excitement growing rapidly more and more intense as bit by bit the description of the stranger became more accurate and minute. She is a steamer.—and a large one! That sounded well, and the hopes of the sanguine rose higher and higher. Brigantine rigged.—and a side-wheel steamer!—so far so good. This answers exactly to the description of the Californian steamers.

A few minutes will decide it now; the *Alabama*'s canvas has some time since been snugly furled, the fires spread and well supplied with fresh fuel, the propeller lowered, and the ship's head turned in a direction to intercept the approaching vessel. Rapidly the chase looms larger and larger, as the two swift steamers approach each other at almost top speed. And now the huge walking-beam can be plainly distinguished, see-sawing up and down between the lofty paddle-boxes, and the decks appear crowded with hundreds of passengers, conspicuous among whom are to be seen the gay dresses of numerous ladies; and—yes, surely that is the glimmer of bayonets, and that military-looking array drawn up on the hurricane-deck is a strong detachment of United States marines!

Swiftly, and in grim silence, the *Alabama* approached her huge but defenceless prey. From her open ports grinned the black muzzles of her six 32 pounders, each with its crew standing round, eager for the word. High above them towered the huge, black pivot-gun, while from the mizzen-peak floated the delusive Stars and Stripes, the sight of which was to tempt the stranger into a confession of his own nationality.

The *ruse* was, as usual, successful, and as the two vessels crossed, the *Alabama* passing a short distance astern of the stranger, the latter also hoisted United States colours, and expectation gave way to certainty among the delighted crew of the Confederate steamer. Down came the Yankee colours from her gaff, and in its stead the white ensign of the Confederacy fluttered gaily in the breeze, while a blank shot from the *Alabama*'s lee bow-chaser summoned the chase to surrender. Surrendering, however, seemed to be the last thing in the chase's thoughts. Already she was ahead of the Confederate cruiser, and trusting to her own well-known speed, appeared determined to make at least one effort to escape. She held steadily on her course, at top speed, without noticing the pursuer's summons; the black smoke that poured in volumes from her funnel, showing no less plainly than the rapid revolutions of her paddles the strenuous exertions she was making to escape.

This state of things, however, could not last long. For a few minutes the chase was permitted to try her speed against that of her pursuer; but the latter soon found that with the highest pressure of steam she had been able to raise during the short period that had elapsed since the enemy first hove in sight, she was by no means overhauling the chase as rapidly as could be desired. So the friendly warning having been disregarded, the adoption of more peremptory measures was decided on, and a shotted gun was ordered to be fired over her.

Boom! went the *Alabama*'s bow-chaser, as she yawed for a moment to permit the gunner to take aim—and boom! at almost the same instant went one of her broadside guns, the enthusiastic captain of which could not contain himself until the order to fire was given, but must needs bring down upon himself a reprimand from the authorities of the quarter-deck for his precipitation. Fortunately, however, this irregular shot did no harm—not improbably, perhaps, from the very fact of its having been launched so totally without consideration.

The first, however, did its errand most effectively, and the shower of white splinters that flew from the chase's foremast as the shell, after grazing the funnel, struck full against it, afforded most satisfactory evidence of the accuracy of the line. Happily, the shell contented itself with cutting the foremast very nearly in two, and did not explode until it had passed safely overboard, otherwise the havoc created by it on the crowded deck of the steamer must have been fearful.

The hint, however, was sufficient. The paddles of the chase ceased to revolve, the huge walking-beam remained poised in midair, and the steamer rounding to, submitted herself to her captors. A boat was now lowered and, sent on board of the prize, which proved to be, as anticipated, the mail steamer *Ariel*, from New York to Aspinwall, having on board one hundred and forty marines on their way to join the enemy's Pacific squadron; several military and naval officers, among the latter of whom was Commander Sartori, on his way to take command of the St. Mary's; and about five hundred other passengers, a large proportion of whom were women and children.

The *Alabama* had "bought an elephant," and now the question arose—what was to be done with her valuable but most unwieldy acquisition? The first step, of course, was to send a prize crew on board. The second to transfer to the *Alabama* sundry important matters, such as the ship's papers, three large boxes of specie, a 24 pounder rifled gun, 125 new rifles, 16 swords, and about 1,000 rounds of ammunition. The marines and officers were then put on parole, the former being disarmed, and all pledged not to fight again against the Confederate States until they should be regularly exchanged.

But this done, Captain Semmes' task was not half accomplished. There was still the ship herself to be disposed of, and with her the remaining five hundred and odd passengers, including among their number a large proportion of women and children. What was to be done? It was clear he could not fire the ship until all these were safely out of her. It was at least equally clear that, squeeze and contrive how he would, he could not possibly transfer such a host of prisoners to his own already sufficiently crowded decks. His only choice, then, was either to release the captured vessel at once, upon a ransom bond, or to keep her by him for a time in the hope that something might turn up to obviate the necessity of so unsatisfactory a step. Captain Semmes decided upon the latter course, and detaining the captain of the *Ariel* on board his own ship, sent a prize crew to take charge of the *Ariel*, with orders to keep company with the *Alabama* through the night.

This done, the *Alabama* returned under easy sail to her station off the Cape, still anxiously looking out for the homeward-bound steamer, which would of course prove a very far richer prize than the one home-bound vessel he had captured. The following afternoon the precaution was taken of disabling the captured vessel, by removing from her engines the "bonnet of the steam chest and a steam valve," which were sent into safe custody on board the *Alabama*; care being also taken to prevent the *Ariel* from availing herself of her sails as a means of escape should the *Alabama* have to start off in pursuit of her homeward-bound consort.

No homeward-bound steamer, however, appeared, and it was now determined to convey the *Ariel* into Kingston, Jamaica, where it was proposed to land the passengers, and after providing the *Alabama*, from the prize, with coal, provisions, and other matters of which she stood in need, to take her out again to sea and burn her. With this view the portions of the machinery which had been removed during the night were restored to their places, and the two vessels made sail towards Jamaica, on or about the line which it was supposed would be taken by the Californian steamer.

The next morning was fine, and, with the prize in company, the island of Navaza was made at about 9.30 p.m., on the port bow; and five hours afterwards the two steamers were in sight of the east end of Jamaica. By half-past seven that evening, the *Alabama* was within about nine miles of Point Morant Light, and checked her speed to enable the prize to come up with her.

And now a catastrophe occurred which, but for the most careful and excellent management, might have had most serious results. At about eight o'clock in the evening chase was given to an hermaphrodite brig, on coming up with which a blank cartridge was fired, and a boat despatched to board her and examine her papers. At this moment, up came the engineer to report that the engine had suddenly become entirely useless from the giving way of some of the valve castings, and that twenty-four hours, at least, would be required before the damage could be repaired. At this untoward intelligence, the captain's first thought was of the chase, and, casting a rapid glance in that direction, to his equal amazement and disgust, he perceived that she had not obeyed the signal to heave to, but was still standing quietly upon her course!

Here was, indeed, a pleasant predicament. Not a step could he stir in pursuit, nor did he dare fire a shot after the departing vessel, for fear, in the darkness of the night, of sending to the bottom his own boat, which was now in full pursuit of her. What if the boat should be led away too far in the ardour of the chase, and of course taking for granted that as soon as the brigantine's contumacy was discovered, the *Alabama* herself would at once be after her? What, too, if the *Ariel* should get scent of her captor's predicament, and take this favourable opportunity of showing her a clean pair of heels, carrying off the unlucky prize crew as a running horse might carry off the unskilful rider who had imprudently bestridden it?

The moment was an anxious one, and great was the relief to the minds of all who were in the secret, when the welcome sound of oars working regularly backwards and forwards in their rowlocks was again heard, and the boat returned, having managed to overhaul the stranger; the wind having fortunately fallen too light for her to escape.

The chase proved to hail from one of the German States, and was just out of Kingston. According to her statement, this latter port was now suffering from a severe visitation of yellow-fever. This intelligence caused an entire change in the *Alabama*'s plans. It had been Captain Semmes' intention to run into Kingston, and endeavour, at all events, to obtain permission to discharge his numerous prisoners; this being, apparently, the only way in which he could hope to disencumber himself of them, except by releasing the ship at the same time.

To turn some seven hundred prisoners, however, many of them delicate women and children, adrift in a place known to be suffering from the fearful scourge of yellow-fever, would have been an act of inhumanity of which the Confederate captain was quite incapable. Sorely to his disappointment, therefore, he felt himself compelled to abandon the Kingston scheme, and forego the pleasure of making a bonfire of the splendid steamer that had fallen into his hands. It is an ill wind that blows nobody any good, and to the yellow-fever were the passengers by the *Ariel* indebted for an uninterrupted voyage, and her owners for the preservation of their valuable vessel.

The question once decided in favour of the *Ariel's* release, it was, of course, under existing circumstances, an object of no small importance to get the matter concluded as speedily as possible. Had she only known her captor's crippled condition she would have had nothing to do but just to have steamed quietly away, taking the prize-crew with her as compensation for the inconvenience to which she had been put by her detention. And any moment might reveal the all-important secret; so without delay, a boat was again sent on board for the master, who was evidently not a little relieved on being told that the vessel was to be released.

Some little discussion now arose as to the amount of ransom to be exacted, but both parties were equally, though not as openly, anxious to conclude the transaction; and the amount was finally fixed at 261,000 dollars—a handsome sum, indeed, but one by no means exorbitant, when the value of the vessel to be ransomed is taken into consideration.

The bond duly signed, and safely deposited among the other securities of the kind, Captain Semmes breathed more freely, and a feeling of satisfaction at having steered safely through a situation of such difficulty, offered some slight compensation for the disappointment arising from the enforced release of the prize. The two vessels now parted company; all parties, both civil, naval, and military, on board of the *Ariel*, uniting their testimony in eulogy of the quiet, orderly, and respectful conduct of their unwelcome guests. So with mutual amenities the two courteous enemies parted, the *Ariel* steering a course to the S.S.W., the *Alabama* still hard at work in the repairs of her machinery, standing off and on within easy distance of the Jamaica coast, and keeping as far as possible from the track of vessels until the untoward disaster should be repaired.

CHAPTER 22

To Sea Again

The exciting episode of the *Ariel* was followed by a period altogether devoid of incident, though by no means destitute either of interest or anxiety for those on board the *Alabama*. From daybreak to dusk the click of the hammer, and the shrill screaming of the file, arose incessantly from the engine room, as the engineer and his staff laboured without a pause to repair the damage to the machinery. The task proved even longer than had been anticipated, and it was not until the afternoon of the third day that the mischief had been finally remedied, and the *Alabama* was pronounced in a condition to resume with safety her destructive career.

Meanwhile, a brighter lookout than ever was kept from her mastheads. There was still a possibility—though but a slight one—of falling in with the homeward-bound Californian, for which they had been waiting so long and so anxiously; whilst it was more than ever necessary to care against surprise from any of the enemy's cruisers, who might fairly be expected to be in considerable force somewhere in the neighbourhood.

The northern shores of Jamaica, however, off which the *Alabama* was now lying, standing along the coast, under easy sail during the day, and at night laying her main-topsail to the mast, appeared to be but little frequented by vessels of any kind, and the cruiser was permitted to carry on her repairs without a single interruption in the way of either a chase, or a call to quarters. And it was perhaps as well that such an interval of rest should have been afforded after the severe strain of the previous few days. For Captain Semmes, at all events, it was a great boon, for on that officer's never very robust constitution, the continued anxiety and constant night-calls on deck, in wind and rain, had had a very serious effect, and he was fairly laid up with cold and fever.

The evening of Friday, December the 12th, saw the repairs of the machinery of the vessel completed, the *Alabama* being at, nightfall about opposite to the little town of St. Anne's. That evening the crew were exercised at quarters; and the next day, after a thorough cleaning of the decks, &c., the vessel ran away to the westward of the Island of Jamaica, *en route* for another point of rendezvous, at which to take in fresh coal, and other needful supplies.

Saturday, December 13th.—Nothing in sight, and I intend to see nothing—unless it be a homeward-bound Californian steamer—at present, as it is important I should make the run I contemplate without being traced. I should have much liked to touch at the Caymans for fruit and vegetables for the crew, but forbear on this account.

Monday, December 15th.—Fresh trade, ship rolling along under topsails. This running down, down, the ever-constant trade wind—to run *up* against it, by and by, under steam—is not very pleasant. Still, God willing, I hope to strike a blow of some importance, and make my way safely out of the Gulf.

Wednesday, December 17th.—The wind blew quite fresh during the night from about N.E. by N. Today it is blowing a moderate gale from about N.N.E. This is probably a *norther* from the American coast, modified by its contact with the N.E. trade wind. The clouds look hard and wintry. Close-reefed at nightfall. The gale has continued all day, with a rough sea, in which the ship is rolling and tumbling about. Weather cloudy and gloomy-looking, and the wind moaning and whistling through the rigging—enough to give one the blues. These are some of the comforts of sea-going, and we have had our share of them in the *Alabama*.

Thursday, December 18th.—The gale continues, with dense clouds in every direction obscuring the heavens so that we get no meridian altitude. I got a glimpse of the sun at about nine minutes past noon. When one's ship is in a doubtful position, how eagerly and nervously one watches the shifting clouds near noon, and how remorsely they sometimes close up their dense masses just at the critical moment, shutting out from us the narrowly-watched face of the sun! One is foolish enough sometimes almost to feel a momentary resentment against inanimate nature—weak mortals that we are!

The gale has drifted us so far to leeward that the wind from its present quarter will no longer permit us to "lay through" the Yucatan passage, so at 2 p.m. we tacked to the southward and eastward. Weather still thick in the afternoon, with light rain at intervals. We had a very ugly sea lashing us this morning—the ship rolling so heavily as to awaken me frequently, though I sleep in a swinging cot; and the water swashing over the decks, and rushing by bucketsful down the companion-way, which we are obliged to keep open to avoid being smothered.

Friday, December 19th.—The gale continues with the tenacity of a norther, this being the third day. This is but a foretaste of the weather we may expect in the Gulf of Mexico. Being now in the Gulf of Honduras, there is but a small strip of land between us and it.

Saturday, December 20th.—As ugly a day as one often sees, with a great variety of wind and weather. In the morning the wind was fresh from the N.E., with flying clouds, and a bright sun, now and then obscured. At about 9 p.m. a cloud bank in the north began to rise, and by 11.30 we had a densely overcast sky, with heavy rain-squalls. I was running for Cape Catoche, and was greatly disappointed at not getting a meridian altitude, especially after the promise of the morning. At about 11.30 made the land—two islands, as described by the man at the masthead. At 4 p.m. sounded in twenty-eight fathoms. Weather threatening a gale. At six, double-reefed the topsails, and sounded in twenty-five fathoms. I shall endeavour to feel my way around the Cape, and gradually bear up for the westward. The bank is apparently clean and safe, but still groping one's way in the dark in strange waters is a somewhat nervous operation.

Sunday, December 21st.—We doubled Cape Catoche very successfully last night, hauling around it gradually in from twenty-five to thirty fathoms, and ran along in the latter depth all night, course W. and W. by S., sounding every hour. The wind blew half a gale, and the weather looked threatening. This morning the wind hauled more to the eastward, and moderated somewhat. The sky still looks wintry, and the sun sheds a lurid light through a semi-transparent stratum of dull grey clouds. At 11 p.m. mustered the crews and at meridian passed a large steamer (hull down) steering to the eastward, probably a French ship of war from Vera Cruz.

Monday, December 22nd.—Ran on during the night in a very regular line of soundings of twenty fathoms, on a W.S.W. course. At 9 p.m., having run within about twenty miles of the Arcas, anchored for the night in twenty fathoms.

Tuesday, December 23rd.—At 9 p.m. called all hands up anchor; and at ten we were under way, steering W.S.W.; at meridian observed six miles to the northward of the Arcas, and altered course to S.W. At 1.30 p.m. made the Arcas half a point on the starboard-bow, distant about twelve miles; and at sunset came to anchor in eleven fathoms of water, with the south Arca bearing N.W. by N. In the course of the afternoon our coal-ship, which I had ordered to rendezvous here, hove in sight, and joined us at the anchorage a few minutes after we came to.

Wednesday, December 24th.—In the forenoon went out of the harbour, and examined the entrances and anchorage. The dangers are all visible, and it is only necessary to give a berth to the reefs that make off from the points. There is an inner reef making off to the westward from the northern island; but it, like the other, is visible, and there is no danger whatever in approaching it. The Arcas are three low keys, lying in a triangle; the northern key being the largest. We found a hut on this latter key, a boat hauled up on the island, a net inside the hut, a boiler or two for trying out oil, and other evidences of the inhabitancy of fishermen or turtlers; but this not being the season for these pursuits, everything had apparently been abandoned for some time.

Numerous birds of the gull species were the only living things found in the island, and of these there were varieties of old birds and their fledglings, and some of the former were still laying and sitting. They seemed to have no fear of our men, and suffered themselves to be caught by the hand, and knocked on the head with sticks. The vegetation found was on the larger island, and on that it consisted of a dense carpeting of sea-kale—not a shrub of any kind. In the transparent waters on the inner reef, a great variety of the living coral was found in all its beauty, imitating the growth of the forest on a small scale. At p.m. we got under way, and stood in and anchored under the south side of the larger island in nine fathoms, and moored ship with an open hawse to the north.

We entered by the S.E. passage between the south and the north islands. The *barque* followed us, coming in by the S.W. passage between the south and the west islands, and anchored a little to the S.E. of us. Our anchorage is open to the S.E., but at this season it does not blow from that quarter, and probably would not bring in much sea if it did. We feel very comfortable tonight in snug berth.

Thursday, December 25th.—Christmas-day!—the second Christmas since we left our homes in the *Sumter*. Last year we were buffeting the storms of the North Atlantic, near the Azores; now we are snugly anchored, in the Arcas: and how many eventful periods have passed in the interval! Our poor people have been terribly pressed in this wicked and ruthless war, and they have borne privations and sufferings which nothing but an intense patriotism could have sustained. They will live in history as a people worthy to be free; and future generations will be astonished at the folly and fanaticism, wickedness and want of principle, developed by this war among the Puritan population of the North. And in this class may nine-tenths of the native population of the Northern States be placed, to such an extent has the "Plymouth Rock" leaven "leavened the whole lump." A people so devoid of Christian charity, and wanting in so many of the essentials of honesty, cannot but be abandoned to their own folly by a just and benevolent God.

Our crew is keeping Christmas by a run on shore, which they all seem to enjoy exceedingly. It is, indeed, very grateful to the senses to ramble about over even so confined a space as the Arcas, after tossing about at sea in a continued state of excitement for months. Yesterday was the first time I touched the shore since I left Liverpool on the 18th August last, and I was only one week in Liverpool after a voyage of three weeks from the Bahamas; so that I have in fact been but one week on shore in five months. My thoughts naturally turn on this quiet Christmas-day, in this lonely island, to my dear family. I can only hope, and trust them to the protection of a merciful Providence. The only sign of a holiday on board tonight is the usual "splicing of the main-brace"—*Anglicè*, giving Jack an extra allowance of grog.

Friday, December 26th.—Weather fine, but the barometer has gone down the tenth of an inch today, and is now (7 p.m.) 29.96. I shall begin to look for a norther in about twenty-four hours. We commenced caulking our leaky decks today, and despatched the launch to assist in ballasting the *barque*. I strolled on the islands today, and amused myself searching for shells along the beach. There are some very pretty diminutive shells to be found, similar to those on the Florida coast; but none of a larger size than the common "conch," of which there are a few.

We have made free with the turtle nets of the fishermen found in the huts, and have set them. As yet, we have only caught two or three small turtle. I landed on the south island today, where they are getting off ballast. This islet is occupied exclusively by the black man-of-war bird; whilst the north islet seems to be divided between the white gannet (with the lower edges of its wings black) and the black warrior; the colonies being quite distinct. The birds are still laying and incubating.

Saturday, December 27th.—The barometer has risen again, and the weather still continues fine. Ballasting the *barque*, and overhauling and setting up our topmast and lower rigging, and caulking decks. Took a stroll in the north island towards sunset. It is dull recreation after the novelty has worn off, with the somewhat tough walking through the sand, and the smell and filth of the clouds of gannet.

Sunday, December 28th.—Weather cloudy, with the wind from the N.E. At 8.30 descried a schooner from aloft in the N.W., the first sail we have seen, and quite an unexpected sight at this season of the year. After we had armed and manned the cutter, to board the sail when it should heave in sight from the deck, it was ascertained that the lookout had been deceived, and that the supposed sail was probably a cloud in the horizon, it having suddenly disappeared.

At 11 p.m. mustered the crew and inspected the ship. A quiet Sabbath. Strolled on the island towards sunset, with the gannets for companions, the surf for music, and the heavy sand for a promenade. The weather cleared at nightfall, with the breeze fresh from the N.N.E. Some of the men are getting tired of their hard service; the chief boatswain's-mate having applied to return to England in the *barque*. Refused him permission, of course. Constant cruising, vigilance against being surprised by the enemy, salt provisions, and a deprivation of the pleasures of port, so dear to the heart of a seaman, are probably what most of them did not expect. A tight rein and plenty of work will cure the evil.

Monday, December 29th.—Weather clear and fine. At daylight hauled the *barque* alongside, and commenced coaling. Another seaman got drunk today, and seized his bag to go on board the *barque* to return to England. Confined him in double irons. Many of my fellows no doubt thought they were shipping in a sort of privateer, where they would have a jolly good time and plenty of license.

They have been woefully disappointed, for I have jerked them down with a strong hand, and now have a well-disciplined ship of war, punishment *invariably* follows immediately on the heels of the offence. It has taken me three or four months to accomplish this, but when it is considered that my little kingdom consisted of one hundred and ten of the most reckless from the groggeries of Liverpool, this is not much.

Tuesday, December 30th.—The weather still continues remarkably fine, with a moderate breeze from the E.S.E. We finished coaling today, and hauled the *barque* off in the afternoon. Getting ready generally for our dash at the enemy's coasts; or rather, at the enemy on our own coasts, of which he is in possession. A brig hove in sight today to the S. and E., approaching the islands on the starboard tack, until she became visible from the bridge, and then tacking—probably a Frenchman, making way from Vera Cruz to the eastward on the banks. Took my usual afternoon stroll on shore.

About nightfall, the sky assumes a peculiarly lurid aspect, becoming dark overhead, whilst the western horizon is lighted up with the rays of the setting sun, although there is not a cloud visible. One witnessing such a scene elsewhere would fancy himself on the eve of a storm; I attribute it to the reflection from the green waters of the bank. We have cleared away all the old eggs from the gannets' nests, and these prolific layers are now supplying us with fresh. Of fish we can catch none, except by trolling. We have no better success with our turtle nets.

Wednesday, December 31st.—The weather has been good all day, though we have had a heavy surf on all the reefs, indicating that there is a gale somewhere in our vicinity—probably a norther, along the Mexican coast to the west of us. The wind is at N.N.E. and moderate, and the barometer has been rising all day, though it has not been a tenth below 30.21; it is now (4 p.m.) 30.15, so we shall probably not feel the gale here.

Thursday, January 1st.—The first day of the new year. What will it bring forth? The Almighty for a wise purpose hides future events from the eyes of mortals, and all we can do is to perform well our parts, and trust the rest to His guidance. Success, as a general rule, attends him who is vigilant and active. It is useful to look back on the first day of the new year and see how we have spent the past; what errors we have committed, and of what faults we have been guilty, that we may in the future avoid the one and reform the other.

Although the wind blew pretty fresh during the past night, we did not feel the gale in any force; and today it has moderated, and the weather become fine again. Still caulking and painting. The former seems to be an interminable job with our small gang of caulkers. In the afternoon a brig approached the island, near enough to be seen, hull up, from the deck. She was beating up the bank to the eastward probably from Vera Cruz.

Friday, January 2nd.—The wind has been fresh all day from the eastward, bringing in some sea, and as we have been riding across the tide, the ship has had some motion. Caulking and painting, tarring down and squaring ratlines, &c. Commenced condensing water to supply the *barque* for her return voyage to England. I must get to sea on Tuesday, though I fear we shall not have finished caulking; but Banks' expedition must be assembling off Galveston, and time is of importance to us if we would strike a blow at it before it is all landed. My men will rebel a little yet. I was obliged today to trice one of them up for a little insolent behaviour.

Saturday, January 3rd.—A gale opened after all from the S.E., which I had hoped to escape, so rare is it to have blows from this quarter at this season of the year. We have veered to forty-five fathoms on each chain, and are in six fathoms water astern (there being nine where the anchors are), and are tailing directly on the surf, with a few hundred feet only between us and it, which of course makes me feel a little solicitude.

We are open to the S.E. winds, though these blow over the bank from landwards. Still the water is deep and the land distant, and a considerable sea comes in. I have ordered the fires to be lighted under another boiler to guard against accidents. The Arcas are a dirty little anchorage for large ships, being but an open roadstead, affording good shelter only from the north. There is a very small basin between the two reefs, running off from the northern island, fit for very small vessels, where they could be made secure against northerly and southerly winds; but everywhere they would be exposed more or less to wind from the westward.

Sunday, January 4th.—Weather clear, with the wind fresh from the S.E., dying away in the afternoon. Having determined to get to sea this evening, we commenced getting our coal-bags on board from the *barque*, omitting the usual Sunday muster. Busy with the seamen, as usual on such occasions, sending home their allotments, &c. The weather begins to portend a norther, so I have directed the engineer to hold on with his steam for the present.

Monday, January 5th.—It did not blow last night as I expected. This morning the wind has gone round again. I cannot wait longer for the norther,[1] so I must get under way. At 11 p.m. got under way, and stood out from the anchorage under steam. Let the steam go down, hoisted the propeller, and put the ship under sail.

---

1. One of the officers of the *Alabama* enters in his journal that on this day, in anticipation of news being received of Lincoln's proclamation, a tombstone, consisting of a board about four feet in length and two in breadth, was sent on shore and placed in the most prominent position the largest island afforded. Inscribed on the tombstone, in black letters on a white ground, was the following:—"In memory of Abraham Lincoln, President of the late United States, who died of nigger on the brain, 1st January, 1863."—"No. 290." Upon a piece of paper, protected from the weather, was written in Spanish—"Will the finder kindly favour me by forwarding this tablet to the United States Consul, at the first point he touches at?" This affair originated with, and was executed by, the steerage officers.

CHAPTER 23

Rescue of the Crew

Contrary to her usual aspirations, the principal wish of the *Alabama*, as she started on this fresh cruise, was to reach her destination without having seen a single vessel. She was now in fact on a service of a kind altogether different from that which had yet occupied her. In his address to the crew, upon taking command off Terceira, Captain Semmes had promised that the first moment they were in a condition of training and discipline, to enable them to encounter the enemy, they should have an opportunity of doing so. That time had come, and laying aside for a short period her more especial *rôle* of annihilating as rapidly as possible the enemy's commerce, the *Alabama* set steadily out in search of a fight.

The grand expedition of General Banks, which had been the subject of so much speculation in the United States, and of which their newspapers had long before duly informed the Confederate cruiser, seemed to offer the most favourable opportunity possible for such an enterprise. The expedition would, of course, be accompanied by one or more armed vessels, but the principal portion of it would be composed of troop-ships, crowded with the enemy's soldiers; and should the *Alabama* but prove victorious in the fight, these transports would be a prize of more practical importance than all the grain and all the oil ever carried in a merchantman's hold.

It was a daring adventure certainly. To steer, with a solitary light-armed sloop, close upon a coast, blockaded from north to south, by hundreds of armed vessels, in deliberate quest of a squadron, not improbably four or five times stronger than herself, was an act of almost reckless hardihood, fully in keeping with the rest of the *Alabama*'s career. The event indeed proved the full danger of the adventure; whilst, at the same time, nothing could have more clearly showed how utterly groundless were the dastardly imputations upon the courage and prowess of her crew, poured out daily from the foul-mouthed organs of the Northern press. There could be no question of the fighting qualities, or disposition, of the Confederate cruiser, after such a test as this.

For five days the *Alabama* kept steadily on her course for Galveston, where she expected to find the fleet of which she was in search. At length, on Sunday, the 11th January—her "lucky day"—the moment so anxiously looked for came.

Our position at noon—writes Captain Semmes—put us just within thirty miles of Galveston, and I stood on, intending either just to sight the shipping at a great distance, without being seen myself, or else to anchor just out of sight until the moon should rise the following night, which would be about half-past eleven, and then run in, and attack, as I hoped, "Banks' expedition." Owing, however, to a little carelessness in the look-out at "masthead," we were permitted to approach the ships anchored off the bar in such plain sight, before they were announced, that we were discovered, although we tacked immediately and stood off, in the hopes of eluding the vigilance of the enemy.

There were three ships found lying off the bar—one heavily-sparred ship, which our look-out took for a sail frigate, but which afterwards proved to be the *Brooklyn* steamer, our old friend that chased us in the *Sumter*, and two steamers supposed to be propellers. Very soon one of the steamers was seen to be getting up steam, and in about an hour and a half afterwards she was reported to be under weigh, standing out for us.

I lowered the propeller, and directed steam to be got in readiness, and awaited the approach of the stranger, who overhauled us very slowly, and seemed to reconnoitre us, as he came along, with great caution.

All this time we were standing on under topsails away from the bar, and the stranger was approaching us stern on. I gave my ship a little motion with the engine occasionally, both to draw the enemy—for I, of course, supposed him to be such—away from his consorts, so that in case of a conflict the latter might not hear our guns, and to prolong the time until dark to enable me to take in my topsails, and close with him in so short a time that the movement should not be noticed by him until too late to escape, which I feared he might attempt, if he saw me turn upon him with the intention of pursuing him.

Accordingly, soon after dark—the enemy in the meantime having approached us so near as not to endanger our losing sight of him—I clewed up, and furled the topsails, beat to quarters, and doubled suddenly upon the stranger. He came in quite boldly, and when within hailing distance of us, hailed us, and inquired—

"What ship is that?"

"Her Majesty's ship *Petrel*. What ship's that?"

To this inquiry there was no reply, and although we repeated it several times there was no rejoinder.

During the colloquy, I endeavoured to place myself in a raking position astern of him, which he as carefully avoided by keeping his broadside to me. From this manoeuvre I knew him pretty certainly to be an enemy, and having approached to within about two hundred yards, I directed my First Lieutenant to repeat the question. "What ship's that?" was accordingly again shouted, and this time there was a reply.

We distinctly heard that he was an United States something or other, but the name we could not make out. I then directed the First Lieutenant to tell him that this was the Confederate States steamer *Alabama*, and to open fire on him immediately, which we did from our starboard battery. He returned our fire in a minute or two, and the action was thus commenced.

We continued to run side by side at a distance ranging from two to five hundred yards, both of us keeping up a rapid fire of both artillery and rifles, when, after the lapse of thirteen minutes, the enemy fired two guns from his off, or starboard side, and showed a light above his deck in token of his being whipped.

At once we ceased firing, and approaching him still nearer, asked him if he surrendered and needed assistance. To both of these questions he replied in the affirmative, and we immediately despatched our quarter boats to him; these, with his own four boats, were busily employed in transporting the crew on board, which had only been accomplished when the ship went down. (See letter following.)

United States Consulate, Kingston,
Jamaica, Jan., 21, 1868.

Sir,—It is my painful duty to inform the Department of the destruction of the United States steamer *Hatteras*, recently under my command, by the rebel steamer *Alabama*, on the night of the 11th instant, off the coast of Texas. The circumstances of the disaster are as follows:—

Upon the afternoon of the 11th inst., at 2.30 p.m., while at anchor in company with the fleet under Commodore Bell, off Galveston, Texas, I was ordered by signal from the United States flag-ship *Brooklyn* to chase a sail to the southward and eastward. I got under weigh immediately, and steamed with all speed in the direction indicated. After some time, the strange sail could be seen from the *Hatteras*, and was ascertained to be a steamer, which fact I communicated to the flag-ship by signal. I continued the chase, and rapidly gained upon the suspicious vessel. Knowing the slow rate of speed of the *Hatteras*, I at once suspected that deception was being practised, and hence ordered the ship to be cleared for action, with everything in readiness for a determined attack and a vigorous defence.

When within about four miles of the vessel, I observed that she had ceased to steam, and was lying broadside and awaiting us. It was nearly seven o'clock, and quite dark; but notwithstanding the obscurity of the night, I felt assured, from the general character of the vessel and her manoeuvres, that I should soon encounter the rebel steamer *Alabama*. Being able to work but four guns on the side of the *Hatteras*—two short 32 pounders, one 30 pounder rifled Parrot gun, and one 20 pounder rifled gun,—I concluded to close with her that my guns might be effective, if necessary.

I came within easy speaking range—about seventy-five yards—and upon asking "What steamer is that?" received the answer, "Her Britannic Majesty's ship *Petrel*." I replied that I would send a boat aboard, and immediately gave the order. In the meantime the vessels were changing positions, the stranger endeavouring to gain a desirable position for a raking fire. Almost simultaneously with the piping away of the boat the strange craft again replied, "We are the Confederate steamer *Alabama*," which was accompanied with a broadside. I at the same moment returned the fire. Being well aware of the many vulnerable points of the *Hatteras*, I hoped, by closing with the *Alabama*, to be able to board her, and thus rid the seas of the piratical craft.

I steamed directly for the *Alabama*, but she was enabled by her great speed and the foulness of the bottom of the *Hatteras*, and consequently her diminished speed, to thwart my attempt when I had gained a distance of but thirty yards from her. At this range musket and pistol shots were exchanged. The firing continued with great vigour on both sides. At length a shell entered amidships in the hold, setting fire to it, and at the same instant—as I can hardly divide the time—a shell passed through the sick bay, exploding in an adjoining compartment, also producing fire. Another entered the cylinder, filling the engine-room and deck with steam, and depriving me of my power to manoeuvre the vessel, or to work the pumps, upon which the reduction of the fire depended.

With the vessel on fire in two places, and beyond human power, a hopeless wreck upon the waters, with her walking-beam shot away, and her engine rendered useless, I still maintained an active five, with the double hope of disabling the *Alabama* and attracting the attention of the fleet off Galveston, which was only twenty-eight miles distant.

It was soon reported to me that the shells had entered the *Hatteras* at the water-line, tearing off entire sheets of iron, and that the water was rushing in, utterly defying every attempt to remedy the evil, and that she was rapidly sinking. Learning the melancholy truth, and observing that the *Alabama* was on my port bow, entirely beyond the range of my guns, doubtless preparing for a raking fire of the deck, I felt I had no right to sacrifice uselessly, and without any desirable result, the lives of all under my command.

To prevent the blowing up of the *Hatteras* from the fire, which was making much progress, I ordered the magazine to be flooded, and afterwards a lee gun was fired. The *Alabama* then asked if assistance was desired, to which an affirmative answer was given.

The *Hatteras* was then going down, and in order to save the lives of my officers and men, I caused the armament on the port side to be thrown overboard. Had I not done so, I am confident the vessel would have gone down with many brave hearts and valuable lives. After considerable delay, caused by the report that a steamer was seen coming from Galveston, the *Alabama* sent us assistance; and I have the pleasure of informing the Department that every living being was conveyed safely from the *Hatteras* to the *Alabama*.

Two minutes after leaving the *Hatteras*, she went down, bow first, with her pennant at the masthead, with all her muskets and stores of every description, the enemy not being able, owing to her rapid sinking, to obtain a single weapon.

The battery upon the *Alabama* brought into action against the *Hatteras* numbered nine guns, consisting of six long 32 pounders, one 100 pounder, one 68 pounder, and one 24 pounder rifled gun. The great superiority of the *Alabama*, with her powerful battery, and her machinery under the water-line, must be at once recognized by the Department, who are familiar with the construction of the *Hatteras*, and her total unfitness for a conflict with a regular built vessel of war.

The distance between the *Hatteras* and the *Alabama* during the action varied from twenty-five to one hundred yards. Nearly fifty shots were fired from the *Hatteras*, and I presume a greater number from the *Alabama*.

I desire to refer to the efficient and active manner in which Acting-master Porter, executive officer, performed his duty. The conduct of the Assistant-surgeon, Edward S. Matthews, both during the action and afterwards, in attending to the wounded, demands my unqualified commendation. I would also bring to the favourable notice of the Department Acting-master's mate McGrath, temporarily performing duty as gunner. Owing to the darkness of the night and the peculiar construction of the *Hatteras*, I am only able to refer to the conduct of those officers who came under my especial attention; but from the character of the contest, and the amount of damage done to the *Alabama*, I have personally no reason to believe that any officer failed in his duty.

To the men of the *Hatteras* I cannot give too much praise. Their enthusiasm and bravery were of the highest order.

I enclose the report of Assistant-surgeon E.S. Matthews, by which you will observe that five men were wounded and two killed. The missing, it is hoped, reached the fleet at Galveston.

I shall communicate to the Department, in a separate report, the movements of myself and my command from the time of our transfer to the *Alabama* until the departure of the earliest mail from this place to the United States.

                I am, very respectfully, your obedient servant,
                H.C. Blake, Lieutenant Commanding.
                    Hon. Gideon Welles,
Secretary of the Navy, Washington.

For a further account of this action from the journal of one of the junior officers, see Appendix.

The prize proved to be the United States gunboat *Hatteras*, Lieutenant-Commanding H.C. Blake, which officer came on board after his crew had been transported, and delivered up his sword. I said to him:—

"I am glad to see you on board the *Alabama*, and we will endeavour to make your time as comfortable as possible."

The *Hatteras* had the following armament, *viz*.:—

32 pounders of 27 cwt.,	4
30 pounders, rifled,	2
20 pounders, rifled,	1
2 pounders, howitzer,	1
total,	8.

The armament of the *Alabama* was:—

32 pounders of 52 cwt.,	6
100 pounders, rifled,	1
24 pounders, rifled,	1
8-inch shell gun,	1
total,	9.

A great disparity in weight of metal in our power; but we equalized this to a considerable extent by the fair fight which we showed the enemy in approaching him so very close as to render his small guns almost as efficient as larger ones.

The tonnage of the *Hatteras* was eleven hundred tons; material, iron, with watertight compartments; age, eighteen months. Her crew numbered a hundred and eight men, and eighteen officers; our own numbering a hundred and eleven men, and twenty-six officers.

The casualties on both sides were slight. On board the enemy two were missing (firemen), supposed to have been killed in the fire-room, and three wounded, one of them severely, and two slightly. On board ourselves, only two slightly wounded.

After the action had been over an hour or more, and whilst I was steaming off on my course, it was reported to me that a boat of the enemy, containing an acting master and five men, which had been lowered before we opened fire upon him, to board "Her Majesty's steamer *Petrel*," had escaped.

As the sea was smooth and the wind blowing gently towards the shore, distant only about nineteen miles, this boat probably reached the shore in safety in five or six hours. The night was clear and starlit, and it would have no difficulty in shaping its course. But for these circumstances, I should have turned back to look for it, hopeless as this task must have proved in the dark. The weather continued moderate all night, and the wind to blow on shore.

It was ascertained that Galveston had been retaken by us, and that the *Brooklyn* and four of the enemy's steam-sloops were off the port, awaiting a reinforcement of three other ships from New Orleans to cannonade the place. So there was no "Banks' expedition," with its transports, heavily laden with troops, &c., to be attacked, and but for the bad lookout of our man at the masthead, we should have got instead into a hornet's nest.

CHAPTER 24

Reinstating the Discipline

The *Alabama*'s little fighting holiday was over, and she returned to her appointed task of annoying the enemy's commerce. Her course lay towards Jamaica, the captain being anxious to relieve himself as soon as possible of the nest of prisoners that crowded his decks, and were necessarily the occasion of considerable inconvenience to both men and officers. The latter especially were most uncomfortably crowded, the captain setting the example of self-sacrifice, by giving up his stateroom for the benefit of Lieutenant Blake, Commander of the sunken *Hatteras*.

It may be supposed that, under these circumstances, the *Alabama* was not very anxious to increase the number of her involuntary passengers. Still duty was duty, and when, on the day following the engagement, a sail was reported from aloft, chase was at once given, and expectation again on tiptoe at the thought of a prize. No prize, however, was to be taken that day. At about half-past two, the *Alabama* came within signal-distance of the chase, and was already busy exchanging the usual information, when the "stranger" *barque* was discovered to be no other than their old friend and faithful tender the *Agrippina*; and the *Alabama* continued her course, not a little amused at her own blunder in thus chasing her most particular friend.

Another week passed by with no event of interest, the *Alabama* working her way towards Jamaica, through a succession of more or less heavy gales, which, in the crowded state of the ship, were anything but comfortable. On the 20th January, she sighted land a little before daybreak, passing Portland at about 3 p.m., and arriving off the lighthouse on Plum Point at half-past four. Here French colours were displayed in case of accident, and a gun fired for a pilot. At about halt-past six, that important individual made his appearance, and in about three-quarters of an hour more the *Alabama* was safely at anchor in Port Royal harbour.

Wednesday, January 21st.—Found here several English men-of-war—the *Jason*, the *Challenger*, the *Greyhound*, &c., the Commanders of all of which called on us. I saw the Commodore (Dunlop) this morning, and requested of the Governor through him permission to land my prisoners, &c., which was readily granted. Made arrangements for coaling and provisioning the ship, and for repairing damages; and in the afternoon ran up to Kingston, and thence proceeded to the mountains with Mr. Fyfe.

Thursday, January 22nd.—Had a delightful ride over a fine, natural McAdamized road, for about ten miles, and thence by horse and bridle-path through the most picturesque of mountainous regions, with its lovely valleys, abrupt precipices, streams of water, luxuriant foliage, &c., to Flamstead, the residence of the Rev. Mr. Fyfe, who soon returned from town and received me most hospitably.[1] Spent a delightful, quiet day, riding to Flamstead, and walking in the afternoon along the winding mountain paths. Jamaica—that is, the south side-is a wilderness, and the town of Kingston a ruin. The negro population idle, thriftless, and greatly subject to diseases of an inflammatory kind. No morals—gross superstition, &c.

Friday, January 23rd.—Rode over to, and spent a day and night at, Blocksburgh, visiting *en route* the English-looking cottage of Captain Kent, now absent in England. Had some lady-visitors at Blocksburgh in the evening.

Saturday, January 24th.—Returned to town today by the way of Mr. Mais' fairy little cottage, kept in the nicest of order, and in a perfect picture of a country. Upon my arrival in town I found that my friends had *kindly* put a notice in the papers, informing the good people that I would be at the Exchange at noon, &c. &c. Was obliged to go, and made a speech to the people, which was well received. Returned on board in the evening.

---

1. As soon as our arrival became known the most intense excitement prevailed. It is impossible to describe the hospitable welcome we received, every one placing their houses at our disposal. Up to 9 p.m. visitors were constantly received, all expressing a most hearty, encouraging sympathy for our cause, and speaking hopefully for our prospects. Still the same enthusiasm prevails: visitors of each sex and every class coming on board, officers and men going on shore, and receiving the most flattering attentions.

Sunday, January 25th.—Workmen still engaged trying to get the ship ready for sea tonight. Returned my visits to the English Captains, all of whom I found very agreeable. Settling the ship's bills, and getting the drunken portion of my crew on board by aid of the police. Three of them in broad daylight jumped into a shore boat and tried to escape; but we pursued and captured them. Work all done, and fires lighted at 5 p.m., and at half-past eight we steamed out of the harbour.

Monday, January 26th.—At 10.30 p.m. descried a sail, which we came up with at 1.20 p.m. She proved to be the *Golden Rule*, from New York for Aspinwall. Captured and burned her, there being no certificate on board of the neutrality of the cargo. This vessel had on board masts, spars, and a complete set of rigging, for the United States brig *Bainbridge*, lately obliged to cut away her masts in a gale at Aspinwall. Nine prisoners. At about 6 p.m., the prize being well on fire, steamed on our course.

CASE OF THE *GOLDEN RULE*

No certificate of the neutral ownership of any portion of the cargo. The only bills of lading found on board are the following:—

Marcial and Co. to Gregorio Miro and Co., 2069.28 dollars; insured against war risk.

Keeler and Vonhiss to John Wilson, 724.20 dollars. Consigned to *order*, and for account and risk of "whom it may concern."

Woolsey, consigned to *order*. Amount not stated, and no letter of advice.

Berner to Field. Amount not stated, and no letter of advice.

Herques and Maseras to Juan Melendez, 41.58 dollars.

F. Hernias to Gillas. Amount not stated, and no letter.

The *Golden Rule* furnished a supply of papers containing an abundance of welcome news. From them the *Alabama* learned of the safe escape of her sister cruiser, the *Florida*, from Mobile, as well as of the foundering of the United States gunboat *Monitor* in a gale, during her passage down the coast. The good news was also received of the entire failure of an attack on Vicksburg.

The time was now pretty much taken up in reinstating the discipline which had been somewhat shaken by the brief stay at Port Royal, and in awarding due punishment for the various offences there committed. On the whole, however, considering the hard service the men had undergone, and the length of the confinement they had sustained without a single "spell" on shore, the offences could not be considered very numerous. A few of the petty officers were disrated, and various minor penalties inflicted, and on the 31st of January the court-martial, which had been employed on this unpleasant but necessary service, terminated its sittings and was dissolved.

Meanwhile another prize had fallen into the *Alabama*'s hands, in the shape of the United States brig *Chastelain*, of Boston, from Martinique and Guadaloupe for Cienfuegos; and the following day, after duly committing her prize to the flames, the *Alabama* arrived at San Domingo, dropping anchor off the town at 6 p.m.

In the harbour were two other vessels: one a New York brig, under English colours. The anchor had not been long down when a visit was received from the captain of the Port, who proved to be an old acquaintance of Captain Semmes, he having piloted the brig *Porpoise* about the island at the time when the latter officer was First Lieutenant of that vessel. He seemed much pleased to renew the acquaintance, and volunteered to take on shore, to the Governor, Captain Semmes' request for permission to land his prisoners.

Soon he returned, bringing with him a commander of the Spanish navy with the required permission. The prisoners were accordingly sent on shore, from whence they shortly returned, somewhat crestfallen, with the intelligence that no one was allowed to land after dark. The captain, however, being anxious to depart, application was made to the authorities, who courteously permitted the prisoners to be sent for the night to the government vessel, undertaking to send them on shore in the morning.

This matter was settled, the *Alabama* again stood out, having thus displayed for the first time, in San Domingo, the flag of the young republic.

The only excitement of the next few days was an alarm of fire, which, on the 2nd of February, occasioned for a short time very considerable anxiety. It came from the carelessness of the captain of the hold, who, in direct violation of the written rules of the ship, took a naked light into the spirit-room to pump off liquor by. The moment he commenced operations, the fumes of the spirit took fire, placing the ship for a few minutes in imminent peril. The danger, however, was brief, for the captain happened to be on deck at the time, and at once gave the order to beat to quarters; before it could be obeyed the fire was extinguished, and the ship's company *quitte pour la peur*. Not so, however, the delinquent captain of the hold, who was at once sent to expiate his fault in the durance vile of a suit of double irons.

The 3rd February brought a small prize in the United States schooner *Palmetto*, from New York for St. John's, Porto Rico, with a mixed cargo of provisions. She, too, laid claim to immunity on the ground of neutrality of cargo; but inquiry soon led to condemnation, and after taking from her a large quantity of biscuit, cheese, &c., the crew were removed on board the *Alabama*, and the schooner burned.

CASE OF THE *PALMETTO*.

The schooner was U.S., per register and flag. The cargo was shipped by Herques and Maseras, of New York, to Vincente Brothers, in San Juan, Porto Rico. There was no affidavit or certificate of neutral property on board, and the cargo would have been condemnable on this ground alone. It being in an enemy's ship, it is presumed to be enemy's property until the contrary be shown by proper evidence under oath. The Master, upon examination, testified that he had no knowledge of the ownership of the cargo; and this, though he was the agent and charterer of the ship, as well as Master. The correspondence found on board—that is to say, a letter from the shippers to the consignee-states that the cargo is shipped, two thirds on account of the consignee, and one third on account of the shippers—the parties being the joint owners of the *undivided* cargo in these proportions. Therefore, whatever may be the general business-relations of the parties, they are, *quoad* this shipment, partners; and the house in the enemy's country having shipped the goods, the other partner's share is condemnable, notwithstanding his residence in a neutral country. See 3rd *Phillimore*, 605; and the *Vigilantia*, 1 Rob., pp. 1-14, 19; the *Susa*, ib., p. 255.

Several days now passed without adventure of any kind, the monotony of alternate gales and calms being only varied by the receipt of a few old newspapers from the schooner *Hero*, of Yarmouth, N.S., giving news of the angry "resolutions" passed by the New York Chamber of Commerce with reference to the *Alabama*; and also—which was of considerably more importance—the information that the *Vanderbilt* and *Sacramento* were both to sail towards the end of January, in pursuit of the Confederate cruiser.

Sunday, the 15th February, dawned dark and gloomy, the wind blowing nearly a whole gale from the north, and the *Alabama* dashing along, with the wind well abeam, under reefed topsails.

This boisterous Sabbath, writes Captain Semmes, is the second anniversary of my resignation from the United States navy, and of course it has called up many reminiscences. I have more and more reason, as time rolls on, to be gratified at my prompt determination to quit the service of a corrupt and fanatical majority, which even then had overridden the constitution, and shown itself in so aggressive and unscrupulous a form as to give us just cause of alarm.

But what shall we say of its course since? If the historian perform his duty faithfully, posterity will be amazed at the wickedness and corruption of the Northern and Western peoples, and will wonder by what process such a depth of infamy was reached in so short a time.

The secret lies here. The politicians had become political stock-jobbers, and the seekers of wealth had become usurers and swindlers; and into these two classes may be divided nearly the whole Yankee population. Such is "Plymouth Rock" in our day, with its Beechers in the pulpit, and its Lincoln in the chair of Washington! With its Sumners and its Lovejoys in Congress, and its Simmonses *et id genus omne* in the contract market!

CHAPTER 25

Patience Rewarded

More than a week passed without the occurrence of any event worthy of record. Saturday, the 21st February, however, brought an exciting chase. By 8 p.m. four vessels had been reported in sight. The first seen proved too far ahead and to windward, to be worth chasing, and sail was then made in the direction of two others, which were observed to be exchanging signals with considerable diligence. Their conversation ended, they parted company and sailed off in different directions, evidently with the object of distracting the attention of the *Alabama* which was now in full chase.

But the *Alabama* was not so easily to be baffled. Devoting her attention first to the vessel which appeared by her slower rate of sailing to offer the promise of an easier capture, she got up steam as she went along, and the black smoke was already poured from her funnel and the propeller beginning to revolve as she came within hail of the chase. A blank cartridge was fired as usual; but the stranger kept doggedly upon his way, evidently determined, if he could not escape himself, at all events to do his best to increase the chances of his consort.

Even this chivalrous determination, however, was of no avail. A second gun from the pursuer quickly followed upon the first, and this time the command was pointed by the emphatic accompaniment of a round shot which went whizzing through the rigging of the chase. Finding his enemy in earnest, the ship now gave up the game, and hove to with the United States colours at her peak. Putting a prize crew on board, the *Alabama* wore round, and started at full speed in the direction of the second vessel, which was making the best of her way off, and was by this time some fifteen miles distant. The *Alabama* was now, however, under a full head of steam, flying through the water at the rate of three to one of the chase, and by the end of a couple of hours, she also was brought to, with the Stars and Stripes flying, and her main-topsail to the mast.

A rapid investigation of papers resulted in the decision that the claim of neutral ownership of the cargo was totally unsustained by evidence, and the crew of the *Olive Jane*[1] were transferred to the *Alabama*, and the *barque* set on fire, whilst her captor again came round and ran down to meet his other prize. On communicating with the prize-master in charge she proved to be the United States ship *Golden Eagle*, from Howland's Island in the Pacific Ocean to Cork for orders.

The following particulars relating to these two vessels, are given in Captain Semmes' journal:—

Case of the *Olive Jane*.

Under United States colours and register—from Bordeaux for New York—cargo consigned generally to houses in New York, with the exception of five of the shipments which are consigned to *order*; but there is no claim among the papers of French property, even in these latter shipments, and *non constat* but that the property is American, and that the consignment on the face of the papers was made in this manner to give a semblance of French ownership, until the property should reach its destination, when the real owner would claim it under a duly-indorsed bill of lading, forwarded to him by steamer. At all events, the presumption of law is, that all property found on board an enemy is enemy's property, until the contrary be shown by proper evidence; and no evidence has been presented in this case at all. The master, though quarter owner of the *barque*, and who, consequently, should be well informed as to her cargo, &c., knows nothing, except that one of the shippers—a Frenchman—told him that forty casks of wine, worth, perhaps, twenty dollars per cask, belonged to him. Vessel and cargo condemned.

Case of the *Golden Eagle*

Ship under United States colours and register. From San Francisco, *via* Howland's Island, for Cork, laden with guano by the American Guano Company. Cargo consigned to "orders." There is no question, therefore, of property. Ship and cargo condemned.

On the morning of the 23rd February four vessels were in sight; but on overhauling them they one and all proved to be under the

---

1. Of Boston, from Bordeaux to New York, with a partial cargo of French wines and "knickknackeries."

protection of neutral flags. One of them, however—a Frenchman from Buenos Ayres to Havre—relieved the *Alabama* of two French prisoners, an artist and his son, captured on board one of the late prizes. One of the other vessels—the *Prince of Wales*, from Melbourne to England—dipped her ensign to the Yankee colours displayed from the *Alabama*, on which the latter, unwilling to appropriate a compliment intended for another, lowered the Stars and Stripes and hoisted her own ensign.

Hardly had the change been effected when a bustle was observed on board the English vessel, and passengers and crew crowded on deck to have a look at the renowned Confederate. The formal compliment accorded to the flag first displayed was renewed with hearty good-will, and this time accompanied by the most enthusiastic demonstrations from all on board, the men cheering and the ladies waving their handkerchiefs in honour of the gallant little cruiser of which they had heard so much.

The next day, the *Alabama* being in the vicinity of the crossing of the 30th parallel by the San Roque and India-bound United States ships, sail was shortened, and a bright lookout kept, but until nearly sunset nothing was seen; and when, at length, "Sail, ho!" was cried, and the Confederate cruiser on nearing the stranger showed the Yankee colours, it was replied to by the tricolour of France. Again, at 9.30 p.m., when another vessel was descried, there was still no prize, although it required two cartridges, a chase of three-quarters of an hour, and vociferous demands in both English and French to compel the vessel to heave to.

When, at last, the Master obeyed the command, it was discovered that the brig was a Portuguese, bound from Pernambuco to Lisbon. The officer despatched to overhaul the chase found, on stepping on board, everything in the wildest confusion, and everybody so alarmed, that neither skipper, mates, nor seamen seemed to know what they were about. So great, indeed, was their trepidation, that upon an explanation being asked of their strange conduct, the excuse given was that they were too frightened to heave to!

The 25th February was a blank, only two sail being seen; the one a Dutchman, the other English. The master of the latter coolly asked the *Alabama* to take to England a discharged British seaman, and on the following morning another master of an English ship made a similar request—both being met with a refusal. On the 26th, no less than thirteen sail were sighted by the *Alabama*, but not one of them displayed the Yankee flag. The only excitement of the day was an obstinate Hamburgh *barque*, which refused to show colours until the Confederate cruiser was nearly upon her, and even then a blank cartridge was required to bring her to.

After the large number of neutrals that the *Alabama* had overhauled, came a prize. On the morning of the 27th February, the United States ship *Washington* was captured. The vessel was the property of the enemy, but as she carried a cargo of *guano* from the Chincha Islands, on account of the Peruvian government, consigned to their agents at Antwerp, the *Washington* was released on giving a ransom bond for 50,000 dollars. The prisoners on board the *Alabama* having been transferred to the capture, the two vessels parted company; the United States ship going on its course, rejoicing that the neutral cargo she carried had saved her from a fiery end. Two days after, another prize was taken. On the 1st March, the *Bethia Thayer*, of Rockland, Maine, was overhauled, and like the *Washington*, having on board *guano* the property of the Peruvian government, was released on a bond of 50,000 dollars.

Shortly after, a suspicious *barque*, with the English flag at the peak, hove in sight. Immediately the *Alabama* set every stitch of canvas, the stranger did the same, and away the two dashed before the fresh southwester that was blowing. The chase was most exciting, and lasted seven hours; but gradually the *Alabama* overhauled the suspicious craft, and at 4.30 p.m. was enabled to signal it. The Confederate hoisted the United States flag, and announced herself by an assumed name. The *barque* replied that she was the *William Edward*, from Bahia, for Liverpool.

After some further communication, which convinced the *Alabama* that the *barque* was English, the cruiser announced her real name, and permitted the *William Edward* to proceed on her course. At nightfall another ship was chased, which, upon being brought to, also proved to be English, the Nile, bound from Akyab to London. The master of this vessel informed the boarding-officer that a United States man-of-war, supposed to be the *Ino*, was in the South Atlantic, in eager search of the *Alabama*!

At daybreak, on the 2nd March, a sail was made out through the hazy atmosphere, slowly steering towards the cruiser. Patiently the Confederate waited, as the light wind from the south bore the stranger towards them; their patience, too, was rewarded, for at 6 p.m., a boarding-officer stepped on board the ship *John S. Parks*, of Hallowall, Maine. The skipper, his wife, and crew, were transferred to the cruiser, together with sundry stores and provisions; and then, after Captain Semmes had carefully examined the papers of the capture, the prize was set fire to, making number thirty-five on the list of the *Alabama*'s successes. With respect to the cargo of the *Parks*, there was a plea of neutrality set up, to which, as the following extracts will show, Captain Semmes gave the fullest consideration:—

Case of the Ship *John S. Parks*

Ship under U.S. colours and register. Cargo, white pine lumber, laden on board at the port of New York. The cargo was shipped by Edward F. Davidson, who appears, from the statement of the master, to be a large lumber dealer, and is consigned to Messrs. Zimmerman, Faris, and Co., at Monte Video, or Buenos Ayres. Annexed to the bill of lading is what purports to be an affidavit sworn to before "Pierrepont Edwards," who signs himself as "vice-consul." Above his name are the words, "by the consul," from which it appears he professes to act for the consul, and not for himself as "vice-consul."[2] The affiant is Joseph H. Snyder, who describes himself as of "128, Pearl Street, New York." He states that the cargo was shipped by Edward F. Davidson, "for and on account of John Fair and Co., of London, &c." First, as to the *form* of this affidavit.

A vice-consul is one who acts in place of a consul when the latter is absent from his post; and when this is the case, he signs himself as vice-consul, and his acts take effect *proprio vigore*, and not as the acts of the consul—which this act purports to do. Further, the Master was unable to verify this document, which, to give it validity, he should have been able to do—he declaring that he could not say whether it was a forgery or not. "Although, as has been said, the ship's papers found on board are proper evidence, yet they are so only when properly verified; for papers by themselves prove nothing, and are a mere dead letter if they are not supported by the oaths of persons in a

---

2. Extract from a letter, captured on the *barque Amazonian*, from Mr. Edward F. Davidson to Messrs. Zimmerman, Faris, and Co., of Monte Video:— "You will learn from London of the loss of the ship *John S. Parks*, and collection there of insurance on her cargo: the freight is insured here, at the Great Western Company. They have thirty days, after receipt of the captain's protest, to pay the loss in. Captain Cooper has arrived in Portland, and gone to his home at Hallowall; and the company require a copy of the protest made in London, certified by the Consul, which I have sent for. In the meantime, I have requested the captain to come to this, and trust not to have to wait receipt of the document from London."

situation to give them validity." 3rd *Phillimore*, 394. Further, "*Valin sur l'Ordonnance*" says, "*Il y a plus, et parceque les pièces en forme trouvées abord, peuvent encore avoir été concertées en fraude, il a été ordonné par arrêt de conseil du 26 Octobre, 1692, que les dépositions contraires des gens de l'équipage prís, prévaudrojent à ces pièces.*"

The latter authority is express to the point, that papers found on board a ship are not to be credited, if contradicted by the oath of any of the crew, and I take it that an inability to verify amounts to the same thing. For if this had been a *bonâ fide* transaction, it was the duty of the party interested to take the master before the consul to witness the taking of the deposition, so that he might verify "the paper," if captured. But why should Mr. Snyder be the party to make this affidavit? He was not the shipper, but Davidson, a lumber dealer; and Davidson, who, if he sold the lumber at all, must have known to whom he sold it, was the proper person to testify to the fact. Further: the master says that Snyder bought the lumber from Davidson, as he was informed by his (the master's) brother, who was the owner of the ship.

If so, then Snyder being the owner of the lumber (whether on his own or foreign account, it matters not) was the real shipper, and not Davidson, and the proper person to consign it to the consignees, either in his own name, or in the name of his principal, if he were an agent. But the bill of lading, and Davidson's letter to the consignees, show that Davidson was both the shipper and the consignor. The ship was also chartered by Davidson, and 13,000,000 dollars freight-money paid in advance, for which Davidson required the owner of the ship to secure him by a policy of insurance against both marine and *war* risk—the policy made payable to him (Davidson) in case of loss.

Two questions arise upon that policy: 1st—why, if the property were *bonâ fide* neutral (the cargo itself was also insured in London) the war clause should be inserted? and, 2nd—why Davidson should make the policy payable to himself? If he advanced this freight money on the credit of the London house, he had no insurable interest in it; and if the lumber really belonged to the London house, and was going to their partners or agents at the port of delivery, why should Davidson pay the freight in advance at all? And if Snyder purchased the lumber of Davidson, why should Snyder not have made the advance for his principal instead of Davidson?

The conclusion would seem to be, that Davidson was shipping this lumber on his own account to agents, in whose hands he had no funds or credit, and as the lumber might not be sold readily, the ship could not be paid her freight unless it were paid in advance? Further: the ship had a contingent destination. She was either to go to Monte Video or Buenos Ayres, as the consignees might find most advantageous. This looks very much like hunting for a market. But further still. Although Davidson prepared a formal letter of consignment to Zimmerman, Faris, and Co., to accompany the consular certificate, he at the same time writes another letter, in which he says, "The cargo of *John S. Parks* I shall have certified to by the British Consul as the property of British subjects. You will find it a very good cargo, and should command the highest prices."

How is Davidson interested in the price which this cargo will bring, if it belongs, as pretended, to the house in London? And if Davidson sold to Snyder, and Snyder was the agent of the house in London, Davidson should have still less concern with it. In that same letter in which a general account of recent lumber shipments is given, the following remarks occur:—"Messrs. Harbeck and Co. have a new *barque, Anne Sherwood,* in Portland, for which they have picked up in small lots a cargo of lumber costing 20,000 dollars. I have tried to make an arrangement for it to go to you (on account of John Fair and Co., of London?); but they as yet only propose to do so, you taking half-interest at twenty-five dollars, and freight at eighteen dollars, payable at yours (port?), which is too much. If I can arrange it on any fair terms, I will do so for the sake of keeping up your correspondence with H. and Co."

This letter would seem to show that Zimmerman, Faris, and Co. are favourite consignees with Davidson, and that he not only consigns his own lumber to them (for it must be remembered that he is a lumber dealer) but endeavours to befriend them by getting them other consignments. It may be that Davidson in New York, John Fair and Co., in London, and Zimmerman, Faris, and Co., in Buenos Ayres, are all connected in this lumber business, and that the trade is attempted to be covered under the name of the London house; or it may be that Davidson is the sole owner, or a joint owner with Zimmerman, Faris, and Co. In either case the property is condemnable, being shipped by the house of trade in the enemy's country. Ship and cargo condemned.

CHAPTER 26

Coaling at Sea Under Difficulties

Captain Cooper, of the *John Parks*, and his wife and two nephews, were fortunate in not being condemned to a long period of captivity. The burning remains of his unlucky vessel were still within sight, when an English *barque* ranged up alongside of the *Alabama*, and an arrangement was soon effected with her captain to convey the whole party to England.

A long interval now, with nothing but the Englishman's excitement—the weather—to break the weary monotony of an eventless voyage. So far, however, as gales of wind could offer a distraction, the *Alabama* had little of which to complain, and the vessel rolled and tumbled about in the heavy seas in a manner which sorely tried the endurance of, at all events, her unfortunate captain.

The gale still continues, writes Captain Semmes, on the 11th March. Wind E.N.E. For four days now we have been rolling and tumbling about, with the wind roaring day and night through the rigging, and rest more or less disturbed by the motion of the ship. Sea-life is becoming more and more distasteful to me. The fact is, I am reaching an age when men long for quiet and repose. During the war my services belong to my country, and ease must not be thought of; but I trust that the end is not afar off. The enemy, from many signs, is on the point of final discomfiture. Nay, a just Providence will doubtless punish the wicked fanatics who have waged this cruel and unjust war upon us, in a way to warn and astonish the nations upon earth. Infidelity and wickedness in every shape let loose upon themselves, must end in total destruction. The Yankee States have yet to go through an ordeal they little dreamed of in the beginning of their unholy crusade against the Southern people.

On the 12th, the vessel was within fourteen degrees of the equator, but so cool did the weather still continue that all hands were still wearing woollen clothing, and sleeping under a couple of blankets. The sky continued grey and overcast, with an occasional slight sprinkle of rain, and a stiff breeze. The barometer falling steadily until, on the 14th March, it had reached as low as 29.96, about the usual standard of the trade winds.

That night brought, however, a slight relief from the long dullness. It was just midnight when the startling cry of "Sail, ho! close aboard!" was heard from the lookout; and in less than five minutes the *Alabama* was within hailing distance of a large ship standing close on a wind towards the northward and westward.

"Ship ahoy!—what ship's that?" rang hoarsely through the speaking-trumpet from the deck of the *Alabama*. But no answer came, and the hail was repeated. Still no answer, the strange sail keeping steadily on her course, regardless of everything, her huge hull towering up high and dark as she passed almost within harpooning distance of the *Alabama*, and shot away again into the darkness, like a phantom that on being spoken to, had vanished away.

But the *Alabama* could have brought-to the *Flying Dutchman* himself, if he had attempted to pass by without answering a hail. "Hands, wear ship!" was the order before the sound of the second summons had well died away. Up went the helm, round came the *Alabama*'s head in the direction in which the stranger had disappeared; and with the reefs shaken out of her topsails, away she went in chase like a greyhound after a hare.

By the time sail was made, and headway got on the ship, the chase was some three miles in advance, and gliding swiftly along with a strong breeze. But though a stern chase is proverbially a long chase, the splendid sailing qualities of the *Alabama* soon made themselves felt, and within three hours after her helm was put up, she was within a few hundred yards of the stranger, who now hove to at the first summons from the cruiser's bow-guns.

She proved to be the United States ship *Punjaub*, of Boston, from Calcutta for London, and having an English cargo on board, as appeared from sworn affidavits among the papers, from the nature of the voyage—from one British port to another—and from the cargo of jute and linseed, she was released on a ransom bond for 55,000 dollars, the remaining prisoners from the *John Parks* being transferred to her for passage home.

The 21st March brought a change of weather, with heavy squalls of rain. The variety was greatly enjoyed by all on board, Captain Semmes recording in his journal his own pleasure at once more hearing the roll of the thunder, for the first time for many months, and the delight with which both officers and men paddled about on the deck with their bare feet, enjoying, "like young ducks," the first heavy rain they had experienced for a considerable time.

On the morning of Monday, March 23rd, a sail hove in sight, which, being overhauled about noon, was found to be the United States ship *Morning Star*, from Calcutta to London. This ship also had a neutral cargo, duly vouched as such by the proper legal certificates; so she, too, was released on ransom bond.

A second prize, however, which fell into the *Alabama*'s hands the same day, was less fortunate. This was the United States schooner *Kingfisher*, of Fairhaven, Massachusetts, some months out on a whaling voyage. It was well for her that she but very recently discharged into another vessel her second cargo of oil, and could only, at present, boast of some twenty barrels, all of which were at once consigned to the flames, together with the unlucky vessel.

The *Kingfisher* brought a piece of intelligence which afforded immense satisfaction to all on board, being of no less a fact than the presence of the United States sloop of war, *Ino*, at Ascension, where the *Kingfisher* had left her but a fortnight before. This was the identical vessel that had assisted in the piratical capture of Messrs. Myers and Tunstall, on neutral ground, scarcely fourteen months before; and all hands were rejoicing in the prospect of an early brush with her, when the outrage then perpetrated might be avenged. Anxious as all were for a fight on any terms, there was possibly not a vessel in the United States navy they would have more gladly encountered.

It was a curious circumstance connected with this schooner, that her master was, according to his account, one of the only three persons in his native place, Fairhaven, who, in the last fatal election of a President for the United States, had voted for the Southern candidate, Breckinridge.

Two more captures were made on the following day—one, the ship *Charles Hill*, of Boston, from Liverpool to Monte Video; the other, the ship *Nora*, also of Boston, from Liverpool for Calcutta. In both cases the usual claim was set up to a neutral ownership of cargo, and as usual on investigation proved to be altogether unsupported by anything like real evidence.

The following are the cases:—

Case of the Charles Hill

Ship under U.S. flag and register, laden with salt (value in Liverpool six shillings per ton), under charter party with H.E. Falk to proceed from Liverpool to Monte Video or Buenos Ayres. No claim of neutral property in the cargo. Ship and cargo condemned.

Case of the Nora

Ship under the U.S. flag; laden with salt, under charter party with W.N. de Mattos, of London, to proceed to Calcutta. In the bill of lading the cargo is consigned to "order;" and on the back of the bill is this endorsement:—

I hereby certify that the salt shipped on board the *Nora* is the property of W.N. de Mattos, of London, and that the said W.N. de Mattos is a British subject, and was so at the time of shipment.

(Signed) H.E. Falk,
Agent for W.N. de Mattos.

At the bottom of the signature is "R.C. Gardner, Mayor," presumed to be intended for the signature of the Mayor of Liverpool. As this statement is not under oath, and as there is no seal attached to it, it does not even amount to an *ex parte* affidavit. Vessel and cargo condemned.

Some valuable supplies were extracted from these two ships, and the prisoners—one of them a female—having been transferred to the *Alabama*, the vessels were fired on the evening of the day after their capture. As was but too frequently the case in boarding prizes, access was by some means obtained to their strong liquor, and that evening saw a good deal of drunkenness on board the *Alabama*. Unfortunately, the delinquents were but too often some of the best men in the ship. They could be trusted with anything in the world but rum or whisky; but against temptation of this kind they were not proof, and the duty of boarding offered only too easy an opportunity of indulging this true sailor's taste. However, if the prizes had their little bit of revenge in thus creating a temporary disorder among their captors, they in this case, at all events, more than made up for it, by contributing an accession of half-a-dozen seamen to the crew, which, notwithstanding the discharge of the men sent home in the——, was now fast growing very strong.

The following extract from a letter found on board the *Charles Hill* may throw some light on the pretensions of that vessel at all events, to the protection of neutrality:—

Captain F. Percival.

Dear Sir,—I have read your several letters from Philadelphia. As a rebel privateer has burned several American ships, it may be well if you can have your bills of lading endorsed as English property, and have your cargo certified to by the English Consul, &c.

After crossing the equator during the night of the 29th-30th March, the *Alabama* experienced a succession of calms and wet weather; at one time chasing a vessel in so thick a mist that, though not more than a mile or two ahead, she was more than once lost sight of for an hour at a time. She was still involved in this misty, uncomfortable weather, when, on the night of the 4th April, she again fell in with an United States ship, the *Louisa Hatch*, deeply laden with that, to the *Alabama*, most invaluable article—coal. An investigation of her papers gave the following result:—

Case of the *Louisa Hatch*

Ship, under U.S. colours. Among the papers is a charter party, dated London, 1st January, 1863, executed between John Pirie and Co., and William Grant, the Master, by which the ship was chartered to take coal to Point de Galle, Ceylon, or Singapore, as ordered, &c. Without any assignment of this contract, as far as appears, the ship seems to have been loaded by entirely new parties, to wit, by one J.R. Smith, who describes himself as the agent of H. Worms, of Cardiff. By the bill of lading, the ship is to proceed to the. Point de Galle, and there deliver the coal to the company of Messageries Imperiales. On the back of the bill of lading is the following certificate:—"I certify that the within-mentioned cargo is French property, having been shipped by order, for the account of the Messageries Imperiales."

This certificate is signed by Mr. Smith, but is not sworn to, nor is the order, nor any copy of the order to ship this cargo to an account of the Messageries Imperiales, found among the papers. As the ship was not chartered by any agent of this company, and as the coal was not shipped by any such agent, Smith being the agent of Worms, and Worms not being described as the agent of the company, the presumption is that, if there was any such order at all in the case, it was a mere general understanding that the company would pay so much per ton for coal delivered for them at their depots, the property remaining in the shippers until delivery. The presumption, in the absence of proof, is, that the cargo being on board an American ship is American; shipped on speculation to the far east, by the owner, or his agent, in Cardiff; and we have seen that there is no legal evidence in the case; the unsworn certificate of Mr. Smith not even amounting to an *ex parte* affidavit. Ship and cargo condemned. Probable value of cargo in Cardiff, 2500 dollars. Cost of coal in Brazil, 15 to 17 dollars per ton.

The *Alabama* now stood away in the direction of Fernando de Noronha, with her prize in company, with the intention of there taking on board a fresh supply of coal. The run was not a little protracted by the light and baffling winds that still prevailed, and as though this was not enough, fortune must needs play her a trick, by sending her off on a chase of fourteen miles after a supposed Yankee whaler, which, when at last overhauled, turned out to be nothing but a poor little green-painted "*Portiguee*."

Rain—rain—rain, the sun sometimes showing himself for an hour or two, just a few minutes too early, or a few minutes too late, for any purposes of observation, and then again retiring behind the dense masses of cloud that hid the whole horizon in one drenching downpour. And all this while every mile of latitude of the last importance, as the *Alabama* groped her way slowly to the southward and eastward in search of the little island at which she was to take in her supplies, and which she might at any moment run past in the darkness altogether! Trying work, indeed, for the patience of men cooped up in their narrow floating prison, and longing to be at work again.

Too trying, at last, to be borne any longer without an effort at action; so a bold attempt was made at coaling while under way upon the open sea! Steam was got up, and the prize taken in tow, and then two boats were lowered, and set to work. But the scheme, bold and ingenious as it was, was soon found to be impracticable. The boats managed to get loaded from the captured collier, but they had then to be warped up alongside the *Alabama*, and the lowest speed that could be given her was too great for them to be hauled up against it. So each time, as they were filled, it was necessary to stop the engine, and thus occasion another difficulty.

We now—says Captain Semmes—began to part our tow lines by these stoppages and startings, and it took a long time to get the line fast again; so after a sleepless night, during which, as I lay in my cot trying to sleep, it seemed as if a dozen stentors on deck were rivalling each other in making the night hideous, I sent word to get the boats run up again, and to continue our course to Fernando de Noronha without interruption.

At daylight we made the peak of the island a long way off, some thirty-eight or forty miles, and in the afternoon at 2.30 came to, with the peak bearing S.W. 1/2 S. and the N.E. end of the Rat Island N.E. by E. 1/2 E., depth of water thirteen and a half fathoms. Anchored the prize near us. But for our steam we should have been still drifting to the S.W., as the day has been nearly calm throughout. Fernando de Noronha, in the wayside of the commerce of all the world, is sighted by more ships, and visited by fewer, than any other spot of earth. It is a broken, picturesque, volcanic rock, in mid ocean, covered with a pleasing coat of verdure, including trees of some size, and the top of the main island is cultivated in small farms, &c. Awfully hot when the sun shines, and indeed, when he does not shine. Just after dark hauled the prize alongside, and commenced coaling.

CHAPTER 27

Landing Prisoners

April 11th.—Light and variable airs; misty from the southward and eastward, and oppressive; ther. 83°. Last night the two vessels lay alongside of each other so roughly, and we received so much damage (our forechannels being crushed in, and our topsail main-yard being carried away) that we were compelled to haul the prize off, and continue coaling by means of our boats.

The authorities on shore having hoisted no colours, we have not set ours today. We were visited this morning by a couple of gentlemen from the shore, bearing a letter from the Governor in reply to an inquiry I had caused the Paymaster to address to him on the subject of supplies. Their interpreter very naively informed me that he was a German, who had been sentenced to banishment here from Rio, and that he had a year and a-half to serve. This was said while my servant was drawing the cork of a champagne bottle. The forger (for such was his offence) taking his glass of wine with the rest! The Governor informed me that I could procure supplies of beef, fresh pork, fowls, &c., and that he would be glad to exchange these articles with me for flour, wine, sugar, coffee, &c.

I was glad to find that he raised no question of neutrality, though he had, no doubt, been informed by a boat's crew from the shore that got the information on board, of the ship in my company being a prize. He kindly invited me to visit the shore. During the night (one o'clock) we had a surprise in the way of a strange steamer making her appearance, coming round the point of Rat Island. I had all hands called to quarters, and the battery made ready, fires extinguished, and chains got right for slipping. Although she came within a mile of us, with the intention, as we thought, of coming to anchor, she kept on her course to the southward and we piped down, the men, much fagged from coaling, not having lost more than half an hour's rest by the operation.

Sunday, April 12th.—The exigencies of war compel me to work today in coaling ship. Weather clear and very hot during morning, clouding about noon and raining for several hours.

I visited the island this morning in company with the Surgeon, and called on the Governor. The surf was too heavy to land, but we found a *bolsa* moored at some distance from the shore, and transferring ourselves to this we were very skilfully put through the surf by three or four naked fellows, two of them not having even a breech-cloth about their loins. Fine, well-made fellows they were too. We found horses in waiting, and rode about a mile to the village and residence of the Governor—a major in the Brazilian army; passing an immense sand-drift, which we had not expected to find on this volcanic rock.

We found the Governor at breakfast, and he insisted on our seating ourselves, and making a second breakfast with him in company with his wife—a sprightly, bright *mulatto*—and a pretty girl, quite white, of about sixteen, and the *padre*. After breakfast we were introduced to a number of what appeared to be the gentry of the island, and who had assembled thus early to meet us. Having smoked and chatted awhile, we remounted for a ride over the island.

We were not in the saddle more than twenty minutes when one of those showers, so sudden in this climate, overtook us, and gave us a complete drenching; we had other showers during the day, but were compensated by the sun hiding himself during the entire ride. We passed under the shadow of the gigantic peak, and soon reached the summit of the island, which spreads out into a most beautiful and productive plain of some two or three hundred acres. The soil is a ferruginous clay of the richest description, and covered with the choicest vegetation of wild grapes, Indian corn, the cotton plant, the castor bean, &c., &c.

We stopped a few minutes to examine a manioc manufactory. Continuing our ride, we passed through a small but dense forest, to a cocoa-nut plantation on the south-west part of the island, where we found the water-melon growing in its choice soil—sand. Here we took shelter again from another heavy rain, and got some fine grapes. Whilst waiting for the shower to pass, I had quite a talk with the Governor on various topics; among others, on the state of the mixed races in the Brazils, &c., &c.

The island, at the season at which we visited it, was a gem of picturesque beauty—exceedingly broken and diversified with dells and rocks, and small streams, &c., &c. It was the middle of the rainy season. The little mountain paths as we returned became small brooks that hummed and purled in their rapid course. I took occasion to inform his Excellency that my tender was a prize, so that he might be under no apprehension. Number of convicts 1000. Whole number of population, 2000. The Governor expressed himself our very good friend, &c., &c. Got on board at 5 p.m.

Monday, April 13th.—Another rainy day. Showers very heavy, but still we continue our coaling. Wind from northward and westward, and though light, there is considerable sea on. The bad weather continued all day, and the night having set in with threatening appearances, I caused everybody to be brought on board from the prize, to guard against the possibility of her being driven on shore, and endangering life. I had the steam got up, and the chain ready for slipping, and was fearful that I should be obliged to slip; but we held on during the night. Night very dark, with heavy rain, and much sea on.

Tuesday, April 14th.—Wind this morning from about W.S.W.; weather still louring. Our friends came off from the shore again this morning, bringing the fresh provisions ordered for the crew. Everything is very dear here. Meat forty cents per pound; but still my crew has been so long on salt diet that flesh is an anti-scorbutic necessity for them. I have arranged to sell forty or more tons of coal for a Brazilian schooner there is in the harbour, and had a proposition for purchasing the prize, which I offered to sell as low as 20,000 dollars; but this sum seemed to alarm them, they saying there was not so much money in Fernando de Noronha. Continued our coaling.

Wednesday, April 15th.—Weather clear, and light wind from the eastward. Finished coaling ship this morning. At about 11 p.m. a couple of whale-boats from two vessels in the offing pulled into the harbour; went on board our prize, and thence to the shore. Although the two masters were told that we were the *Iroquois*, they seemed at once to have comprehended the true state of the case, and to make haste to put themselves out of harm's way. We were an hour and more getting up steam and weighing our anchor for the chase; and if in the meantime these whaling captains had pulled out to their ships, and run into shore so as to get within the league, they might have saved them. We gave chase, and came up with both of them on the south side of the island, about half-past 3 p.m., and captured them—both of them being without the league.

One the hermaphrodite brig *Kate Cory*, of Westport, and the other the *barque Lafayette*, of New Bedford; the *barque* we burned, and the brig we brought into the anchorage, arriving after dark, about 7 p.m. We sounded in thirteen fathoms on a bank on the south side, on the southern extremity of which there is a breaker lying out from two and a half to three miles. There is also a reef off Tobacco Point running out half a mile. We saw no other dangers.

With reference to these captures, the following amusing account is extracted from the private journal of the officer of the *Alabama* who was prize-master on board the *Louisa Hatch*:—

> At noon, on the 15th of April, two vessels were descried to the south, standing off and on, under reduced sail. At 12:30 two boats were observed pulling towards us, asking my ship's name, the port I hailed from, &c. I answered correctly. The person in charge of the other boat then inquired if the war-steamer was the *Alabama*. I replied, 'Certainly not, she was the *Iroquois* U.S. steamer.' 'Have you any news of the *Alabama*?' 'Yes, we had heard of her being in the West Indies, at Jamaica or Costa Rica, &c.' A conversation ensued, by which I learned that the boats belonged to the two vessels in the distance, that they were both whalers put in for supplies, and that seeing the steamer they were rather dubious as to her nationality, and had therefore spoke me, to gain the required information. A brisk conversation was then kept up; my object in engaging them in it was to enable the *Alabama* to get under way ere the whalers took the alarm, feeling certain that the preparations were being made to go after them.
>
> I then invited the masters to come on board my ship, which they cheerfully consented to do, and were within a boat's length, when a cry of alarm broke from the steersman in the foremost boat. Shouting to his crew to 'Give way, men; give way for your lives!' he with a few well-directed, vigorous strokes, turned his boat's head round, and made for the shore, the other boat following, blank astonishment being depicted on the face of each member of the crews. To the frantic inquiries of the person in charge of the other boat as to the cause of his (the steersman's) extraordinary conduct, his only reply was, 'There!' pointing to a small Confederate flag of about fifteen inches long and six inches broad, which I had inadvertently left flying at the gaff;

the gaff being lowered down, the little flag having been used as a dog-vane, in order to tell the direction of the wind, &c. No sooner did the men perceive it than they redoubled their exertions to gain the shore; one of the masters calling out that they had spoken a ship a week ago, from whom they had obtained news of peace. No credence, however, could be, or was placed in this statement.

Immediately after they left I despatched a boat to the *Alabama* informing them of the character of my visitors. At 9.15 the *Alabama* was observed to get under way, steaming out of the anchorage after the two vessels.

The larger island being between the scene of the *Alabama*'s operations and the *Louisa Hatch*, I was not, of course, an eye witness of the captures. But at 5.30 I observed a dense column of smoke, which, as it grew later, turned into a ruddy glare, leaving no doubt in our minds as to the fate of the whalers. At 7 p.m. observed the *Alabama* coming round the northern part of the island with a vessel in tow, both anchoring at 7.30. The next morning I learnt that the captures were the *barque Lafayette*, of New Bedford, and the brig *Kate Cory*, of Westport. The *barque* was burnt and the brig kept, it being our intention to send off all the prisoners we had on board, consisting of 140, including the women stewardesses, in her; but on communicating with the authorities, it was resolved to land them on the island, a Brazilian schooner engaging to convey them to Pernambuco. For this purpose provisions for twenty-one days were sent ashore, the prisoners, after being paroled, following.

The remainder of the day was spent in transferring provisions, &c., for ship's use. The next evening the prizes, the *Louisa Hatch* and *Kate Cory*, slipped cables, and stood seaward. When about five miles from land both vessels were set fire to; Mr. Evans, the officer in charge of the brig, returning on board long before me, the strong westerly current rendering it extremely difficult to stem it.

We remained painting and cleaning ship until the 22nd. At 9.30 p.m. we got under way, steering and cruising towards Bahia, at which place we arrived on the 11th of May, having captured and burnt four vessels between Fernando and Bahia.

'The news of our doings off the islands had preceded us, of course with additions and manipulations *ad lib.*, the schooner having left Noronha the day previous to our departure. The Governor of Pernambuco had sent three war vessels to the islands to enforce the neutrality of the place, which, according to Yankee representations, had been infringed. Not content with this, the American representatives had succeeded in procuring the recall of the Governor, whose only crime was that he had let us anchor off the place—a crime of which he was necessarily guiltless, because he had no power to prevent our anchoring if we insisted on it.

Whilst at Bahia I was shown a letter from the master of one of the whaling *barques* to an agent, in which he wrote that he would spare no money or time to follow to the uttermost ends of the earth, and bring to justice, the man who had so cruelly deceived him. This sentence had reference to my denial of the *Alabama* and the substitution of the U.S. steamer *Iroquois* for that of C.S. steamer *Alabama*. The ingratitude of some people!!

On the 16th April Captain Semmes resumes his diary as follows:- Weather clear; wind light from the southward and eastward. Our banner, last night a lurid flame, is a tall column of smoke advertising us for twenty-five or thirty miles round. My first intention was to ship all my prisoners, amounting to about one hundred and ten, in the prize brig, but the Governor having consented to my landing them, I am busy today getting them on shore, with their baggage and provisions, and receiving prisoners from the *Louisa Hatch*. Sun very warm. The Governor paid me a visit this morning, and requested that I would write him on the subject of the captures yesterday, stating the fact (with which he was satisfied, or at least, to which he made no objection) that they were captured beyond the league from the land, and requesting leave to land the prisoners, in order that our understanding should assume an official shape, which I did.

Friday, April 17th.—The weather still continues very warm; wind light from the S.E., and cloudy. Busy receiving and stowing away provisions, replacing the coal consumed, and getting ready for sea generally. The landing of so many prisoners amid so small a population has created a very great stir, and the excitable Brazilians are discussing among themselves and with the Yankee captains the question of the American war with great vehemence. Several sail have been reported as usual. The afternoon set in rainy, and the rain continued all night. Towards nightfall sent the prizes, *Louisa Hatch* and *Kate Cory*, a league outside the island, and burned them. Received four recruits from the *Louisa Hatch*, and more volunteered, but I am full.

Saturday, April 18th.—Morning cloudy, with wind light from the S.E. Loosed sails today. I am anxiously expecting the arrival of the *Agrippina*, my store ship, from England, which was ordered to rendezvous here—not so anxiously, however, as if my coal-bunkers were empty. But she has a couple of additional guns on board, that would make an important addition to my battery.

Sunday, April 19th.—Rain in the morning, with light airs. Our steam-tubes leak badly, and I am afraid the leaks will increase so as to give us trouble. Every time we get up steam, even a few pounds for condensing water, we find that large quantities of hot water flow into the hold; eight inches escaped in about twelve hours yesterday. Unfortunately, too, this tubing is laid so low in the bottom of the ship, as to be out of reach for examination or repairs without being taken up. The Governor sent me off a fine turkey and some fruit, and his lady a bouquet of roses. The roses were very sweet, and made me homesick for a while.

Monday, April 20th.—A dull, heavy, rainy day—the rain coming down at intervals in torrents, as it is wont to do in these regions. Still laying at our anchors, waiting for the *Agrippina*. She should be out thirty-five days, today, from Cardiff. In the afternoon the rain ceased, except an occasional light sprinkle, but the dull canopy of clouds did not break, and we had a strong breeze from the S.E. for four or five hours, indicating the approach of the trades to this latitude.

Tuesday, April 21st.—Morning clear, wind light from S.E. The Island after the rain is blooming in freshness and verdure, and as my eye roams over its green slopes I long for repose and the quiet of peace in my own land: I do not think it can be far off. Fresh "trade" in the afternoon. Towards night the Brazilian steamer sailed with a load of our prisoners.

Wednesday, April 22nd.—Cloudy, with squalls for rain. At 9.30 got under way under steam, and stood to the eastward. Cut away four whale-boats that the islanders might have a scramble for them. They soon started in chase! Steamed due east, about forty-five miles, let the steam go down, and put the ship under sail. No sail seen.

CHAPTER 28

Homesick

A curious prize was the next that fell into the clutches of the all-devouring *Alabama*. A whaling *barque*, the *Nye*, of New Bedford, eleven months out, without having once put into port! Three whole months before the launching of the *Alabama*, had that patient little vessel been ploughing the seas, gathering, as it turned out, only additional fuel for her own funeral pyre. A weary voyage to have so sad a termination!

Among her crew, transferred as prisoners to her captor, was a lieutenant of Marines from the Quaker State, serving on board the whaler in the capacity of steward!

Next came the *Dorcas Prince*, of and from New York, for Shanghai. Cargo chiefly coal, probably intended for United States ships of war in the East Indies—a supposition that undoubtedly gave additional zest to the bonfire, which—no claim to neutrality being found among her papers—in due course followed on her capture.

*Saturday, May 2*nd.—An anniversary with me—writes Captain Semmes—my marriage-day. Alas! this is the third anniversary since I was separated from my family by this Yankee war! And the destruction of fifty of their ships has been but a small revenge for this great privation.

On that day two more were added to the long list, and the *barque Union Jack*, of Boston, and ship *Sea Lark*, of New York, shared the fate of their fifty predecessors. The former of these two vessels added three women and two infants to the already far too numerous colony of the weaker sex, by which the *Alabama* was now encumbered.

There was no claim of neutral property among the papers of either of these ships, except in the case of one Allen Hay, who was the shipper of five cases of crackers, and ten barrels of butter, on board the *Union Jack*. In this case, a Thomas W. Lielie made oath before the British Consul at New York, that the said articles were shipped "for and on account of Her Britannic Majesty." This certificate was of no force or effect, for its *indefiniteness*, as decided in other cases. A claim of property must point out the owner or owners, and not aver that it belongs to the subjects of a nation generally. There must be someone designated who has a right to the possession of the property under the bill of lading. The certificate was accordingly set aside, and the ship and cargo condemned.

Besides the women and children, the *Union Jack* furnished also another prisoner of a somewhat unusual character, in the person of the Rev. Franklin Wright, late editor of a religious paper, and newly-appointed consul at Foo Chow. The worthy clergyman's entry, however, upon his new duties was for the time indefinitely postponed by the confiscation of his appointment, along with the other public papers in his charge. So, for a time, Foo Chow had to exist without the advantages arising from the presence of a functionary from the United States.

Monday, May 11th.—Showed the United States colours to a Spanish brig. In the afternoon ran in and anchored in the harbour of Bahia. A Portuguese steamer, the only vessel of war found here. No Yankee man-of-war had been here for some months. The health officer came on board, just at nightfall. The *Agrippina* not here, and I begin to fear that some disaster has befallen her.

Tuesday, May 12th.—This morning the President sent a messenger to me with a copy of the *Diario de Bahia* of the 8th May, in which appears a sort of proclamation or request, addressed to me by the President of Pernambuco, desiring that I should leave Fernando de Noronha in twenty-four hours after the receipt of the same. This paper seems to be based on certain false statements carried to Pernambuco by the Yankee prisoners whom I had sent to this place. It is alleged that I violated the neutrality of the island, &c. I replied to the President, that there was no truth in this statement; but that, on the contrary, I had paid respect to the neutrality of Brazil.

In reply to my communication, the President informed me that I should be admitted to the usual hospitalities of the port; but the bearer of his despatch took occasion to say that he hoped I would not stop more than three or four days, as the President was afraid of being compromised in some way. The master of an English *barque* came on board and informed me that he had coal and provisions for the Confederate steamer Japan, which was to meet him here on the 6th instant.

Wednesday, May 13th.—Early this morning a strange steamer was discovered at anchor about half a mile from us; and at 8 p.m., when we hoisted our colours, to our great surprise and delight, she too hoisted the Confederate flag. We then exchanged the established signals; and on sending a boat on board of her, we ascertained that she was the *Georgia*, Lieutenant Commanding Maury. Chapman and Evans, two of my *Sumter* lieutenants, were on board of her. The *Georgia* sailed from England about the 2nd of April, and armed off Ushant. Our ship has been crowded with visitors ever since we came in.

Thursday, May 14th.—At 12.15 p.m. with a party of officers from the *Georgia* and my own ship, I took a steam-tug and proceeded up the harbour to the railroad depot, at the invitation of the manager of the road, for an excursion into the country, which proved to be very pleasant. We passed along the whole port of Bahia, the lower town skirting the water, and the upper town the crests of a semicircular height, the intermediate space being filled with trees and shrubbery. The houses are mostly white, and many of them very picturesque. The terminus of the road is a beautiful and spacious iron building, situated in the middle of a great square; and the road itself is a very substantial job.

We rode out twenty-four miles through a picturesque country, the road bordered for most of the way by the bay and lagoons, with beautiful little valleys occasionally opening on either hand, with their patches of sugar-cane and cotton. On our return we sat down to a beautiful lunch, with champagne. Our hosts were attentive and agreeable, and we returned on board at dusk, after a very pleasant day. The English residents here have been very attentive to us. Our tug-man, who was a Thames waterman, dodged in and out among the launches and vessels in a way that only a Thames man can do. The French mail came in today, and brought us news that the *Florida* was at Pernambuco.

Friday, May 15th.—This morning a person in citizen's dress came on board and said that the President had requested him to ask me to show him my commission. I replied that I could have no objection to show my commission, but it must be to an officer of my own rank, and that this officer must come on board in his uniform for the purpose; that I could not show my commission to any person who might come on board in citizen's dress, bringing me a mere verbal message, and without any credentials of his rank, &c. I remarked, however, that it would give me very great pleasure to call on the President myself and exhibit it. To this he readily assented; and having appointed an hour for the interview, I went on shore, accompanied by my *aide*, and had a long and agreeable chat with his Excellency, who was a man of about thirty-five years of age, tall and delicate-looking, with black eyes and hair.

We discussed various points relating to the subject of neutral and belligerent rights, &c.; and I took occasion to repeat the assurances I had previously given him in my letter, that I had paid due attention to the neutral rights of Brazil during my visit to Fernando de Noronha, &c. I told him I only desired him to extend to me and to the *Georgia* the same hospitality as he would extend to a Federal cruiser; but that I might say to him as an individual, that we were entitled to the warm sympathies of Brazil, &c.

I arranged about coaling the *Georgia* and this ship by means of launches, as there were port objections to the ship being hauled alongside. He seemed anxious that our stay should be as short as possible, lest our delay might compromise his neutrality in some way. He said my sailors had been behaving very badly on shore, and indeed I knew they had. I told him he would oblige me by securing the rioters and putting them in prison. This evening we were entertained very handsomely at the residence of Mr. Ogilvie, where we met all the English society of the place.

Saturday, May 16th.—This day the ship (*Castor*), from which the *Georgia* was coaling, was ordered to be hauled off, and the operation suspended, the Yankee Consul having alleged to the Government that she had munitions of war on board.

Sunday, May 17th.—In the morning an officer came on board and read me a despatch from the President, expressing displeasure at my remaining so long in the port, and directing me to proceed to sea in twenty-four hours. The same paper was read on board the *Georgia*. I replied that the Government itself had caused our delay, by prohibiting us from coaling from the ship from which we had purchased our coal; and that I could go to sea in twenty-four hours after this prohibition was removed, &c., &c. A party of English ladies and gentlemen visited the ship this afternoon. We were crowded all day, besides, with miscellaneous visitors.

Tuesday, May 19th.—This morning, at the request of the President, I went on shore to see him, and we had a long and animated discussion, in which he stated he had certain proofs, adduced by the United States Consul, to the effect that the coal-ship *Castor* had been sent here to meet us, &c.; and that under these circumstances (the ship being charged, besides, with having munitions of war on board), he felt it his duty to prevent us from coaling from her, but that we might have free access to the market, &c. The Consul, too, had told him that I had shipped one of the prisoners after landing him: the fact being that, although many of them volunteered, I refused to receive any of them, having already a full crew on board. In the afternoon addressed a letter to the President, insisting upon the right to coal from the *Castor*.

Wednesday, May 20th.—We were promised lighters with coal from the shore this morning; but not one has yet come off—half-past twelve. Just at nightfall a lighter came alongside, and during the night we filled up. The next day we got under way and steamed out of the harbour.

Sunday, May 24th.—I am quite homesick this quiet Sunday morning. I am now two *long, long* years away from my family, and there are no signs of an abatement of the war; on the contrary, the Yankees seem to become more and more infuriated, and nothing short of a war of invasion is likely to bring them to terms, unless indeed it be the destruction of their commerce; and for this, I fear, we are as yet too weak. If we can get and hold Kentucky, the case may be different. Well, we must sacrifice our natural yearnings on the altar of our country, for without a country we can have no home.

Chapter 29

Short of Provisions

The 25th May witnessed the capture of the ship *Gildersliene* and the *barque Justina*. The latter having a neutral cargo, was ransomed on a bond for 7000 dollars; the former condemned and burned, after an investigation terminating in the following decision:—

CASE OF THE *GILDERSLIENE*

Ship under the United States colours and register. Charter-party with Messrs. Halliday, Fox, and Co., of London, who describe themselves as merchants and freighters, to make a voyage to Calcutta and back to London or Liverpool. Cargo taken in at Sunderland, and consisting of coal, said to be shipped for the "service of the Peninsular and Oriental Steam Navigation Company," but not even averred to be on "their account and risk." No certificate or other evidence of property; ship and cargo condemned. Master knows nothing of property except what appears by the papers.

Friday, May 29th.—We had another chase last night from about 2 p.m., but with better success than the two previous nights, since at 7.30 p.m. we came up with and captured the ship *Jabez Snow*, of Rockport, Maine. Just at daylight, being within about four miles of her, we hoisted our own colours, and fired a gun. She did not show any colours in return, and stood a second gun before heaving to; she finally showed her colours. Got on board from the prize a quantity of provisions and cordage; transhipped the crew, and about sunset set her on fire. Found a letter on board, the writer of which referred to American ships being under a cloud "owing to dangers from pirates, more politely styled privateers," which our kind friends in England are so willing "should slip out of their ports to prey on our commerce." This letter was dated Boston, November 25th, 1862.

Case of the *Jabez Snow*

Ship under United States colours, cargo coals, from Cardiff for Monte Video. On the face of the bill of lading is the following:

> We certify that the cargo of coals per *Jabez Snow*, for which this is the bill of lading, is the *bonâ fide* property of Messrs. Wilson, Holt, Lane, & Co., and that the same are British subjects and merchants; And also that the coals are for their own use.
>
> Jno. Powell & Sons.

As this certificate was not sworn to, it added no force to the bill of lading, as every bill of lading is an unsworn certificate of the facts it recites. There being no legal proof among the papers to contradict the presumption that all property found under the enemy's flag is enemy's property, and as the master, who was the charterer and agent of the ship, and whose duty it was to know about all the transactions in which he was engaged, swore that he had no personal knowledge of the owner of the cargo, except such as he derived from the ship's papers, the cargo, as well as the ship, is condemned as prize of war. The following significant extract from a letter of the Master to his owners, dated Penrith Roads, April 19th, 1863, was found on board, though not produced by the master:—

> I have my bills of lading certified by the mayor, that the cargo is *bonâ fide* English property. Whether this will be of any service to me in the event of my being overhauled by a Southern pirate, remains to be proved.

The certificate above recited seems, therefore, to have been procured by the master to protect his ship from capture, and not to have been a spontaneous act of the pretended neutral owners to protect the cargo. The cargo and advance freight were insured against war-risk, the ship paying the premium. No effort was made by Wilson, Holt, Lane, & Co., to protect the cargo, and they were the proper parties to make the oath. The agent who shipped the coal for this firm, and who wrote the above-quoted certificate, could only know, of course, that he had shipped them by order of his principal. Why, then, did Wilson, Holt, Lane, & Co., decline to make the necessary oath to protect the cargo? They should have taken the necessary steps to protect either themselves or the insurers, but they did no such thing. It would seem, probably, that they were the agents of some American house, and that they could not, in conscience, take the oath required by law.

The next prize was the *Amazonian*, of Boston, from New York to

Monte Video, captured, after a long chase, on the 2nd of June, but not until two blank shots had failed to bring her to, and the stronger hint of a round from the rifled gun had convinced her of the impossibility of escape.

Case of the *Barque Amazonian*

Ship under United States colours; has an assorted cargo on board, and is bound from New York to Monte Video. There are two claims of neutral property—one for twenty cases of varnish and fifty casks of oil, claimed as shipped on "account of Messrs. Galli & Co., French subjects." This claim is sworn to by a Mr. Craig, before a notary. It does not aver that the property is in Messrs. Galli & Co., but simply that it was shipped "on their account." There is no outside evidence of the truth of this transaction, as the master knows nothing about it.

Right glad was the *Alabama* to fall in, on the day after this last capture, with an English brigantine, the master of which proved willing, in consideration of a gift from Captain Semmes of one of his noble collection of captured chronometers, to relieve him of the crowd of prisoners with which he was encumbered. To the number of forty-one they were forthwith transferred, along with a stock of provisions sufficient for a fortnight's consumption; and the *Alabama* breathed freely again, relieved of her disagreeable charge.

It may not be an uninstructive, and it is most assuredly an amusing comment, upon the claims of neutrality so loudly insisted upon, to quote the following extract from a New York letter, captured on board one of the recent prizes. It is dated April 7th, and addressed to a correspondent in Buenos Ayres:—

> When you ship in American vessels, it would be as well to have the British Consul's certificate of English property attached to the bill of lading and invoices; as in the event of falling in with the numerous privateers, it would save both cargo and vessel, in all probability. An American ship, recently fallen in with, was released by the *Alabama* on account of a British Consul's certificate showing the greater part of the cargo to be English property. If you ship in a neutral vessel, we save five *per cent*, war insurances.

Another prize. *The Talisman*, a fine ship of 1100 tons, under United States colours and register, with no claim of neutral property in cargo; and before the glare of her funeral pyre had faded from the horizon, another hove in sight, so evidently American, that notwithstanding the English ensign flying at her peak, she was at once brought to and boarded. And American she proved to be in her origin; but her owners had been wise, and, so far as her papers went, she had been regularly transferred to the protection of the British flag—humiliating, perhaps, to the proud "Yankee nation," but effective as a precaution against capture; though, had the Confederate cruiser been able to send her into port for adjudication, the transfer might very possibly, when the evidence came to be sifted, have proved but a "bogus transaction" after all.

So the "Englishman" had to be released, consenting, however, to relieve the *Alabama* of a prisoner and his wife, recently captured on board the *Talisman*. A week passed away, and then came another instance of a similar transfer under the strong pressure of fear, the whilom Yankee *barque Joseph Hall*, of Portland, Maine, now seeking a humiliating safety as the "British" *Azzopadi*, of Port Lewis, Isle of France!

Alas! for the Stars and Stripes, the *Azzopadi* was not hull down on the horizon ere the once-renowned Yankee clipper Challenger lay humbly, with her main-topsail to the mast, in the very place in which her countryman had just been performing a similar penance, claiming, as the British-owned *Queen of Beauty*, a similar immunity.

At last, however, as the impatient crew of the *Alabama* were beginning to think that their enemy's flag had finally vanished from the face of the ocean, an adventurous *barque* hove in sight, with the old familiar bunting at her peak. She proved to be the *Conrad*, of Philadelphia, from Buenos Ayres for New York, partly laden with wool, the ownership of which was, as usual, claimed as neutral. On investigation, the claim proved an evident-fabrication, the facts of the case being as follows:—

Case of the *Conrad*

Ship under American colours and register. A Mr. Thomas Armstrong, who describes himself as a British subject doing business at Buenos Ayres, makes oath before the British Consul that a part of this wool belongs to him and a part to Don Frederico Elortando, a subject of the Argentine Republic. This may or may not be true, but the master is unable to verify the document, he not having been present when it was prepared, and not knowing anything about it. There is, besides, so strong a current of American trade with Buenos Ayres, that the presumption is, from the very fact that this wool was going to New York in an American *barque*, under the imminency of capture, which our presence in these seas—well known at Buenos Ayres when the *barque* sailed—must have shown, that the property is American, and that the certificate is an attempt to cover it; Mr. Armstrong probably being a brother or a partner in the transaction with some American house. Ship and cargo condemned.

Further Examination of Case of Conrad

From an examination of the correspondence in this case, brought on board after the ship's papers had been examined, it appeared that Mr. Armstrong, the party shipping a part of the cargo, swears before *his* consul that he and one Don Frederico Elortando, are the *owners* of the property, and swears before the United States Consul that he is the sole *owner* of the property. Both of these oaths cannot be true. It further appears that, whilst the property in the bill of lading is consigned to Simon de Visser, Esq., in the letters of Messrs. Kirkland and Von Sachs it is spoken of as consigned to them. The letters make no mention of any joint-ownership with Armstrong, but treat the consignment as his sole property. But though, like so many of her countrymen, condemned, the *Conrad* was not to die.

A nobler fate was in store for her—no less a destiny than that of carrying the proud young flag to which she had succumbed, and taking the sea, under a new name, as the consort of her captor. Accordingly, Acting-Lieutenant Low was appointed to the command, assisted by Acting-Master Sinclair and two master's mates. The two rifled pounders captured in the *Talisman* were mounted on board, a due complement of rifles, revolvers, ammunition, &c., supplied, and then the transformed *barque* fired her first gun, ran up the Confederate ensign to her peak, and amid a burst of cheering from her own crew and that of her consort, made a fresh start in life as the Confederate States sloop-of-war *Tuscaloosa*.

The *Alabama* was now bound for the Cape of Good Hope, where her faithful tender, the *Agrippina*, was again to meet her. On the 27th of June, however, when in lat. 20.01 S., long. 28.29 W., it was discovered that a great portion of the supposed month's supply of bread had been destroyed by weevils, and that there was not enough left for the run. A visit to some port nearer at hand thus became inevitable, and the ship's course was accordingly shaped for Rio Janeiro.

CHAPTER 30

The Capture off Cape Town

Sunday, June 28th.—At 4.30 this evening brought-to a heavy ship with a blank cartridge; or rather she seemed to come-to of her own accord, as she was evidently outsailing us, and was, when we fired, at very long range. Soon after heaving-to she burned a blue light, and whilst our boat, with a light in it, was pulling towards her, she burned another. She afterwards said she would not have hove-to but that she thought we might be in distress. The boarding officer reported us as the United States ship *Dacotah*, and demanded to see the ship's papers, which were refused, the Master stating that we had no right to see his papers.

The boarding officer having been informed of her name (the *Vernon*), and that she was from Melbourne, for London, and being satisfied, from observation, that she was really an English ship, she being one of the well-known frigate-built Melbourne packets, returned on board, and the ship filled away; and she was already at considerable distance from us when I received the boarding officer's report. Under all these circumstances, I did not chase him afresh to enforce my belligerent right of search. *Cui bono*, the vessel being really English? Although, indeed, the resistance to search by a neutral is good cause of capture, I could only capture to destroy; and I would not burn an English ship (being satisfied of her nationality) if the Master persisted to the law in not showing his papers. Nor did I feel that the Confederate States flag had any insult to revenge, as the insult, if any, was intended for the Yankee flag. Most probably, however, the ship being a packet-ship, and a mail-packet, the Master erred from ignorance.

Lat. 26.35, long. 32.59.30, current S.E. thirty miles; ship rolling and tumbling about, to my great discomfort. The fact is, I am getting too old to relish the rough usage of the sea. Youth sometimes loves to be rocked by the gale, but when we have passed the middle stage of life, we love quiet and repose.

Tuesday, June 30th.—The bad weather of the past week seems at length to have blown itself out; and this morning we have the genial sunshine again, and a clear, bracing atmosphere. With a solitary exception, the Cape pigeons, true to their natures, have departed. There is still some roughness of the sea left, however, and the ship is rolling and creaking her bulk-heads, as usual. Wind moderate from about East.

Another prize on the 2nd of July, the *Anna, F. Schmidt*, of Maine, from Boston for San Francisco; and another cautious Yankee transformed into an Englishman; and then came a large ship flying before the wind, with all sail set to her royals, and answering the *Alabama*'s challenge with a gun from her own bow port.

A man-of-war this, from her fashion of replying, even had the fact not been sufficiently apparent from the cut of her heavy yards and lofty spars. An enemy, perhaps! And wild with the hope of a fight, though it be with an enemy not much less than double her size, away flies the *Alabama*, at top speed of sail and steam, in chase. The sea was smooth, though with a strong breeze; and ere long the saucy little cruiser ranged up alongside of the fine frigate, with ten black muzzles grinning through his ports on either side.

"This is the Confederate States ship *Alabama!*" rang out from the quarter-deck, as the two ships flew through the water, side by side:- "What ship's that?"

But there was to be no fight that day. The chase contented herself with the laconic reply, "Her Britannic Majesty's ship *Diomede;*" and went tearing along upon her course under the tremendous press of canvas, beneath which her spars were bending like a whip, and was soon out of sight, evidently bound on some errand that would not brook delay.

Some small compensation for this disappointment was found two days afterwards in the capture of the fine ship *Express*, of Boston, from Callao for Antwerp, loaded with *guano*, the particulars of which are recorded as follows:—

Case of the Ship *Express*

Ship under United States colours and register; cargo *guano*, shipped by Senan, Valdeavellano and Co., at Callao, and consigned to J. Sescau and Co., at Antwerp. On the back of this bill of lading is the following endorsement:

> *Nous soussignés chargé d'affaires et consul général de France à Lima, certifions que la chargement de mille soixante douze de register de Huano spécifié au présent connaissement, est propriété neutre.*
> *Fait à Lima, le 27 Janvier, 1863.*
> (Signed and impressed with the Consular seal.)

This certificate fails to be of any value as proof, for two reasons: first, it is not sworn to; and secondly, it simply avers the property to be neutral (the greater part of it, for it does not touch the guano in sacks), instead of pointing out the owner or owners. A Consul may authenticate evidence by his seal, but when he departs from the usual functions of a Consul, and becomes a witness, he must give his testimony under oath, like other witnesses. This certificate, therefore, does not even amount to an *ex parte* affidavit. If the property had been in the shipper's or consignee's name, it would have been quite as easy to say so as to put the certificate in its present shape.

Why, then, was the simple declaration that the property was neutral made use of?—the law with which every Consul, and more especially a *chargé d'affaires*, is supposed to be acquainted with, declaring them to be insufficient? The conclusion from these two facts—*viz.*, that there was no oath taken, and that there was no owner named—seemed to be that the Consul gave a sort of matter-of-course certificate, upon the application of someone who declared the property to be neutral, perhaps with a knowledge to the fact, or contrary to the fact, neither party taking any oath. Now, the presumption of law being, that goods found in an enemy's ship belong to the enemy, unless a distinct neutral character be given to them, by pointing out the *real owner*, by proper documentary proof, as neither the bill of lading nor the certificate, which is a mere statement of a fact, like the bill of lading, not under oath, nor the master's testimony, who knows nothing (see his deposition) except as he has been told by the shipper, amounts to proper documentary proof, the ship and cargo are both condemned.

It must be admitted that this is a case in which, perhaps, a prize court would grant "further proof;" but as I cannot do this, and as a distinct neutral character is not impressed upon the property by former evidence, I must act under the presumption of law. Sect. 3rd, *Phillimore*, 596. The charter-party in this case describes the charterers, J. Sescau and Co., of Antwerp, as agents of the supreme Peruvian Government. But if so, why was it not certificated by the government, as was done in the case of the Washington, captured and released on bond by this ship? And then the master swears that *the shippers told him* that the cargo belonged to them; and if the Peruvian Government must resort to a French official for a certificate, why not, then, on oath made before him? and why did he not state the fact that it so belonged, which would have protected it?

The *Alabama* was now again heading for the Cape, the *Anna Schmidt* having yielded a supply of bread sufficient, with strict economy, to last out the passage. There she arrived on the 29th July, anchoring in Saldanha Bay, at about 1.45 p.m.

Thursday, July 30th.—Last night the sky and atmosphere were singularly brilliant. Landed this morning at eight, to get sight for my chronometers, this being the first time that I ever set foot on the Continent of Africa. Saldanha is a gloomy, desert-looking place, the shore comprised of sand and rock, without trees, but with green patches here and there. There are three or four farm-houses in sight, scattered over the hills. The farmers here are mostly graziers. The cattle are fine and good; a great number of goats graze on the hills, and sheep-raising is extensive, the mutton being particularly fine. Small deer are abundant. We had a venison steak for breakfast. The little islands in the bay abound in rabbits, and there is good pheasant-shooting in the valleys. Already a party of officers has gone out to stretch their limbs, and enjoy the luxury of shooting.

July 31st.—Took a stroll on shore, and walked round some fine oat-fields. The soil resembles our hummock land in Florida, and produces finely. Engaged caulking, painting, &c. An abundance of wild-flowers in bloom. Huge blocks of granite lie about the sand, and from the tops of projections, &c.

Saturday, Aug. 1st.—I returned on board, after a stroll on shore, at 2 p.m. During my walk I met some farmers in a four-horse wagon coming to see the ship. They brought me a wild peacock—not quite so large as our wild turkey. It was without the gorgeous plumage of the domestic bird. The schooner *Atlas* came in this afternoon, with letters for me from some merchants at Cape Town, offering their services to supply me with coal, &c., and expressing their good-will, &c., &c. I took occasion by this vessel, which returned immediately, to write to the Governor, Sir Philip B. Wodehouse, informing him of my presence here.

Sunday, Aug. 2nd.—The inhabitants say that this winter has been remarkable for its general good weather, and for the few gales they have had. Crowds of country people, from far and near, came on board to look at the ship today.

Monday, Aug. 3rd.—Another crowd of visitors today, who came in their country wagons and on horseback. They all speak Dutch, and it is rare to find one among them who speaks English. Although it is nearly half a century since England took final possession of the colony, the English language has made but little progress, the children being taught by a Dutch schoolmaster, and the papers being, many of them, printed in Dutch. There was an intelligent young *boer* (about twenty-three) among them, who had never been on board a ship before. He was quite excited by the novelty of everything he saw. Some of the female visitors were plump, ruddy, Dutch girls, whose large rough hands, and awkward bows and curtsies, showed them to be honest lasses from the neighbouring farms, accustomed to milking the cows and churning the butter. I found the geranium growing wild in my rambles today. Just as we were going to sun-down quarters, a boat came alongside with the body of Third Assistant-engineer Cummings, who accidentally shot himself with his gun.

Tuesday, Aug. 4th.—In the afternoon, at three, the funeral procession started from shore with the body of the deceased engineer. He was taken to a private cemetery about a mile and a half distant, and interred with the honours due to his grade, the First Lieutenant reading the funeral service. This is the first burial we have had from the ship.

Wednesday, Aug. 5th.—At 6 p.m. got up the anchor, and getting under way, steamed out of the bay and shaped our course for Cape Town. At 9.30 descried a sail a point on the starboard bow, and at 10.30 came up with and sent a boat on board of the Confederate *barque Tuscaloosa*, and brought Lieutenant Lowe on board. He reported having captured, on the 31st July the American ship *Santee*, from the eastward, laden with rice, certificated as British property, and bound for Falmouth. He released her on ransom for 150,000 dollars. I directed Lieutenant Lowe to proceed to Simons Bay for supplies. Steamed in for the town. At 12.30 made a *barque*, two points on starboard bow; gave chase, and at about 2 p.m. came up with and hove the chase, she having up United States colours.

This was a close pursuit, as the *barque* was not more than five or six miles from the shore when we came up with her. The Master might have saved himself if he had stood directly in for the land; but we ran down upon him under English colours, and he had no suspicion of our character until it was too late. The United States consul at once protested against our violation of British waters (!). The Governor telegraphed to the Admiral (Walker), at Simon's Bay, to send a man-of-war round; and about 10 p.m. her Majesty's steamship *Valorous*, Captain Forsyth, came in and anchored. Some correspondence has passed between the Governor and myself on the subject of the capture, and I believe he is satisfied as to distance, &c. Put a prize crew on board the prize (*Sea Bride*), and directed her to stand off and on until further orders. The moment our anchor was dropped we were crowded with visitors.

Thursday, Aug. 6th.—Notwithstanding the bad weather, the ship has been crowded with visitors all the morning, and my cabin has been constantly filled with people pressing to shake hands with me, and to express sympathy for my cause. During the night we had some thunder and lightning, first from the S.E., and then from the N.W.; and the wind springing up, very gently at first, freshened to a gale by morning, with showers of rain and hail. Communicated with the prize, and directed the Prizemaster, in case he should be blown off by a gale, to rendezvous at Saldanha Bay by the fifteenth of the month. Captain Forsyth, of the *Valorous*, came on board. Returned his visit.

Friday, Aug. 7th.—I should have been under way for Simons Bay this morning but for the gale. The wind is blowing very fresh from northward and westward, with dense clouds climbing up and over the Table, Lion's head, &c.—presenting a very fine spectacle, with the rough waters, the ships with struck upper yards, and the town half enveloped with flying mists, &c. The bold watermen in all the gale are cruising about the bay under reefed sails, some of them with anchors and cables, ready to assist any ships that may require it. Last night, in the first watch, a sail was reported to be on the shore near the lighthouse and firing signal guns. Very soon we saw two or three boats put out to her assistance. In the morning we heard that it was a Brazilian brig, and that the crew was saved. The brig is fast breaking up in the gale.

CHAPTER 31

A Night Scene

Saturday, August 8th, 1863.—The gale broke last night, but there is still some breeze blowing, and the sea is quite rough. Last night a Bremen brig was wrecked off Point Monille. We heard her firing guns, and I feared at first it was our prize; and yet I could not conceive how my Prizemaster, who was acquainted with the soundings, could have made such a mistake. The weather has checked the throng of visitors, and yet a few get off to us, asking for autographs, and looking curiously at the ship. We are finishing our repairs, and getting supplies on board. Our prize has not made her appearance today. She will rendezvous at Saldanha Bay on the 15th inst.

Sunday, August 9th, 1863.—Weather has again become fine. At 6 p.m. precisely, we moved out of the bay, and steamed along the coast towards the Cape. We gave chase to two sail off the mouth of False Bay, and overhauling them, one proved to be an English, and the other an American *barque*. The latter we boarded; but when I came to get bearings and plot my position, it unfortunately turned out that I was within a mile, or a mile and a quarter, of a line drawn from the Cape Lighthouse to the opposite headland of the bay, and therefore within the prescribed limit of jurisdiction.

The master of the *barque*, in the meantime, having come on board, I informed him of those facts, and told him to return to, and take possession of his ship, as I had no authority to exercise any control over him; which he did, and in a few minutes more, we were under steam standing up the bay. What a scene for the grim old Cape to look down upon. The vessel boarded was the *Martha Wenzell*, of Boston, from Akyab for Falmouth. At 2 p.m. anchored in Simon's Bay, and was boarded by a Lieutenant from the flag-ship of Admiral Walker.

Monday, August 10th.—Weather fine. I called on Admiral Walker at his residence, and was presented by him to his family, and spent an agreeable half hour with them, giving them a brief outline of our quarrel and war. Dined on board the Chinese gunboat *Kwang-Tung*, Commander Young. This is one of Laird's side-wheel steamers, built for Captain Sherrard Osborne's fleet. Capt. Bickford, of the *Narcissus*, and Lieutenant Wood, flag Lieutenant, dined with us.

Tuesday, August 11th.—Weather fine. Visited the flag-ship of Rear-Admiral Sir Baldwin W. Walker and the *Kwang-Tung*. Employed caulking and refitting ship. Many visitors on board.

Wednesday, August 12th.—Wind fresh from the southward and eastward. Photographers and visitors on board. The *Kwang-Tung* made a trial trip of her engines, after having repaired them, with the Admiral's family on board. Wind freshened to a gale towards night.

Thursday, August 13th.—Weather cloudy; blowing a moderate gale from the S.E. The *Tuscaloosa* is ready for sea, but is detained by the weather. Dined with Rear-Admiral Walker; Governor Sir Philip Wodehouse and lady were of the party. My sailors are playing the devil as usual. They manage to get liquor on board the ship, and then become insubordinate and unruly. We have to force some of them into irons. The man Weir, whom I made a quartermaster, has run off; also two of the stewards, and two dingy boys; the latter were apprehended and brought on board.

Friday, August 14th.—We have a dense fog today and calm. The *Tuscaloosa*, which went out at daylight, anchored some four or five miles outside the harbour. The mail steamer from England arrived at Cape Town today, bringing us news of Lee's invasion of Maryland and Pennsylvania. Finished our repairs this evening.

Saturday, August 15th.—We were ready to get under way at daylight this morning, but were delayed by the dense fog until eleven o'clock, when we moved out of the harbour. As we neared the Cape another fog bank rolled over and enveloped us for a couple of hours. At 2.30, boarded an English *barque*. At 3, let the steam go down, and raised the propeller. Weather threatening. Barometer 29.80. Took single reefs in the topsails. At 11 p.m. a steamer passed close, to leeward of us.

Light winds and thick weather now for rather more than a week, varied by a stiff northwester on the 22nd August, lasting over the greater part of two days.

Tuesday, August 25th.—Dense, cloudy morning. Got a glimpse of the sun and latitude at twelve o'clock. Our freshwater condenser is about giving out, the last supply of water being so salt as to be scarcely drinkable. This will be a serious disaster for us if we cannot remedy it at Cape Town, for we have no tank room for more than eight days' supply, and no place to store casks except on deck, where they would interfere with the guns. And so I have borne up to run for Angra Pequena, where I expect to pick up my prize-crew that I may return to Simon's Bay to see what can be done, without further delay. I am quite knocked up with cold and fever, but sick as I may be, I can never lie by and be quiet, the demands of duty being inexorable and incessant.

Thursday, August 27th.—Morning fine; made all sail at early daylight and stood in for the land, having every promise of getting latitude at meridian for position, and running in to an anchor early in the afternoon. But an ominous fog-bank, that we had noticed hanging over the land for a short time before, suddenly enveloped us at eight, and shut us in so completely as to render it difficult to see a hundred yards in any direction; the wind the while blowing fresh from the south; weather cool and uncomfortable, and the rigging dripping rain. Hove to, and awaited anxiously the disappearance of the fog; but hour after hour passed, and still no change—six, seven bells struck, and the fog appeared to grow more dense, and the wind to increase; wore ship, and put her head off shore; went below, and turned in, in supreme disgust.

At 1.30 aroused by the report that there was a topsail schooner close aboard. She ran down for us, when we backed main topsail, and sent a boat and brought the Master on board. Being like ourselves bound for Angra, he consented to pilot us in. Filled away, and made sail. We were today, at noon, by computation, W.S.W. from Pedestal Point (Angra); distance about ten miles. The fog continued most relentlessly until 4 p.m., when it disappeared, and we wore ship for the land, and were probably on the point of making it just at sunset, when the fog came on again, and enveloped everything in impenetrable darkness. Wore ship seaward, and stood off and on during the night: the weather blustering.

Friday, August 28th.—Morning cloudy, wind blowing half a gale. At 8.50 took a single reef in the topsail—the schooner in sight to leeward. At 9.30 made the land, and soon came in full view of it. My would-be pilot could not recognise it, until the schooner, having run in ahead of us, ran down, to leeward, by which we knew that she had made out our position. I followed her, and ran in, and anchored in Sheerwater Bay; my pilot being of no sort of assistance to me, he seeming to have a very imperfect knowledge of the locality. Soon after anchoring, a boat came out of the lagoon to us, and we recognised some of our prize-crew of the *Sea Bride* in her.

In effect the *Tuscaloosa* and the prize had both been three days in the harbour of Angra Pequena. In the afternoon we got up our anchor again, and ran into the lagoon, and anchored near the *Sea Bride* in seven fathoms of water. A number of the officers are off this evening to visit the *Tuscaloosa*—no doubt to get a *good drink of fresh water*. I have sent my pitcher for some, being nearly parched up with the salt-water we have been drinking for the last three days. We are lying in *smooth water*, in a snug harbour, and I hope to get what I have not had for several nights—a good night's rest. A more bleak and comfortless prospect, in the way of landscape, could scarcely present itself to the eye. Nothing but land and rock—not a sprig of vegetation of any kind to be seen. In fact it never rains here, and this is consequently a *guano* region. We passed a bank of *guano* in Halifax island, a shanty, a few labourers, and a large army of penguins spread out with much solemnity on the island.

Saturday, August 29th.—Getting on board flour, &c., from the *Sea Bride*, and water from the schooner—1500 gallons, which will enable us to cruise some twenty days. Hauled a borrowed sieve in the afternoon, and caught a fine lot of fish.

Sunday, August 30th.—At 10.30 mustered the crew, and landed James Adams, O.S., discharged by sentence of court-martial, with forfeiture of pay and prize-money.

Monday, August 31st,—At 7 p.m. got under way, and stood out of the harbour.

The *Alabama* was now visited by a succession of the heavy gales prevalent during winter time in the neighbourhood of the Cape. On the 7th Sept.—Captain Semmes writes—we had a rough, ugly night of it, with a continuance, and even increase of the gale, and a short and abrupt sea, in which the ship occasionally rolled and pitched with violence, frequently thumping my cot against the beams overhead and awaking me. Shipped large quantities of water through the propeller well; cabin-deck leaking.

Tuesday, September 8th.—Weather cloudy, the sun shining faintly through the grey mass. Gale continues; the wind (E.S.E.) not having varied a hair for the last sixteen hours. Barometer gradually falling; ship rolling and pitching in the sea, and all things dreary-looking and uncomfortable. I am supremely disgusted with the sea and all its belongings; the fact is, I am past the age when men ought to be subjected to the hardships and discomforts of the sea.

Seagoing is one of those constant strifes which none but the vigorous, the hardy, and the hopefu—in short, the youthful, or at most, the middle-aged—should be engaged in. The very roar of the wind through the rigging, with its accompaniments of rolling and tumbling, hard, overcast skies, gives me the blues. This is a double anniversary with me. It was on the 8th of September that I received my first order for sea-service (1826); and it was on the 8th of September that Norton's Division fought the battle of Moline del Ray (1847).

What a history of the United States has to be written since the last event! How much of human weakness and wickedness and folly has been developed in these years! But the North will receive their reward, under the inevitable and rigorous laws of a just government of the world.

Another week passed with a solitary excitement in the shape of an obstinate English skipper, who stoutly refused to heave to. The following account of this affair is extracted from the journal of one of the *Alabama*'s officers:—

Towards evening of the 10th of September the wind fell considerably. At 8.30 p.m. a sail in sight on weather bow. Immediately we turned to windward, and stood in chase. At 9.45 fired a gun to heave chase to. Chase, however, still kept on her course. At 10.35 we ran up alongside, and the officer of the deck hailed her—"Ship ahoy!"

"Halloa! heave to, and I will send a boat on board."

"What do you want me to heave to for?"

"That's my business."

"Are you a vessel of war?"

Captain Semmes then waxing wroth, replied, "I'll give you five minutes to heave to in." "You have no right to heave me to unless you tell me who you are."

"I'll let you know who I am."

To officer of the deck—"Load that gun with shot, sir, and rain on that fellow—he's stupid enough to be a foreigner."

"Tell me who you are," yelled out the master of the ship. "If you are not hove to in five minutes I'll fire into you."

Addressing the officer of the watch, Captain Semmes asked, "Is that gun ready for firing, sir?"

"All ready, sir."

"Then stand by to fire."

The captain of the ship beginning to realize the fact that we were in earnest, rolled out a volley of oaths, not only loud, but deep also. That little ebullition being finished, he hauled his mainsail up and lay to. Captain Semmes then gave me orders to board and ascertain who the vessel was, as the reluctance to heave to was suspicious in itself.

On boarding, the mate met me at the gangway and introduced me to a tall, burly man, who proved to be the Master. With the utmost suavity I inquired, "What ship is this?"

"Who are you?" he blurted out.

"What ship is this, captain?" I repeated.

"I sha'n't tell you," was the polite reply.

"Captain, what vessel is this?"

"Are you a man-of-war?" asked he.

"Of course we are," replied I.

"Who are you?" queried he.

With the greatest distinctness possible, and with the utmost sternness, I said, "We are—we are the United States steamer *Iroquois*, Captain Palmer, on a cruise; and now, having told you this, I have something more to tell you—namely, that I am come on board to ask questions, not to answer them; further, I have asked you three times who you are, and have not yet received an answer. So just step down into the cabin, and produce the ship's papers."

With a very ill grace he descended into the cabin, I following, and I had just removed my cap when he roared out, "Who are you? Are you English? Say you are an English man-of-war, and I will let you look at my papers."

Said I, "Captain, either you are crazy or else you think I am. Here we fire a gun, and any man with a grain of sense would have understood that it was meant for a ship to heave to, more especially when a nation is at war. You are told to heave to, are boarded, and asked a question. Instead of replying, you ask, perfectly savagely, 'Who are you?' I tell you we are the United States ship *Iroquois*, and then you ask, 'Are you English? Tell me you are an English man-of-war!' It's absurd, I tell you."

"Mr. Officer," yelled he, "'crazy!' 'sense!' 'absurd!' By G—d, sir, if an English man-of-war were here, no Yankee dare set foot on this deck, sir. Who are you?" "Captain," I said to the man, "it is time this piece of folly were ended. Now understand me. Look at that clock: it wants twelve minutes to eleven; I want to see your papers; I give you two minutes to produce them in. If, at ten minutes to eleven, the papers are not forthcoming, I shall adopt measures to place them in my possession."

I then sat down. Question after question did the worthy skipper ask, but no reply did I deign to give. At length it wanted but a few seconds to the time specified, when with a bad grace the irate Master produced his key, unlocked his safe, and brought forth his papers. Upon examination I found it was the ship *Flora*, of and to Liverpool, from Manilla, with a general cargo.

While looking over his papers, a ceaseless string of interrogations was kept up by the Master, to which I returned no answer, merely returning the papers, and remarking that he had given himself and us also, some really causeless detention. "Have you any news, captain?" I asked. "Yes, I have some news; news that some three or four of you would like to be acquainted with, but news that one of you would rather not know. But I'd see you Yankees sunk forty fathoms deep before I would tell you it." "Come, captain, don't be uncharitable; you know what is written in the Bible."

He then went on to state what a bad passage he had made so far, having met with a succession of baffling winds ever since he had left Manilla; that he had made all sail for a fair wind, and which had only lasted for a few hours, the wind coming ahead again; and it looking threatening, he had reduced sail considerably, and was making but slow progress when he was stopped by us.

"Stopped by a Yankee, too! That's something I won't forget in a hurry," said he.

I could not help laughing at the "offended majesty" air he assumed, and wishing him a speedy passage, returned on board. From one of my boat's crew I learnt that the *Flora* had either seen or been boarded a couple of days ago by a two-masted long-funnelled steamer, supposed by the Master to have been a Confederate, though showing Yankee colours.

Wednesday, September 16th.—At 3 p.m. doubled the Cape of Good Hope and steamed into the anchorage at Simon's Town, which we reached at about 4.30 p.m. The *Vanderbilt* had left on Friday last, and was reported to have hovered near the Cape for a day or two. Greatly disarranged by the news from home—Vicksburg and Port Hudson fallen; Rosecrans' army marching southwards; and Lee having recrossed the Potomac. Our poor people seem to be terribly pressed by the Northern hordes.

But we shall fight it out to the end, and the end will be what an all-wise Providence shall decree.

Thursday, September 17th.—Called on the Admiral, and received a visit from the captain of the *Narcissus*.

Various misrepresentations had been made to the Admiral as to my proceedings since I left, &c., by the United States Consul, which I explained away. Spent an agreeable half-hour with the Admiral and his lady. There being no coal here—the *Vanderbilt* having taken it all—I made arrangements for it to be sent to me from Cape Town.

Saturday, September 19.—The steamer *Kadie* arrived with coals for me from Cape Town. Hauled her alongside, and commenced coaling. Walked on shore, and lunched with Captain Bickford. Dispatched letters for the mail-steamer for England. Liberty-men drunk, and few returning. Dined with the Admiral. A very pleasant party, composed entirely of naval officers, including the Captains of the ships present, the Captain-superintendent of the dockyard, &c. After dinner the young ladies made their appearance in the drawing-room, and we had some music.

Sunday, September 20th.—Hauled the ship over to get at the copper around the blow-pipe, which was worn off. Visited the shore at half-past nine, took a long walk, dropped in upon the Post-captain, and went to church—Father Kiernan saying mass. He is an earnest, simple-minded Irish priest, with a picturesque little church on the hill-side, and a small congregation composed chiefly of soldiers and sailors—a seaman serving mass. Captain Coxon and a couple of the Lieutenants of the squadron being present. Liberty-men returning in greater numbers today—the money is giving out.

Monday, September 21st.—At daylight, hauled the steamer alongside again, and recommenced coaling. Called to see the ladies at the Admiral's after dinner, and walked through their quite extensive garden, winding up a ravine with a rapid little stream of water passing through it.

Tuesday, September 22nd.—A large number of liberty-men on shore yet. The Yankee Consul, with his usual unscrupulousness, is trying to persuade them to desert. With one or two exceptions, the whole crew have broken their liberty—petty officers and all. With many improvements in the character of the seaman of the present day, in regard to intelligence, he is, in some respects, as bad as ever. Finished coaling this evening.

Wednesday, September 23rd.—Refitting the foretopmasts. Some twenty men still absent. A few are picked up by the Simon's Town police for the sake of the reward. And the sailor-landlords, those pests of all sea-ports, are coming on board and presenting bills for board, &c. Of course these claims are not listened to. It is a common contrivance with Jack and these sharks, to endeavour to extort money out of their ships.

The process is simple enough. The landlord gives Jack a glass or two of bad liquor, and it may be, a meal or two, and it is agreed between them that a bill of twenty times the value received shall be acknowledged. The land-shark charges in this exorbitant way for the risk he runs of not being able to get anything, so he has nothing to complain of when he happens to come across a captain who is disposed to protect his seamen from such extortion. Knowing the villains well, I did not permit them to impose upon me.

Thursday, September 24th.—Waiting for the chance of getting over my deserters from Cape Town. Informed by telegraph, in the afternoon, that it was useless to wait longer, as the police declined to act. It thus appears that the authorities declined to enable me to recover my men—fourteen in number, enough to cripple my crew. This is another of those remarkable interpretations of neutrality in which John Bull seems to be so particularly fertile. Informed by telegrams from Cape Town that vessels had arrived reporting the *Vanderbilt* on two successive days off Cape Aguthas and Point Danger. The moon being near its full, I preferred not to have her blockade me in Simon's Bay, as it might detain me until I should have a "dark moon," and being all ready for sea, this would have been irksome; so the gale having lulled somewhat, towards 9 p.m., I ordered steam to be got up, and at half-past eleven, we moved out from our anchors.

The lull only deceived us, as we had scarcely gotten under way, before the gale raged with increased violence, and we were obliged to buffet it with all the force of our four boilers. The wind blew fiercely; but still we drove her between five and six knots per hour in the very teeth of it.

Nothing could exceed the peculiar weird-like aspect of the scene, as we struggled under the full moonlight with the midnight gale. The surrounding mountains and high lands, seemingly at a great distance in the hazy atmosphere, had their tops piled with banks of fleecy clouds, remaining as motionless as snow-banks, which they very much resembled—the cold south wind assisting the illusion; the angry waters of the bay breaking in every direction, occasionally dashing on board of us; the perfectly clear sky, with no sign of a cloud anywhere to be seen, except those piled on the mountains already mentioned;- the bright full moon, shedding her mysterious rays on all surrounding objects—illuminating, yet distancing them—all these were things to be remembered. And last, the revolving light on the Cape, at regular intervals, lighting up the renowned old headland.

We passed the Cape at about 3 p.m., and bearing away gave her the trysails reduced by their bonnets, and close-reefed topsails; and I turned in to snatch a brief repose, before the trials of another day should begin.

Friday, September 25th.—Delivered the jail—as usual, upon getting to sea. It will take several days, I am afraid, to work the grog out of the crew, before they are likely to settle down into good habits and cheerfulness.

The next fortnight's run through the heavy gales that prevail almost incessantly in the higher latitudes of the Indian Ocean, brought the *Alabama* some 2400 miles upon her course. Two days more brought her off the Island of St. Paul's, a distance of 2840 miles. Another couple of days, and she had made about sufficient easting, and began to shape her course towards the north—the "sunny north."

A few short extracts from the *journal* will give sufficient idea of the period thus passed through:—

October 16th.—Lat. 35.23; Long. 89.55; no observations for current; distance some 135 miles. The gale in which we lay-to ten hours, having broken in upon our day's work. Bar. 29.57, and on a stand; running before the wind, under close-reef and reefed foresail. Afternoon gale increased, and between twelve and one it blew furiously, the whole sea being a sheet of foam, the air rendered misty by the spray, and the heavy seas threatening to jump on board of us, although we were scudding at the rate of very little less than fifteen knots—the whole accompanied by an occasional snow-squall from dark, threatening-looking clouds.

It is not often that a wilder scene is beheld: in the meantime the Cape pigeons are whirling around us, occasionally poising themselves against the stern, as serenely, apparently, as if the elements were at rest. The barometer has remained perfectly stationary at 29.57 during this blow for seven hours (from morning to 7 p.m.), without varying a single hair's breadth, during all of which time the gale was raging with unmitigated violence from about S.W. by W. to S.W.

During this period, we were travelling about on an average speed of eleven knots; and of course this must have been the rate of speed of the vortex—distant from us probably 150 to 200 miles. At 7 p.m. the mercury began to rise slowly, and at 8 was at 27.60, the weather looking less angry, and the squalls not so frequent or violent. Verily, our good ship, as she is darted ahead on the top of one of those huge, long Indian Ocean waves that pursue her, seems like a mere cock-boat.

It is remarkable that this is the anniversary of the cyclone we took off the banks of Newfoundland.

October 18th—Observing has been particularly vexatious during the past week. What with the heavy seas constantly rising between the observer and the horizon, preventing him from producing a contact at the very instant, it may be, that he is ready for it, the passage of a flying cloud under the sun when his horizon is all right, and the heavy rolling of the ship requiring him to pay the utmost care to the preservation of his balance, and sometimes even to "lose his sight"—from the necessity of withdrawing one hand suddenly from his instrument to grasp the rail or the rigging to prevent himself from falling—what with all these things, the patience of even as patient a man as myself is sorely tried. Perhaps this stormy tumbling about at sea is the reason why seamen are so calm and quiet on shore. We come to hate all sorts of commotion, whether physical or moral.

At last the region of endless gales was passed, and escaping entirely the southern belt of calms, the *Alabama* dashed along in the S.E. trade. On the 26th October, as she was nearing the Line, news reached her from an English *barque*, that the United States sloop *Wyoming* was on guard in the Sunda Straits, accompanied by a three-masted schooner. This sloop being about the *Alabama*'s own size, hopes of a fight were again rife among both officers and men; and great was their impatience when the trade at length parted from them, and light, variable winds again began to baffle the eager ship.

Drawing slowly nearer to the Straits, news still came from passing ships of the enemy's presence there, reports going at length so far as to state, that she had been specially dispatched thither by the United States consul at Batavia, in search of the *Alabama* herself.

At last, on the 6th November, came another prize, the first since leaving the Cape of Good Hope, nearly six weeks before. She proved to be the *barque Amanda*, from Manilla to Queenstown for orders, the following being the particulars of her case:—

CASE OF THE BARQUE AMANDA

Ship under U.S. colours and register. Cargo, sugar and hemp. Charter-party to proceed to Europe or the United States. On the face of each of the three bills of lading appears the following certificate for the British Vice-consul at Manilla:—

I hereby certify that Messrs. Ker and Co., the shippers of the merchandize specified in this bill of lading, are British subjects established in Manilla, and that according to invoices produced, the said merchandize is shipped by order, and for account of Messrs. Halliday, Fox, and Co., British subjects of London, in Great Britain.

As nobody swears to anything, of course this certificate is valueless, and the presumption of law prevails, *viz.*, "that all property found under the enemy's flag is enemy's property," until the contrary be shown by competent and credible testimony under oath, duly certified to by a Consul or another officer. Ship and cargo condemned.

CHAPTER 32

Yankee Ships Scarce

The 8th of November saw the *Alabama* again in sight of land, and after anchoring for a night off Flat Point, and sending a boat ashore, in the vain hope of finding in the Malay villages a supply of some sort of fresh provision, she again lifted her anchor and proceeded to sea under steam.

Tuesday, November 10th.—Passed between the islands of Beezee and Sonbooko, both high and picturesque, the channel about a mile wide, some villages under the groves of cocoa-nut trees on the former. The naked natives coming down to the beach to gaze at us. We ran through the Strait of Sunda about 2 p.m., passing to the westward of Thwart-the-Way.

Soon after passing out of the Strait and shaping our course, we discovered a clipper-looking ship, under topsails, standing towards North Island. Gave chase, although we were in the midst of a rain squall, and in the course of fifteen or twenty minutes we were near enough to him to make him show his colours. They were United States, and upon being boarded he proved to be the *Winged Racer,* a vessel for which we had been hunting outside the Strait. We captured him and sent him to anchor about three miles from North Island (the Island bearing about W.S.W.), and ran up and anchored near him ourselves.

By working hard we were enabled to get everything we wanted out of him by 2 o'clock p.m.; and having despatched her crew, together with the crew of the *Amanda,* in the boats of the prize, at their own request, we got under way at 4 p.m., and steamed out of sight of the coast by daylight. We were fortunate enough to get some fowls, fruits, and vegetables from a bum-boat of Malays, who made a business of supplying ships. The boat reported that, when she left Angra about two days before, the *Wyoming* was there. Fired the ship.

CASE OF THE *WINGED RACER*

Ship under United States colours and register, and no claim of the neutrality of the cargo among the papers; ship bound to New York. Ship and cargo condemned.

Wednesday, November 11th.—Made the North Watcher soon after daylight, and finding that if I continued on at the same speed, I should be up with Gasper Strait early in the night, and should be obliged to anchor until daylight, I ordered the steam to be let down, and we were about making arrangements for getting up the propeller, when a sail was descried on the port bow, close hauled on the starboard tack. She soon proved to be a rakish-looking ship, evidently United States. Kept away from her from time to time as she passed towards our bow, and when we came near enough we showed her the United States colours. She replied with the same. I then fired a gun and hoisted our own colours (new flag).

Instead of obeying this signal to heave to, she made sail and ran. We at once started the fires afresh, the steam having gone entirely down, and made all sail in pursuit. The chase at this time was about four miles from us, and for a long time we gained scarcely any thing upon her. We threw a rifleshot astern him, but he disregarded this also. Finally, after an exciting chase of one hour and a half (shifting guns, and sending men aft to trim ship, and giving her a full head of steam), we came near enough to him to throw a 32 pound shot between his masts, when he shortened sail, came to the wind, and hove to.

If the wind had been *very* fresh (it was blowing a good breeze) he would probably have ran away from us. He proved to be the clipper ship *Contest*, from Yokohama (Japan) for New York. Captured him, and anchored in the open sea in fourteen fathoms of water, and took from the prize such supplies as we wanted. All our people having returned on board about nightfall, it was discovered soon after that the prize was dragging her anchor, which she did so fast in the freshened breeze that a boat which was sent to board and fire her sculled until the officer nearly lost sight of us, and fearing that if he continued he might lose sight of us altogether in a rain squall, returned. Got up steam immediately and weighed anchor, and ran down to the prize, sent a boat crew on board of her and burned her.

CASE OF THE *CONTEST*

Ship under United States colours and register, and no claim for cargo; ship and cargo condemned.

Concluding, that on receiving intelligence of the *Alabama*'s arrival, the *Wyoming*, if, in truth, she was near the Strait, would run at once for Gaspar Passage in search of her, Captain Semmes now determined to double upon his enemy, and gave her the start of him, holding himself for a few days in the Java Sea, a little east of the Strait. A week passed by without any incident worthy of record. At length a change came.

Thursday, November 19th.—At 3.30 p.m. boarded the English ship *Avalanche* (transferred) two or three days from Singapore, with newspapers from England of the 10th of October—only forty days! Gratified at the general good aspect of the news, and particularly at our victory at Chicamauga. Reports several American ships laid up at Singapore, and a general stagnation of American trade. This ship came to anchor some two miles astern of us, and we sent off the prisoners of the *Contest* by her, the Master consenting to take them for a chronometer which I sent him. He will probably put them on shore at Angra Point. We first hoisted the Dutch flag, and sent a German, Master's mate we had, on board of him; but the Master, when told that we were a Dutch ship of war, said, "Oh! that won't do; I was on board of her in Liverpool, when she was launched!"

Friday, November 20th.—Lowered and rigged the cutter, and sent her to board a couple of *barques*, which reported four American ships at Bankok; there about to lay up, lest they should fall in with us, and one American ship at Manilla.

Saturday, November 21st.—At 3 p.m. got under way under sail, with the wind from the south-west.

Sunday, Nov. 22nd.—At 3 p.m. lowered the propeller, and went ahead under steam. Passed within about four miles of Direction Island at 5.15 p.m.

Monday, Nov. 23rd.—At 8 p.m. made Seraia.

Thursday, Nov. 26th.—Lat. 5.36; Long. 111.42, or within fifty miles of dangerous ground, towards which the current is setting us. No anchoring ground. 47 fathoms. After noon, the calm still continuing, let go a kedge in 50 fathoms of water—mud—and veered to 150 fathoms.

Friday, Nov. 27th.—Noon. The struggle against the current is hopeless in the death-like calm that prevails, and so we have come-to again with the kedge.

Sunday, Nov. 29th.—After five days of dead calm, we took the monsoon this morning at daylight, settling in lightly, and at 9 p.m. we got under way, and stood to the northward and westward.

Thursday, Dec, 3rd.—At daylight we discovered a small vessel at anchor near the head of the harbour of the Island of Condore, with French colours, and awnings and other indications of her being a vessel of war. Sent a boat in to examine water. Boat returned at 1 p.m. with the commander of the vessel—a French vessel of war—and I was quite surprised to learn that we had arrived in civilized waters, and that the Island of Condore was in the possession of the French. There was a small garrison of 50 or 60 at the village on the east side.

There had been a recent revolt of the natives, the French officers said; and for this reason there were few vegetables or fruits to be had, and most of the natives had betaken themselves to the mountains. Got underway and ran into the harbour, the Frenchman politely showing me the way, and anchored in nine fathoms. Got a spring out, so as to present our port broadside to any enemy that might be disposed to violate neutrality, and, to save coal, permitted all the fires to go out. A couple of ships, running before the wind, passed in sight during the day—the ships prudently running a little out of the track to sight the island in this uncertain sea.

Friday, December 4th.—The harbour is picturesque, with mountains rising abruptly from the water to the height of 1800 feet, clothed with dense verdure from water's edge to top, many of the trees being of large size. The soil is very rich, but there is little cultivated land, the mountain-sides being too steep. The French have constructed two or three huts on the northern shore, and a couple of rude jetties, or landing places of loose stone. Landed on one of these to get sight for the chronometers. Found a Frenchman overseeing three or four Chinese seamen chopping wood and thatching a hut. The French make slaves, both here and on the mainland, of prisoners of war. The island is under the government of an *Enseign de Vaisseau*.

The commander of the Junk is a midshipman, so that we have gotten among high dignitaries. Landed at noon, at an inviting little sand-beach on the south shore, to get latitude—8° 39' 10". Found the ruined hut of a Frenchman, with his grave close by, and his name carved on the bark of a tree on the beach. A picturesque burial spot, amid eternal shades, with the lullaby of the ocean.

Saturday, December 5th.—Amused this morning, watching some sedate old baboons sitting on the sand-beach opposite, and apparently observing the ship very attentively. Large numbers of these caricatures of humanity inhabit these islands; yesterday, when a boat landed, great numbers of young ones were seen gambolling about; but one of the old ones having called out to them, they soon all disappeared in the thick wood. Returned the visit of the Frenchman. He is on board a miserable country craft, of about 40 tons burthen.

Sent a boat to the village on the east side to call on the Governor, and see if we could get some fruit and vegetables. Boat returned at nightfall. The village is a mere military port, the native inhabitants, except a few prisoners or slaves, having fled to the mountains, and no supplies were to be had. The Governor's residence is a *thatched* hut, as are all the other houses, with no industry or taste displayed in their structure. A few patches of cultivation were visible—rice, fruit, and cotton—the latter looking rather unpromising.

The destroyers of their rice were the monkeys. There are several varieties of fine large pigeons here, and in abundance. They are beautiful in feather and fat. A common variety has a green back and golden tail. This must be a paradise for monkeys, so abundant is their food in the forests, almost every tree bearing a fruit or nut of some sort. These French officers had heard and believed that we sunk or burned every ship we took, *with all on board*, and received the Paymaster rather coolly at first, but became quite cordial when they observed we were *Christians*, and did not commit this wholesale murder.

Sunday, December 6th.—Another lonely Sabbath-day—lonely, though in the midst of one hundred and fifty people. Away, away from home, by half the circumference of the globe! One of the most frequent and unpleasant of my experiences since I entered the China Sea, is an *oppressive* sense of *great* distance from home, and the utter strangeness of everything around me, almost as though I had entered another planet.

Monday, December 7th.—The commander of the island, M. Bizot, visited me today. He is an agreeable and intelligent young man of twenty-four or five years of age, and appeared very friendly and expressed sympathy for our cause. His position is a flattering one for a man of his age and rank, and he seems to have entered upon his duties with pride and zeal. He brought me a chart of the island, surveyed last year. The French have been in possession two years and a half. He spoke of my having hoisted the English flag upon first anchoring, and seemed surprised that we had not heard of the possession of the island by the French, which, he said, had been notified to all the Powers.

I pleasantly told him that I had had some notion of taking possession of it myself, but that I had found the French ahead of me. He brought down for me the welcome present of a *pig* and some little fruit, and told me he had a *potato patch* on shore, which he would share with me. Fresh provisions of all kinds are so scarce here that I fear my generous friend has been robbing himself. He told me that he had one hundred and forty *forçats*—slave-prisoners—at the village, whom he meant to put to good use in constructing store and dwelling-houses, &c. The hunters brought on board today an East India bat, or vampire, measuring two feet ten inches from tip to tip of wing. Its head resembled that of a dog or wolf more than any other animal, its teeth being very sharp and strong. Among the curiosities of the island is a locust, that has a whistle almost as loud as that of a railroad.

Tuesday, Dec. 8th.—The commander of the Junk came on board, and brought me a couple of fowls. The apes here are very large, and quite fierce. They will not run from you, but come around you, and grin and chatter at you. An officer shot one, and he died like a human being, throwing his hands over his wound and uttering piercing cries! This monkey was afterwards buried in the sand by his comrades, though the interment was not quite complete when the operators were interrupted. This is the reason why nobody ever sees a dead monkey, any more, as the Singhalese proverb says, than a white crow or a straight cocoa-nut tree.

A curious vegetable product was brought on board today, it being to all appearance a finely-made Havana cigar. The fibre is woody, covered with a smooth bark, and the colour of dark tobacco. It comes from the tree perfect in shape, and is not a seed-pod or fruit. One is at a loss to conceive its use or functions. The illusion caused by its appearance is perfect. We had no success with the sieve, the fish here being all jumpers, and jumping out of the net.

Wednesday, Dec. 9th.—The excessive heat and moisture of the climate here is very enervating. We begin to feel its effects already. It weighs upon us like a vapour-bath, and we feel indisposed to take the least exercise; a walk on shore of half a mile or so quite overcomes us.

Thursday, Dec. 10th.—At about 2.30 p.m. a French steamer passed the Gap, going to the southward. Afterwards informed by the commander that it was the mail steamer from Saigon, for Singapore. The Saigon people are expecting us there.

Friday, Dec. 11th.—In the afternoon the commander and surgeon came on board, bringing us a *bullock!* and some vegetables.

Sunday, Dec. 13th.—The crew dined off the commander's bullock today, being the first meal of fresh meat since leaving Simon's Town, nearly three months ago; and yet we have *no one* on the sick list! Causes—good water, temperance, strict government, and, as a consequence, a reasonable degree of contentment, and moderate and constant employment. The crew has had several runs on shore, too, without the possibility of getting drunk. A present of cocoa-nuts this morning from the commander. This young Frenchman is very attentive to us.

Monday, Dec. 14th.—Today we applied the principle of the cofferdam to the replacement of the copper around our delivery or blowpipe, some three feet below water. The operation proved quite simple and easy of accomplishment. Getting ready for sea. The news of our "whereabouts" probably reached Singapore on the evening of Saturday, and it is only two days from Singapore here, for a fast steamer; and so, whilst the enemy, should there be one at Singapore, is coming hitherward, we must be going thitherward to seek coal and provisions.

Tuesday, Dec. 15th.—At daylight got under way, under sail, and stood out of the harbour—lighting and banking the fires. On account of our proximity to the shore, and the very light breeze, we had barely room to pass the point—not more than a ship's length to spare, in case we had been obliged to let go our anchor. I felt quite nervous for a few minutes, but held on, and we caught a light breeze that soon sent us ahead out of danger.

Well, we are on the sea once more, with our head turned *westward*, or *homeward*. Shall we ever reach that dear home which we left three years ago, and which we have yearned after so frequently since? Will it be battle, or shipwreck, or both, or neither? And when we reach the North Atlantic, will it still be war, or peace? When will the demon-like passions of the North be stilled? These are solemn and interesting questions for us, and an all-wise Providence has kindly hidden the answers behind the curtain of Fate. A lengthened cruise would not be politic in these warm seas.

The homeward trade of the enemy is now quite small—reduced probably to twenty or thirty ships per year; and these may easily evade us by taking the different passages to the Indian Ocean, of which there are so many, and so widely separated. The foreign coasting trade (as between one port in China and another, and the trade to and from Calcutta and to and from Australia), besides facilities for escape, are almost beyond our reach—at least we could only ransom the ship, the cargoes being all neutral—that is to say, *such of them as get cargoes, now not many*. And then there is no cruising or chasing to be done here successfully, or with safety to oneself, without plenty of coal; and we can only rely upon coaling once in three months at some English port.

At the other ports there would probably be combinations made against us, through the influence of the Yankee Consuls. So I will try my luck around the Cape of Good Hope once more; then to the coast of Borneo; and thence perhaps to Barbadoes, for coal; and thence—? If the war be not ended, my ship will need to go into dock, to have much of her copper replaced, now nearly destroyed by such constant cruising, and to have her boilers overhauled and repaired; and this can only be properly done in Europe. Our young officers, who had had so agreeable a change from the cramped ship to the shores and forests of Condore, with their guns and their books, had become so attached to the island that they left it with some regret.

CHAPTER 33

Getting at the Truth

The *Alabama* was now steering for Singapore, and for three or four days kept her course without the occurrence of anything particularly noteworthy. On the 19th December she anchored for a time in the bay on the south-east side of the island of Aor, with its lofty hills clothed with green to their summits, and its little sandhills and groves of cocoa-nut trees. The island is unclaimed by any European nation.

Sunday, Dec, 20th.—Today being Sunday, and the weather being still thick, and blowing, I have resolved to remain until tomorrow before making the run for Singapore. Weather improved this morning, however, and the barometer going up. Several islands visible that were hid from us yesterday. Pulo Aor looking beautiful and picturesque. Some of the natives on board with their scant stores of fowls, eggs, and cocoa-nuts. They are larger than the natives of Condore, and stouter, and more developed, but with countenances not very prepossessing. The Governor, a rough-looking, middle-aged fellow, above the common height, pulled out some greasy papers, the recommendations of former visitors, and desired that I also would give him one, which I declined, as I knew nothing about him.

Their canoes are light and graceful, and occasionally they present quite a picture with their gaily-dressed or half-dressed occupants. We heard their *tom-toms* and *banjoes* last night as evening set in, but a music much sweeter to our ears was a chorus from some *frogs*, with notes somewhat finer than their relatives on our side of the earth. These islanders are nothing more than marine nomads, that lead an idle, vagabond life, intermixed with a good deal of roguery. They have a fine *physique*, as might be supposed from their open-air mode of life, in which they have plenty of healthful exercise without being overworked, as Mother Nature feeds them spontaneously, and they require little more clothing than they brought into the world with them.

In the afternoon some of the officers visited the shore, and were hospitably received. There were from ninety to one hundred natives, men, women, and children, visible, and there were probably as many more on the other side of the island, as they have a S.W. monsoon village there. They seemed to have plenty of fowls, and they are very expert fishermen. They were gambling—such a thing as labour being out of the question. The island seems originally to have been a solid mass of rock, the rocky walls of the mountains peeping out in many places from the midst of the dense forest, and gradually as time and the elements disintegrated portions of it, plants and trees took root, until the island became what it is now, a mass of luxuriant vegetation.

There were some fine large boats carefully hauled up on the beach, quite large enough for piratical purposes, for which they were probably intended, and some swivels were lying near the chief man's door. The cocoa-nut tree has climbed the mountain sides, and waves its feathery foliage from the crests of the ridges. It is food, and cordage, and light to the natives. Several delightful little valleys presented themselves, upon which, and on the adjacent steeps or the mountains, were thatched huts. Probably to the mere animal part of our nature, the life that these people lead is happier than any other; wants few and easily supplied, labour not too pressing, and the simple tastes satisfied with such pleasures as they find.

Rain, rain, in the afternoon. Most of the moisture is deposited on the mountain-tops, and the clouds sweep over it. And now for Singapore, God willing.

Monday, Dec. 21st—At 3.30 p.m. we got under way, under steam and sail, and steered S. by E. 32 1/2 miles, South 18 miles, and S. by W. 14 miles; and the weather setting in very thick, with heavy rain, obscuring all things, we were obliged to come to in 10 ½ fathoms, with the north point of Bintang island bearing, and within 11 miles by computation of the Pedra Branca lighthouse. We have thus to war against the weather as well as our enemies. Soon after daylight we made a ship-rigged steamer on our port bow, bound also for Singapore. She anchored near us astern. It clearing a little at noon, we got hold of the marks and got under way, and taking a Malay pilot, anchored off Singapore at 5.30 p.m.

Tuesday, Dec. 22nd.—At 9.30 p.m. the pilot came on board, and we ran up into New Harbour alongside of the coaling *depôt*, and commenced coaling. Singapore is quite a large town, with an air of prosperity—a large number of ships in the harbour. The country is beautiful, and green, with an abundance of fine fruit, &c.; the country around highly improved with tasteful houses and well-laid-out grounds. The English residents call it the Madeira of the East, in allusion to its healthfulness. Some twenty-two American merchant ships here, most of them laid up! The *Wyoming* was here twenty days ago, and left for Rhio Strait, where she remained for some days. Finished coaling last night, the operation having occupied no more than ten hours. Received provisions.

Wednesday, Dec. 23rd.—Weather variable, with occasional showers of rain—raining heavily in the afternoon. Visited the city, and was astonished at its amount of population and business. There are from eighty to one hundred thousand Chinese on Singapore island, nearly all of them in the city, from twelve to fifteen thousand Malays, and about fifteen hundred Europeans. Singapore being a free port, it is a great *entrepôt* of trade. Great quantities of Eastern produce reach it from all quarters, whence it is shipped to Europe.

The business is almost exclusively in the hands of the Chinese, who are also the artisans and labourers of the place. The streets are thronged with foot-passengers and vehicles, among which are prominent the ox, or rather the buffalo cart, and the hacks for hire, of which latter there are nine hundred licensed. The canal is filled with country boats of excellent model, and the warehouses are crammed with goods. Money seems to be abundant and things dear. They are just finishing a tasteful Gothic church, with a tall spire, which is a notable landmark as you approach; they are also completing officers' quarters on a hill which commands the town. Barracks for three or four regiments lie unoccupied a couple of miles outside the city, and a large court-house.

The moving multitude in the streets comprises every variety of the human race, every shade of colour, and every variety of dress, among which are prominent the gay turbans and fancy jackets of the Mahomedan, Hindu, &c. Almost all the artisans and labourers were naked, except a cloth or a pair of short trousers tucked about the waist. The finest dressed part of the population was decidedly the *jet-black*, with his white flowing mantle and spotted turban. The upper class of Chinese merchants are exceeding polite, and seem intelligent. I visited the establishment of Whampoa and Co. Whampoa was above the middle height, stout, and with a large, well-developed head. I was told that his profits some years amounted to forty or fifty thousand pounds!

He was sitting in a small, dingy, ill-lighted little office on the ground floor, and had before him a Chinese calculating machine, over the numerous small balls of which, strung on wires, he was running his hands for amusement, as a gambler will sometimes do with his checks. At the suggestion of the gentleman who was with me, I requested him to multiply four places of figures by three places, naming the figures, and the operation was done about as rapidly as I could write down the result. Their shaved heads, and long queues, sometimes nearly touching the ground, are curious features of their personal appearance. The workshops front upon the streets, and in them busy, half-naked creatures may be seen, working away as industriously as so many beavers all day long, seeming never to tire of their ceaseless toil.

Amid all this busy population I saw but one female in the streets, and she was of the lower class. Dined in the country with Mr. Beaver. The ride out was over good roads flanked by large forests and ornamental trees, among which was the tall, slender, graceful palm of the betel-nut. The Botanical Gardens are on an elevation commanding a fine view of the town and the sea, and are laid out with taste, ornamented with flowering trees and shrubs, and flowers. Hither a band of music comes to play several times a week, when the townspeople turn out to enjoy the scene. A few miles beyond the town the whole island is a jungle, in which abounds the ferocious Bengal tiger. It is said that one man and a half per day is the average destruction of human life by these animals. Visited opium-preparation shop. It pays an enormous licence.

All this beauty fails to reconcile the European lady to this country, I was told. The eternal sameness of summer, and the heat and moisture, weigh upon them, and their husbands being away all day on business, they pine for their European homes. The life seems agreeable enough to the men. The Governor of the "Straits Settlement" is a Colonel.

Thursday, Dec. 24.—Cloudy; five of my men deserted last night. The *Kwang-tung* got under way at 8.30 p.m., and we followed her and steered for the strait of Malacca. Several sails in sight; Malay pilot on board. Passed the Kwang-tung very rapidly. At about 1 p.m. we fired a gun and hove to an American-looking *barque*, under English colours, with the name, "*Martaban,* of Maulmain," on her stern. Sent a boat on board; and the officer reporting that she was an American-built ship, with English register, and that the master refused to come on board, I went on board myself to examine the case. There being no bill of sale, the transaction being recent, the master and mate, &c., being Americans, I had no doubt that the transfer was fraudulent, and captured and burned her.

The cargo had no paper on board connected with it, except the ordinary bill of lading. It consisted of rice, and was shipped in Maulmain by a Mr. Cohen, and consigned to his order at Singapore, whither the ship was bound. Of course, the cargo followed the fate of the ship under such circumstances. Upon examination of the Master (Pike), under oath, he admitted that the transfer was a sham, and made to protect the ship from capture. At 11.30 p.m. came to anchor about four miles distant from Malacca, bearing N., in fifteen fathoms water, for the purpose of landing our prisoners.

The boarding officer's journal furnishes the annexed description of the interview with the master of the prize:—

I was sent on board to examine her papers. The *barque* was American built, had a new English flag, and on her stern was painted "*Martaban*, of Maulmain." We knew that many Yankee vessels had been transferred to English owners, and of course had to have an English flag; but the question arose—Was there not some jobbery in this case? Nearing the *Martaban* I saw that she was newly painted; pulling round and under the stern, I saw that a name had been painted over, but could not see what the name was. I further observed that the last four letters of Maulmain had been painted much more recently than the other ones, so I determined to most rigidly scrutinize her papers. Upon my arrival on board, I inquired after the Captain's health, and then expressed a wish to make a few inquiries respecting his vessel.

He with the utmost affability was equally ready to afford me any information required, at the same time informing me I should find "everything correct." The vessel I found was the *Martaban* of Maulmain, Captain Pike, from Maulmain to Singapore, rice laden. I then requested to see the ship's papers, which request was readily granted. Accordingly the register, clearance bills of lading, and crew list, were speedily produced and examined, not omitting the Master's certificate. These but corroborated what I previously knew. Putting a few questions to the Captain, and comparing his answers with the papers, I learned the following facts—*viz.*, that the *barque* was American built, that she had been upwards of five months in Maulmain; that she had been transferred on the 10th December, after the cargo was in, and on the day in which she cleared, and only one day previous to her sailing; that the captain had no certificate or bill of sale, nor, in fact, any papers respecting the transfer on board; that he, the Captain, was an American, and had commanded the *barque* previous to her transfer.

Taking the register up again and closely scrutinizing it, I observed what had previously escaped my attention—*viz.*, that the register, which is a printed form, with spaces for written insertions, had been first written with a lead pencil, and over that with ink. No professional registrar or shipmaster would, I felt certain, have so prepared it. Looking again at the crew list I made another discovery, that all the names of the crew were written in one handwriting, from the mate to the boys. Now I well knew that some of the crew, and especially the mates, would be able to write, and of the mate's ability to use a pen I speedily satisfied myself by making him produce his logbook, wherein his name, &c., was written; or, if unable to write, the usual X, his mark, would have been affixed to each name.

I had now no doubt about the papers, believing them to be false. I then requested the master to take his papers and go on board the *Alabama*, which, however, he positively refused to do, unless forcibly compelled; stating that "this was an affair that flag (pointing to the English colours flying at his peak) wouldn't stand." He still persisting in his refusal to go on board our ship, I took possession of his vessel, pending Captain Semmes' decision.

Finding that the *Mountain wouldn't come to Mahomet, Mahomet went to the Mountain*; for, after calling a man out of my boat and stationing him at the wheel, I dispatched the boat back to the *Alabama* with a report of the irregularity of the papers, and a request for further instructions. To my surprise, Captain Semmes came himself and stopped at the gangway, and told the captain he had come to examine the ship's papers. Captain Pike signifying his assent, we went into the cabin, and the papers being produced, I pointed out some of the discrepancies and acts previously mentioned.

Captain Semmes then sharply interrogated Pike, insisting upon additional documents to prove the legality of the transfer. None being forthcoming, Captain Semmes put some questions, as only a lawyer can (Captain Semmes not only having studied, but practised law), the answers to which only convinced Captain Semmes that what he had suspected was true—*viz.*, that the ship was sailing under false colours, and was to all intents and purposes an American vessel.

Captain Pike of course protested, to which Captain Semmes replied by ordering the destruction of the vessel. Captain Semmes returning to the *Alabama*, I ordered the English flag to be hauled down, and directed the mates and crew to pack their luggage, and hold themselves in readiness to go on board our ship. The First Lieutenant coming off, our boats got off a few stores, and the prisoners were transferred to the *Alabama*.

By 5.20 had applied the torch, and regained our ship 5.30. The steamer *Kwang-Tung* was observed near our burning prize. We then shaped our course for Malacca, intending to land our prisoners there.

About 7.30 the same evening, Mr. Smith, captain's clerk, and self had the boatswain and a seaman down in the steerage; and putting them on oath obtained the following additional particulars—*viz.*, that they shipped on board the *Martaban* at Hong Kong and Singapore respectively; that she was then an American vessel, and called the *Texan Star*, of Galveston or Boston (she having had two American registers); that she left Maulmain as the *Texan Star*, and on leaving there hoisted American colours; that the name *Martaban*, of Maulmain, was painted by the captain's nephew two days after leaving that port; that the English flag was hoisted for the first time when the *Alabama* hove in sight this day; and that no articles were signed by them at Maulmain; nor, indeed, was any agreement made by the crew to serve in a British vessel, all hands, in fact, believing her to be American. The mate having also made a few admissions, they and the preceding depositions were shown to Captain Semmes, who, after sending for Captain Pike, put the following questions to him—*viz.*:

What is your name?
Samuel B. Pike.

Where were you born?
At Newbury Port, Massachusetts.

Are you a naturalized citizen of any foreign government?
I am not.

How long have you been in command of the *Martaban*, formerly the *Texan Star*?
Two years and a half.

In what part of the United States was the *Texan Star* registered?
She was built and registered at Boston.

Has she but one register in America?
There was a change of owners, and she has had two American registers.

Who were the owners under the last American register?
John Alkerm, Samuel Stevens, George L. Rogers, and myself.

What proportion of the ship did you own?
One-sixth.

When did you sail from the last port in the United States?
A year ago last July.

It is stated in the present British register that Mr. Mark Currie is the owner?
That is as I understand it.

Do you state upon your oath that the sale was a *bonâ fide* sale?
I do not state that.

Do you not know that it was intended merely as a cover to prevent capture?
Yes, I do know it.

This closed the matter; nothing more was necessary. Here was admission enough to destroy any legal doubt that might have arisen from the destruction of a vessel under the English flag. What added to our triumph was the copy of a letter from Captain Pike to his owners, in which he stated that "he had taken such precautions as would deceive Semmes and all the Confederates." Had the *Texan Star* escaped, how Yankee cuteness would have been extolled! Why, as the Bostonians have presented a gold chronometer to the master of the *barque Urania* for such a daring deed as hoisting the American flag over his American vessel in a neutral port (Cape Town), whilst the *Alabama* was lying there, I say, had the *Texan Star* escaped from the *Alabama*, nothing short of the Presidency, or a statue in marble, or the deed graved in letters of gold, or some other equally ridiculous token of admiration, would have awaited the gallant master, and the fame of his clever trick would have been handed down to Yankee posterity.

Captain Semmes thus resumes his diary on the 25th December:- At daylight sent the prisoners of the *Texan Star* on shore, with a note to the Commander. Malacca is a pretty little village, or at least the sea-point, viewed from our anchorage, with a picturesque hill in the rear, on which is situated the fort and lighthouse. The flagstaff was decorated with flags and signals in honour of Christmas Day. A couple of boats with some English officers and citizens ran off, and visited us for a few minutes. Got under way at 9.30, under steam; at night anchored near Parceelar Hill in 25 fathoms water.

Saturday, December 26th.—At 6 p.m. got under way, and stood out for the lightship, and soon made a couple of American-looking ships ahead, at anchor; steamed up to the first, which refused to show colours. Sent a boat on board, when she proved to be the American ship Senora, from Singapore. Captured her, and steamed to the second, which in like manner refused to show colours. Upon sending a boat on board, she proved to be the American ship *Highlander*, also from Singapore. Captured her. Both of these ships were very large, being over a thousand tons each. They were both in ballast, bound to Aycaab for rice. At 10 p.m., having sent off the crews of the two prizes in their own boats, at their own election, fired the ships, and steamed out. Passed the lightship at about 11 p.m., and discharged the pilot.

From the 26th December to the 13th of January the *Alabama* steadily pursued her course, meeting with little adventure. Only four sail were seen in the period, and these all proved to be neutrals. On the last day of the year 1863 the North Indian Ocean was entered, and the ship's head once more laid in the direction of the Cape.

CHAPTER 34

Off Again

On the 14th January, as the *Alabama* was lazily drifting in a northeasterly direction, near the Malabar coast, a ship was discovered running down towards her. The useful decoy—the United States flag—was at once hoisted, and the same colours were run up by the stranger. A gun brought the Yankee vessel to, and the *Alabama* forthwith took possession of the *Emma Jane* of Bath, Maine, bound from Bombay to Amherst in ballast, and at 8.30 p.m. the prize was set fire to.

About this period the cruiser experienced a series of calms, and she drifted with the current rather than sailed. On the 16th of January the Ghaut Mountains were made, and Captain Semmes makes the following entry in his journal.

Saturday, January 16th.—At meridian made the town of Quilon, and bore up east 1/2 south for the town of Angenga, which we made about 2 p.m. At 4.30 came to in the road abreast of the fort, and despatched a Lieutenant on shore to see about landing my prisoners. In the evening the residing magistrate's son came on board, and I arranged the matter with him. There being no external trade or shipping at Angenga, the prisoners could not well get away by sea; but my visitor stated that there was lagoon navigation inland all the way to Cochin, some seventy-five miles to the northward, and that at Cochin there were always means of reaching Bombay and other ports.

Native boats were passing every day between Angenga and Cochin, and if I would send the necessary provisions on shore for the prisoners, his father would see them transported to Cochin. I sent a lieutenant on shore after night with the son, to arrange the matter with the father; and as the boat was delayed much beyond her time, and we heard some firing as of revolvers and muskets, and as there was also some surf running, I became uneasy, and despatched the First Lieutenant in another boat to look into the matter. The chief magistrate had only been at public worship—the cause of the detention of the boat. Both boats returned about 11.30 p.m.

Sunday, January 17th.—At daylight I sent all the prisoners on shore, where they were landed apparently in the presence of half the village—the native boats taking them through the surf—and at 9.30 got under way. The town of Angenga was formerly of some importance as a shipping port for the produce of the country—cocoa-nut oil, pepper, &c. But all its trade has passed to its more prosperous rival—Cochin. It is about fifty miles from Travancore, the residence of the *Rajah*. There is water communication all the way, and the journey is generally made (in canoes) in the night to avoid the heat of the sun. The natives are nearly as black as the Africans, but with straight hair and European features. A large number of them visited the ship this morning. They were fine specimens of physical development, and wore scarcely any other covering than a cloth about the loins. They were sprightly and chatty, and in their quaint canoes made quite a picture.

On the 17th January the *Alabama* left Angenga, arriving without further adventure on the 21st at the Island of Minicoy, and after three weeks more of fine weather, found herself off the island of Comoro.

Tuesday, February 9th.—At 3.30 p.m. passed in sight of the N.E. end of Comoro. Soon after daylight made the Islands of Johanna and Mohilla. At 1.30 p.m. came to anchor about three-quarters of a mile from the shore. Despatched the Paymaster to the-town to arrange for fresh provisions. In the afternoon visited by several canoes, with a couple of poles lashed across the gunwales, attached to a float in each, to maintain their stability. Stalwart naked negroes were for the most part their occupants. Many of them spoke a little English. Among others, a dignitary of the church came on board with the compliments of the chief priest (Mahommedan).

We made arrangements with him for the supply of the ship. One of his companions asked me to which of the belligerent parties I belonged to, the North or the South. I replied, to the South. "Then," said he, "you belong to the side which upholds slavery." "Yes," said I, "we belong to the country where the black man is better taken care of than in any other part of the world." The churchman seeing me put on the defensive, as it were, came to my aid, and said: "Oh, we are slaveholders here; being Mahommedans, we have no prejudices that way; our only trouble is, we cannot get slaves enough. The English, who have no control over us, we being an independent government, are strong enough to interfere in everybody's business, and to say to us, that we bring over from the main no more slaves. The slaves themselves would gladly come to us, as they are much better off than under their native chiefs, who are continually making war upon and enslaving one another."

My informant was himself a full-blooded African negro, as black as the ace of spades, but with an immaculate white turban on his head, and the flowing robe and loose jacket of the Mahommedan.

Wednesday, February 10th.—Visited by the King's Dragoman this morning, who came to pay the respects of the authorities, to say he was glad to see us in Johanna. In the course of conversation, he was pleased to say that our ship was well known to him, and the news of our having appeared off the Cape some months ago had driven off all the Yankee whalers, several of which had been accustomed to resort hither. King Abdallah, he said, resided on the east side of the island. The king himself would come to see us, but was very busy just now patting up a sugar-mill, which he had just received from the Mauritius.

The island is a beautiful, picturesque spot. There is quite a mountain in the interior, and the higher parts of Johanna are densely wooded; the mountain-sides being in some places so steep that the tops of some trees touch the trunks and roots of others.

The inhabitants are a mixture of Arabs and negroes. They are intelligent and sprightly, and had not only heard of the American war, but said it bore heavily on them, as they were now compelled to pay a much higher price for their goods, which are mostly cotton. We have driven away, they say, all their Yankee trade. The *Sultan* is a young man of twenty-eight, with a moderate harem of only five wives.

Thursday, February 11th.—Visited the town to get sights for my chronometers—which puts the town at 44.26.30 N., just 30" less than Captain Owen's determination. The town, as viewed from the anchorage, is a picturesque object, with its tall minaret, its two forts, one perched on a hill commanding the town, and the other on the sea-beach, and its stone houses; but the illusion is rudely dispelled on landing. You land on a beach of rocks and shingle, through a considerable surf even in the calmest weather. The beach was strewn with the washed clothes of the ship, and a set of vagabonds of all colour, save only that of the Caucasian, were hanging about looking curiously on. The town is dilapidated and squalid to the last degree—the houses of rough stones, cemented and thatched; the streets five feet wide, and rendered, as it would seem, purposely crooked.

It was the second day of the fast of Ramadan, and groups of idlers were congregated in the narrow porticoes reading the Koran. The language, which is peculiar to the island, is very soft and pleasing to the ear. We visited one of the principal houses. The walls were filled with a number of small niches, receptacles for everything imaginable—coffee-cups, ornaments, &c. A number of couches were ranged round the room.

A crowd of half-clad, dirty children gathered round us, but no female made her appearance. We took our sights among the gaping multitude, all of whom were very civil and polite, and returned on board about 5 p.m., having seen all the outside life that was to be seen at Auzuan. The inside life was, of course, out of our reach.

Upon coming on deck this morning I was struck with the soft picturesque beauty of the hills, as shone upon by the morning sun lighting up the tops and sides, and throwing the valleys and ravines into shade. At night I am lulled by the roar of the sea upon the beach. It is delightful to sniff the fragrance of the land as it comes off to us upon the dew-laden wings of the softest of breezes. My fellows on shore looked rueful and woe-begone—nature had no charms for them—there was no liquor to be had! If I were to remain here long, I should send them on shore as a punishment.

Friday, February 12th.—This is the Mahommedan Sabbath, but they do not keep it so grimly as the Puritans. We had a number of visitors on board, and among others, several princes, cousins-german of the Sultan, one of them being the commander-in-chief of the army. He gave me an account of the affair of the Dale. Some years ago two Yankee whalers came in. One of them obtained provisions to the amount of two hundred and fifty dollars, telling the people he was too poor to pay for them in money, but that he would give them a bill on the Consul at Zanzibar. To this they assented; the skipper then ran off with his ship in the night, without giving the bill. They seized the other captain and took him on shore, to keep him as a hostage while his ship should go in pursuit of the runaway and get the promised bill.

But they thought better of it in a few hours, and released him. The Dale came the next season and demanded twenty-five thousand dollars, threatening to burn the town if the money was not paid. They could not pay them, there being probably not so much money in the island. The Yankees then set fire to one end of the town, cannonaded the fort, doing some damage, and withdrew. This is about the usual origin of Yankee shipmasters' complaints to their government. I made a present of a captured Yankee clock to each of the princes, and gave them a package of writing-paper. They seemed anxious to get some finery for their wives, but I told them we were not in that line, like Yankee whalers.

Saturday, February 13th.—Visited the town again today. Called at the houses of a couple of the princes, in which I found everything dirty, with an attempt at tawdry finery. A black *houri* was set to fan me. We were served with rose syrup. Walked to the prince's garden—a beautiful wilderness of cocoa and betel nuts, sweet orange and mango, with heterogeneous patches of rice, sweet potatoes and beans, and here and there a cotton plant. Two or three slave huts were dotted about, and walls of loose stones ran along crooked lanes and bye-ways. As we came off, some of the inhabitants were at evening prayer, and others preparing to take their evening meal. People met us everywhere with kindly greetings, and the *Cadi*, a venerable-looking old man, wished me a safe return to my own country.

Sunday, February 14th.—Visited in force again today by the princes, and other chief men. In the afternoon the high-priest visited me. He was a fine-looking man—Arab by descent—with a well-developed forehead, and easy, gentlemanly bearing. He wore a sword, and was evidently looked upon with great respect by his attendants. He expressed much sympathy with our cause, and said he would pray to Allah for our success. The Yankee whalers, he said, invariably stole some of their slaves. Said they could not do very well without the whalers, as they were the only traders to the island, and brought them many useful things.

Monday, February 15th.—Received on board some bullocks and fruit; paid our bills, and were taken leave of affectionately by the simple people. At meridian moved out of the anchorage under steam, amid the cheers, given in real English fashion, by the many boatmen that surrounded us.

CHAPTER 35

At Cherbourg

From the middle to the 28th February there was but little excitement on board the *Alabama*. On that day the usual routine of life on a man-of-war was broken by the cry of "Man overboard." The vessel was at once hove to, but before a boat could be lowered a gallant fellow, Michael Mars, leapt overboard, and swimming to the rescue of his shipmate, fortunately succeeded in saving the man's life.

On the third of March they saw the first Cape pigeon and albatross, and on the 4th Captain Semmes writes as follows:—

The gale still continues, though moderating very fast; sea not so turbulent, though the surf is thundering into it now and then, and keeping the decks flooded. 'Tis three years today since I parted with my family in Washington, on the day in which Washington's great republic was humiliated by the inauguration as President of a vulgar democratic politician, in whom even the great events in which, by a singular destiny, he has been called to take a part, have not been able to sink the mountebank. These three years of anxiety, vigilance, exposure, and excitement, have made me an old man, and sapped my health, rendering repose necessary, if I would prolong my life. My ship is wearing out, too, as well as her commander, and will need a general overhauling by the time I can get her into dock. If my poor services be deemed of any importance in harassing and weakening the enemy, and thus contributing to the independence of my beloved South, I shall be amply rewarded.

The *Alabama* still kept on through gales, with creaking cordage and jerking tiller ropes, until on the 11th of March the Cape was sighted, off which they were knocked about until the 20th instant; lying in the track of vessels bounding before the gale at the rate of ten or twelve knots an hour, and only able to see them when within a mile of the ship.

Arrived in Table Bay, Captain Semmes received intelligence of the seizure of the *Tuscaloosa*, upon which he at once wrote a despatch to Admiral Walker.[1]

The Cape was left on the 25th of March, the vessel's head being laid towards Europe, and on the 29th the following entry is found in the journal:—

"I have at length had a little leisure to read the late papers received at the Cape. The Yankee Government and people, and with them a great portion of the English press and people, seem to have jumped suddenly to the conclusion that we are beaten, and that the war must soon end by our submission! Mr. Lincoln has even gone so far as to prescribe the terms on which our States may re-enter the rotten "concern"—to wit, by a reorganization of the States government by one-tenth of the people. Verily, the delusion of these men in the matter of this war is unaccountable. No power on earth can subjugate the Southern States, although some of them have been guilty of the pusillanimity of making war with the Yankees against their sisters. History will brand them as traitors and cowards. As for the tone of the English press, I am not surprised at it. England is too rich to be generous. Our war for her is a sort of prize-fight, and she is looking on in about the same spirit with which her people lately viewed the prize fight between King and Heenan. Hurrah one; well done the other."

From March 29th to April 22nd there were no events calling for special attention, save that on the sixteenth the intelligence was learned from the master of a French ship that there were no American vessels at the Chincha Islands, though in July, 1863, there were between seventy and eighty American sail there. This speaks volumes of the terror the *Alabama* had excited.

The night of the 22nd of April was employed in giving chase to a strange sail, which was overhauled at daybreak on the following morning; and the United States flag having been responded to by a display of the same colours, the *Alabama* boarded and took possession of the *guano*-laden ship, *Rockingham*, which was employed as a target, and then set fire to. The cargo being claimed as the property of

---

1. For papers relating to the seizure of this vessel, see Appendix.

neutrals, Captain Semmes examined the ship's papers and entered the following in his journal:—

CASE OF THE *ROCKINGHAM*

"Ship under United States colours and register. Is from Callao, bound to Cork for orders, and loaded with *guano*. This *guano* purports to be shipped by the Guano Consignment Company to Great Britain. One Joseph A. Danino, who signs for Danino and Moscosa, certifies that the *guano* belongs to the Peruvian Government; and Her Britannic Majesty's Acting Consul at Lima certifies that the said Joseph A. Danino appeared before him and 'voluntarily declared' 'that the foregoing signature is of his own handwriting, and also that the cargo above mentioned is truly and verily the property of the Peruvian Government.'

"As this is the only certificate of the neutrality of the cargo among the papers, and as nobody swears to anything in this certificate, there is no testimony at all. The ship being enemy's property, and the cargo being presumed to be enemy's property also, from being found on board the ship, it was incumbent on the neutral parties, if there are any such in the case, to have documented their property by sworn certificates; and this rule of law is so well known, that the absence of an oath would seem to be conclusive as to the fraudulent attempt to cover. Ship and cargo condemned."

This capture was followed by that of the *Tycoon*, on the 27th of the same month; and as no claim of neutrality of cargo was made, the ship was burned. This, as it afterwards turned out, was the last of the *Alabama*'s prizes. Nineteen other vessels were overhauled before she reached Cherbourg, but not one of them sailed under the Stars and Stripes. When it is remembered that no less than sixty-five American ships had been taken by the gallant cruiser, it is not much to be wondered at that the Yankee flag was a *rara avis* on the high seas.

From the 25th of May to the 10th of June the *Alabama* was making her way north, and on the last-named date she was abreast of the Lizard, and was boarded by a Channel pilot. "I felt," writes Captain Semmes, "great relief to have him on board, as I was quite knocked up with cold and fever, and was too ill-qualified physically for exposure to the weather and watching through the night. And thus, thanks to an all-wise Providence, we have brought the cruise of the *Alabama* to a successful termination."

Little could Captain Semmes have imagined, when he penned

these lines, that the cruising days of his vessel were so soon to end. The vessel entered Cherbourg on the morning of the 11th. Two days after news was received that the *Kearsarge* would shortly arrive there, intelligence which was confirmed next day by the appearance of that vessel.

CHAPTER 36

The Informing Spirit

It was written that the *Alabama* was never to behold the ports of her country!

The latest entries in the diary of Captain Semmes are of an interest too great to permit us to exclude them, prior to the narration of the memorable duel which closes the history of a vessel whose renown, short as her career has been, may challenge that of any ship that has spread a sail upon the waters, and casts a lustre even upon the heroic history of the Confederate States.

On Tuesday, June 14th, Captain Semmes writes:—

Great excitement on board, the *Kearsarge* having made her appearance off the eastern entrance of the breakwater, at about 11 p.m. Sent an order on shore immediately for coal (one hundred tons), and sent down the yards on the mizzen-mast, and the topgallant yards, and otherwise preparing the ship for action.

Wednesday, June 15th.—The Admiral sent off his *aide* to say that he considered my application for repairs withdrawn upon my making application for coal, to which I assented. We commenced coaling this afternoon. The *Kearsarge* is still in the offing; she has not been permitted to receive on board the prisoners landed by me, to which I had objected in a letter to the Admiral. Mailed a note yesterday afternoon for Flagofficer Barrow, informing him of my intention to go out to engage the enemy as soon as I could make my preparations, and sent a written notice to the U.S. consul, through Mr. Bonfils, to the same effect. My crew seems to be in the right spirit, a quiet spirit of determination pervading both officers and men. The combat will no doubt be contested and obstinate; but the two ships are so equally matched, I do not feel at liberty to decline it. God defend the right, and have mercy upon the souls of those who fall, as many of us must!"

It has been denied that the captain of the *Kearsarge* sent a challenge to the *Alabama*. Captain Semmes, indeed, says nothing of it himself. What the *Kearsarge* did—and with a particular object, there cannot be a doubt—was, as recorded, to enter the breakwater at the east end, and "at about 11 p.m., on Tuesday, she *passed through the west end without anchoring.*" These are the words of a French naval captain, who speaks of what he saw. Few will deny that among brave men this would be considered something equivalent to a challenge. It was more than a challenge—it was a defiance. The officer we have quoted adds, that "anyone could then see her outside protection." It is easy to see everything after the event. The *Kearsarge* looked bulky in her middle section to an inspecting eye; but she was very low in the water, and that she was *armed* to resist shot and shell it was impossible to discern.

It is distinctly averred by the officers of the *Alabama* that from their vessel the armour of the *Kearsarge* could not be distinguished. There were many reports abroad that she was protected on her sides in some peculiar way; but all were various and indistinct, and to a practical judgment untrustworthy. Moreover, a year previous to this meeting, the *Kearsarge* had lain at anchor close under the critical eye of Captain Semmes. He had on that occasion seen that his enemy was not artificially defended. He believes now that the reports of her plating and armour were so much harbour-gossip, of which during his cruises he had experienced enough.

Now the *Kearsarge* was an old enemy, constantly in pursuit, and her appearance produced, as Captain Semmes has written, great excitement on board the *Alabama*. And let us here call attention to what the officers and men of the illustrious Confederate ship had been enduring for the space of two years. During all this time they had been homeless, and without a prospect of reaching home. They had been constantly crowded with prisoners, who devoured their provender-of which they never had any but a precarious supply. Their stay in any neutral harbour was necessarily short as the perching of a hawk on a bough. Like the hawk's in upper air, the *Alabama's* safety as well as her business was on the high seas.

Miserably fed, hunted, eluding, preying, destroying—is this a life that brave men would willingly have to be continuous? They were fortified by the assurance of a mighty service done to their country.

They knew that they inflicted tremendous damage upon their giant foe. They were, perhaps, supported by the sense that their captain's unrivalled audacity had done more harm to the United States than the operations of many thousand men. But their days were wretched; their task was sickening; it demands an imagination that can fix its eye upon stern, barren duty as a planet never darkened, always visible, for such a life as this to be carried on uncomplainingly and without a passionate longing for the bare exercise of hard blows.

In addition, they read of the reproaches heaped upon them by comfortable shore-men. They were called pirates, and other gloomy titles. The execrations of certain of the French and English, and of all the United States press, sounded in their ears across the ocean; but from their own country they heard little. The South was a sealed land in comparison with the rest of the world. Opinion spoke loudest in Europe, and though they knew that they were faithfully, gallantly, and marvellously serving their country in her sore need, the absence of any immediate comfort, either physical or moral, helped to make them keenly sensitive to virulent criticism, even to that of avowed and clamorous enemies.

It was this state of mind through the whole crew which caused the excitement on board the *Alabama* when the *Kearsarge* steamed in and out of the breakwater. Now, and at last, our day of action has come! was the thought of every man on board. The chivalrous give and take of battle was glorious to men who had alternately hunted and fled for so dreary a term. They trusted for victory; but defeat itself was to be a vindication of their whole career, and they welcomed the chances gladly.

The application for coal at a neutral port was in itself a renunciation of any further hospitality from the harbour, as Captain Semmes was aware. The Port-admiral contented himself with pointing it out to him. A duel is not an unpopular thing in France. The prospective combat of two apparently equally-matched ships of war would have been sufficient to have melted any scruples entertained by Frenchmen in authority; they were only too happy to assist towards an engagement between Federals and Confederates, the latter being as popular in France as in England, to say nothing for the sympathy excited for the *Alabama*.

French officers agreed with Captain Semmes in thinking that there was marked offence and defiance in the manoeuvres of the *Kearsarge*, and that he could hardly do less than go out and meet her. We have done our best to show that the Captain, whether in his heart he felt the mere chances to be equal or not, was anxious to persuade himself that they were so. He knew his opponent to be the heavier in ship, battery, and crew, but "I did not know that she was also iron-clad," he says. Personally he desired the battle; the instigations of an enthusiastic crew, unanimous for action, as also of friendly foreign officers, are to be taken into account.

Those who venture, now that we are enabled to measure by results, to cast blame upon him, should first, in justice, throw themselves into his position. President Davis may deplore the loss of a vessel that did a mighty service, but we doubt not that he will endorse the honourable words of Mr. Mason in his justification of Captain Semmes, and rejoice that the man who was the ship, is saved for further service to the Confederacy.

On Sunday, in the morning, being the 19th June, the *Alabama* steamed out of Cherbourg harbour by the opening to the west, and steered straight to meet the *Kearsarge*, accompanied by the French iron-clad *La Couronne*. The late foul weather had given way to a gentle breeze, and the subsiding swell of the Atlantic wave under a clear sky made the day eminently favourable for the work in hand. All Cherbourg was on the heights above the town and along the bastions and the mole. Never did knightly tournament boast a more eager multitude of spectators.

It chanced fortunately that an English steam-yacht, the *Deerhound*, with its owner, Mr. John Lancaster, and his family, on board, was in harbour at the time. The *Deerhound* followed the *Alabama* at a respectful distance, and was the closest witness of the fight. Some French pilot-boats hung as near as they considered prudent. At the limit of neutral waters the *Alabama* parted company with her, escort, and the *Couronne* returned to within a league of the shore.

Left to herself at last, the *Alabama* made her final preparations for the coming struggle. Mustering all his ship's company upon the deck, Captain Semmes addressed them as follows;—

Officers and Seamen of the *Alabama*:
You have, at length, another opportunity of meeting the enemy—the first that has been presented to you since you sunk the *Hatteras*! In the meantime, you have been all over the world, and it is not too much to say that you have destroyed, and driven for protection under neutral flags, one-half of the enemy's commerce, which, at the beginning of the war, covered every

sea. This is an achievement of which you may well be proud; and a grateful country will not be unmindful of it. The name of your ship has become a household word wherever civilization extends. Shall that name be tarnished by defeat? The thing is impossible! Remember that you are in the English Channel, the theatre of so much of the naval glory of our race, and that the eyes of all Europe are at this moment upon you. The flag that floats over you is that of a young republic, which bids defiance to her enemy's, whenever and wherever found. Show the world that you know how to uphold it. Go to your quarters.[1]

It took three-quarters of an hour for the *Alabama* to come within range of the *Kearsarge*. At the distance of one mile, the *Alabama* opened fire with solid shot. The *Kearsarge* took time to reply. After ten minutes the firing was sharp on both sides.

According to the statement of the Captain of the *Kearsarge*, her battery consisted of seven guns—to wit, two 11-inch Dahlgrens-very powerful pieces of ordnance; four 32 pounders, one light rifle 28 pounder. She went into action with a crew of 162 officers and men.

The armament of the *Alabama* consisted of one 7-inch Blakeley rifled gun, one 8-inch smooth-bore pivot gun, six 32 pounders, smooth-bore, in broadside. The *Alabama*'s crew numbered not more than 120. On this head Captain Winslow speaks erroneously. He sets down the *Alabama*'s crew at 150 officers and men. The *Alabama* had a formidable piece in the Blakeley rifled gun, but she was destitute of steel shot.

It will thus be seen that there was inequality between the antagonists. Captain Winslow speaks of the *Alabama* having "one gun more" than the *Kearsarge*. His two great Dahlgrens gave the balance altogether in his favour. But in an estimate of the rival capabilities of the two vessels, the deteriorated speed of the *Alabama* should be considered as her principal weakness. Cherbourg had done little to repair the copper of her bottom, which spread out in broad fans and seriously impeded her cutting of the water; and it had been found impossible to do more than to patch up the boilers for the day's business.

They were not in a state to inspire the engineers with confidence. The *Kearsarge*, on the other hand, was in first rate condition and well

---

1. The above is a correct report of Captain Semmes' address on this occasion. Various statements have appeared as to the way in which it was continued: received. Captain Semmes states, "The only replies that were made were shouts from the seamen of 'Never! never!' when I spoke of the name of their ship being tarnished by defeat."

in hand. She speedily showed that she could overhaul the *Alabama*. In fact, the *Alabama* entered the lists when she should have been lying in dock. She fought with an exhausted frame. She had the heroism to decide upon the conflict, without the strength to choose the form of it. After some little manoeuvring this became painfully evident to Captain Semmes. The *Kearsarge* selected her distance at a range of five hundred yards, and being well protected she deliberately took time and fired with sure effect.

Captain Semmes had great confidence in the power of his Blakeley rifled gun, and we believe it is a confidence not shaken by its failure to win the day for him. He wished to get within easy range of his enemy, that he might try this weapon effectively; but any attempt on his part to come to closer quarters was construed by the *Kearsarge* as a design to bring the engagement between the ships to a hand-to-hand conflict between the men. Having the speed, she chose her distance, and made all thought of boarding hopeless.

It was part of the plan of Captain Semmes to board, if possible, at some period of the day, supposing that he could not quickly decide the battle with artillery. It was evidently Captain Winslow's determination to avoid the old-fashioned form of a naval encounter, and to fight altogether in the new style; his superior steam power gave him the option. When the *Alabama* took her death-wound she was helpless. We must interpret the respectful distance maintained by the *Kearsarge* up to the very last, and the persistent plying of her guns while the side of the sinking ship was visible, as a settled resolution on Captain Winslow's part to trust to guns alone, and throughout, so that a dangerous proximity might be shunned. That much homage was paid by him to the hostile crew, and that his manoeuvre was creditably discreet, few will deny.

The crew of the *Alabama*, seamen and officers, were in high spirits throughout the engagement, though very early the slaughter set in and the decks were covered with blood. Their fire was rapid and admirable. It has been said in the House of Lords by no less a person than the Duke of Somerset, that her firing was positively bad; and that she hit the *Kearsarge* only three times during the action. By Captain Winslow's own admission the *Kearsarge* was hit twenty-eight times by shot and shell—or once to every fifth discharge.

No seaman knowing anything of an actual engagement on the deep will object to the accuracy of such an aim. Had the *Kearsarge* shown the same blank sides as the *Alabama*, another tale might have been told.

Captain Semmes, however, perceived that his shell rebounded after striking her, and exploded harmlessly. This led him to rely upon solid shot. The *Alabama*, not being thus or in any way shielded, was pierced with shell, and soon showed vast rents in her after-part. Her pivot-gun was a distinct mark for the enemy, and a single shell exploding near it killed and wounded half the number of men by whom it was worked. Each ship fought her starboard broadside, and steamed in a circle to keep that side to the enemy. So, for an hour, this, to a distant spectator, monotonous manoeuvre continued, without perceptibly narrowing the range.

Captain Semmes was standing on the quarter-deck when the chief engineer sent word to say that the ship was endangered by leakage. The first lieutenant, Mr. Kell, was sent below to inspect the damage. He returned with word that the ship was sinking. Captain Semmes at once ordered the ship to be put about and steered towards shore. But the water was rising in her: the fires were speedily extinguished. The *Alabama*'s shot from slackening had now ceased. It was evident to all on board that she was doomed. To have continued firing would have been to indulge a stupid rancour, and to act in such a manner is not in the nature of a seaman like Captain Semmes. On the contrary, his thoughts were directed towards saving the lives of his crew. He gave command for the Confederate flag to be hauled down.

Many wild stories are being told of something like a mutiny of the crew at this desecration of the Southern banner; of how they implored the captain to spare them the disgrace of it; and of a certain quartermaster drawing his cutlass, daring any hand on board to haul down the flag, and being dramatically threatened with a loaded pistol by Mr. Kell, the first lieutenant, and so brought to his senses. The fact is, that the flag came down quietly and decorously. All on board perceived that there was no help for it, and that it would be a shocking breach of humanity to imperil the lives of the wounded men.

The general detestation of the Yankee was yet more strongly instanced when the men were struggling for life in the water. The head of every man was pointed away, as if instinctively, from the vessel that stood nearest to rescue him. One who was hailed from the *Kearsarge* with the offer of a rescue, declined it civilly, and made his way for the neutral flag. The men swam as if they had still an enemy behind them, and not one that was ready to save. Tardy as were the boats of the *Kearsarge* in descending to perform this office, they found many of the poor fellows still painfully supporting themselves above the surface. Of these, both men and officers, when, after being hauled into the boats, they had dashed the blinding salt water from their eyes and discovered among whom they were, many sprang overboard again, preferring any risk to the shelter of the Federalists. Hatred to the flag of the old Union and love of their Captain appear to have been their chief active passions. When taken on board the *Deerhound*, the question as to the safety of Captain Semmes was foremost in every mouth.

Captain Semmes asserts that shots were fired at the *Alabama* after the signal of surrender. We will not attempt to substantiate a charge like this: but French officers maintain it to be an undeniable fact that, after the Confederate flag had been lowered, the *Kearsarge* fired no less than five shots into her. We believe that Captain Winslow does not deny the charge; but asserts that he was unaware of the act of surrender. In his letter to the *Daily News*, he declares the accusation that he had been guilty of this act to be "twaddle" (we quote his own phrase).

The master's mate of the *Alabama*, Mr. Fullam, was despatched in the dingy to the *Kearsarge* with a request that assistance might immediately be given in rescuing the lives of the wounded men. It was promised, but the fulfilment of the promise, owing, as we trust it may be proved, to circumstances incidental to the fight, was, as we have said, tardy. Captain Winslow expressed himself in kindly terms with regard to his old shipmate in the days when the Union was not a mockery of its name; Captain Semmes having served with him in the same vessel many years back. During Mr. Fullam's absence the *Alabama* had gone down stern foremost. All the wounded had been stretched in the whale-boat for transmission to the *Kearsarge*.

The surgeon of the *Alabama*, an Englishman, Mr. David Herbert Llewellyn, son of an incumbent of a Wiltshire parsonage, and godson of the late Lord Herbert of Lea, was offered a place in this boat. He refused it, saying that he would not peril the wounded men, and he sank with the *Alabama*. The rest of the crew, with their captain, were already in the waves. Mr. Lancaster meantime had steamed up to the *Kearsarge*, requesting permission to assist in saving life, and he was soon among them, throwing lines from the yacht, and picking up many exhausted men in his boats.

The loss of men by drowning was nineteen, including an officer (Mr. Llewellyn), carpenter, and assistant-engineer. The loss in killed and wounded was twenty-eight, of whom seven were killed. Not a wrack of the *Alabama* was secured by the victors in this memorable sea-fight. The captain and his officers dropped their swords into the deep; the men drove their oars into the bottoms of the boats. One spirit—the spirit of the unconquerable Confederation of the Southern States—animated all. Not a man who was able to support himself in the water, swam towards the *Kearsarge*.

So sank the *Alabama*. It would have been glorious for her to have won, but it was not disgraceful that the day went against her. She fought against odds such as brave commanders are not in the habit of declining; she fought to the water's edge. An end like this, and the splendid antecedents she points to, have made her name and that of her captain household words. Her flag has been indeed a "meteor flag," and that it shall "yet terrific burn" we may reckon to be probable, when it is remembered that the informing spirit, of which the good vessel was but the gross body, is alive, and prepared once more to offer himself to the land of his choice for service upon the seas.

Appendix

No. 1

CAPTURES OF THE SUMTER.

Ably Bradford—Of New York, from New York to Puerto Caballo. Captured 25th July, 1861, N.E. of Laguayra, Venezuela.

Sent to New Orleans. Recaptured by enemy.

Albert Adams—Of Massachusetts. Captured 5th July, 1861, four leagues off Cienfuegos.

Sent to Cienfuegos. Released by Captain-General of Cuba.

Arcade—Of Maine, from Portland, Maine, to Guadaloupe. Captured 26th November, 1861, in lat. 20° 27' N., long. 57° 15' W.

Burned.

Ben Dunning—Of Maine. Captured 5th July, 1861, four leagues off Cienfuegos.

Sent to Cienfuegos. Released by Captain-General of Cuba.

Cuba—Of Maine, from Trinidad to English ports. Captured 4th July, 1861, in lat. 21° 29' N., long. 84° 06' W.

Sent to Cienfuegos. Retaken by enemy.

Daniel Trowbridge—Of Connecticut, from New York to Demerara. Captured 27th October, 1861, in lat. 17° 54' N., long. 56° 30' W.

Burned.

Ebenezer Dodge—Of Massachusetts, from New Bedford to South Pacific (whaling). Captured 8th December, 1861, in lat. 30° 57' N., long. 51° 49' W.

Burned.

Golden Rocket—Of Bangor, Maine. Captured 3d July, 1861, in lat. 21° 29' N., long. 84° 06' W. Valued at $35,000.

Burned.

Investigator—Of Maine, from Spain to Newport, Wales. Captured

18th January, 1862, in Straits of Gibraltar. Valued at $15,000,

Released on ransom bond.

Joseph Maxwell—Of Pennsylvania. Captured 27th July, 1861, seven miles from Puerto Caballo.

Sent to Cienfuegos. Released by Governor-General of Cuba.

Joseph Parkes—Of Massachusetts, from Pernambuco to Boston. Captured 25th September, 1861, in lat. 6° 20' N., long. 42° 24' W.

Burned.

Louisa Kilham—Of Massachusetts. Captured 6th July, 1861, five miles from Cienfuegos.

Sent to Cienfuegos. Released by Captain-General of Cuba.

Machias—Of Maine, from Trinidad to an English port. Captured 4th July, 1861, in lat. 21° 29' N., long. 84° 06' W.

Sent to Cienfuegos. Released by Captain-General of Cuba.

Montmorency—Of Maine, from Newport, Wales, to St. Thomas. Captured 25th November, 1861, in lat. 18° 30' N., long. 58° 40' W. Valued at $20,000.

Released under ransom bond.

Naiad—Of New York. Captured 6th July, 1861, five miles from Cienfuegos.

Sent to Cienfuegos. Released by Captain-General of Cuba.

Neapolitan—Of Massachusetts, from Messina to Boston. Captured 18th January, 1862, in Straits of Gibraltar.

Burned.

Vigilans—Of Maine, from New York to Island of Sombrero. Captured 3d December, 1861, in lat. 29° 10' N., long. 57° 22' W. Valued at $40,000.

Burned.

West Wind—Of Rhode Island. Captured 6th July, 1861, five miles off Cienfuegos.

Sent to Cienfuegos. Released by Captain-General of Cuba.

Captures of the *Alabama*

Alert—Of New London, from New London to the Indian Ocean (whaling). Captured 9th September, 1862, off Flores. Valued at $20,000.

Burned.

Altamaha—Of New Bedford, from New Bedford (whaling). Captured 13th September, 1862, in lat. 40° 34' N., 25° 24' W. Valued at $3,000.

Burned.

Amanda—Of United States, from Manilla to Queenstown. Captured 6th November, 1863, in lat. 7° 00' S., long. 103° 19' E. Valued at $104,442.

Burned.

Amazonian—Of New York, from New York to Monte Video. Captured 2d June, 1863, in lat. 15° 09', long. 55° 04'. Valued at $97,665.

Burned.

Anna F. Schmidt—Of Maine, from Boston (_via_ St. Thomas) to San Francisco. Captured 2nd July, 1863, in lat. 26° 14', long. 37° 51'. Valued at $350,000.

Burned.

Ariel—Of New York, from New York to Aspinwall. Captured 7th Dec., 1862, off Cape Maize. Valued at $261,000.

Released on bond.

Baron de Castine—Of Castine, from Bangor to Cardenas. Captured 29th October, 1862, in lat. about 39° 18' N., long. about 69° 12' W. Valued at $6,000.,

Released on bond.

Benjamin Tucker—Of New Bedford, from New Bedford (whaling). Captured 14th September, 1862, off Flores. Valued. at $18,000.

Burned.

Bethia Thayer—Of Maine. Captured 1st March, 1863, in lat. 29° 50' N., long. 38° 31' W. Valued at $40,000.

Released on bond.

Brilliant—Of New York, from New York to Liverpool. Captured 3d October, 1862, in lat. 39° 58' N., long. 50° 00' W. Valued at $164,000.

Burned.

Charles Hill—Of Boston, from Liverpool to Monte Video. Captured 25th March, 1863, in lat. 1° 22', long. 26° 08'. Valued at $28,450.

Burned.

Chastelaine—Of Boston, from Martinique to Cienfuegos. Captured 27th January, 1863, in lat. 17° 19' N., long. 72° 21' W. Valued at $10,000. Burned.

Contest—Of the United States, from Yokohama, Japan, to New York. Captured 11th November, 1863, in lat. 4° 48' S., long. 106° 49' E. Valued at $122,815.

Burned.

Courser—Of Province Town, from Province Town (whaling). Captured 16th September, 1862, off Flores. Valued at $7,000.

Burned.

Crenshaw—Of New York, from New York to Glasgow. Captured 26th October, 1862, in lat. 40° 11' N., long. 64° 32' W. Valued at $33,869.

Burned.

Dorcas Prince—Of New York, from New York to Shanghai. Captured 26th April, 1862, in lat. 7° 36', long. 31° 57'. Valued at $44,108.

Burned.

Dunkirk—Of New York, from New York to Lisbon. Captured 7th October, 1862, in lat. about 41° 00' N., long. 53°. Valued at $25,000.

Burned.

Elisha Dunbar—Of New Bedford, from New Bedford (whaling). Captured 18th September, 1862, in lat. 39° 50' N., long. 35° 25' W. Valued at $25,000.

Burned.

Emily Farnum—Of New York, from New York to Liverpool. Captured 3d October, 1862, in lat. 39° 58' N., long. 50° 00' W.

Neutral cargo, Released and made a Cartel.

Emma Jane—Of Maine, from Bombay to Amherst (in ballast). Captured 14th January, 1864, in lat. 7° 57' S., long. 76° 09' W. Valued at $40,000.

Burned.

Express—Of Callao, from Callao to Antwerp. Captured 6th July, 1863, in lat. 28° 28', long. 30° 20. Valued at $121,300.

Burned.

Gildersliene—Of London, from Sunderland to Calcutta. Captured 25th May, 1863, in lat. 12° 04', long. 35° 10'. Valued at $62,783.

Burned.

Golden Eagle—Of United States, from San Francisco (_via_ Howland's Island) to Cork. Captured 21st February, 1863, in lat. 29° 28' N., long. 44° 58' W. Valued at $61,000.

Burned.

Golden Rule—Of New York, from New York to Aspinwall. Captured 26th January, 1863, off Jamaica. Valued at $112,000.

Burned.

Hatteras—Of United States Navy, gunboat. Sunk 11th January, 1863, off Galveston. Valued at $160,000.

Sunk.

Highlander—Of the United States, from Singapore to Aycaab (in ballast). Captured 26th December, 1863. Valued at $75,965.

Burned.

Jabez Snow—Of Cardiff, from Cardiff to Monte Video. Captured 29th May, 1863, in lat. 12° 54', long. 35° 18'. Valued at $72,881.

Burned.

John A. Parks—Of Maine, from New York to Monte Video. Captured 2d March, 1863, in lat. 29° 25' N., long. 37° 47' W. Valued at $66,157.

Burned.

Justina—Of the United States. Captured 25th May, 1863, in lat. 12° 04', long. 35° 10'. Valued at $7,000.

Ransomed.

Kate Cory—Of Westport (whaler). Captured 15th April, 1863, in lat. 4° 08', long. 32° 01'. Valued at $10,568.

Burned.

Kingfisher—Of Massachusetts, from Fair Haven (on whaling expedition). Captured 23d March, 1863, in lat. 2° 08' N., long. 26° 08' W. Valued at $2,400.

Burned.

Lafayette (1)—Of New York, from New York to Belfast. Captured 23d October, 1862, in lat. 39° 34' N., long. 63° 26' W. Valued at $110,337.

Burned.

Lafayette (2)—Of New Bedford (whaler). Captured 15th April, 1863, in lat. 4° 08', long. 32° 01. Valued at $20,908.

Burned.

Lamplighter—Of Boston, from New York to Gibraltar. Captured 15th October, 1862, in lat. 41° 32' N., long. 54° 17' W. Valued at $117,600.

Burned.

Lauretta—Of Boston, from New York to Madeira and Mediterranean. Captured 28th. October. 1862, in lat. 39° 18' N., long. 67° 35' W. Valued at $32,880.

Burned.

Levi Starbuck—Of New Bedford, from New Bedford to the Pacific (whaling). Captured 2d November, 1862, in lat. 36° 13' N., long. 66° 01' W. Valued at $25,000.

Burned.

Louisa Hatch—Of Rockland, from Cardiff to Point de Galle. Captured 4th April, 1863, in lat. 3° 12', long. 26° 9'. Valued at $38,315.

Burned.

Manchester—Of New York, from New York to Liverpool. Captured 11th October, 1862, in lat. 41° 08' N., long. 55° 26' W. Valued at $164,000.
Burned.
Morning Star—Of Boston, from Calcutta to London. Captured 23d March, 1863, in lat. 2° 08' N., long. 26° 08' W. Valued at $61,750.
Released on bond.
Nora—Of Boston, from Boston to Calcutta. Captured 25th March, 1863, in lat. 1° 22', long. 26° 08'. Valued at $76,-636.
Burned.
Nye—Of New Bedford, from New Bedford (whaling *barque*). Captured 24th April, 1863, in lat. 5° 45', long. 31° 53'. Valued at $31,127.
Burned.
Ocean Rover—Of Massachusetts, from Massachusetts (out whaling). Captured 8th September, 1862, off Flores. Valued at $70,000.
Burned.
Ocmulgee—Of Edgartown. Captured 5th September, 1862, in about lat. 37° 20' N., long. 28° 08' W. Valued at $50,000.
Burned.
Olive Jane—Of the United States, from Bordeaux to New York. Captured 21st February, 1863, in lat., 29° 28' N., long. 44° 58' W. Valued at $43,208.
Burned.
Palmetto—Of New York, from New York to St. John's, Porto Rico. Captured 3d February, 1863, in lat. 27° 18' N., long. 6° 16' W. Valued at $18,430.
Burned.
Parker Cook—Of Boston, from Boston to Aux Cayes. Captured 30th November, 1862, in lat. 18° 59' N., long. 68° 45' W. Valued at $10,000.
Burned.
Punjaub—Of Boston, from Calcutta to London. Captured 15th March, 1863, in lat. 8° 36' N., long. 31° 43' W. Valued at $55,000.
Released on bond.
Rockingham—Of the United States, from Callao to Cork. Captured 23d April, 1864, in lat. 15° 52' S., long. 31° 44' W. Valued at $97,878.
Burned.
Sea Lark—Of New York, from New York to San Francisco. Captured 3d May, 1863, in lat. 9° 39' S., long. 32° 44' W. Valued at $550,000.

Burned.

Sonora—Of the United States, from Singapore to Aycaab (in ballast). Captured 26th December, 1863, off Malacca. Valued at $46,545.
Burned.

Starlight—Of Boston, from Fayal to Boston. Captured 7th September, 1862, off Flores. Valued at $4,000.
Burned.

Talisman—Of New York, from New York to Shanghai. Captured 5th June, 1863, in lat. 14° 35', long. 36° 26'. Valued at $139,195.
Burned.

Texan Star—Of the United States, from Maulmein to Singapore. Captured 24th December, 1863, off Malacca. Valued at $97,628.
Burned.

Tonawanda—Of Philadelphia, from Philadelphia to Liverpool. Captured 9th October, 1862, in lat. 40° 03' N., long. 54° 38' W. Valued at $80,000.
Released on ransom bond.

Tycoon—Of the United States, from New York to San Francisco. Captured 27th April, 1864. in lat. 11° 16', long. 32° 6'.
Burned.

Union—Of Baltimore, from Baltimore to Jamaica. Captured 5th December, 1862, off Cape Maise. Valued at $15,000.
Released on bond.

Union Jack—Of Boston, from Boston to Shanghai. Captured 3d May, 1863, in lat. 9° 39', long. 32° 44'. Valued at $77,000.
Burned.

Virginia—Of New Bedford, from New Bedford (whaling). Captured 17th September, 1862, in lat. 40° 03' N., long. 32° 46' W. Valued at $25,000.
Burned.

T. B. Wales—Of Boston, from Calcutta to Boston. Captured 8th November, 1862, in lat. 29° 15' N., long. 57° 57' W. Valued at $245,625.
Burned.

Washington—Of New York, from Chincha Islands to Antwerp. Captured 27th February, 1863, in lat. 30° 19' N., long. 40° 01' W. Valued at $50,000.
Released on bond.

Wave Crest—Of New York, from New York to Cardiff. Captured 7th October, 1862, in lat. about 41° 00' N., long. 53°. Valued at $44,000.

Burned.

Weather Gauge—Of Province Town, from Province Town (whaling). Captured 9th September, 1862, off Flores. Valued at $10,000.
Burned.

Winged Racer—Of the United States, from Manilla to New York. Captured 10th November, 1863, in Strait of Sunda. Valued at $150,000.
Burned.

No. 2

COURSE OF THE SUMTER

From NEW ORLEANS, *30 June*, 1861, *to* GIBRALTAR, 18 *January*, 1862.

1861.
July	1	Lat. 26.18 N.	Long. 87.23 W.
	2	23.04	86.13
	3	21.29	84.06
	4	No observation.	
	5	Off the Jardinelles.	
	6	At Cienfuegos, Cuba.	
	7	Ditto ditto.	
	8	Off the Caymans.	
	9	Off Jamaica.	
	10 to 15	No observation.	
	16 to 24	At St. Anne's, Curaçao.	
	25 to 27	At and off Puerto, Cabulla.	
	28	Off Tortuga.	
	29 to	At Port of Spain.	
Aug.	5		
	6	9.14	59.10
	7	8.31	56.12
	8	7.19	53.34
	9	6.10	50.48
	10	4.29	48.25

Aug.	11	Lat. 2.38 N.	Long. 47.48 W.
	12	4.10	49.37
	13	4.56	50.55
	14	4.49	51.19
	15–16	At Cayenne.	
	17	5.56	
	18	Off the mouth of the Surinam.	
	19 to 31	At Paramaribo.	
Sept.	1	No observation.	
	2	4.50	50.20
	3	3.05	48.44
	4	00.44	47.12
	5	1.03	44.48
	6 to 15	At Maranham.	
	16	00.17 S.	42.59
	17	2.19 N.	41.29
	18	3.38	40.57
	19	4.33	40.41
	20	4.46	41.00
	21	5.12	41.59
	22	5.37	42.12
	23	5.25	42.19
	24	5.35	42.27
	25	6.20	42.27
	27	6.24	43.10
	28	6.10	44.20
	29	6.55	45.08
	30	7.33	45.28
Oct.	1	7.39	45.55
	2	8.19	46.23
	3	8.30	46.21
	4	8.55	46.58
	5	9.13	47.21

Oct.	6	Lat. 8.31 N.	Long. 47.08 W.
	7	8.13	47.13
	8	8.52	46.44
	9	7.21	46.30
	10	6.22	45.48
	11	6.38	45.13
	12	6.56	44.41
	13	7.04	44.47
	14	8.31	45.46
	15	9.36	48.11
	16	10.22	50.05
	17	11.37	51.49
	18	13.01	53.12
	19	13.33	53.46
	20	13.46	54.06
	21	14.00	54.07
	22	14.21	54.16
	23	14.36	54.37
	24	15.20	54.51
	25	16.54	55.30
	26	18.13	56.04
	27	17.54	56.30
	28	17.03	57.07
	29	16.54	57.33
	30	16.40	58.16
	31	16.54	57.59
Nov.	1	16.52	57.25
	2	16.32	56.55
	3	16.35	57.38
	4	16.43	57.45
	5	17.10	59.06
	6	16.39	59.54
	7	16.00	60.46
	8		
	9	15.08	61.54
	10 to 23	At Martinique.	

Date	Lat.	Long.
Nov. 24	16.12 N.	
25	18.11	58.48 W.
26	20.07	57.12
27	22.22	56.27
28	24.22	57.12
29	25.51	57.36
30	27.16	58.29
Dec. 1	27.38	58.20
2	28.12	58.09
3	29.10	57.22
4	30.03	55.09
5	30.19	53.02
6	29.35	52.02
7	29.27	51.35
8	30.57	51.49
9	31.35	51.14
10	32.39	49.47
11	32.48	49.32
12 } 13 }	33.28	47.03
14	33.49	44.47
15	34.00	42.05
16	33.24	40.43
17	33.24	40.00
18	33.53	38.43
19	34.30	36.40
20	34.17	35.31
21	35.17	33.05
22	No observation.	
23	36.29	32.32
24	27.31	31.30
25	36.08	28.42
26	35.09	25.56
27	35.00	22.49
28	35.17	20.53
29	35.43	18.59
30	35.39	17.33
31	35.22	16.27

1862.
Jan. 1   Lat. 35.53 N.   Long. 13.14 W.
    2   35.52   9.36
    3   35.49   7.00

On the 4th of January the Sumter reached Cadiz, and on the 17th left for Gibraltar. She entered that port on the following day, where she was finally put out of commission.

COURSE OF THE ALABAMA.

1862.
Aug. 25   Lat. 39.15 N.   Long. 26.30 W.
     26   39.39   26.07
     27   39.59   24.34
     28   39.58   21.30
     29   38.56   19.23
     30   37.23   19.06
     31   Lat. by acc. 36.23   21.54
Sept. 1   Lat. 35.33   22.17
     2   35.29   24.22
     3   36.16   25.56
     4   37.22   28.08
     5   No observation.
     6 ⎫
    to ⎬ Off Flores.
    11 ⎭
     12   40.17   34.05
     13   40.34   35.24
     14   40.12   33.02
     15   40.03   32.46
     16   Off Flores.
     17   40.03   32.46
     18   39.50   35.25
     19   38.32   35.03
     20   37.20   36.26
     21   36.35   36.58

Sept.	22	Lat. 35.21 N.	Long. 37.26 W.
	23	34.43	38.38
	24	34.52	48.28
	25	34.59	41.10
	26	35.35	41.36
	27	37.12	43.13
	28	37.40	42.00
	29	37.09	43.13
	30	38.37	45.03
Oct.	1	40.27	46.31
	2	40 to 40.30	48 to 48.20
	3	39.58	50.00
	4	39.52	50.41
	5	40.19	51.14
	6	41.02	53.50
	7	No observation.	
	8	Lat.(D.R.)41.00	Long.(D.R.)55.43
			Long. Chro. 54.37
	9	Lat. 40.03	Long. 54.38
	10	41.13	53.45
	11	41.08	55.26
	12	41.42	56.48
	13	Assumed 40.30	59.28
	14	41.21	59.31
	15	41.32	59.17
	16	(D.R.)42.16	59.18
	17	(D.R.)42.06	59.46
	18	Supposed 41.25	59.10
	19	40.21	62.08
	20	40.28	62.40
	21	40.18	62.40
	22	By acct. 40.16	64.17
	23	39.34	63.26
	24	40.04	62.05
	25	39.57	63.18
	26	40.11	64.32
	27	39.47	68.06
	28	39.18	67.35

Oct.	29	No observation.	
	30	Lat. 39.18 N.	Long. 69.12 W.
	31	37.51	67.34
Nov.	1	36.15	65.55
	2	36.13	66.01
	3	35.17	67.11
	4	34.27	63.30
	5	31.34	61.27
	6	29.05	61.22
	7	29.03	59.23
	8	29.15	57.57
	9	27.51	58.24
	10	25.40	57.50
	11	24.05	57.36
	12	22.58	57.37
	13	22.08	57.43
	14	21.11	57.49
	15	20.40	58.24
	16	18.00	59.27
	17	15.51	60.20
	18	13.15	63.01
	21	12.10	64.35
	22 to 25	At Island of Blanquilla.	
	26	13.12	65.30
	28	16.19	66.06
	29	17.45	67.15
	30	18.59	68.45
Dec.	1	19.40	69.49
	2	20.04	71.50
	3	20.12	72.58
	4 to 12	Off Cape Maise, Jamaica, and Cuba.	
	13	18.47	78.27
	14	18.16	80.43
	15	18.39	83.06

Dec.	16	Lat.	19.16 N.	Long.	84.10 W.
	17		19.18		04.25
	18		19.47		85.46
	19		20.00		85.31
	20		21.20		86.32
	21		22.06		88.40
	22		21.26		91.15
	23		20.18		91.50
	24 to 31	} At the Arcas.			

1863.

Jan.	1 to 5	} At the Arcas.			
	6		21.11		93.13
	7		22.35		94.26
	8		24.36		94.45
	9		26.19		94.11
	10		27.45		94.42
	11		28.51		94.55
	12		28.03		93.08
	13		27.05		90.37
	14		25.58		88.58
	15		26.16		88.35
	16		23.43		87.35
	17		21.45		85.34
	18		19.50		82.51
	19		18.30		80.34
	20 to 25	} At Port Royal.			
	26		17.50		74.52
	27		17.19		72.21
	28		17.56		70.28
	29	At San Domingo.			
	30		19.31		67.38

Jan.	31	Lat. 21.45 N.	Long. 68.06 W.
Feb.	1	24.08	68.18
	2	26.17	68.06
	3	27.18	66.10
	4	28.00	64.11
	5	27.10	61.30
	6	25.44	60.32
	7	26.36	60.15
	8	25.41	58.48
	9	24.51	57.55
	10	24.32	56.53
	11	24.52	56.34
	12	25.15	56.36
	13	26.08	55.32
	14	27.09	53.17
	15	28.29	50.07
	16	28.45	46.57
	17	28.11	45.01
	18	28.15	44.37
	19	28.04	44.29
	20	28.32	45.05
	21	29.28	44.58
	22	29.33	44.57
	23	30.31	43.55
	24	30.32	42.50
	25	30.22	41.03
	26	30.23	40.42
	27	30.19	40.01
	28	30.07	39.38
March	1	29.50	38.31
	2	29.25	37.47
	3	28.42	36.59
	4	27.02	35.44
	5	26.04	35.23
	6	24.09	32.20
	7	24.30	35.12
	8	22.36	34.32
	9	20.22	33.53

Date	Lat.	Long.
March 10	18.26 N.	33.17 W.
11	16.18	32.36
12	13.57	31.47
13	11.31	31.25
14	9.24	31.48
15	8.36	31.43
16	7.46	30.21
17	7.53	30.34
18	7.14	29.26
19	5.59	28.01
20	4.32	27.00
21	2.47	26.23
22	2.11	26.24
23	2.08	26.08
24	1.41	26.13
25	1.22	26.08
26	1.12	26.32
27	No observation.	
28	00.46	26.19
29	00.18	26.10
30	00.34 S.	25.35
31	00.39	25.19
April 1	1.00	25.20
2	2.10	26.02
3	2.52	25.58
4	3.12	26.09
5	3.25	27.04
6	3.46	28.00
7	3.57	30.07
8	4.01	Long.(D.R.) 31.17
9	4.08	32.01
10 to 22	At Fernando de Noronha.	
23	4.42	31.49
24	5.45	31.53
25	6.22	31.44
26	7.36	31.57

April	27	Lat. 8.16 S.	Long. 32.18 W.
	28	8.19	31.40
	29	8.22	31.07
	30	9.02	31.39
May	1	9.17	32.17
	2	9.37	32.34
	3	9.39	32.44
	4	8.48	32.34
	5	10.06	32.45
	6	10.24	32.30
	7	12.08	33.07
	8	12.30	33.52
	9	12.55	34.49
	10	13.29	36.07
	11 to 21	At Bahia.	
	22	13.04	37.36
	23	12.33	36.39
	24	11.34	34.54
	25	12.04	35.10
	26	11.39	34.47
	27	12.15	35.05
	28	12.54	35.18
	29	13.31	35.38
	30	14.19	35.36
	31		
June	1	14.44	35.15
	2	15.01	34.56
	3	15.09	35.04
	4	14.46	34.57
	5	14.35	36.26
	6	15.17	35.26
	7	16.07	35.37
	8	15.55	35.28
	9	16.55	35.36
	10	16.17	34.35
	11	15.32	33.46

June	12	Lat. 17.25 S.	Long. 34.24 W.
	13	19.21	35.37
	14	19.54	35.18
	15	22.38	35.11
	16	23.41	35.36
	17	23.54	35.53
	18	24.16	37.15
	19	24.57	39.01
	20	25.48	40.18
	21	25.46	40.16
	22	25.55	40.21
	23	25.24	38.40
	24	25.19	36.36
	25	25.56	33.44
	26	Lat.(D.R.) 26.40	30.16
	27	26.01	28.29
	28	25.57	30.31
	29	26.35	32.59
	30	25.56	35.12
July	1	25.38	36.38
	2	26.14	37.51
	3	26.31	37.33
	4	27.27	34.37
	5	27.58	31.43
	6	28.28	30.20
	7	29.45	27.36
	8	30.00	24.20
	9	29.57	21.16
	10	29.29	17.47
	11	28.00	15.12
	12	26.44	13.32
	13	28.13	13.27
	14	29.21	11.31
	15	30.07	8.06
	16	Lat.(D.R.) 30.39	4.05
	17	30.16	00.20
	18	29.54	3.04 E.
	19	Lat.(D.R.) 29.47	5.32

July 20	Lat. 29.57 S.	Long. 7.23 E.
21	30.43	10.19
22	31.33	12.37
23	31.59	14.12
24	33.24	14.51
25	33.56	15.34
26	33.26	16.37
27	33.46	17.17
28	33.46	17.31
29 to Aug. 16	At Saldanha Bay, and the Cape.	
17	Lat. 34.03	Long. 17.11 E.
18	33.24	16.56
19	32.52	17.09
20	32.45	16.55
21	33.14	15.41
22	32.13	16.08
23	31.43	15.30
24	31.24	14.34
25	31.18	13.37
26	27.57	14.12
27	No observation.	
28 to 30	At Angra Pequena	
31	26.51	14.40
Sept. 1	No observation.	
2	28.37	10.13
3	29.43	8.59
4	30.04	8.46
5	30.24	9.28
6	30.35	11.16
7	31.17	11.07
8	31.41	11.16
9	32.30	12.49
10	33.16	15.20
11	33.10	16.37

Sept.	12	Lat. 33.43 S.	Long. 16.03 E.
	13	33.51	17.34
	14	34.28	17.43
	15	34.26	17.30
	16 to 24	At Simon's Town.	
	25	35.26	18.15
	26	37.28	17.58
	27	37.52	19.03
	28	39.02	23.07
	29	39.02	27.20
	30	39.12	31.59
Oct.	1	39.15	35.46
	2	38.27	39.02
	3	38.46	42.49
	4	38.43	46.56
	5	38.47	49.29
	6	38.44	53.33
	7	37.51	57.30
	8	38.04	60.23
	9	38.16	64.15
	10	38.26	68.57
	11	38.28	72.40
	12	38.46	77.12
	13	38.15	80.29
	14	37.47	83.42
	15	35.23	89.55
	16	35.23	89.55
	17	32.59	93.28
	18	30.59	96.17
	19	28.26	98.43
	20	25.33	99.43
	21	22.41	100.12
	22	21.13	100.10
	23	18.52	100.19
	24	15.45	101.25
	25	Lat. (D.R.) 12.26	Long. (D.R.) 102.00

Oct.	26	Lat. 10.27 S.	Long. (D.R.) 102.13 E.
	27	9.55	Long. 101.50
	28	9.38	101.51
	29	9·20	101.53
	30	9.09	102.14
	31	8.53	102.50
Nov.	1	8.55	103.51
	2	9.30	103.28
	3	9.17	103.31
	4	8.31	103.06
	5	7.22	103.15
	6	7.00	103.19
	7	6.59	103.27
	8 to 10	Off Flat Point.	
	11	4.48	106.49
	12	4.19	108.00
	13	3.59	107.25
	14	3.44	109.05
	15	3.03	109.27
	16	2.44	109.16
	17 to 23	Off the Malaya.	
	24	3.40 N.	109.45
	25	Supposed 3.50	Supposed 110.30
	26	4.36	111.42
	27	4.51	111.54
	28	4.51	111.54
	29	5.01	111.47
	30	6.14	110.31
Dec.	1	7.30	108.42
	2	8.30	107.15
	3 to 14	At Cindore.	
	15	8.24	106.48

Dec. 16		Lat. 7.18 N.	Long. 107.27 E.
17		(D.R.) 6.11	106.12
18		4.48	105.10
19 and 20	} At island of Aor.		
21 to 26	} At and off Singapore.		
27		4.08	100.11
28		Supposed 4.46	99.40
29		Supposed 5.29	98.16
30		5.39	96.40
31		Off N. end of Sumatra.	
1864. Jan. 1		6.23	93.35
2		5.39	93.08
3		5.29	92.33
4		6.05	Long. (D.R.) 91.40
5		6.29	90.37
6		6.07	88.40
7		5.39	87.22
8		5.22	84.53
9		5.05	82.09
10		5.14	79.50
11		5.49	78.25
12		7.26	76.02
13		7.33	76.01
14		7.57	76.09
15		8.25	76.08
16		At Quilon.	
17		8.40	76.32
18		8.31	76.30
19		8.05	75.05
20		7.29	74.28
21		No observation.	
22		7.52	70.22
23		7.04	67.17

Jan. 24	Lat. 7.03 N.	Long. 64.28 E.
25	6.27	61.49
26	5.33	59.19
27	5.01	56.36
28	4.02	53.46
29	2.43	51.00
30	00.50	48.42
31	1.31 S.	47.20
Feb. 1	3.15	46.13
2	4.48	45.40
3	6.47	44.44
4	8.24	44.26
5	10.18	43.47
6	10.42	44.00
7	10.44	43.50
8	10.45	43.42
9 to 16	At Islands of Johanna and Mohilla.	
17	13.41	43.04
18	14.15	42.45
19	15.03	42.24
20	16.00	41.45
21	17.02	41.31
22	18.43	41.20
23	19.49	41.23
24	20.29	41.19
25	21.18	41.44
26	23.36	41.15
27	25.31	40.00
28	27.11	37.51
29	29.16	36.17
March 1	31.32	34.37
2	33.20	32.22
3	35.05	29.49
4	35.11	23.28
5	35.51	26.43
6	39.09	24.58

March 7	Lat. 35.10 S.	Long. 24.03 E.
8	35.49	21.39
9	35.46	20.29
10	35.42	20.13
11	35.08	18.21
12	33.57	17.06
13	33.35	16.10
14	34. 3	15.20
15	33.48	15.23
16	32.50	16.31
17	33.10	16.22
18	No observation.	
19	32.57	15.55
20	33.51	17.31
21 to 24	At the Cape.	
25	34.02	18.10
26	33.41	15.52
27	31.50	12.39
28	31.36	10.09
29	30.25	8.25
30	28.53	6.55
31	28.00	4.50
April 1	26.13	2.40
2	24.17	0.24
3	22.35	1.29 W.
4	21.01	3.13
5	19.37	4.44
6	18.41	4.22
7	17.15	3.44
8	17.42	5.50
9	18.00	8.53
10	18.12	11.47
11	18.25	14.42
12	18.47	17.13
13	18.55	19.43
14	18.58	22.33

April	15	Lat. 19. 9 S.	Long. 25.—W.
	16	19.17	26.42
	17	19.12	27.33
	18	19.22	28.57
	19	19.13	29.36
	20	18.49	30.01
	21	18.18	30.26
	22	17.23	30.56
	23	15.52	31.44
	24	15.19	32. 6
	25	13.59	32. 4
	26	13. 5	32.22
	27	11.16	32. 6
	28	10. 5	31.46
	29	8. 9	31.29
	30	5.26	30.12
May	1	2.25	30.38
	2	00.13	30.41
	3	1.43 N.	31.28
	4	3.30	32.38
	5	5. 6	34.19
	6	7.15	36. 7
	7	9.40	37.36
	8	11.54	38.43
	9	14.13	39.43
	10	16.43	40.33
	11	18.37	41. 9
	12	20.10	41.25
	13	20.33	41.19
	14	20.53	41. 9
	15	21.12	40.55
	16	22.05	41.16
	17	22.57	41.50
	18	24.33	41.57
	19	26.32	41.50
	20	28.04	41.33
	21	29.24	40.42
	22	30.25	39.54

May 23	Lat. 31.39 N.	Long. 38.39 W.
24	33.13	36.49
25	35.51	35.41
26	37.43	33.53
27	38.42	32.50
28	39.23	32.31
29	39.51	(D.R.) 32.25
30	40.25	30.22
31	40.54	27.15
June 1	41.35	24.15
2	42.07	22.15
3	42.18	20.30
4	42.10	18.04
5	41.58	16.31
6	42.31	15.42
7	43.47	14.12
8	45.45	(D.R.) 12.06
9	47.34	9.07
10	49.18	6.03
11	On this day the Alabama entered Cherbourg harbour.	

No. 3

Mr. Laird's Speech on the *Alabama*

The following is a full report of Mr. Laird's speech in the House of Commons on Friday night:—After the discussion that has taken place about the *Alabama*, I shall not trouble the house with many remarks. I can only say, from all I know and all I have heard, that from the day the vessel was laid down to her completion everything was open and above-board in this country. (Cheers.) I also further say that the officers of the Government had every facility afforded them for inspecting the ship during the progress of building. When the officers came to the builders they were shown the ship, and day after day the customs officers were on board, as they were when she finally left, and they declared there was nothing wrong. ("Hear," from Mr. Bright.)

They only left her when the tug left, and they were obliged to declare that she left Liverpool a perfectly legitimate transaction. (Hear, hear.) One point has been overlooked in this discussion. If a ship without guns and without arms is a dangerous article, surely rifled guns and ammunition of all sorts are equally—(cheers)—and even more dangerous. (Cheers.) I have referred to the bills of entry in the custom houses of London and Liverpool, and I find there have been vast shipments of implements of war to the Northern States through the celebrated houses of Baring and Co.—(loud cheers and laughter)- Brown, Shipley and Co., of Liverpool, and a variety of other names, which I need not more particularly mention, but whose Northern tendencies are well known to this house. (Hear, hear.)

If the member for Rochdale, or the honourable member for Bradford, wishes to ascertain the extent to which the Northern States of America have had supplies of arms from this country, they have only to go to a gentleman who, I am sure, will be ready to afford them every information, and much more readily than he would to me or to any one else calling upon him—the American consul in Liverpool. Before that gentleman the manifest of every ship is laid, he has to give an American pass to each vessel; he is consequently able to tell the exact number of rifles which have been shipped from this country for the United States—information, I doubt not, which would be very generally desired by this house. (Loud cries of "Hear.") I have obtained from the official custom house returns some details of the sundries exported from the United Kingdom to the Northern States of America from the 1st of May, 1861, to the 31st of December, 1862.

There were—muskets, 41,500 (hear, hear); rifles, 341,000 (cheers); gun flints, 26,500; percussion caps, 49,982,000 (cheers and laughter); and swords, 2,250. The best information I could obtain leads me to believe that from one-third to a half may be added to these numbers for items which have been shipped to the Northern States as hardware. (Hear, hear.) I have very good reason for saying that a vessel of 2,000 tons was chartered six weeks ago for the express purpose of taking out a cargo of "hardware" to the United States. (Cheers.) The exportation has not ceased yet. From the 1st of January to the 17th March, 1863, the custom bills of entry show that 23,870 gun-barrels, 30,802 rifles, and 3,105,800 percussion caps were shipped to the United States. (Hear, hear). So that if the Southern States have got two ships, unarmed, unfit for any purpose of warfare—for they procured their armaments somewhere else—the Northern States have been well supplied from this country through the agency of some most influential persons. (Hear, hear.)

Now, it has been stated—and by way of comparison treated as matter of complaint—that during the Crimean war the Americans behaved so well that the honourable member for Bradford and the member for Birmingham both lauded their action as compared with that of our own Government. Now, I have heard that a vessel sailed from the United States to Petropaulovski. (Cries of "Name.") If honourable members will allow me I will go on, and first I propose to read an extract from the *Times*, written by their correspondent at San Francisco, dated the 29th of January, 1863:—

> Now, this case of the *Alabama* illustrates the saying that a certain class should have a good memory. During the Crimean war, a man-of-war (called the *America*, if I remember) was built in America for the Russian Government, and brought out to the Pacific, filled with arms and munitions, by an officer in the United States navy. This gentleman took her to Petropaulovski, where she did service against the allied squadron, and she is still in the Russian navy. (Cries of 'No,' and 'Hear, hear.') We made no such childish fuss about this act of 'hostility' by a friendly Power, which we could not prevent, as our friends are now making about the *Alabama*, whose departure from England our Government could not stop.

The *America* was commanded by a Lieutenant Hudson, who—if my information be correct, and I have no doubt that it is—was then, or had been just previously, a lieutenant in the American navy; he was the son of a most distinguished officer in the same service, Captain Hudson. I am further informed that some doubts having arisen about the character of this ship, the American men-of-war in the different ports she called at protected her; and, on her arrival in Russia, the captain who took her out was, I know, very handsomely rewarded for his services. (Hear, hear.) Now, I will go a step further about the Northern States.

In 1861, just after the war broke out, a friend of mine, whom I have known for many years, was over here, and came to me with a view of getting vessels built in this country for the American Government—the Northern Government. (Hear, hear.) Its agents in this country made inquiries; plans and estimates were given to my friend, and transmitted to the Secretary of the American Navy. I will read an abstract from this gentleman's letter, dated the 30th of July, 1861. It is written from Washington, and states—

> Since my arrival here I have had frequent interviews with our 'Department of Naval Affairs,' and am happy to say that the

Minister of the Navy is inclined to have an iron-plated ship built out of the country. (Hear, hear.) This ship is designed for a specific purpose, to accomplish a definite object. I send you herewith a memorandum handed me last evening from the department, with the request that I would send it to you by steamer's mail of tomorrow, and to ask your immediate reply, stating if you will agree to build such a ship as desired, how soon, and for how much, with such plans and specifications as you may deem it best to send me.

(Loud cheers.) The extract from the memorandum states that "the ship is to be finished complete, with guns and everything appertaining." (Renewed cheering and laughter.) On the 14th of August I received another letter from the same gentleman, from which the following is an extract:

I have this morning a note from the Assistant-Secretary of the Navy, in which he says, 'I hope your friends will tender for the two-iron plated steamers.'

(Hear, hear.) After this, the firm with which I was lately connected, having made contracts to a large extent with other persons, stated that they were not in a position to undertake any orders to be done in so short a time. This was the reply:

I sent your last letter, received yesterday, to the Secretary of the Navy, who was very desirous to have you build the iron-plated or bomb-proof batteries, and I trust that he may yet decide to have you build one or more of the gunboats.

(Loud cheers.) I think, perhaps, in the present state of the law in America, I shall not be asked to give the name of my correspondent (hear), but he is a gentleman of the highest respectability. If any honourable member wishes, I should have no hesitation in handing the whole correspondence, with the original letters, into the hands of you, sir, or the First Minister of the Crown, in strict confidence, because there are communications in these letters respecting the views of the American Government which I certainly should not divulge, which I have not mentioned or alluded to before. But seeing that the American Government are making so much work about other parties, whom they charge with violating or evading the law, though in reality they have not done so, I think it only fair to state those facts. (Cheers.)

As I said before, they are facts. (Hear, hear.) I do not feel at liberty to state those points to which I have referred, as being of a confidential character, but, if any honourable gentleman feels a doubt regarding the accuracy of what I have stated, I shall feel happy to place the documents in the hands of the Speaker, or of the First Minister of the Crown, when he will see that they substantiate much more than I have stated. (Cheers.) I do not wish to occupy the House longer; but I must say this, that to talk of freedom in a land like the Northern States of America is an absurdity. Almost every detective that can be got hold of in this country is employed. (Hear, hear.)

I believe there are spies in my son's works in Birkenhead, and in all the great establishments in the country. A friend of mine had detectives regularly on his track in consequence of some circumstances connected with his vessels. If that be freedom, I think we had better remain in the position in which we now are. (Cheers and laughter.) In conclusion, I will allude to a remark which was made elsewhere last night—a remark, I presume, applying to me or to somebody else, which was utterly uncalled for. (Hear.) I have only to say that I would rather be handed down to posterity as the builder of a dozen *Alabama*s than as the man who applies himself deliberately to set class against class (loud cheers), and to cry up the institutions of another country, which, when they come to be tested, are of no value whatever, and which reduce liberty to an utter absurdity. (Cheers.)

No. 4

THE ENGAGEMENT WITH THE *HATTERAS*

From the Journal of an Officer of the Alabama.

Sunday, 11th.—Fine moderate breeze from the eastward. Read Articles of War. Noon: Eighteen miles from Galveston. As I write this some are discussing the probability of a fight before morning. 2.25 p.m.: Light breeze; sail discovered by the look-out on the bow. Shortly after, three, and at last five, vessels were seen; two of which were reported to be steamers. Every one delighted at the prospect of a fight, no doubt whatever existing as to their being war-vessels—blockaders we supposed. The watch below came on deck, and of their own accord began preparing the guns, &c., for action. Those whose watch it was on deck were engaged in getting the propeller ready for lowering; others were bending a cable to a kedge and putting it over the bow—the engineers firing up for steam, officers looking to their side-arms, &c., and discussing the size of their expected adversary or adversaries.

At 2.30 shortened sail and tacked to the southward. 4 p.m.: A steamer reported standing out from the fleet toward us. Backed maintopsail and lowered propeller. 4.50: Everything reported ready for action. Chase bearing N.N.E., distant ten miles. Twilight set in about 5.45. Took in all sail. At 6.20 beat up to quarters, manned the starboard battery, and loaded with five second shell; turned round, stood for the steamer, having previously made her out to be a two-masted sidewheel, of apparent 1,200 tons, though at the distance she was before dark we could not form any correct estimate of her size, &c.

At 6.30 the strange steamer hailed and asked, "What steamer is that?" We replied (in order to be certain who he was), "Her Majesty's ship *Petrel*! What steamer is that?" Two or three times we asked the question, until we heard, "This is the United States steamer———," not hearing the name. However, United States steamer was sufficient. As no doubt existed as to her character, we said, at 6.35, that this was the "Confederate States steamer, *Alabama*," accompanying the last syllable of our name with a shell fired over him. The signal being given, the other guns took up the refrain, and a tremendous volley from our whole broadside given to him, every shell striking his side, the shot striking being distinctly heard on board our vessel, and thus found that she was iron.

The enemy replied, and the action became general. A most sharp spirited firing was kept up on both sides, our fellows peppering away as though the action depended on each individual. And so it did. Pistols and rifles were continually pouring from our quarter-deck messengers most deadly, the distance during the hottest of the fight not being more than forty yards! It was a grand, though fearful sight, to see the guns belching forth, in the darkness of the night, sheets of living flame, the deadly missiles striking the enemy with a force that we could *feel*. Then, when the shells struck her sides, especially the percussion ones, her whole side was lit up, and showing rents of five or six feet in length. One shot had just struck our smoke-stack, and wounding one man in the cheek, when the enemy ceased his firing, and fired a lee gun; then a second, and a third.

The order was given to "Cease firing." This was at 6.52. A tremendous cheering commenced, and it was not till everybody had cleared his throat to his own satisfaction, that silence could be obtained. We then hailed him, and in reply he stated that he had surrendered, was on fire, and also that he was in a sinking condition. He then sent a boat on board, and surrendered the U.S. gunboat, *Hatteras*, nine guns,

Lieutenant-Commander Blake, 140 men. Boats were immediately lowered and sent to his assistance, when an alarm was given that another steamer was bearing down for us. The boats were recalled and hoisted up, when it was found to be a false alarm. The order was given, and the boatswain and his mates piped "All hands out boats to save life;" and soon the prisoners were transferred to our ship—the officers under guard on the quarter deck, and the men in single irons.

The boats were then hoisted up, the battery run in and secured, and the main brace spliced. All hands piped down, the enemy's vessel sunk, and we steaming quietly away by 8.30, all having been done in less than two hours. In fact, had it not been for our having the prisoners on board, we would have sworn nothing unusual had taken place—the watch below quietly sleeping in their hammocks. The conduct of our men was truly commendable. No flurry, no noise—all calm and determined. The coolness displayed by them could not be surpassed by any old veterans—our chief boatswain's mate apparently in his glory. "Sponge!"—"Load with cartridge!"—"Shell-fire seconds!"—"Runout!"—"Well, down compressors!"—"Left, traverse!"—"Well!"—"Ready!"—"Fire!"—"That's into you!"—"Damn you! that kills your pig!"—"That stops your wind!" &c., &c., was uttered as each shot was heard to strike with a crash that nearly deafened you.

The other boatswain's mate seemed equally to enjoy the affair. As he got his gun to bear upon the enemy, he would take aim, and banging away, would plug her, exclaiming, as each shot told—"That's from the scum of England!"—"That's a British pill for you to swallow!" the New York papers having once stated that our men were the "scum of England." All other guns were served with equal precision. We were struck seven times; only one man being hurt during the engagement, and he only received a flesh-wound in the cheek. One shot struck under the counter, penetrating as far as a timber, then glancing off; a second struck the funnel; a third going through the side across the berth-deck, and into the opposite side; another raising the deuce in the lamp room; the others lodging in the coal-bunkers.

Taking a shell up and examining it, we found it filled with sand instead of powder. The enemy's fire was directed chiefly towards our stern, the shots flying pretty quick over the quarter-deck, near to where our captain was standing. As they came whizzing over him, he, with his usual coolness, would exclaim—"Give it to the rascals!"—"Aim low, men!"—"Don't be all night sinking that fellow!" when for all or anything we knew, she might have been an iron-clad or a ram.

On Commander Blake surrendering his sword, he said that "it was with deep regret he did it." Captain Semmes smacked his lips and invited him down to his cabin. On Blake giving his rank to Captain Semmes, he gave up his state-room for Blake's special use, the rest of the officers being accommodated according to their rank in the wardroom and steerages, all having previously been paroled, the crew being placed on the berth-deck, our men sleeping anywhere, so that the prisoners might take their places. Of the enemy's loss we could obtain no correct accounts, a difference of seventeen being in their number of killed, the *Hatteras* having on board men she was going to transfer to other ships. Their acknowledged loss was only two killed and seven wounded.

A boat had been lowered just before the action to board us; as we anticipated, and learnt afterwards, it pulled in for the fleet and reached Galveston. From conversation with her first-lieutenant, I learnt that as soon as we gave our name and our first broadside, the whole after division on board her left the guns, apparently paralyzed; it was some time before they recovered themselves. The conduct of one of her officers was cowardly and disgraceful in the extreme. Some of our shells went completely through her before exploding, others burst inside her, and set her on fire in three places. One went through her engines, completely disabling her; another exploding in her steam chest, scalding all within reach. Thus was fought, twenty-eight miles from Galveston, a battle, though small, yet the first yard-arm action between two steamers at sea.

She was only inferior in weight of metal—her guns being nine in number, *viz.*, four thirty-two pounders, two rifled thirty pounders, carrying 60lb. shot (conical), one rifled twenty pounder, and a couple of small twelve pounders. On account of the conflicting statements made by her officers, we could never arrive at a correct estimate of her crew. Our prisoners numbered seventeen officers, one hundred and one seamen.

We further learnt that the *Hatteras* was one of seven vessels sent to recapture Galveston, it being (although unknown to us) in the possession of our troops.

We also found that the flag-ship *Brooklyn*, twenty-two guns, and the *Oneida*, nine guns, sailed in search of us. By their account of the course they steered they could not fail to have seen us.

No. 5

THE *ALABAMA* IN TABLE BAY

[From the *Cape Argus*.]

*August 6*th, 1863.

Yesterday, at almost noon, a steamer from the northward was made down from the signal-post, Lion's-hill. The Governor had, on the previous day, received a letter from Captain Semmes, dated Saldanha Bay, informing his Excellency that the gallant captain had put his ship into Saldanha Bay for repairs. This letter had been made public in the morning, and had caused no little excitement. Cape Town, that has been more than dull—that has been dismal for months, thinking and talking of nothing but bankruptcies—bankruptcies fraudulent and bankruptcies unavoidable—was now all astir, full of life and motion.

The stoop of the Commercial Exchange was crowded with merchants, knots of citizens were collected at the corner of every street; business was almost, if not altogether suspended. All that could be gleaned, in addition to the information in Captain Semmes' letter to the Governor, a copy of which was sent to the United States Consul immediately it was received, was that the schooner *Atlas* had just returned from Malagas Island, where she had been with water and vegetables for men collecting guanos there.

Captain Boyce, the master of the *Atlas*, reported that he had himself actually seen the steamer *Alabama*; a boat from the steamer had boarded his vessel, and he had been on board her. His report of Captain Semmes corroborated that given by everyone else. He said the captain was most courteous and gentlemanly. He asked Captain Boyce to land thirty prisoners for him in Table Bay, with which request Captain Boyce was unable to comply. Captain Semmes said that the *Florida* was also a short distance off the Cape, and that the *Alabama*, when she had completed her repairs, and was cleaned and painted, would pay Table Bay a visit. He expected to be there, he said, very nearly as soon as the *Atlas*.

Shortly after the *Atlas* arrived, a boat brought up some of the prisoners from Saldanha Bay, and amongst them one of the crew of the *Alabama*, who said he had left the ship. All these waited on the United States Consul, but were unable to give much information beyond what we had already received. The news that the *Alabama* was coming into Table Bay, and would probably arrive about four o'clock this afternoon, added to the excitement. About noon a steamer from the north-west was made known by the signal-man on the hill. Could this be the *Alabama*? or was it the *Hydaspes*, from India, or the *Lady Jocelyn*, from England? All three were now hourly expected, and the city was in doubt.

Just after one it was made down, "Confederate Steamer *Alabama*, From the N.W., and Federal *Barque* From The S.E." Here was to be a capture by the celebrated Confederate craft, close to the entrance of Table Bay. The inhabitants rushed off to get a sight. Crowds of people ran up the Lion's-hill, and to the *Kloof*-road. All the cabs were chartered—every one of them; there was no cavilling about fares; the cabs were taken and no questions asked, but orders were given to drive as hard as possible. The *barque* coming in from the south-east, and, as the signal-man made down, five miles off; the steamer, coming in from the north-west, eight miles off, led us to think that the *Kloof*-road was the best place for a full view.

To that place we directed our Jehu to drive furiously. We did the first mile in a short time; but the *Kloof*-hill for the next two and-a-half miles is uphill work. The horse jibbed, so we pushed on, on foot, as fast as possible, and left the cab to come on. When we reached the summit, we could only make out a steamer on the horizon, from eighteen to twenty miles off. This could not be the *Alabama*, unless she was making off to sea again. There was no *barque*. As soon as our cab reached the crown of the hill, we set off at a breakneck pace down the hill, on past the Roundhouse, till we came near Brighton, and as we reached the corner, there lay the *Alabama* within fifty yards of the unfortunate Yankee.

As the Yankee came round from the south-east, and about five miles from the bay, the steamer came down upon her. The Yankee was evidently taken by surprise. The *Alabama* fired a gun, and brought her to. When first we got sight of the *Alabama*, it was difficult to make out what she was doing; the *barque's* head had been put about, and the *Alabama* lay off quite immovable, as if she were taking a sight at the "varmint!" The weather was beautifully calm and clear, and the sea was as smooth and transparent as a sheet of glass. The *barque* was making her way slowly from the steamer, with every bit of her canvas spread. The *Alabama*, with her steam off, appeared to be letting the *barque* get clear off. What could this mean? no one understood. It must be the *Alabama*.

"There," said the spectators, "is the Confederate flag at her peak; it must be a Federal *barque*, too, for there are the Stars and the Stripes of the States flying at her main." What could the *Alabama* mean lying there—

As idly as a painted ship
Upon a painted ocean.

What it meant was soon seen. Like a cat watching and playing with a victimized mouse, Captain Semmes permitted his prize to draw off a few yards, and he then up steam again, and pounced upon her. She first sailed round the Yankee from stem to stern, and stern to stem again. The way that fine, saucy, rakish craft was handled was worth riding a hundred miles to see. She went round the bark like a toy, making a complete circle, and leaving an even margin of water between herself and her prize of not more than twenty yards. From the hill it appeared as if there were no water at all between the two vessels. This done, she sent a boat with the prize crew off, took possession in the name of the Confederate States, and sent the *barque* off to sea. The *Alabama* then made for the port.

We came round the *Kloof* to visit Captain Semmes on board. As we came we found the heights overlooking Table Bay covered with people; the road to Green Point lined with cabs. The windows of the villas at the bottom of the hill were all thrown up, and ladies waved their handkerchiefs, and one and all joined in the general enthusiasm; over the quarries, along the Malay burying-ground, the Gallows Hill, and the beach, there were masses of people—nothing but a sea of heads as far as the eye could reach.

Along Strand Street and Adderley Street the roofs of all the houses from which Table Bay is overlooked, were made available as standing-places for the people who could not get boats to go off to her. The central, the north, the south, and the coaling jetties, were all crowded. At the central jetty it was almost impossible to force one's way through to get a boat. However, all in good time, we did get a boat, and went off in the midst of dingies, cargo-boats, gigs and wherries, all as full as they could hold.

Nearly all the city was upon the bay; the rowing clubs in uniform pulled off with favoured members of their respective clubs on board. The crews feathered their oars in double-quick time, and their pulling, our "stroke" declared, was "a caution, and no mistake." Just before getting alongside, we passed Captain Wilson in the port-boat, who told us that the prize taken was the *Sea Bride*, and that there was no difficulty in hearing from Captain Semmes himself the whole story of the capture.

We passed the Federal *barque Urania* at her anchorage, and that ship, disregardful of the privateer, sported all her bunting with becoming pluck. The Stars and Stripes floated defiantly from her-mizzen peak, and her name from her main. On getting alongside the *Alabama*, we found about a dozen boats before us, and we had not been on board five minutes before she was surrounded by nearly every boat in Table Bay, and as boat after boat arrived, three hearty cheers were given for Captain Semmes and his gallant privateer. This, upon the part of a neutral people, is, perchance, wrong; but we are not arguing a case- we are recording facts. They did cheer, and cheer with a will, too. It was not, perhaps, taking the view of either side, Federal or Confederate, but in admiration of the skill, pluck, and daring of the *Alabama*, her captain, and her crew, who now afford a general theme of admiration for the world all over.

Visitors were received by the officers of the ship most courteously, and without distinction, and the officers conversed freely and unreservedly of their exploits. There was nothing like brag in their manner of answering questions put to them. They are as fine and gentlemanly a set of fellows as ever we saw; most of them young men. The ship has been so frequently described, that most people know what she is like, as we do who have seen her. We should have known her to be the *Alabama* if we had boarded her in the midst of the ocean, with no one to introduce us to each other. Her guns alone are worth going off to see, and everything about her speaks highly for the seamanship and discipline of the commander and his officers. She has a very large crew, fine, lithe-looking fellows, the very picture of English men-of-war's men.

The second officer told us that it was the *Sea Bride* they had captured, and pointed out her captain, who stood aft conversing with a number of people who had gathered round him. "This, sir," said the officer, "is our fifty-sixth capture; we have sent her off with about ten of our men as a crew, and we left a few of her own men on board of her." We asked him how he liked Saldanha Bay, and his answer was, "It is a very charming place. Why did you not build Cape Town there?" Our answer was, "Because we never do anything properly at the Cape." "Ah, sir!" he said; "that is a great mistake to leave so fine a bay without harbour conveniences.

It is a great deal better than Table Bay. We enjoyed ourselves capitally there, had some good shooting; one of us shot an ostrich, a fine fellow, but he got away. Unfortunately, we lost one of our officers there—one whom we all respected—as fine an officer as ever trod this ship's deck. He was in a boat in the bay, shooting wild fowl; he drew his gun towards him, the barrel in his hand; the trigger caught, the charge passed through his lung, and his only dying words were, 'Oh, me!' and he fell back a corpse. But for that circumstance, we should always remember Saldanha Bay with pleasure. The gun was within an inch of his breast when it went off."

After this melancholy recital, we walked across to get a little chat with the prisoner so recently captured. He is a superior man, and spoke of the loss of his ship in the spirit of a philosopher. He was leaning against a rail just opposite the cabin. "What can't be cured must be endured," said he. In answer to our remark, that an hour more would have saved him, he said, "Yes, it would; I had not the remotest idea of a capture at this end of the world. I never supposed that she was in this direction. I was in my cabin, washing," said he, "and my mate came down and said there was a steamer in sight. 'Capital!' I said; 'it is the English mail-steamer; I shall be just in time for my letters.' He went up again, and shortly returning, said, 'She is going to hail us.' 'Hail us!' I said; 'what the deuce can she want to hail us for?' and I went on deck. I looked at that (pointing to the Confederate flag), and I soon saw who we were falling into the hands of. I said, 'Goodbye, mate; we shall not be long here.' This, sir," he went on to say, "is the second time I have been captured coming to the Cape. I left New York in the M.J. Calcon, and was captured by the *Florida* in 33° West and between 28° and 29° North. I went home all right, and left New York again on the 28th of May, direct for the Cape." This gentleman's name is Mr. H. Spaling.

The next we had an opportunity of conversing with was the chief officer. This gentleman who, by the way, stands six feet four out of his shoes, showed us round the ship with just pride. He pointed out to us the peculiar qualities of the magnificent guns. One of Blakeley's rifle pieces is a terrible-looking weapon. It throws conical shells of a hundred weight; and he remarked, "When we fought the *Hatteras*, these conical shells struck one after the other in capital style; they exploded with magnificent effect, and lit up her whole broadside." Many of the captured crew we observed in irons.

We were now introduced to Captain Semmes, who up to this time had been engaged in the cabin with Mr. W.J. Anderson, of Anderson, Saxon, and Co., upon the subject of supplies, which are to be provided by the firm. We received a very cordial greeting from the gallant gentleman, who remarked that at Bahia, and indeed everywhere he had been, both his officers and himself had received very great attention from the English residents. We had always concluded that Captain Semmes, of the *Powhattan*, a fine steamer belonging to the States, to whom we were introduced some years since by the late Mr. D.M. Huckins, American Consul, was the captain of the *Sumter* and *Alabama*; but we found we were mistaken, and on remarking this to the captain, he said, "Captain Semmes of the *Powhattan* is of the same family as myself—he is, indeed, my cousin; but he was born in the North, his interests are all there, and he remains in the Federal service."

Having desired us to take a seat, he said he should be happy to give us any information in his power; he had no secrets, and bade us take notes if we wished so to do. He then informed us that he had taken fifteen ships since he left Bahia. We told him that Captain Bartlett, of the ship *Fortuna*, stated that on the 2nd of July he saw a ship on fire. Our readers will recollect that the particulars were given in a paragraph immediately after the *Fortuna* arrived. It was as follows:—

On the 2nd of July, Captain Bartlett saw some smoke rising up on the horizon, which he supposed to be the smoke from a steamer. Later in the day, however, a strong reflection of light was seen in the sky, and which the captain at once believed to be a ship on fire. All hands were then called up 'to bout ship,' and they stood towards the spot from whence the light proceeded. This was about six o'clock; and at two o'clock on the morning of the 3rd July, and in lat. 25° 57' South, and in long. 38° 20' West, the *Fortuna* ran up within forty yards of a large vessel of 800 or 1000 tons, which was enveloped in one mass of flame from stem to stern.

Nothing remained of her but her hull; the whole of her rigging, masts, and decks had already been consumed. As the *Fortuna* ran towards the wreck, another vessel—the *Oaks*—bound to Calcutta, joined her, and the two vessels spoke one another. From what Captain Bartlett could make out, the captain of the *Oaks* told him that in the evening, about half-past six, an English man-of-war had passed him, and whilst passing she fired two guns, from which it was concluded that the crew of the burning vessel had been rescued by the man-of-war." Captain Semmes said Captain Bartlett was quite right in supposing that the ship had been set on fire by himself. She was the Annie F.

Schmidt, from New York to San Francisco, with a general cargo on board; but the supposition of the man-of-war coming to the rescue of the crew was a mistake. "We set her on fire in the night," said Captain Semmes, "and shortly after we had done so, we heard a couple of guns. We thought it was another Yankee, and we up steam and fired a gun for her to heave-to. On coming alongside her, we found she was Her Majesty's frigate *Dido*. 'We did not take her, sir,' said the captain, with a laugh; 'in fact, we never attempt to take any of Her Majesty's frigates.'"

We said we would mention that, and we do, as Captain Semmes's last. "The *Dido* people," he went on to say, "asked us if we had set the ship on fire, and I answered we had, and had got the crew safe on board. 'All right!' was the answer, and we parted. She was a vessel of about 1000 tons." We asked Captain Semmes if he could give us the names of the vessels he had captured. He answered that he could. "For," he said, "you English people won't be neighbourly enough to let me bring my prizes into your ports, and get them condemned, so that I am obliged to sit here a court of myself, try every case, and condemn the ships I take. The European powers, I see, some of them complain of my burning the ships; but what, if they will preserve such strict neutrality as to keep me out of their ports, what am I to do with these ships when I take them but burn them?"

He then fetched his record books, and we took the following down from his lips:—"The ships we have captured were—the *Ocmulgee*, of 400 tons, thirty-two men on board; we burned her. The *Alert*, a whaler of 700 tons; we burned her. The whaling schooner *Weathergauge*; we burned her. The whaling brig *Altamaha*; we burned her. The whaling ship *Benjamin Tucker*, we burned her. The whaling schooner *Courser*, we burned her. The whaling *barque* Virginia; we burned her. The *barque* Elisha Dunbar, a whaler; we burned her. The ship *Brilliant*, with 1000 tons of grain on board; we burned her. The *Emily Farnum* we captured and released as a cartel, and having so many prisoners we put some of them on board her, and sent them off.

"The *Wave Crest*, with a general cargo on board for Europe, we set on fire. The *Dunkirk* brig, with a general cargo on board, we burned. The ship *Tonawanda* we captured, with a valuable freight on board, and released her, after taking a bond for a thousand dollars. The ship *Manchester*, with a cargo of grain, we burned. The *barque Lamplighter*, with an assorted cargo for Europe, we burned. The *barque Lafayette*, with an assorted cargo, we burned. The schooner *Crenshaw*, with an assorted cargo for the West Indies, we burned. The *barque Lauretta*, with an assorted cargo on board for Europe, we burned. The brig *Baron de Custine* we took a bond for and released. The whaling ship *Levi Starbuck* we burned. The *T.B. Wales*, from Calcutta to Boston, with a valuable cargo on board, we burned. The *barque Martha*, from Calcutta to West Indies, with an assorted cargo, we burned.

"The schooner *Union* we, after boarding, found had some English property on board, and we released her on bond. The mail steamer *Ariel* running between New York and Aspinwall, we captured. Unfortunately she was going, not returning, or we should have had a lot of gold. We released her on bond. The United States gunboat *Hatteras*, who came out to fight us, had the same number of guns and crew. Our guns were a little heavier than hers, but we equalized them by permitting her to fight us at 300 yards. We sunk her in thirteen minutes by the watch. The *barque Golden Rule*, with an assorted cargo, we burned. She belonged to the same company as the *Ariel*. The brig *Chastelaine* we burned. The schooner *Palmetto* we burned.

"The *barque Olive Jane* we burned. The *Golden Eagle*, laden with *guano*, we burned. The *Washington*, from the Pacific, with *guano*, we released on bond. The *Bethia Thayer*, from East India, with a valuable cargo on board, was released on bond. The *John A. Parker*, with flour and lumber, from Boston to Buenos Ayres, we burned. The *Punjaub*, from East India, we found to have some English cargo on board, we released on bond. The ship *Morning Star* we released on bond. The whaling schooner *Kingfisher* we burned. The ship *Nora*, from Liverpool to West Indies, with salt on board, we burned. The *barque Lafayette* we burned. The whaling brig *Kate Cory* we burned. The whaling *barque Nye* we burned. The *Charles Hall*, from Liverpool, with coal, we burned.

"The ship *Louisa Hatch*, from Cardiff to West Indies, we burned. The ship *Dorcas Prince*, with a general cargo, we burned. The ship *Sea Lark*, with a general cargo from the East Indies, we burned. The *barque Union Jack*, from Boston to Shanghai, we burned. We captured a Yankee consul on board of her; he was on his way to Foochin; we landed him at the Brazils. The ship *Gildersliene*, from New York to the East Indies, we burned. The *barque Justina* we released on bond, to take home prisoners. The ship *Jabez Snow*, from New York to the East Indies, we burned. The *barque Amazonian*, from Boston to Buenos Ayres, we burned. The ship *Talisman*, from New York to the East Indies, we burned. The *barque Conrad*, fitted up as a Federal cruiser, a tender to a man-of-war, we captured and burned. After these came the *Anne F.*

Schmidt, mentioned before, and the *Sea Bride*—and the *Sea Bride* you saw us take today. The estimated value of these captures is 4,200,000 dollars."

The American Consul, Mr. Graham, has handed to his Excellency the Governor a protest against the capture of the *Sea Bride*, on the ground that the vessel was in British waters at the time of her being stopped by the *Alabama*. His Excellency told Mr. Graham that the decision of the case remained purely on evidence, but he would see there was no breach of neutrality. The captain of the *Sea Bride* says he is prepared to show by bearings that he was within two and a half miles of Robben Island.

No. 6
Correspondence Respecting the *Tuscaloosa*
Rear-Admiral Sir B. Walker to the Secretary to the Admiralty, August 19, 1863.

I beg you will be pleased to acquaint my Lords Commissioners of the Admiralty with the following particulars relative to the proceedings of the Confederate States ships of war *Alabama*, her reported tender *Tuscaloosa*, and the *Georgia*, which have recently arrived at the Cape of Good Hope.

2. On the 28th of July an English schooner arrived in Table Bay, and reported that on the previous day she had been boarded by the Confederate steamer *Alabama*, fifteen miles north-west of Green Point. After some inquiries the *Alabama* left her, steering south-east.

3. Upon the receipt of this intelligence I ordered Captain Forsyth, of the *Valorous*, to hold himself in readiness to proceed to any of the ports in this colony where the *Alabama* might anchor, in order to preserve the rules of strict neutrality.

4. By a letter addressed to the Governor of this Colony by Captain Semmes, copy of which was telegraphed to me on the 4th instant, it appears that the *Alabama* had proceeded to Saldanha Bay for a few days, anchoring there on the 29th of July.

5. On the 5th instant I received a private telegram to the effect that the *Alabama* was off Table Bay, when I directed the *Valorous* immediately to proceed to that anchorage; and shortly afterwards a telegram reached me from the Governor stating "that the *Alabama* had captured a vessel (American), which was in sight, and steering for Table Bay." The *Valorous* reached that Bay at 10.15 p.m., where the *Alabama* had anchored at 3 o'clock in the afternoon of the same day.

6. Captain Forsyth having informed me that the tender to the *Alabama* had been ordered by Captain Semmes to Simon's Bay for provisions, and having learned that this vessel had been captured off the coast of Brazil, and not been condemned in any Prize Court, I had doubts as to the legality of considering her in the light of a tender, being under the impression that it was a ruse to disguise the real character of the vessel. I therefore wrote to the Governor to obtain the opinion of the Attorney-General of the Colony upon this subject, which correspondence is inclosed.

7. On the 8th of August the tender *Tuscaloosa*, a sailing *barque*, arrived in Simon's Bay, and the boarding officer having reported to me that her original cargo of wool was still on board, I felt that there were grounds for doubting her real character, and again called the Governor's attention to this circumstance. My letter and his reply are annexed. And I would here beg to submit to their Lordships' notice that this power of a captain of a ship of war to constitute every prize he may take a "tender," appears to me to be likely to lead to abuse and evasion of the laws of strict neutrality, by being used as a means for bringing prizes into neutral ports for disposal of their cargoes, and secret arrangements—which arrangements, it must be seen, could afterwards be easily carried out at isolated places.

8. The *Alabama*, after lying three days in Table Bay, came to this anchorage to caulk and refit. She arrived here on the 9th, and sailed again on the 15th instant. Captain Semmes was guarded in his conduct, and expressed himself as most anxious not to violate the neutrality of these waters.

9. I should observe that, from the inclosed copy of a letter from Captain Forsyth to the Governor, it would appear that the vessel *Sea Bride*, taken by the *Alabama* off Table Bay, was beyond the jurisdiction of neutral territory.

10. During his passage to this port Captain Semmes chased another American vessel, the *Martha Wentzel*, standing in for Table Bay. On my pointing out to him that he had done so in neutral waters, he assured me that it was quite unintentional, and, being at a distance from the land, he did not observe that he had got within three miles of an imaginary line drawn from the Cape of Good Hope to Cape Hanglip, but on discovering it he did not detain the vessel. The explanation I considered sufficient.

11. The tender *Tuscaloosa*, having been detained by a strong south-easter, got under way for the purpose of going to sea on the 14th

instant, but anchored again a little distance from the Roman Rock lighthouse in consequence of thick fog prevailing.

12. The *Alabama* did not take in any coal, either here or at Table Bay, but after being caulked she proceeded to sea on the 15th instant, followed by the *Tuscaloosa*. Their destinations are unknown.

13. On the 16th instant, the Confederate States steamer *Georgia*, Commander Maury, anchored in this bay. She requires coal, provision, and caulking. This vessel did not meet the *Alabama* outside.

14. The *Florida*, another Confederate States steamer, is reported to be off this coast, probably cruising to intercept the homeward-bound American ships from China; indeed, it is with that object these ships are on this part of the Station.

15. I have learnt, since the departure of the *Alabama*, and her so-called tender, that overtures were made by some parties in Cape Town to purchase the cargo of wool, but, being unsatisfactory, they were not accepted. It is reported to be Captain Semmes' intention to destroy the *Tuscaloosa* at sea.

16. The *Alabama* is a steamer of about 900 tons, with 8 guns, and 150 men. The *Georgia* is an iron steamer of about 700 tons, with 5 guns, and 110 men. The *Tuscaloosa* is a sailing-*barque* of 500 tons, having 2 small guns and 10 men.

Captain Semmes, C.S.N., to Governor Sir P. Wodehouse,
August 1, 1863.

An opportunity is offered me by the coasting schooner *Atlas*, to communicate with the Cape, of which I promptly avail myself.

I have the honour to inform your Excellency that I arrived in this bay on Wednesday morning last, for the purpose of effecting some necessary repairs. As soon as these repairs can be completed I will proceed to sea, and in the meantime your Excellency may rest assured that I will pay the strictest attention to the neutrality of your Government.

Rear-Admiral Sir B. Walker to Governor Sir P. Wodehouse.
August 7, 1863.

Captain Forsyth having informed me that the *Alabama* has a tender outside captured by Captain Semmes on the coast of America, and commissioned by one of the *Alabama*'s Lieutenants, and as this vessel has been ordered into Simon's Bay for provisions, may I request your Excellency will be good enough to obtain the opinion of the Law Officers whether this vessel ought still to be looked upon in the light of a prize, she never having been condemned in a Prize Court; the instructions, copy of which I inclose, strictly forbidding prizes captured by either of the contending parties in North America being admitted into our ports.

Governor Sir P. Wodehouse to Rear-Admiral Sir B. Walker, August 8, 1863.

I have the honour to acknowledge the receipt of your Excellency's letter of yesterday's date, and to inclose the copy of an opinion given by the Acting Attorney-General to the effect that the vessel to which you refer ought to be regarded as a tender and not as a prize.

I shall take care to submit this question to Her Majesty's Government by the next mail, but in the meantime I conclude that your Excellency will be prepared to act on the opinion of the Attorney-General in respect to any vessels which may enter these ports in the character of prizes converted into ships of war by the officers of the navy of the Confederate States.

EXTRACTS FROM *WHEATON'S ELEMENTS OF INTERNATIONAL LAW.*

What constitutes a setting forth as a vessel of war has been determined by the British Courts of Prize, in cases arising under the clause of the Act of Parliament, which may serve for the interpretation of our own law, as the provisions are the same in both. Thus it has been settled that where a ship was originally armed for the Slave Trade, and after capture an additional number of men were put on board, but there was no commission of war and no additional arming, it was not a setting forth as a vessel of war under the Act. But a commission of war is decisive if there be guns on board; and where the vessel after the capture has been fitted out as a privateer, it is conclusive against her, although, when recaptured, she is navigating as a mere merchant-ship; for where the former character of a captured vessel had been obliterated by her conversion into a ship of war, the Legislature meant to look no further, but considered the title of the former owner forever extinguished.

Where it appeared that the vessel had been engaged in a military service of the enemy, under the direction of his Minister of the Marine, it was held as a sufficient proof of a setting forth as a vessel of war; so where the vessel is armed, and is employed in the public military service of the enemy by those who have competent authority so to employ it, although it be not regularly commissioned. But the mere employment in the enemy's military service is not sufficient; but if there be a fair semblance of authority, in the person directing the vessel to be so employed, and nothing upon the face of the proceedings to invalidate it, the Court will presume that he is duly authorized; and the commander of a single ship may be presumed to be vested with this authority as commander of a squadron.

Rear-Admiral Sir B. Walker to Governor Sir P. Wodehouse.,
August 8, 1863.

I have the honour to acknowledge the receipt of your Excellency's letter of this day's date, covering the written opinion of the Acting Attorney-General of this Colony as to the legality of the so-called tender to the Confederate States armed ship *Alabama*, and for which I beg to express my thanks.

The vessel in question, now called the *Tuscaloosa*, arrived here this evening, and the boarding officer from my flag-ship obtained the following information:

That she is a *barque* of 500 tons, with two small rifled 12 pounder guns and ten men, and was captured by the *Alabama* on the 21st June last, off the coast of Brazil: cargo of wool still on board.

The admission of this vessel into port will, I fear, open the door for numbers of vessels captured under similar circumstances being denominated tenders, with a view to avoid the prohibition contained in the Queen's instructions; and I would observe that the vessel *Sea Bride* captured by the *Alabama* off Table Bay a few days since, or all other prizes, might be in like manner styled tenders, making the prohibition entirely null and void.

I apprehend that to bring a captured vessel under the denomination of a vessel of war, she must be fitted for warlike purposes, and not merely have a few men and two small guns put on board of her (in fact nothing but a prize crew) in order to disguise her real character as a prize.

Now this vessel has her original cargo of wool still on board, which cannot be required for warlike purposes, and her armament and the number of her crew are quite insufficient for any services other than those of a slight defence.

Viewing all the circumstances of the case, they afford room for the supposition, that the vessel is styled a "tender" with the object of avoiding the prohibition against her entrance as a prize into our ports, where, if the captors wished, arrangements could be made for the disposal of her valuable cargo, the transhipment of which, your Excellency will not fail to see, might be readily effected on any part of the coast beyond the limits of this Colony.

My sole object in calling your Excellency's attention to the case is to avoid any breach of strict neutrality.

Governor Sir P. Wodehonse to Rear-Admiral Sir B. Walker.,
August 10, 1863.

I have the honour to acknowledge the receipt of your Excellency's letter of the 8th instant, on which I have consulted the Acting Attorney-General.

The information given respecting the actual condition of the *Tuscaloosa* is somewhat defective, but referring to the extract from Wheaton transmitted in my last letter, the Attorney-General is of opinion that if the vessel received the two guns from the *Alabama* or other Confederate vessel of war, or if the person in command of her has a commission of war, or if she be commanded by an officer of the Confederate navy, in any of these cases there will be a sufficient setting forth as a vessel of war to justify her being held to be a ship of war; if all of these points be decided in the negative, she must be held to be only a prize, and ordered to leave forthwith.

Rear-Admiral Sir B. Walker to Governor Sir P. Wodehouse,
August 11, 1863.

I have the honour to acknowledge the receipt of your Excellency's letter, dated yesterday, respecting the Confederate *barque Tuscaloosa* now in this bay.

As there are two guns on board, and an officer of the *Alabama* in charge of her, the vessel appears to come within the meaning of the cases cited in your above-mentioned communication.

Governor Sir P. Wodehouse to the Duke of Newcastle,
August 19, 1863.

(Extract.)

I beg to take this opportunity of making your Grace acquainted with what has occurred here in connection with the visit of the Confederate States steamer *Alabama.*

On Tuesday, the 4th instant, I received a letter from the Commander of that vessel, dated the 1st August at Saldanha Bay, announcing his having entered that bay with a view to effecting certain repairs, and stating that he would put to sea as soon as they were completed, and would strictly respect our neutrality.

When this intelligence was received, the United States Consul called on me to seize her, or at any rate to send her away instantly; but as the vessel which brought the news reported that the *Alabama* was coming immediately to Table Bay, I replied that I could not seize her, but would take care to enforce the observance of the neutral regulations.

On the next day, about noon, it was reported from the signal station that the *Alabama* was steering for Table Bay from the north, and that a Federal *barque* was coming in from the westward; and soon after, that the latter had been captured and put about. A little after 2 p.m. the United States Consul called to state that he had seen the capture effected within British waters; when I told him he must make his statement in writing, and an investigation should be made. I also, by telegram, immediately requested the Naval Commander-in-Chief to send a ship of war from Simon's Bay.

The *Alabama*, leaving her prize outside, anchored in the bay 3.30 p.m., when Captain Semmes wrote to me that he wanted supplies and repairs, as well as permission to land thirty-three prisoners. After communicating with the United States Consul, I authorized the latter, and called upon him to state the nature and extent of his wants, that I might be enabled to judge of the time he ought to remain in the port. The same afternoon he promised to send the next morning a list of the stores needed, and announced his intention of proceeding with all despatch to Simon's Bay to effect his repairs there. The next morning (August 6th) the Paymaster called on me with the merchant who was to furnish the supplies, and I granted him leave to stay till noon of the 7th.

On the night of the 5th, Her Majesty's ship *Valorous* had come round from Simon's Bay. During the night of the 6th the weather became unfavourable; a vessel was wrecked in the bay, and a heavy sea prevented the *Alabama* from receiving her supplies by the time arranged. On the morning of the 8th, Captain Forsyth, of the *Valorous*, and the Port Captain, by my desire, pressed on Captain Semmes the necessity for his leaving the port without any unnecessary delay; when he pleaded the continued heavy sea and the absence of his cooking apparatus, which had been sent on shore for repairs, and had not been returned by the tradesman at the time appointed, and intimated his own anxiety to get away. Between 6 and 7 p.m., on Sunday, the 9th, he sailed, and on his way round to Simon's Bay captured another vessel; but on finding that she was in neutral waters he immediately released her.

In the meantime, the United States Consul had, on the 5th August, addressed to me a written statement that the Federal *barque Sea Bride* had been taken "about four miles from the nearest land," and "already in British waters;" on which I promised immediate inquiry. The next day the Consul repeated his protest, supporting it by an affidavit of the master of the prize, which he held to show that she had been taken about two miles and a half from the land; and the agent for the United States underwriters, on the same day, made a similar protest. On the 7th, the Consul represented that the prize had, on the previous day, been brought within one mile and a half of the lighthouse, which he considered as much a violation of the neutrality as if she had been there captured, and asked me to have the prize crew taken out and replaced by one from the *Valorous*, which I declined.

I had, during this period, been seeking for authentic information as to the real circumstances of the capture, more particularly with reference to the actual distance from the shore, and obtained through the Acting Attorney-General statements from the keeper of the Green Point Lighthouse (this was supported by the Collector of Customs), from the signal-man at the station at the Lion's Rump, and from an experienced boatman who was passing between the shore and the vessels at the time. Captain Forsyth, of the *Valorous*, also made inquiries of the captain of the *Alabama* and of the Port Captain, and made known the result to me. And upon all these statements I came to the conclusion that the vessels were not less than four miles distant from land; and on the 8th I communicated to the United States Consul that the capture could not, in my opinion, be held to be illegal by reason of the place at which it was effected.

In his reply of the 10th, the Consul endeavoured to show how indefensible my decision must be, if, in these days of improved artillery, I rested it on the fact of the vessels having been only three miles from land. This passage is, I think, of considerable importance, as involving an indirect admission that they were not within three miles at the time of capture. And I hope your Grace will concur in my view that it was not my duty to go beyond what I found to be the distance clearly established by past decisions under international law.

An important question has arisen in connection with the *Alabama*, on which it is very desirable that I should, as soon as practicable, be made acquainted with the views of Her Majesty's Government. Captain Semmes had mentioned after his arrival in port, that he had left outside one of his prizes previously taken, the *Tuscaloosa*, which he had equipped and fitted as a tender, and had ordered to meet him in Simon's Bay, as she also stood in need of supplies. When this became known to the naval commander-in-chief, he requested me to furnish him with a legal opinion; and whether this vessel could he held to be a ship of war before she had been formally condemned in a prize court; or whether she must not be held to be still a prize, and, as such, prohibited from entering our ports. The Acting Attorney-General, founding his opinion on Earl Russell's despatch to your Grace, of the 31st January, 1862, and on "Wheaton's International Law," states in substance that it was open to Captain Semmes to convert this vessel into a ship of war, and that she ought to be admitted into our ports on that footing.

On the 8th August the vessel entered Simon's Bay, and the Admiral wrote that she had two small rifled guns, with a crew of ten men, and that her cargo of wool was still on board. He was still doubtful of the propriety of admitting her.

On the 10th August, after further consultation with the Acting Attorney-General, I informed Sir Baldwin Walker that, if the guns had been put on board by the *Alabama*, or if she had a commission of war, or if she were commanded by an officer of the Confederate Navy, there must be held to be a sufficient setting forth as a vessel of war to justify her admission into port in that character.

The Admiral replied in the affirmative on the first and last points, and she was admitted.

The *Tuscaloosa* sailed from Simon's Bay on the morning of the 14th instant, but was becalmed in the vicinity until the following day, when she sailed about noon. The *Alabama* left before noon on the 15th instant. Neither of these vessels was allowed to remain in port longer than was really necessary for the completion of their repairs.

On the 16th, at noon, the *Georgia*, another Confederate war steamer, arrived at Simon's Bay in need of repairs, and is still there.

Before closing this despatch I wish particularly to request instructions on a point touched on in the letter from the United States Consul of the 17th instant, *viz*.: the steps which should be taken here in the event of the cargo of any vessel captured by one of the belligerents being taken out of the prize at sea, and brought into one of our ports in a British or other neutral vessel.

Both belligerents are strictly interdicted from bringing their prizes into British ports by Earl Russell's letter to the Lords of the Admiralty of the 1st June, 1861, and I conceive that a colonial government would be justified in enforcing compliance with that order by any means at its command, and by the exercise of force if it should be required.

But that letter refers only to "prizes;" that is, I conceive, to ships themselves, and makes no mention of the cargoes they may contain. Practically the prohibition has been taken to extend to the cargoes; and I gathered, from a conversation with Captain Semmes on the subject of our neutrality regulations, that he considered himself debarred from disposing of them, and was thus driven to the destruction of all that he took.

But I confess that I am unable to discover by what legal means I could prevent the introduction into our ports of captured property purchased at sea, and tendered for entry at the custom-house in the usual form from a neutral ship. I have consulted the Acting Attorney-General on the subject, and he is not prepared to state that the customs authorities would be justified in making a seizure under such circumstances; and therefore, as there is great probability of clandestine attempts being made to introduce cargoes of this description, I shall be glad to be favoured with the earliest practicable intimation of the views of Her Majesty's Government on the subject.

Captain Semmes, C.S.N., to Sir P. Wodehouse.,
August 5, 1863.

I have the honour to inform your Excellency of my arrival in this bay, in the Confederate States steamer *Alabama* under my command. I have come in for supplies and repairs, and in the meantime I respectfully ask leave to land in Cape Town thirty-three prisoners, lately captured by me on board two of the enemy's ships destroyed at sea. The United States Consul will doubtless be glad to extend such hospitality and assistance to his distressed countrymen, as required of him by law.

Sir P. Wodehouse to Captain Semmes, C.S.N.
August 5, 1863.

I have the honour to acknowledge the receipt of your letter announcing your arrival in this port, and to state that I have no objection to offer to your landing the prisoners now detained in your ship.

I have further to beg that you will be good enough to state the nature and extent of the supplies and repairs you require, that I may be enabled to form some estimate of the time for which it will be necessary for you to remain in this port.

Captain Semmes, C.S.N., to Sir P. Wodehouse.,
August 5, 1863.

I have had the honour to receive your letter of this day's date, giving me permission to land my prisoners, and requesting me to state the nature of the supplies and repairs which I may require. In the way of supplies I shall need some provisions for my crew, a list of which will be handed you tomorrow by the paymaster, and as for repairs my boilers need some iron work to be done, and my bends require caulking, being quite open. I propose to take on board the necessary materials here, and to proceed with all despatch to Simon's Bay for the purpose of making these repairs.

Mr. Adamson to Captain Semmes C.S.N.
August 6, 1863.

I am directed by the Governor of this colony to acquaint you that he has received from the Consul for the United States at this port a representation, in which he sets forth that an American *barque* was yesterday captured by the ship which you command, in British waters, in violation of the neutrality of the British Government, and claims from him redress for the alleged outrage.

His Excellency will be glad, therefore, to receive from you any explanation you may wish to give as to the circumstances in which the capture was effected.

Captain Semmes, C.S.N., to Mr. Adamson.,
Cape Town, August 6, 1863.

I have had the honour to receive your communication of this day's date, informing me that the United States Consul at this port had presented to his Excellency the Governor a representation in which he sets forth that an American *barque* was yesterday captured by this ship under my command in British waters, in violation of the neutrality of the British Government, and requesting me to make to his Excellency such representation as I may have to offer on the subject.

In reply, I have the honour to state that it is not true that the *barque* referred to was captured in British waters, and in violation of British neutrality; she having been captured outside all headlands, and a distance from the nearest land of between five and six miles. As I approached this vessel I called the particular attention of my officers to the question of distance, and they all agreed that the capture was made from two to three miles outside the marine league.

U.S. Consul to Sir P. Wodehouse,
August 4, 1863.

From reliable information received by me, and which you are also doubtless in possession of, a war steamer called the *Alabama* is now in Saldanha Bay, being painted, discharging prisoners of war, &c.

The vessel in question was built in England to prey upon the commerce of the United States of America, and escaped therefrom while on her trial trip, forfeiting bonds of £20,000, which the British Government exacted under the Foreign Enlistment Act.

Now, as your Government has a treaty of amity and commerce with the United States, and has not recognised the persons in revolt against the United States as a Government at all, the vessel alluded to should be at once seized and sent to England, from whence she clandestinely escaped. Assuming that the British Government was sincere in exacting the bonds, you have doubtless been instructed to send her home to England, where she belongs.

But if, from some oversight, you have not received such instructions, and you decline the responsibility of making the seizure, I would most respectfully protest against the vessel remaining in any port of the colony another day. She has been at Saldanha Bay four [six] days already, and a week previously on the coast, and has forfeited all right to remain an hour longer by this breach of neutrality. Painting a ship does not come under the head of "necessary repairs," and is no proof that she is unseaworthy; and to allow her to visit other ports after she has set the Queen's proclamation of neutrality at defiance would not be regarded as in accordance with the spirit and purpose of that document.

Mr. Adamson to U.S. Consul,
August 5, 1863.

I am directed by the Governor to acknowledge the receipt of your letter of yesterday's date relative to the *Alabama*.

His Excellency has no instructions, neither has he any authority, to seize or detain that vessel; and he desires me to acquaint you that he has received a letter from the Commander, dated the 1st instant, stating that repairs were in progress, and as soon as they were completed he intended to go to sea. He further announces his intention of respecting strictly the neutrality of the British Government.

The course which Captain Semmes here proposes to take is, in the Governor's opinion, in conformity with the instructions he has himself received relative to ships of war and privateers belonging to the United States and the States calling themselves the Confederate States of America visiting British ports.

The reports received from Saldanha Bay induce the Governor to believe that the vessel will leave that harbour as soon as her repairs are completed; but he will immediately, on receiving intelligence to the contrary, take the necessary steps for enforcing the observance of the rules laid down by Her Majesty's Government.

Mr. Graham (U.S. Consul) to Sir P. Wodehouse,
August 5, 1863.

The Confederate steamer *Alabama* has just captured an American *barque* off Green Point, or about four miles from the nearest land (Robben Island). I witnessed the capture with my own eyes, as did hundreds of others at the same time. This occurrence at the entrance of Table Bay, and clearly in British waters, is an insult to England and a grievous injury to a friendly Power, the United States.

Towards the Government of my country and her domestic enemies the Government of England assumes a position of neutrality; and if the neutrality can be infringed with impunity, in this bold and daring manner, the Government of the United States will no doubt consider the matter as one requiring immediate explanation.

Believing that the occurrence was without your knowledge or expectation, and hoping you will take such steps to redress the outrage as the exigency requires, I am, &c.

Mr. Rawson to Mr. Graham. August 6, 1863.

I am directed by the Governor to acknowledge the receipt of your letter of yesterday's date respecting the capture of the *Sea Bride* by the *Alabama*, and to acquaint you that he will lose no time in obtaining accurate information as to the circumstances of the capture.

I have, &c.,
(Signed)   Rawson W. Rawson,
                Colonial Secretary.

Mr. Graham to Sir P. Wodehouse. August 6, 1863.

I have the honour to acknowledge the receipt of your despatch of this date.

I beg now to enclose for your Excellency's perusal, the affidavit of Captain Charles F. White, of the *Sea Bride*, protesting against the capture of the said *barque* in British waters. The bearings taken by him at the time of capture conclusively show that she was in neutral waters, being about two and a half miles from Robben Island. This statement is doubtless more satisfactory than the testimony of persons who measured the distance by the eye.

I believe that there is no law defining the word "coast" other than international law. That law has always limited neutral waters to the fighting distance from land, which, upon the invention of gunpowder, was extended to a distance of three nautical miles from land on a straight coast, and by the same rule, since the invention of Armstrong rifled cannon, to at least six miles.

But all waters inclosed by a line drawn between two promontories or headlands are recognised by all nations as neutral, and England was the first that adopted the rule, calling such waters the "King's chambers." By referring to *Wheaton's Digest*, page 234, or any other good work on international law, you will find the above rules laid down and elucidated.

The fact that the prize has not already been burned, and that her fate is still in suspense, is clear proof that Captain Semmes had misgivings as to the legality of the capture, and awaits your Excellency's assent. If you decide that the prize was legally taken, you will assume a responsibility which Captain Semmes himself declined to take.

Affidavit of C.F.White

On this 6th day of August, A.D. 1863, personally appeared before me, Walter Graham, Consul of the United States at Cape Town, Charles F. White, master of the *barque Sea Bride*, of Boston, from New York, and declared on affidavit that on the 3rd day of August instant, he sighted Table Mountain and made for Table Bay, but that on the 4th instant, night coming on, he was compelled to stand out. On the 5th instant, he again made for the anchorage, and about two p.m. saw a steamer standing toward the *barque*, which he supposed was the English mail steamer, but on nearing her, found her to be the Confederate steamer *Alabama*.

He, Captain White, was peremptorily ordered to heave his vessel to as a prize to the *Alabama*. One gun was fired, and immediately after the demand was made another gun was fired. Two boats were lowered from the *Alabama* and sent on board the *barque*. The officer in charge of these boats demanded the ship's papers, which the said master was compelled to take on board the said steamer. This happened about a quarter before three o'clock. He and his crew were immediately taken from his vessel and placed as prisoners on board the *Alabama*, the officers and crew being put in irons. The position of the *barque* at the time of capture was as follows:—Green Point Lighthouse bearing south by east; Robben Island Lighthouse north-east.

The said appearer did further protest against the illegal capture of said vessel, as she was in British waters at the time of capture, according to bearings.

Mr. Graham to Sir P. Wodehouse. August 7, 1863.

Understanding from your letter of this date, received this morning,[1] that the case of the *Sea Bride* is still pending, I enclose the affidavits of the first officer of that vessel and the cook and steward, which I hope will throw additional light on the subject.

From the affidavit of the first officer, it appears that the alleged prize was brought within one and a half miles of Green Point Lighthouse yesterday at one o'clock p.m. Now, as the vessel was at that time in charge of a prize crew, it was a violation of neutrality as much as if the capture had been made at the same distance from land.

Pending your decision of the case I would most respectfully suggest that the prize crew on board the *Sea Bride* be removed, and that the vessel be put in charge of a crew from Her Majesty's ship *Valorous*.

Affidavit of James Robertson

On the day and date hereof before me, Walter Graham, Consul for the United States of America at Cape Town, personally came and appeared James Robertson, cook and steward of the *barque Sea Bride*, an American vessel, and made affidavit that he was on board said *barque* on the night of the 5th day of August instant, after the said *barque* had been captured as a prize by the Confederate steamer *Alabama*, and a prize crew put on board. That at about five minutes before two o'clock p.m. of the 6th instant, the prize crew on board the said *barque* received a signal from the *Alabama* aforesaid to burn the said *barque*, and immediately all hands were called to execute that order. That the sails were clewed, a tar barrel taken from underneath the topgallant forecastle and placed in the forecastle, and a bucketful of tar, with other combustibles and ammunition, ordered on the cabin table, but that when these arrangements were completed, another signal was received from the said *Alabama*, countermanding the order to burn the said prize, and to stand off and on the land until daylight, which orders were obeyed.

---

1. A formal acknowledgment omitted here as superfluous.

Affidavit of John Schofield

On the day and date hereof before me, Walter Graham, Consul for the United States of America at Cape Town, personally came and appeared John Schofield, first officer of the *barque Sea Bride*, of Boston, who made affidavit that he was on board of said vessel at one o'clock p.m. yesterday, the 6th day of August instant, while she was in possession of a prize crew of the steamer *Alabama*; that he took the bearings of said *barque* at that time, which were as follows: Robben Island Lighthouse bore north-east by north one-half north, Green Point Lighthouse bore south-west one-half west.

He also deposed that the officer in command of the *barque* came on deck about that time, and stamping his foot as if chagrined to find her so near the land, ordered her further off, which was done immediately.

I am directed by the Governor to acknowledge the receipt of your letter of this date, inclosing two affidavits relative to the *Sea Bride*, and to state that his Excellency is not prepared to admit that the fact of that vessel having been brought by the prize crew within one and a half miles of the Green Point Lighthouse "was a violation of the neutrality as much as if the capture had taken place at the same distance from land," although both the belligerents are prohibited from bringing their prizes into British ports.

The Governor does not feel warranted in taking steps for the removal of the prize crew from the *Sea Bride*.

Mr. Rawson to Mr. Graham. August 8, 1863.

With reference to the correspondence that has passed relative to the capture by the Confederate States steamer *Alabama*, of the *barque Sea Bride*, I am directed by the Governor to acquaint you that, on the best information he has been enabled to procure, he has come to the conclusion that the capture cannot be held to be illegal, or in violation of the neutrality of the British Government, by reason of the distance from land at which it took place.

His Excellency will, by next mail, make a full report of the case to Her Majesty's Government.

Mr. Graham to Sir P. Wodehouse. August 10, 1863.

Your decision in the case of the *Sea Bride* was duly received at four o'clock p.m. on Saturday. In communicating that decision you simply announce that the vessel was, in your opinion, and according to evidence before you, a legal prize to the *Alabama*; but you omit to state the principle of international law that governed your decision, and neglect to furnish me with the evidence relied upon by you.

Under these circumstances I can neither have the evidence verified or rebutted here, nor am I enabled to transmit it as it stands to the American Minister at London, nor to the United States Government at Washington. An invitation to be present when the *ex parte* testimony was taken was not extended to me, and I am therefore ignorant of the tenor of it, and cannot distinguish the portion thrown out from that which was accepted. If your decision is that the neutral waters of this colony only extend a distance of three miles from land, the character of that decision would have been aptly illustrated to the people of Cape Town had an American war-vessel appeared on the scene, and engaged the *Alabama* in battle. In such a contest with cannon carrying a distance of six miles (three overland), the crashing buildings in Cape Town would have been an excellent commentary on your decision.

But the decision has been made, and cannot be revoked here, so that further comment at present is, therefore, unnecessary. It can only be reversed by the Government you represent, which it probably will be when the United States Government shall claim indemnity for the owners of the *Sea Bride*.

An armed vessel named the *Tuscaloosa*, claiming to act under the authority of the so-called Confederate States, entered Simon's Bay on Saturday the 8th instant. That vessel was formerly owned by citizens of the United States, and while engaged in lawful commerce was captured as a prize by the *Alabama*. She was subsequently fitted out with arms by the *Alabama* to prey upon the commerce of the United States, and now, without having been condemned as a prize by any Admiralty Court of any recognized Government, she is permitted to enter a neutral port in violation of the Queen's Proclamation, with her original cargo on board. Against this proceeding I hereby most emphatically protest, and I claim that the vessel ought to be given up to her lawful owners. The capture of the *Sea Bride* in neutral waters, together with the case of the *Tuscaloosa*, also a prize, constitute the latest and best illustration of British neutrality that has yet been given.

Mr. Rawson to Mr. Graham. August 10, 1863.

I am directed by the Governor to acknowledge the receipt of your letter of this date, and to state with reference to that part of it which relates to the *Tuscaloosa*, that his Excellency is still in correspondence with the commander-in-chief respecting the character of that vessel, and the privileges to which she is entitled.

Mr. Graham to Sir P. Wodehouse. August 12, 1863.

Upon receiving your last communication to me dated the 10th instant, I deemed it simply a report of progress on one subject treated of in my last letter to your Excellency, and I have therefore waited anxiously for the receipt of another letter from the Colonial Secretary communicating the final result in the case. Failing to receive it, and hearing yesterday p.m. that the *Tuscaloosa* would proceed to Sea from Simon's Bay today, I applied for an injunction from the Supreme Court to prevent the vessel sailing before I had an opportunity of showing by witnesses that she is owned in Philadelphia in the United States, and her true name is *Conrad*; that she has never been condemned as a prize by any legally constituted Admiralty Court; and that I am *ex officio* the legal agent of the owners, underwriters, and all others concerned. I have not yet learned the result of that application, and fearing that delay may allow her to escape, I would respectfully urge you to detain her in port until the proper legal steps can be taken.

I am well aware that your Government has conceded to the so-called Confederate States the rights of belligerents, and is thereby bound to respect Captain Semmes' commission; but having refused to recognize the "Confederacy" as a nation, and having excluded his captures from all the ports of the British Empire, the captures necessarily revert to their real owners, and are forfeited by Captain Semmes as soon as they enter a British port.

Hoping to receive an answer to this and the preceding letter as early as possible, and that you will not construe my persistent course throughout this correspondence on neutral rights as importunate, or my remarks as inopportune, I have, &c.

Mr. Rawson to Mr. Graham. August 12, 1863.

I am directed by the Governor to acknowledge the receipt of your letter of this date, and to acquaint you that it was not until late last evening that his Excellency received from the naval commander-in-chief information that the condition of the *Tuscaloosa* was such as, as his Excellency is advised, to entitle her to be regarded as a vessel of war.

The Governor is not aware, nor do you refer him to the provisions of international law by which captured vessels, as soon as they enter our neutral ports, revert to their real owners, and are forfeited by their captors. But his Excellency believes that the claims of contending parties to vessels captured can only be determined in the first instance by the Courts of the captor's country.

The Governor desires me to add that he cannot offer any objection to the tenor of the correspondence which you have addressed to him on this subject, and that he is very sensible of the courtesy you have exhibited under such very peculiar circumstances!!! He gives you credit for acting on a strict sense of duty to your country.

Mr. Graham to Sir P. Wodehouse. August 17, 1863.

I have delayed acknowledging the receipt of your last letter, dated the 12th August, on account of events transpiring, but which have not yet culminated so as to form the subject of correspondence.

Your decision that the *Tuscaloosa* is a vessel of war, and by inference a prize, astonishes me, because I do not see the necessary incompatibility. Four guns were taken from on board the *Talisman* (also a prize), and put on board the *Conrad* (*Tuscaloosa*), but that transfer did not change the character of either vessel as a prize, for neither of them could cease to be a prize till it had been condemned in an Admiralty Court of the captor's country, which it is not pretended has been done. The *Tuscaloosa*, therefore, being a prize, was forbidden to enter Simon's Bay by the Queen's Proclamation, and should have been ordered off at once; but she was not so ordered. Granting that Her Majesty's Proclamation affirmed the right of Captain Semmes as a belligerent to take and to hold prizes on the high seas, it just as emphatically denied his right to hold them in British ports. Now, if he could not hold them in Simon's Bay, who else could hold them except those whose right to hold them was antecedent to his—that is, the, owners?

The *Tuscaloosa* remained in Simon's Bay seven days with her original cargo of skins and wool on board. This cargo, I am informed by those who claim to know, has been purchased by merchants in Cape Town; and if it should be landed here directly from the prize, or be transferred to other vessels at some secluded harbour on the coast beyond this Colony, and brought from thence here, the infringement of neutrality will be so palpable and flagrant that Her Majesty's Government will probably satisfy the claims of the owners gracefully and at once, and thus remove all cause of complaint. In so doing it will have to disavow and repudiate the acts of its executive agents here—a result I have done all in my power to prevent.

Greater cause of complaint will exist if the cargo of the *Sea Bride* is disposed of in the same manner, as I have reason to apprehend it will be when negotiations are concluded; for being originally captured in neutral waters, the thin guise of neutrality would be utterly torn into shreds by the sale of her cargo here.

The *Georgia*, a Confederate war-steamer, arrived at Simon's Bay yesterday, and the *Florida*, another vessel of the same class, has arrived, or is expected hourly at Saldanha Bay, where she may remain a week without your knowledge, as the place is very secluded. The *Alabama* remained here in Table Bay nearly four days, and at Simon's Bay six days; and as the *Tuscaloosa* was allowed to remain at Simon's Bay seven days, I apprehend that the *Georgia* and *Florida* will meet with the same or even greater favours. Under such circumstances further protests from me would seem to be unavailing, and I only put the facts upon record for the benefit of my Government and officials possessed of diplomatic functions.

Mr. Rawson to Mr. Graham. August 19, 1863.

I am directed by the Governor to acknowledge the receipt of your letter of the 17th instant, and to state that he has, during the recent transactions, endeavoured to act in strict conformity with the wishes of Her Majesty's Government; he will in like manner pursue the same course in any future cases which may arise.

I am to add that His Excellency has no reason to believe that either the *Alabama* or the Tuscaloosa have been allowed to remain in the ports of the Colony for a greater length of time than the state of the weather, and the execution of the repairs of which they actually stood in need, rendered indispensable.

Statement of Joseph Hopson.

Joseph Hopson, keeper of the Green Point Lighthouse, states:

I was on the lookout on Wednesday afternoon when the *Alabama* and *Sea Bride* were coming in. When I first saw them the steamer was coming round the north-west of Robben Island, and the *barque* bore from or about five miles west-northwest. The *barque* was coming in under all sail with a good breeze, and she took nothing in when the gun was fired. I believe two guns were fired, but the gun I mean was the last, and the steamer then crossed the stern side of the *barque*, and hauled up to her on the starboard side.

He steamed ahead gently, and shortly afterwards I saw the *barque* put round with her head to the westward, and a boat put off from the steamer and boarded her. Both vessels were then good five miles off the mainland, and quite five, if not six, from the north-west point of

Robben Island.

Statement of W.S. Field, Collector of Customs.

I was present at the old Lighthouse, Green Point, on Wednesday afternoon, at 2 p.m., and saw the *Alabama* capture the American *barque Sea Bride*, and I agree with the above statement as far as the position of the vessels and their distance from shore.

I may also remark that I called the attention of Colonel Bisset and the lighthouse keeper Hopson to the distance of the vessels at the time of the capture, as it was probable we should be called upon to give our evidence respecting the affair, and we took a note of the time it occurred.

Statement of John Roe.

I was yesterday, the 5th day of August, 1863, returning from a whale chase in Hunt's Bay, when I first saw the *barque Sea Bride* standing from the westward on to the land. I came on to Table Bay, and when off Camps Bay I saw the smoke of the *Alabama* some distance from the westward of Robben Island. When I reached the Green Point Lighthouse the steamer was standing up towards the *barque*, which was about five miles and a half to the westward of Green Point, and about four and half from the western point of Robben Island. This was their position (being near each other at the time) when the gun was fired.

Statement of Signalman at the Lion's Rump Telegraph Station.

On Wednesday last, the 5th day of August, 1863, I sighted the *barque Sea Bride* about seven o'clock in the morning, about fifteen or twenty miles off the land, standing into Table Bay from the south-west. There was a light breeze blowing from the north-west, which continued until after midday. About midday I sighted the *Alabama* screw steamer standing from due north towards Table Bay, intending, as it appeared to me, to take the passage between Robben Island and the Blueberg Beach. She was then between fifteen and eighteen miles off the land.

After sighting the steamer, I hoisted the demand for the *barque*, when she hoisted the American flag, which I reported to the Port Office, the *barque* then being about eight miles off the land from Irville Point. No sooner had the *barque* hoisted the American flag than the steamer turned sharp round in the direction of and towards the *barque*. The steamer appeared at that time to have been about twelve miles off the land from Irville Point, and about four or five miles outside of Robben Island, and about seven miles from the *barque*.

The steamer then came up to and alongside of the *barque*, when the latter was good four miles off the land at or near the old Lighthouse, and five miles off the Island. The steamer, after firing a gun, stopped the further progress of the *barque*, several boats were sent to her, and after that the *barque* stood out to sea again, and the *Alabama* steamed into Table Bay.

Captain Forsyth to Sir P. Wodehouse. August 6, 1863.

In compliance with the request conveyed to me by your Excellency, I have the honour to report that I have obtained from Captain Semmes a statement of the positions of the Confederate States steamer *Alabama* and the American *barque Sea Bride*, when the latter was captured yesterday afternoon.

Captain Semmes asserts that at the time of his capturing the *Sea Bride*, Green Point Lighthouse bore from the *Alabama* south-east about six or six and a half miles.

This statement is borne out by the evidence of Captain Wilson, Port Captain of Table Bay, who has assured me that at the time of the *Sea Bride* being captured, he was off Green Point in the port boat, and that only the top of the *Alabama*'s hull was visible.

I am of opinion, if Captain Wilson could only see that portion of the hull of the *Alabama*, she must have been about the distance from the shore which is stated by Captain Semmes, and I have therefore come to the conclusion that the *barque Sea Bride* was beyond the limits assigned when she was captured by the *Alabama*.

Rear-Admiral Sir B. Walker to the Secretary to the Admiralty., September 17, 1863.

With reference to my letters dated respectively the 19th and 31st *ultimo*, relative to the Confederate States ship of war *Alabama*, and the prizes captured by her, I beg to inclose, for their Lordships' information, the copy of a statement forwarded to me by the Collector of Customs at Cape Town, wherein it is represented that the *Tuscaloosa* and *Sea Bride* had visited Ichaboe, which is a dependency of this Colony.

2. Since the receipt of the above-mentioned document, the *Alabama* arrived at this anchorage (the 16th instant), and when Captain Semmes waited on me, I acquainted him with the report, requesting he would inform me if it was true. I was glad to learn from him that it was not so. He frankly explained that the prize *Sea Bride* in the first place had put into Saldanha Bay through stress of weather, and on being joined there by the Tuscaloosa, both vessels proceeded to Angra

Pequena, on the West Coast of Africa, where he subsequently joined them in the *Alabama*, and there sold the *Sea Bride* and her cargo to an English subject who resides at Cape Town. The *Tuscaloosa* had landed some wool at Angra Pequena and received ballast, but, he states, is still in commission as a tender. It will, therefore, be seen how erroneous is the accompanying report. I have no reason to doubt Captain Semmes' explanation; but he seems to be fully alive to the instructions of Her Majesty's Government, and appears to be most anxious not to commit any breach of neutrality.

3. The *Alabama* has returned to this port for coal, some provisions, and to repair her condensing apparatus.

4. From conversation with Captain Semmes, I find that he has been off this Cape for the last five days, and as the *Vanderbilt* left this on the night of the 11th instant, it is surprising they did not see each other.

The Duke of Newcastle to Sir P. Wodehouse,
November 4, 1863.

I have received your despatch of the 19th August last, submitting for my consideration various questions arising out of the proceedings at the Cape of Good Hope of the Confederate vessels *Georgia*, *Alabama*, and her reputed tender, the *Tuscaloosa*.

I will now proceed to convey to you the views of Her Majesty's Government on these questions.

The capture of the *Sea Bride*, by the *Alabama*, is stated to have been effected beyond the distance of three miles from the shore—which distance must be accepted as the limit of territorial jurisdiction, according to the present rule of international law upon that subject. It appears, however, that the prize, very soon after her capture, was brought within the distance of two miles from the shore; and as this is contrary to Her Majesty's orders, it might have afforded just grounds (if the apology of Captain Semmes for this improper act, which he ascribed to inadvertence, had not been accepted by you) for the interference of the colonial authorities upon the principles which I am about to explain.

With respect to the *Alabama* herself, it is clear that neither you nor any other authority at the Cape could exercise any jurisdiction over her; and that, whatever may have been her previous history, you were bound to treat her as a ship of war belonging to a belligerent Power.

With regard to the vessel called the *Tuscaloosa*, I am advised that this vessel did not lose the character of a prize captured by the *Alabama*, merely because she was, at the time of her being brought within British waters, armed with two small rifled guns, in charge of an officer, and manned with a crew of ten men from the *Alabama*, and used as a tender to that vessel under the authority of Captain Semmes.

It would appear that the *Tuscaloosa* is a *barque* of 500 tons, captured by the *Alabama*, off the coast of Brazil, on the 21st of June last, and brought into Simon's Bay on or before the 7th of August, with her original cargo of wool (itself, as well as the vessel, prize) still on board, and with nothing to give her a warlike character (so far as is stated in the papers before me), except the circumstances already noticed.

Whether, in the case of a vessel duly commissioned as a ship of war, after being made prize by a belligerent Government, without being first brought *infra praesidia*, or condemned by a court of prize, the character of prize, within the meaning of Her Majesty's orders, would or would not be merged in that of a national ship of war, I am not called upon to explain. It is enough to say that the citation from Mr. Wheaton's book by your attorney-general does not appear to me to have any direct bearing upon the question.

Connected with this subject is the question as to the cargoes of captured vessels, which is alluded to at the end of your despatch. On this point I have to instruct you that Her Majesty's orders apply as much to prize cargoes of every kind which may be brought by any armed ships or privateers of either belligerent into British waters as to the captured vessels themselves. They do not, however, apply to any articles which may have formed part of any such cargoes, if brought within British jurisdiction, not by armed ships or privateers of either belligerent, but by other persons who may have acquired or may claim property in them by reason of any dealings with the captors.

I think it right to observe that the third reason alleged by the attorney-general for his opinion assumes (though the fact had not been made the subject of any inquiry) that "no means existed for determining whether the ship had or had not been judicially condemned in a court of competent jurisdiction," and the proposition that, "*admitting her to have been captured by a ship of war of the Confederate States*, she was entitled to refer Her Majesty's Government, in case of any dispute, to the court of her States in order to satisfy it as to her real character." This assumption, however, is not consistent with Her Majesty's undoubted right to determine within her own territory whether her own orders, made in vindication of her own neutrality, have been violated or not.

The question remains what course ought to have been taken by the authorities of the Cape—

1st. In order to ascertain whether this vessel was, as alleged by the United States Consul, an uncondemned prize brought within British waters in violation of Her Majesty's neutrality; and

2ndly. What ought to have been done if such had appeared to be really the fact.

I think that the allegations of the United States Consul ought to have been brought to the knowledge of Captain Semmes while the *Tuscaloosa* was still within British waters, and that he should have been requested to state whether he did or did not admit the facts to be as alleged. He should also have been called upon (unless the facts were admitted) to produce the *Tuscaloosa's* papers. If the result of these inquiries had been to prove that the vessel was really an uncondemned prize, brought into British waters in violation of Her Majesty's orders made for the purpose of maintaining her neutrality, I consider that the mode of proceeding in such circumstances, most consistent with Her Majesty's dignity, and most proper for the vindication of her territorial rights, would have been to prohibit the exercise of any further control over the *Tuscaloosa* by the captors, and to retain that vessel under Her Majesty's control and jurisdiction until properly reclaimed by her original owners.

Sir P. Wodehouse to the Duke of Newcastle. December 19, 1863.

I have had the honour to receive your Grace's despatch of the 4th *ultimo*, from which I regret to learn that the course taken here relative to the Confederate war steamer *Alabama* and her prizes has not in some respects given satisfaction to Her Majesty's Government.

I must only beg your Grace to believe that no pains were spared by the late Acting Attorney-General or by myself to shape our course in what we believed to be conformity with the orders of Her Majesty's Government and the rules of international law, as far as we could ascertain and interpret them.

Mr. Denyssen has been so constantly engaged with professional business since the arrival of the mail that I have been prevented from discussing with him the contents of your despatch; but I think it right, nevertheless, to take advantage of the first opportunity for representing to your Grace the state of uncertainty in which I am placed by the receipt of this communication, and for soliciting such further explanations as may prevent my again falling into error on these matters. In so doing I trust you will be prepared to make allowance for the difficulties which must arise out of this peculiar contest, in respect of which both parties stand on a footing of equality as belligerents, while only one of them is recognized as a nation.

In the first place, I infer that I have given cause for dissatisfaction in not having more actively resented the fact that the *Sea Bride*, on the day after her capture, was brought a short distance within British waters.

Your Grace demurs to my having accepted Captain Semmes' apology for this improper act, which he ascribed to inadvertence. You will pardon my noticing that the fact of the act having been done through inadvertence was established by the United States Consul himself, one of whose witnesses stated, "the officer in command of the *barque* came on deck about that time, and stamping his foot as if chagrined to find her so near the land, ordered her further off, which was done immediately."

I confess that on such evidence of such a fact I did not consider myself warranted in requiring the commander of Her Majesty's ship *Valorous* to take possession of the *Alabama*'s prize.

The questions involved in the treatment of the Tuscaloosa are far more important and more embarrassing; and first let me state, with reference to the suggestion that Captain Semmes should have been required to admit or deny the allegations of the United States Consul, that no such proceeding was required. There was not the slightest mystery or concealment of the circumstances under which the *Tuscaloosa* had come into, and then was in possession of the Confederates. The facts were not disputed. We were required to declare what was her actual status under those facts. We had recourse to Wheaton, the best authority on International Law within our reach—an authority of the nation with whom the question had arisen—an authority which the British Secretary for Foreign Affairs had recently been quoting in debates on American questions in the House of Lords.

Your Grace intimates that the citation from this authority by the Acting Attorney-General does not appear to have any direct bearing upon the question.

You will assuredly believe that it is not from any want of respect for your opinion, but solely from a desire to avoid future error, that I confess my inability to understand this intimation, or, in the absence of instructions on that head, to see in what direction I am to look for the law bearing on the subject.

The paragraph cited made no distinction between a vessel with cargo and a vessel without cargo; and your Grace leaves me in ignorance whether her character would have been changed if Captain Semmes had got rid of the cargo before claiming for her admission as a ship of war. Certainly, acts had been done by him which, according to Wheaton, constituted a "setting forth as a vessel of war."

Your Grace likewise states, "Whether in the case of a vessel duly commissioned as a ship of war, after being made prize by a belligerent Government without being first brought *infra praesidia*, or condemned by a Court of Prize, the character of prize, within the meaning of Her Majesty's orders, would or would not be merged in a national ship of war, I am not called upon to explain."

I feel myself forced to ask for further advice on this point, on which it is quite possible I may be called upon to take an active part. I have already, in error apparently, admitted a Confederate prize as a ship of war. The chief authority on International Law, in which it is in my power to refer, is Wheaton, who apparently draws no distinction between ships of war and other ships when found in the position of prizes; and I wish your Grace to be aware that within the last few days the commander of a United States ship of war observed to me that if it were his good fortune to capture the *Alabama*, he should convert her into a Federal cruiser.

I trust your Grace will see how desirable it is that I should be fully informed of the views of Her Majesty's Government on these points, and that I shall be favoured with a reply to this despatch at your earliest convenience.

Rear-Admiral Sir B. Walker to the Secretary to the Admiralty, January 5, 1864.

I request you will be pleased to acquaint my Lords Commissioners of the Admiralty that the *barque* called the *Tuscaloosa*, under the flag of the Confederate States of North America (referred to in my letter of the 19th of August last), termed a tender to the *Alabama*, returned to this anchorage on the 26th ultimo from cruising off the coast of Brazil.

2. In order to ascertain the real character of this vessel, I directed the boarding officer from my flag-ship to put the questions, as per inclosure No. 1, to the officer in command, Lieutenant Low, of the *Alabama*; and having satisfied myself from his answers that the vessel

was still an uncondemned prize captured by the *Alabama* under the name of the *Conrad*, of Philadelphia, I communicated the circumstances to the Governor of this Colony, who, concurring in opinion with me that she ought to be retained under Her Majesty's control and jurisdiction until reclaimed by her proper owners, for violation of Her Majesty's orders for the maintenance of her neutrality, I caused the so-called *Tuscaloosa* to be taken possession of; informing Lieutenant Low, at the same time, of the reason for doing so.

3. Lieutenant Low has entered a written protest against the seizure of the vessel, a copy of which, together with the reply of the Governor, I inclose for their Lordships' information, as well as a copy of all the correspondence which has passed on this subject.

4. Lieutenant Low having informed me that he expects the *Alabama* shortly to arrive at this place, I have allowed him and his crew to remain on board the Conrad for the present; but should the *Alabama* not make her appearance I have acquainted him that I will grant him and his officers (probably only one besides himself) a passage to England in one of the packets. The crew he wishes to discharge if there is no opportunity of their rejoining the *Alabama*.

5. The vessel in question is at present moored in this bay, in charge of an officer and a few men belonging to Her Majesty's ship *Narcissus*, where she will remain until she can be properly transferred to her lawful owners, as requested by the Governor.

Questions to be put to the Officer in Command or Charge of the barque Tuscaloosa, carrying the Flag of the so-called Confederate States of America.

Ship's name and nation?
Tuscaloosa. Confederate.

Name and rank of officer in command?
Lieutenant Low, late *Alabama*.

Tonnage of the ship?
500.

Number of officers and men on board?
4 officers and 20 men.

Number and description of guns on board?
3 small brass guns, 2 rifled 12 pounders, 1 smooth-bore-pounder.

Where is she from?
St. Katherine's, Brazils.

Where is she bound?

Cruising.

For what purpose has the ship put into this port?
For repairs and supplies.

Is it the same ship that was captured by the *Alabama*, and afterwards came to this port on the 9th of August last?
Yes.

What was her original name, on being captured by the *Alabama*?
Conrad, of Philadelphia.

When was she captured by *Alabama*?
21st June, 1863.

To what nation and to whom did she belong before her capture?
Federal States of America.

Has she been taken before any legally constituted Admiralty Court of the Confederate States?
No.

Has she been duly condemned as a lawful prize by such Court to the captors?
No.

What is she now designated?
Tender to the *Alabama*.

What papers are there on board to constitute her as the Confederate *barque Tuscaloosa*?
The commission of the Lieutenant commanding the *Tuscaloosa* from Captain Semmes. The officers also have commissions to their ship from him.

Are the papers which belonged to her before she was seized by the *Alabama* on board?
No.

Is there any cargo on board, and what does it consist of?
No cargo—only stores for ballast.

    (Signed)   John Low,
                                    Lieut.-Commander,
                                      Confederate States *barque Tuscaloosa*.
    (Signed)   Francis L. Wood,
                                    Lieutenant and Boarding Officer,
                                    Her Majesty's ship *Narcissus*.

Rear-Admiral Sir B. Walker to Lieutenant Low, C.S.N.
December 27, 1863.

As it appears that the *Tuscaloosa*, under your charge and command, is a vessel belonging to the Federal States of America, having been captured by the Confederate States ship of war *Alabama*, and not having been adjudicated before any competent Prize Court, is still an uncondemned prize, which you have brought into this port in violation of Her Britannic Majesty's orders for the maintenance of her neutrality, I have the honour to inform you that, in consequence, I am compelled to detain the so-called *Tuscaloosa* (late *Conrad*) with a view of her being restored to her original owners, and I request you will be so good as to transfer the charge of the vessel to the officer bearing this letter to you.

Rear-Admiral Sir B. Walker to Sir P. Wodehouse.,
December 28, 1863.

I have the honour to inform your Excellency that, acting upon your concurrence in my opinion with reference to the instructions received from home by the last mail, I have detained the *barque Tuscaloosa* (late *Conrad* of Philadelphia), because she is an uncondemned prize, taken by the Confederate States ship of war *Alabama*, and brought into British waters in violation of Her Majesty's Orders for maintaining her neutrality, and with the view to her being restored to her original owners.

I shall be ready to hand her over to the Consul of the United States at Cape Town, or to any person you may appoint to take charge of her.

I should add that Lieutenant Low has given up the *Tuscaloosa* (late *Conrad*) under protest, which he is about to make in writing, a copy of which shall be transmitted to your Excellency as soon as received.

Lieutenant Low, C.S.N., to Sir P. Wodehouse,
December 28, 1863

As the officer in command of the Confederate States ship *Tuscaloosa*, tender to the Confederate States steamer *Alabama*, I have to record my protest against the recent extraordinary measures which have been adopted towards me and the vessel under my command by the British authorities of this Colony.

In August last the *Tuscaloosa* arrived in Simon's Bay. She was not only recognised in the character which she lawfully claimed and still claims to be, *viz.*, a commissioned ship of war belonging to a belligerent Power, but was allowed to remain in the harbour for the period of seven days, taking in supplies and effecting repairs with the full knowledge and sanction of the authorities.

No intimation was given that she was regarded in the light of an ordinary prize, or that she was considered to be violating the laws of neutrality. Nor, when she notoriously left for a cruise on active service, was any intimation whatever conveyed that on her return to the port of a friendly Power, where she had been received as a man-of-war, she would be regarded as a "prize," as a violater of the Queen's proclamation of neutrality, and consequently liable to seizure. Misled by the conduct of Her Majesty's Government, I returned to Simon's Bay on the 26th instant, in very urgent want of repairs and supplies; to my surprise I find the *Tuscaloosa* is now no longer considered as a man-of-war, and she has by your orders, as I learn, been seized for the purpose of being handed over to the person who claims her on behalf of her late owners.

The character of the vessel, *viz.*, that of a lawful commissioned man-of-war of the Confederate States of America, has not been altered since her first arrival in Simon's Bay, and she, having been once fully recognised by the British authorities in command in this Colony, and no notice or warning of change of opinion or of friendly feeling having been communicated by public notification or otherwise. I was entitled to expect to be again permitted to enter Simon's Bay without molestation.

In perfect good faith I returned to Simon's Bay for mere necessaries, and in all honour and good faith, in return, I should on change of opinion or of policy on the part of the British authorities, have been desired to leave the port again.

But by the course of proceedings taken, I have been (supposing the view now taken by your Excellency's Government to be correct) first misled and next entrapped.

My position and character of my ship will most certainly be vindicated by my Government. I am powerless to resist the affront offered to the Confederate States of America by your Excellency's conduct and proceedings.

I demand, however, the release of my ship; and if this demand be not promptly complied with, I hereby formally protest against her seizure, especially under the very peculiar circumstances of the case.

Mr. Rawson to Lieutenant Low, C.S.N.
December 29, 1863.

I am directed by the Governor to acknowledge the receipt of your letter of yesterday's date protesting against the seizure of the *Tuscaloosa*, whose character you represent to be the same as when, in August last, she was admitted into the port of Simon's Bay, and I am to acquaint you in reply that a full report was submitted to Her Majesty's Government of all that took place on the first visit of the *Tuscaloosa*, and that the seizure has now been made in conformity with the opinion expressed by them on that report.

Your protest will of course be transmitted for their consideration.

Rear-Admiral Sir B. Walker to Sir P. Wodehouse,
December 29, 1863.

Lieutenant Low, the officer belonging to the Confederate States ship of war *Alabama*, late in charge of the *barque* called the *Tuscaloosa* (properly the Conrad of Philadelphia), having sent me a copy of the protest which he has forwarded to your Excellency against the detention of that vessel, I think it right to inclose for your information the copy of my letter to Lieutenant Low [2] explaining the circumstances under which the so-called *Tuscaloosa* is detained.

Sir P. Wodehouse to the Duke of Newcastle,
January 11, 1864.

I very much regret having to acquaint your Grace that the Confederate prize vessel the *Tuscaloosa* has again entered Simon's Bay, and that the Naval Commander-in-chief and myself have come to the conclusion that, in obedience to the orders transmitted to his Excellency by the Admiralty, and to me by your Grace's despatch of the 4th November last, it was our duty to take possession of the vessel, and to hold her until properly claimed by her original owners. The Admiral, therefore, sent an officer with a party of men from the flag-ship to take charge of her, and to deliver to her commander a letter in explanation of the act.

Copies of his protest, addressed to me, and of my reply, are inclosed. He not unnaturally complains of having been now seized, after he had on the previous occasion been recognised as a ship of war. But this is manifestly nothing more than the inevitable result of the overruling by Her Majesty's Government of the conclusion arrived at on the previous occasion by its subordinate officer.

---
2. This letter is not given in the Blue Book.

The Consul for the United States, on being informed of what had taken place, intimated his inability to take charge of the ship on account of the owners, and expressed a desire that it should remain in our charge until he was put in possession of the requisite authority. Accordingly, after taking the opinion of the Attorney-General, it was arranged that the vessel should remain in the charge of Sir Baldwin Walker.

I ought to explain that the seizure was made without previous reference to the Attorney-General. I did not consider such a reference necessary. The law had been determined by Her Majesty's Government on the previous case. The Admiral was of opinion that we had only to obey the orders we had received, and on his intimating that opinion I assented.

Your Grace will observe that at the request of the officers of the Tuscaloosa the Admiral has permitted them to remain on board, in expectation of the immediate arrival of the *Alabama*, to which ship they wish to return. I should otherwise have thought it my duty to provide them with passages to England at the cost of Her Majesty's Government, by whom, I conclude, they would be sent to their own country; and it is probable that if the *Alabama* should not soon make her appearance, such an arrangement will become necessary.

I have only to add that I have thought it advisable, after what has now occurred, to intimate to the United States Consul that we should probably be under the necessity of adopting similar measures in the event of an uncondemned prize being fitted for cruising, and brought into one of our ports by a Federal ship of war. I did not speak positively, because I have been left in doubt by your Grace's instructions whether some distinction should not be drawn in the case of a ship of war of one belligerent captured and applied to the same use by the other belligerent, but the Consul was evidently prepared for such a step. Copies of all the correspondence are inclosed.

Mr. Rawson to Mr. Graham. December 28, 1863.

I am directed by the Governor to acquaint you that the *Tuscaloosa* having again arrived in Simon's Bay, will, under instructions lately received from Her Majesty's Government, be retained under Her Majesty's control and jurisdiction until properly reclaimed by her original holders.

Mr. Graham to Sir P. Wodehouse. December 28, 1863.

I have to acknowledge the receipt of your letter of yesterday's date in reference to the *Tuscaloosa*.

By virtue of my office as Consul for the United States of America in the British possessions of South Africa, of which nation the original owners of the *Conrad alias Tuscaloosa* are citizens, I possess the right to act for them when both they and their special agents are absent, I can institute a proceeding *in rem* where the rights of property of fellow-citizens are concerned, without a special procuration from those for whose benefit I act, but cannot receive actual restitution of the *res* in controversy, without a special authority. (See *United States Statutes at Large*, vol. 1., p. 254, notes 2 and 3.)

Under these circumstances I am content that the vessel in question should for the present, or until the properly authenticated papers and power of attorney shall be received from the owners in America, remain in possession and charge of Her Majesty's naval officers. But should it hereafter be determined to give the vessel up to any party other than the real owners, I desire to have sufficient notice of the fact, so that I may take the proper steps to protect the interests of my absent fellow-citizens.

With regard to the property of American citizens seized here at the Custom-house, and which was formerly part of the *Sea Bride's* cargo, I would suggest that it also be held by the Colonial Government, subject to the order of the original owners. An announcement to that effect from you would be received with great satisfaction by me.

Rear-Admiral Sir B. Walker to the Secretary to the Admiralty., January 18, 1864.

With reference to my letter of the 5th instant, I have the honour to submit, for their Lordships' information, a further correspondence between the Governor of this Colony and myself relative to the American vessel *Conrad*, of Philadelphia, lately called the *Tuscaloosa*.

2. Lieutenant Low, belonging to the Confederate States ship of war *Alabama*, lately in charge of the *Tuscaloosa*, having paid off and discharged his crew, finally quitted the vessel on the 9th instant; and I have ordered him a passage to England by the mail-packet *Saxon*, together with his first officer, Mr. Sinclair.

3. The *Conrad* now remains in charge of a warrant officer and two ship-keepers, awaiting to be properly claimed or disposed of as the Government may direct.

Rear-Admiral Sir B. Walker to Sir P. Wodehouse,
January 6, 1864.

With reference to your Excellency's communication of yesterday's date, I have the honour to inform you that I will make arrangements for the safe custody of the *Conrad*, of Philadelphia (late *Tuscaloosa*), by mooring her in this bay, and putting ship-keepers in charge of her, until she can be properly transferred to her lawful owners.

Lieutenant Low has requested to be allowed to remain on board the vessel, together with his crew, for the present, as he expected the *Alabama* to arrive here shortly, to which arrangement I have made no objection.

There are some guns and other articles on board the *Conrad* said to belong to the *Alabama*, a list of which I have already forwarded to your Excellency. It is a matter for consideration how these things should be disposed of.

I think, as a precautionary measure, it may be desirable that some person on the part of the United States Consul should visit the *Conrad*, to observe the state she is in, on being taken into British custody, to prevent any question thereon hereafter.

The Duke of Newcastle to Sir P. Wodehouse,
March 4, 1864.

I have received your despatches of the 11th and 19th January, reporting the circumstances connected with the seizure of the Confederate prize-vessel *Tuscaloosa*, under the joint authority of the Naval Commander-in-chief and yourself. I have to instruct you to restore the *Tuscaloosa* to the Lieutenant of the Confederate States who lately commanded her, or, if he should have left the Cape, then to retain her until she can be handed over to some person who may have authority from Captain Semmes, of the *Alabama*, or from the Government of the Confederate States, to receive her.

You will receive a further communication from me on this subject by the next mail.

The Duke of Newcastle to Sir P. Wodehouse.,
March 10, 1864.

In my despatch of the 4th instant, I instructed you to restore the *Tuscaloosa* to the Lieutenant of the Confederate States who lately commanded her, or, if he should have left the Cape, then to retain her until she could be handed over to some person having authority from Captain Semmes, of the *Alabama*, or from the Government of the Confederate States, to receive her.

I have now to explain that this decision was not founded on any general principle respecting the treatment of prizes captured by the cruisers of either belligerent, but on the peculiar circumstances of the case. The *Tuscaloosa* was allowed to enter the port of Cape Town and to depart, the instructions of the 4th of November not having arrived at the Cape before her departure. The captain of the *Alabama* was thus entitled to assume that he might equally bring her a second time into the same harbour, and it becomes unnecessary to discuss whether, on her return to the Cape, the *Tuscaloosa* still retained the character of a prize, or whether she had lost that character, and had assumed that of an armed tender to the *Alabama*, and whether that new character, if properly established and admitted, would have entitled her to the same privilege of admission which might be accorded to her captor, the *Alabama*.

Her Majesty's Government have, therefore, come to the opinion, founded on the special circumstances of this particular case, that the *Tuscaloosa* ought to be released, with a warning, however, to the captain of the *Alabama*, that the ships of war of the belligerents are not to be allowed to bring prizes into British ports, and that it rests with Her Majesty's Government to decide to what vessels that character belongs.

In conclusion, I desire to assure you that neither in this despatch, nor in that of the 4th November, I have desired in any degree to censure you for the course you have pursued. The questions on which you have been called upon to decide, are questions of difficulty, on which doubts might properly have been entertained, and I am by no means surprised that the conclusions to which you were led have not, in all instances, been those which have been adopted on fuller consideration by Her Majesty's Government.

Captain Semmes, C.S.N., to Rear-Admiral Sir B. Walker, dated C.S.S. Alabama; Table Bay, March 22, 1864.

Sir:—I was surprised to learn upon my arrival at this port of the detention by your order of the Confederate States *barque Tuscaloosa*, a tender to this ship. I take it for granted that you detained her by order of the Home Government, as no other supposition is consistent with my knowledge of the candour of your character—the *Tuscaloosa* having been formerly received by you as a regularly commissioned tender, and no new facts appearing in the case to change your decision. Under these circumstances I shall not demand of you the restoration of that vessel, with which demand you would not have the power to comply, but will content myself with putting this my protest against this detention on the record of the case for the future consideration of our respective Governments.

Earl Russell, in reaching the decision which he has communicated to you, must surely have misapprehended the facts, otherwise I cannot conceive him capable of so misapplying the law. The facts are briefly these:—1st. The *Tuscaloosa* was formerly the enemy's ship *Conrad*, lawfully captured by me on the high seas, as a recognized belligerent; 2ndly. She was duly commissioned by me as a tender to the Confederate States steamer *Alabama*, then, as now, under my command; and 3rdly. She entered English waters not only without intention of violating Her Britannic Majesty's orders of neutrality, but was received with hospitality, and no question was raised as to her right to enter under the circumstances.

These were the facts up to the time of Earl Russell's issuing to you his order in the premises. Let us consider, then, a moment, and see if we can derive from them, or any of them, just ground for the extraordinary decision to which Earl Russell has come.

My right to capture and the legality of the capture will not be denied. Nor will you deny, in your experience as a naval officer, my right to commission this, or any other ship lawfully in my possession, as a tender to my principal ship. Your admirals do this every day, on distant stations; and the tender, from the time of her being put in commission, wears a pennant, and is entitled to the immunities and privileges of a ship of war, the right of capture inclusive.

Numerous decisions are to be found in your own prize law to this effect. In other words, this is one of the recognised modes of commissioning a ship of war, which has grown out of the convenience of the thing, and become a sort of naval common law, as indisputable as the written law itself. The only difference between the commission of such a ship and that of a ship commissioned by the sovereign authority at home is that the word "tender" appears in the former commission and not in the latter. The *Tuscaloosa* having then been commissioned by me in accordance with the recognised practice of all civilized nations that have a marine, can any other Government than my own look into her antecedents? Clearly not.

The only thing which can be looked at upon her entering a foreign port is her commission. If this be issued by competent authority, you cannot proceed a step further. The ship then becomes a part of the territory of the country to which she belongs, and you can exercise no more jurisdiction over her than over that territory. The self-respect and the independence of nations require this; for it would be a monstrous doctrine to admit that one nation may inquire into the title by which another nation holds her ships of war. And there can be no difference in this respect between tenders and ships originally commissioned. The flag and the pennant fly over them both, and they are both withdrawn from the local jurisdiction by competent commissions.

On principle you might as well have enquired into the antecedents of the *Alabama*, as of the *Tuscaloosa*. Indeed, you had a better reason for inquiring into the antecedents of the former than of the latter, it having been alleged that the former escaped from England in violation of your Foreign Enlistment Act. Mr. Adams, the United States Minister, did in fact demand that the *Alabama* should be seized, but Earl Russell, in flat and most pointed contradiction of his late conduct in the case of the *Tuscaloosa*, gave him the proper legal reply, to wit: that the *Alabama* being now a ship of war, he was estopped from looking into her antecedents.

One illustration will suffice to show you how untenable your position is in this matter. If the *Tuscaloosa's* commission be admitted to have been issued by competent authority, and in due form (and I do not understand this to be contested except on the ground of her antecedents), she is as much a ship of war as the *Narcissus*, your flag-ship. Suppose you should visit a French port, and the port admiral should request you to haul down your flag on the ground that you had had no sufficient title to the ship before she was commissioned, or that she was a contract ship and you had not paid for her, and the builder had a lien on her, or that you had captured her from the Russians, and had not had her condemned by a prize court, what would you think of the proceeding?

And how does the case supposed differ from the one in hand? In both it is a pretension on the part of a foreign power to look into the antecedents of a ship of war—neither more nor less in the one case than in the other. I will even put the case stronger. If it be admitted that I had the right to commission a tender, and the fact had been that I had seized a French ship and put her in commission, you could not inquire into the fact. You would have no right to know but that I had the orders of my Government for this seizure. In short, you would have no right to inquire into the matter at all.

My ship being regularly commissioned, I am responsible to my Government for my acts, and my Government, in the case supposed, would be responsible to France, and not to you. If this reasoning be correct—and with all due submission to his lordship I think it is sustained by the plainest principles of the international code—it follows that the condemnation of a prize in a prize court is not the only mode of changing the character of a captured ship. When the sovereign of the captor puts his own commission on board such a ship, this is a condemnation in its most solemn form, and is notice to all the world. On principle, if a ship thus commissioned were recaptured, the belligerent prize court could not restore her to her original owner, but must condemn her as a prize ship of war of the enemy to the captors; for prize courts are international courts, and cannot go behind the pennant and commission of the cruiser.

Further, as to this question of adjudication, your letter to Lieutenant Low, the late commander of the *Tuscaloosa*, assumes that, as the *Tuscaloosa* was not condemned, she was therefore the property of the enemy from whom she had been taken. Condemnation is intended for the benefit of neutrals, and to quiet the titles of purchasers, but is never necessary as against the enemy. His right is taken away by force, and not by any legal process, and the possession of his property *manu forte* is all that is required against him.

Earl Russell having decided to disregard these plain principles of the laws of nations, and to go behind my commission, let us see what he next decides.

His decision is this, that the *Tuscaloosa* being a prize, and having come into British waters in violation of the Queen's orders of neutrality, she must be restored to her original owner. The ship is not seized and condemned for the violation of any municipal law, such as fraud upon the revenue, &c.—as, indeed, she could not be so seized and condemned without the intervention of a court of law—but by the strong arm of executive power he wrests my prize from me, and very coolly hands her over to the enemy.

It is admitted that all prizes, like other merchant ships, are liable to seizure and condemnation for a palpable violation of the municipal law; but that is not this case. The whole thing is done under the international law. Now, there is no principle better established than that neutrals have no right to interfere in any manner between the captor and his prize, except in one particular instance, and that is where the prize has been captured in neutral waters and afterwards comes of her own accord within the neutral jurisdiction. In that case, and in that case alone, the neutral prize court may adjudicate the case, and if they find the allegation of *infra terminos* proved, they may restore the property to the original owner.

If a lawful prize, contrary to prohibition, come within neutral waters, the most the neutral can do is to order her to depart without interfering in any manner with the captor's possession.

It is admitted that if she obstinately refuses to depart, or conducts herself otherwise in an improper manner, she may be compelled to depart, or may, indeed, be seized and confiscated as a penalty for her offence. But there is no plea of that kind set up here. To show how sacred is the title of mere possession on the part of a captor, permit me to quote from one of your own authorities. On page 42 of the first volume of *Phillimore* on International Law, you will find the following passage: "In 1654 a treaty was entered into between England and Portugal, by which, among other things, both countries mutually bound themselves not to suffer the ships and goods of the other taken by enemies and carried into the ports of the other to be conveyed away from the original owners or proprietors."

"Now, I have no scruple in saying (observes Lord Stowell in 1798) that this is an article incapable of being carried into literal execution according to the modern understanding of the law of nations; for no neutral country can intervene to wrest from a belligerent prizes lawfully taken. This is perhaps the strongest instance that could be cited of what civilians call the *consuetudo obrogatoria*._

This being the nature of my title, the reasons should be very urgent which should justify my being forcibly dispossessed of it. But there are no such reasons apparent. It is not contended that there was any misconduct on the part of the *Tuscaloosa*, unless her entry into a British port as a Confederate cruiser be deemed misconduct. As stated in the beginning of this letter, she had no intention of violating any order of the Queen. Her error, therefore, if it were an error, is entitled to be considered with gentleness and not with hardship.

Her error was the error of yourself and his Excellency the Governor, as well as myself. We all agreed, I believe, that she was a lawfully commissioned ship, and that her commission estopped all further enquiry. In the meantime, she proceeds to sea thus endorsed, as it were, by the Colonial authorities; your Home Government overrules your decision; the *Tuscaloosa* returns in good faith to your port to seek renewed hospitality under your orders of neutrality. And what happens? An English officer, armed with your order, proceeds on board of her, turns her commander and officers out of her, and assumes possession on the ground that she has violated the Queen's orders; and this without any warning to depart or any other notice whatever. In the name of all open and fair dealing—in the name of frankness, candour, and good faith, I most respectfully enter my protest against such an extreme, uncalled-for, and apparently unfriendly course.

But the most extraordinary part of the proceeding has yet to be stated. You not only divest me of my title to my prize, but you tell me that you are about to hand her over to the enemy! On what principle this can be done I am utterly at a loss to conceive. Although it may be competent to a Government, in an extreme case, to *confiscate to the Exchequer* a prize, there is but one possible contingency in which the prize can be restored to the opposite belligerent, and that is the one already mentioned of a capture within neutral jurisdiction. And this is done on the ground of the nullity of the original capture.

The prize is pronounced not to have been lawfully made, and this being the case, and the vessel being within the jurisdiction of the neutral whose waters have been violated, there is but one course to pursue. The vessel does not belong to the captor, and as she does not belong to the neutral, as a matter of course she belongs to the opposite belligerent, and must be delivered up to him. But there is no analogy between that case and the one we are considering. My capture cannot be declared a nullity. My title is as good against the enemy as though condemnation had passed. The vessel either belongs to me or to the British Government. If she belongs to me, justice requires that she should be delivered up to me. If she belongs (by way of confiscation) to the British Government, why should that Government make a gratuitous present of her to one of the belligerents rather than the other?

My Government cannot fail, I think, to view this matter in the light in which I have placed it; and it is deeply to be regretted that a weaker people struggling against a stronger for very existence should have so much cause to complain of the unfriendly disposition of a Government from which, if it represents truly the instincts of Englishmen, it had the right to expect at least sympathy and kindness in the place of rigour and harshness.

No. 7

Measurements of the *Alabama*

We are indebted to Messrs. Laird Brothers, of Birkenhead, for the following measurements of the *Alabama*:

Length	About	230	feet.
Length between perpendiculars,	"	213.8	"
Breadth of beam extreme,	"	032.0	"
Depth moulded,	"	019.9	"
Draft of water when complete, with about 300 tons coal in bunkers and stores on board for a six months' cruise,	"	015.0	"

Engines.—300 horse power collective.

Rig.—Three-masted schooner, with long lower masts and yards on fore and mainmasts.

The hull of the vessel built of wood, the general arrangement of scantling and materials being the same as in vessels of similar class in Her Majesty's navy.

The vessel and machinery throughout were built by Messrs. Laird Brothers at their works at Birkenhead.

ALSO FROM LEONAUR
AVAILABLE IN SOFTCOVER OR HARDCOVER WITH DUST JACKET

CAPTAIN OF THE 95th (Rifles) *by Jonathan Leach*—An officer of Wellington's Sharpshooters during the Peninsular, South of France and Waterloo Campaigns of the Napoleonic Wars.

BUGLER AND OFFICER OF THE RIFLES *by William Green & Harry Smith* With the 95th (Rifles) during the Peninsular & Waterloo Campaigns of the Napoleonic Wars

BAYONETS, BUGLES AND BONNETS *by James 'Thomas' Todd*—Experiences of hard soldiering with the 71st Foot - the Highland Light Infantry - through many battles of the Napoleonic wars including the Peninsular & Waterloo Campaigns

THE ADVENTURES OF A LIGHT DRAGOON *by George Farmer & G.R. Gleig*—A cavalryman during the Peninsular & Waterloo Campaigns, in captivity & at the siege of Bhurtpore, India

THE COMPLEAT RIFLEMAN HARRIS *by Benjamin Harris as told to & transcribed by Captain Henry Curling*—The adventures of a soldier of the 95th (Rifles) during the Peninsular Campaign of the Napoleonic Wars

WITH WELLINGTON'S LIGHT CAVALRY *by William Tomkinson*—The Experiences of an officer of the 16th Light Dragoons in the Peninsular and Waterloo campaigns of the Napoleonic Wars.

SURTEES OF THE RIFLES *by William Surtees*—A Soldier of the 95th (Rifles) in the Peninsular campaign of the Napoleonic Wars.

ENSIGN BELL IN THE PENINSULAR WAR *by George Bell*—The Experiences of a young British Soldier of the 34th Regiment 'The Cumberland Gentlemen' in the Napoleonic wars.

WITH THE LIGHT DIVISION *by John H. Cooke*—The Experiences of an Officer of the 43rd Light Infantry in the Peninsula and South of France During the Napoleonic Wars

NAPOLEON'S IMPERIAL GUARD: FROM MARENGO TO WATERLOO *by J. T. Headley*—This is the story of Napoleon's Imperial Guard from the bearskin caps of the grenadiers to the flamboyance of their mounted chasseurs, their principal characters and the men who commanded them.

BATTLES & SIEGES OF THE PENINSULAR WAR *by W. H. Fitchett*—Corunna, Busaco, Albuera, Ciudad Rodrigo, Badajos, Salamanca, San Sebastian & Others

---

AVAILABLE ONLINE AT **www.leonaur.com**
AND OTHER GOOD BOOK STORES

ALSO FROM LEONAUR
AVAILABLE IN SOFTCOVER OR HARDCOVER WITH DUST JACKET

WELLINGTON AND THE PYRENEES CAMPAIGN VOLUME I: FROM VITORIA TO THE BIDASSOA by *F. C. Beatson*—The final phase of the campaign in the Iberian Peninsula.

WELLINGTON AND THE INVASION OF FRANCE VOLUME II: THE BIDASSOA TO THE BATTLE OF THE NIVELLE by *F. C. Beatson*—The second of Beatson's series on the fall of Revolutionary France published by Leonaur, the reader is once again taken into the centre of Wellington's strategic and tactical genius.

WELLINGTON AND THE FALL OF FRANCE VOLUME III: THE GAVES AND THE BATTLE OF ORTHEZ by *F. C. Beatson*—This final chapter of F. C. Beatson's brilliant trilogy shows the 'captain of the age' at his most inspired and makes all three books essential additions to any Peninsular War library.

NAVAL BATTLES OF THE NAPOLEONIC WARS by *W. H. Fitchett*—Cape St. Vincent, the Nile, Cadiz, Copenhagen, Trafalgar & Others

SERGEANT GUILLEMARD: THE MAN WHO SHOT NELSON? by *Robert Guillemard*—A Soldier of the Infantry of the French Army of Napoleon on Campaign Throughout Europe

WITH THE GUARDS ACROSS THE PYRENEES by *Robert Batty*—The Experiences of a British Officer of Wellington's Army During the Battles for the Fall of Napoleonic France, 1813.

A STAFF OFFICER IN THE PENINSULA by *E. W. Buckham*—An Officer of the British Staff Corps Cavalry During the Peninsula Campaign of the Napoleonic Wars

THE LEIPZIG CAMPAIGN: 1813—NAPOLEON AND THE "BATTLE OF THE NATIONS" by *F. N. Maude*—Colonel Maude's analysis of Napoleon's campaign of 1813.

BUGEAUD: A PACK WITH A BATON by *Thomas Robert Bugeaud*—The Early Campaigns of a Soldier of Napoleon's Army Who Would Become a Marshal of France.

TWO LEONAUR ORIGINALS

SERGEANT NICOL by *Daniel Nicol*—The Experiences of a Gordon Highlander During the Napoleonic Wars in Egypt, the Peninsula and France.

WATERLOO RECOLLECTIONS by *Frederick Llewellyn*—Rare First Hand Accounts, Letters, Reports and Retellings from the Campaign of 1815.

AVAILABLE ONLINE AT **www.leonaur.com**
AND OTHER GOOD BOOK STORES

www.ingramcontent.com/pod-product-compliance
Lightning Source LLC
Chambersburg PA
CBHW030218170426
43201CB00006B/123